JOHN LITTLE AND ROBERT WOLFF, PH.D.

ONE MORE REP!

LESSONS FROM THE WORLD'S BIGGEST, STRONGEST, AND BEST BODYBUILDERS

McGraw Hill

New York   Chicago   San Francisco   Lisbon   London   Madrid   Mexico City
Milan   New Delhi   San Juan   Seoul   Singapore   Sydney   Toronto

The *McGraw·Hill* Companies

Library of Congress Cataloging-in-Publication Data

Little, John R., 1960–
    One more rep! : lessons from the world's biggest, strongest, and best bodybuilders
/ John Little & Robert Wolff.
        p.   cm.
    Includes index.
    ISBN 0-07-147515-X (alk. paper)
    1. Bodybuilding—Handbooks, manuals, etc.   2. Bodybuilding—Training.
3. Bodybuilders—Biography.   I. Wolff, Robert, Ph. D.   II. Title.

GV546.5.L545   2007
613.7'13—dc22   2006022863

Photography credits
Steve Reeves photos courtesy of George Helmer and the Steve Reeves International
Society. Manfred Hoeberl photos by Kevin Horton used by permission of Little-Wolff
Creative Group, Inc. Candid photos by John Little and Robert Wolff.
All other interior photographs by Robert Gardner.

1 2 3 4 5 6 7 8 9 10 11 12 13 14 15 16 17 18 19 20   VLP/VLP   0 9 8 7 6

ISBN-13: 978-0-07-147515-0
ISBN-10:   0-07-147515-X

McGraw-Hill books are available at special quantity discounts to use as premiums and
sales promotions, or for use in corporate training programs. For more information, please
write to the Director of Special Sales, Professional Publishing, McGraw-Hill, Two Penn
Plaza, New York, NY 10121-2298. Or contact your local bookstore.

This book and the information contained herein is for educational and entertainment
purposes only and does not advocate or prescribe a specific exercise or nutritional plan
for anyone, regardless of age, sex, or experience level.

Like all bodybuilding, exercise, fitness, health, and nutrition books, we strongly advise
that you get the approval of a qualified medical/health authority before beginning any
exercise program or making any dietary changes. The authors, publisher, people featured,
or anyone associated with this book in any way shall not be held liable for anyone's
actions either directly or indirectly.

This book is printed on acid-free paper.

Also by John Little

Advanced Max Contraction Training

High Intensity Training the Mike Mentzer Way (with Mike Mentzer)

Max Contraction Training

Power Factor Training (with Peter Sisco)

Static Contraction Training (with Peter Sisco)

The Wisdom of Mike Mentzer (with Joanne Sharkey)

Also by Robert Wolff, Ph.D.

Bodybuilding 101

Bodybuilding 201

Dr. Robert Wolff's Great Body, Great Life Program

Home Bodybuilding

Robert Wolff's Book of Great Workouts

Contents

PART 4   Go Ahead and Ask: 20 Questions with Some Greats

PART 5 My Most Productive Workout Routine

PART 6 Personality Profiles

Preface

Over the years, we've spoken to and interviewed (often many times) the people you'll find in this book. A common thing we observed was that these bodybuilding and strength stars were innovators. They were searchers who would look for new and different ways to take their training and bodies to new levels. They were refiners that would take tried-and-true training methods and perhaps change them ever so slightly (or hugely) to give them the results they were searching for.

And while some of them may not, over the years, have changed much of the core foundational principles that built their physiques, others often found new and different ways to take their training to new levels.

But let it be known that one way is not better than another; it all comes down to what works best for your body and your goals. The people in this book didn't become great by accident. They found what worked best for them and kept refining it. You can do the same.

The information you're about to read comes from just some of the wonderful conversations and lessons we learned from them. However, we want to make it very clear that what you'll read is what these bodybuilding and strength athletes did at the times when we spoke to them, and many have changed their techniques from that time to now. So the information you will read here is not set in stone or the last word on the subject of their training, mental, or nutritional approach, nor could it be. The best in any field of endeavor are constantly growing and looking for ways to be better, and these great athletes are no exception. What worked then may or may not be the method these athletes use today, but one of the lessons we learned from them is never be afraid to change, to try, to experiment, to experience.

This book will give you a snapshot and a glimpse into a moment in time in these great athletes' lives, a chance to see greatness growing and uncover a bit of the magic of what it takes to be great from those in the sport who—to countless numbers of fans—were and still are considered great bodybuilders.

After you read these pages, we highly recommend that you go on the Web and find out what these great athletes are saying now—today. Go to your favorite search engine and type in the name of your favorite athlete and see what you'll find. Find out if they have books, videos, courses, or other products that you may wish to order and try.

Listen to the top performers. Watch them. Read them. Learn from them. They all have something good to say, and their words and ideas can be incredibly helpful.

ABOUT THE PHOTOS

With the exception of perhaps a handful of photos, the majority of the photos you'll see in this book were taken by Robert Gardner. We first met Bob and his wife Gail many years ago when we began our writing careers for Joe Weider's magazines. In our opinion (and that of many, many others), no one can touch Bob Gardner when it comes to taking awe-inspiring photos of bodybuilders, men and women in their absolute peak condition.

Bob Gardner was always Joe Weider's main photographer for capturing these champions at their best, and Joe and Bob's

Robert and Gail Gardner

friendship goes back more than 50 years. For anyone who knows about bodybuilding and bodybuilders—especially at the elite level—achieving peak condition is an amazing event, and one that can, and often does, last for a very brief time.

Joe Weider and Bob Gardner knew this, and that's why Joe made sure that bodybuilders who competed in bodybuilding's biggest shows (the Mr. and Ms. Olympia, the Arnold Classic, Night of Champions, NPC Nationals, and others) would go to Bob and Gail Gardner as their first stop—only minutes after they had walked off stage—to be photographed by Bob and captured in their best condition.

If you could create the ideal environment and time to capture bodybuilding champions on film in their best condition, this was it, and Bob Gardner was the one to do it. But don't just take our word for it. Open this book and see for yourself. Friend, it just doesn't get any better than this.

WHY WE CHOSE THEM

So why did we choose the athletes you'll read about in this book? A few reasons. Most of these athletes were very popular at the time we wrote for Joe Weider's magazines. A great many of them became friends, and we respected and admired their commitment to their dreams and all the hard work and sacrifice that went into achieving them. Some of them inspired us when we began training, and as a tribute to them and their inspiration we felt it fitting to share a bit of their story with you.

We included many in the book because, well, over the years you've asked us about them most. Perhaps your reasons were like many of ours. Perhaps they were different. Whatever it may be, to many people, these people were and still are fondly remembered, and we hope they will be more so once you reach the last page.

There were so many others we wanted to include (such as Larry Scott, Frank Zane, Sergio Oliva, and Franco Columbu, just to name a few), but space limitations wouldn't allow it. Perhaps in the next book. We'd like that. We think you would too.

For now, you've got a lot of people waiting to speak to you through the pages of this book. We have a feeling that what they've got to say will bring a smile to your face for many a night to come. Enjoy!

Acknowledgments

We'd like to thank our families and friends who have always been there to support us. A big thank-you goes to all the people at McGraw-Hill for their belief in the book and helping turn our dreams for it into a reality.

We want to give thanks to Joe Weider for giving us the opportunities of a lifetime. To all the people and friends we've met along our bodybuilding and writing roads, we say thank you.

And finally, a very special thanks goes to our good friends Bob and Gail Gardner. We'll always cherish our worldly travel adventures with you, and we thank you for the amazing photography for our book.

Introduction

The sale of Joe Weider's publishing empire in 2002 signaled the end of an era. Not only in terms of a bodybuilding icon who devoted over 60 years of his life to creating the worldwide fitness movement as we know it, but the Golden Era of the interaction and teachings of the greatest bodybuilders of all time.

Starting with only seven dollars and a mimeograph machine, brothers Joe and Ben Weider created their first publication, a newsletter called *Your Physique*, which was the beginning of an empire that captured the world and millions of men and women who changed their bodies and lives because of Joe Weider and the champions his magazines featured.

Every day was a magical day at Weider Headquarters in Woodland Hills, California. People would travel from all parts of the world and wait many hours to meet with Joe Weider. And for good reason.

No one in the history of bodybuilding and fitness could create champions like Joe Weider did, and if you had the rare combination of talent, looks, charisma, knowledge,

Joe Weider with Lee Haney (center) and Franco Columbu (right)

Cory Everson

Shawn Ray

Jean-Pierre Fux

Flex Wheeler

Lenda Murray

Paul Dillett

Dorian Yates

Ronnie Coleman (left) and Ben Weider

Kevin Levrone

Robby Robinson (left) and Gary Strydom

and a body unlike any other, your destiny could change in a matter of days with your picture and story in next month's magazine issue. Many called on Joe Weider, but only a handful were given the keys to bodybuilding fame, fortune, and immortality.

(l to r) Rich Gaspari, Lee Haney, and Berry DeMey

On any given day, writers at Weider Publications would see the greatest body-builders of all time come through the doors—names such as Schwarzenegger, Ferrigno, Haney, Scott, Mentzer, Reeves, and, of course, Joe Weider himself. All of these champions had something to say or lessons to teach.

However, few writers were trusted enough by Joe to be given access and opportunity to once-in-a-lifetime moments to sit one-on-one with the immortal greats and world-champion bodybuilding and strength athletes he held guardedly close to his heart.

Two were.

John Little worked as a senior writer at Weider's *FLEX* magazine; Bob Wolff was the editor of *Muscle & Fitness*. Both came to work for Weider in 1992 with small-town dreams (John from Canada and Bob from Missouri) of meeting the champions they grew up

Joe Weider and John Little

Joe Weider and Bob Wolff

reading about in the pages of Joe's magazines.

Yet the hand that destiny dealt them would far surpass any dreams or imaginations their impressionable minds held, for in the years that followed, Little and Wolff would learn the secrets of bodybuilding at the feet of the champions and, of course, Joe Weider himself.

And learn they did.

Together they interviewed, conversed with, or trained alongside the greatest champions the sport of bodybuilding and strength has ever produced—from the legendary John Grimek, Steve Reeves, and Reg Park to Mike Mentzer, Dorian Yates, Rachel McLish, Cory Everson, Ronnie Coleman, Lenda Murray, Arnold Schwarzenegger, Lee Haney, and so many others.

To Joe Weider, Little and Wolff were always the first-call writers he could trust to get inside these champions' heads and

extract the real training jewels and wisdom these athletes possessed that turned them from average into world champions. And Joe Weider knew, when such knowledge was revealed to the readers of his magazine, he would change innumerable lives and create a dynasty that made his magazine and his champions the most popular in the world.

On Joe Weider's request, John Little and Bob Wolff flew all over the world to interview and spend time with the most exceptional, the most gifted, the most awesome bodybuilding and strength athletes the world has ever seen. From China to Austria to Korea, Guam and any destination in between, Little and Wolff amassed a library of articles, interviews, firsthand experience, and knowledge unmatched by any writer before or since.

This book is a result of some of those teachings they received from these remarkable athletes and the priceless lessons they learned.

J

PART 1

History and Legends

The Legends of Iron

When one talks about the pioneers of bodybuilding and weight lifting, it's amazing how many people think that Arnold Schwarzenegger goes back to "the good old days." But he doesn't. That era was years before Arnold was even born—a time when bodybuilding success was largely determined by trial and error, tenacity, experimentation, and innovation.

Yes, diet and nutrition was a bit primitive by today's standards, yet when we look more closely at what those early champions ate and how they exercised, much of what we do today is simply the reworking of exercise and nutritional principles that these exceptional athletes pioneered way back then.

And then there's the question of how different the physiques looked back then compared to today. There is no question that nutrition advances have helped today's athletes. And there's little disputing the fact that more than a small number of athletes use or have used drugs at least one time in their workout lives. That choice is and will always be yours, so choose wisely.

For those who want to train, grow, and get stronger naturally, the tips and inspiration from yesterday's champions can be a godsend. They did not have access to the amazing kinds of foods you have; they also didn't have the variety and availability of gyms and equipment. But they did have one thing that's been missing big time today: they knew how to train. Keep this in mind: if their principles were effective for them then, you can rest assured they'll be of benefit to you right now.

Let's look back at the lives of two of bodybuilding's most influential, groundbreaking legends: Eugene Sandow and John Grimek.

EUGENE SANDOW

"It is my firm conviction that few men have done more for this country during

our generation than he. . . . Every word which he writes upon the subject deserves the most careful consideration, not only of the general public, but also of the medical faculty with whom he has always loyally worked."

Sir Arthur Conan Doyle

Eugene Sandow was born Frederick Mueller on April 2, 1867, in Konigsburg, East Prussia, and prior to the turn of the century, Sandow would be the most popular bodybuilder in history. Years later, only two other men, Steve Reeves and Arnold Schwarzenegger, would be known to a larger worldwide audience.

While Sandow may not have been what we would call today an unbelievable physical specimen, his body did turn heads wherever he was seen. But Sandow's body was only part of his mystique. The man possessed an amazing amount of knowledge of the human body and was considered by many to be a prophet of exercise, diet, and health. Consider some of his accomplishments:

- For nearly 30 years, Sandow's physique was revered as the greatest of all time.
- He was a bestselling author.
- He spoke many languages fluently and traveled and lectured all over the world.
- He was one of the very first physique contest promoters.
- He personally trained the leaders and royalty of Europe.

His book *Life Is Movement* brought testimonials from royal families (nine kings and queens), politicians (including Woodrow Wilson and William Taft), the clergy, medical professionals, business tycoons, and the mass public.

Sandow's "strongest man in the world" life story is still fascinating to this day. Perhaps equally fascinating is the kind of body he created by his never-ending fascination and interest in knowing and understanding the body.

Here's just a sample of words of wisdom from the great Sandow (from *Life Is Movement*, 1929).

SANDOW ON TRAINING METHODS

"Remember that it is not so much the number of movements made, but the amount of contraction put into each movement that counts. This enhances the benefit of each contraction by assisting in the elimination of the waste caused by the contraction and the bringing up of greater supplies of nutriment by the blood circulation. . . . It is best to use only one arm or leg at a time, except where otherwise advised, as this enables you to concentrate more fully and put more effort into the contraction."

SANDOW ON HEALTH AND MUSCLE POWER

"Strength means health. One cannot be healthy without being strong. In short, an individual's health is mainly contingent on his muscle power, for as I have shown, the nervous system, which regulates all the functions of the body, depends for its supplies upon the muscular system, and the better developed and balanced his muscular system, visible and invisible, the healthier and better functioned the nervous system must be. This muscle power and balance can only be obtained and developed through balanced movement of the voluntary muscles in a scientific way."

JOHN GRIMEK

Over the years, two schools of belief emerged as to what made a real man. The first school believed big muscles, power, and strength made the man, but building large muscles just to have large muscles was a waste of time. The second school held that how the body and muscles looked—the aesthetics—were more important than strength. These two schools came together in the mid 1930s, courtesy of John C. Grimek.

Grimek was a guy who had it all. Born in Perth Amboy, New Jersey, in 1909, John Grimek was an inextricable link to the real old-timers of the Golden Era of bodybuilding. He also had the honor to retire undefeated in bodybuilding contest history (including two tough victories over the great Steve Reeves in 1948 and 1949).

If it was strength you wanted, Grimek could easily press 370 pounds overhead or simultaneously press 125-pound and 110-pound dumbbells. He was an Olympic

athlete and winner of the American Weightlifting Championship and was on the American Olympic team, with his totals in the 1936 Olympic Games the best on the team.

Grimek had amazing flexibility and could jump up into a handstand during his posing routine, then arch over until his feet were on the ground and then release his hands and go into a full splits while hitting a double biceps pose. John Grimek was the epitome of fitness and strength and went head-to-head with the early doomsayers who warned that weight lifting was unnecessary and harmful. Grimek proved them wrong.

John Grimek was a legend, and even up to the time of his death he commanded the respect of those young and old that marveled at the man and his accomplishments. Always easily approachable, happy, easygoing, and quick to joke and smile, Grimek was a fount of knowledge. Here is some of what he said.

GRIMEK ON HIS MOST PRODUCTIVE TRAINING TECHNIQUE

"After I'd been training a while I hit on a system of training that I called 'Triple Progressive.' I'd begin with a fairly light weight for a warm-up set, and then with each successive set I'd add more weight and drop the repetitions until I'd ultimately reach a point where I couldn't perform more than one to three repetitions. When three repetitions became obtainable with this weight, I'd add more weight. And if I could only manage a single repetition, I'd stick with it until it became easier to perform. This was the best technique I ever used."

GRIMEK ON BRINGING UP THE BODY'S STUBBORN PROBLEM AREAS

"I found that it worked better for me to train a problem area after having already performed my regular workout. I got more results from this than from specializing on a certain area on a specific day of the week like you see a lot of bodybuilders doing with their 'split routines' of today. I found that if I had already gone through part of a routine or a whole body routine—which I often

did—then I already hit that problem area some time during that routine. By doing 1 or 2 sets of maximum weights for that body part at the end of my workout brought that lagging body part up in a hurry."

GRIMEK ON THE IMPORTANCE OF TRAINING VARIETY

"I always advocated variety in training. I was constantly seeking something new and different that would make my body grow bigger and stronger. My thing was I always had to feel something from my workout or I would change it."

GRIMEK ON BEING AN EXPERIMENTER

"It's my personal opinion that one set of rules governing repetitions, sets, etc., cannot be applied to one and all. I believe that you should work your muscles until they're thoroughly congested and feel firm to a touch . . . then do a few more reps for good measure."

John Grimek's Bodybuilding Titles
1940—Mr. America (AAU)
1941—Mr. America (AAU)
1946—America's Most Muscular Man
1948—Mr. Universe (AAU)
1949—Mr. U.S.A. (won at age 40)

HERE COME THE TRAILBLAZERS

Back in the early days of bodybuilding and weight lifting, life wasn't easy for those who wanted to become bigger and stronger. Good information about training and nutrition was next to null. Training equipment was crude, and gyms, if you could find them, were small and scarce.

Perhaps that was one of the reasons why those who trained back then forged amazingly tight bonds and alliances with others that did the same. Each had a common goal, and it was in everyone's best interest to share what they learned and discovered with those who still hadn't tried it.

Yes, it can be said with certainty that Sandow and Grimek were pioneers of bodybuilding and strength. However, it was trailblazers Steve Reeves, Reg Park, and Bill Pearl that took many of those ideas of the past,

discovered their own, and refined them all into methods that have become so much a part of how people train today.

It's been said that knowledge is power, and that's only partially true. Knowledge is only potential power unless and until it is used. It's time for an in-the-gym lesson from the trailblazers that used it so well. Let's begin with Steve Reeves.

STEVE REEVES

In many people's minds, Steve Reeves had the most beautiful physique ever. It was Steve Reeves who bridged the gap between bodybuilding and bodybuilders and mainstream public acceptance.

At 6'1" and 215 pounds, Reeves not only had the physique, he had the looks. The great George Eiferman once said that Reeves could cause traffic accidents simply by walking down the sidewalk and that huge crowds used to follow him whenever he went for a stroll down the beach. Just imagine that.

Steve took his charisma, good

looks, and body and, during the 1950s and 1960s, parlayed all of it into a highly lucrative film career. With films like *Morgan the Pirate*, *The Last Days of Pompeii*, and his immortal *Hercules* films, Reeves was a worldwide bona fide movie star with millions of fans.

But his influence didn't stop at the theater. Steve Reeves was admired by great leaders like Winston Churchill, movie legends like James Dean, and the best body-builders the sport has ever produced including Arnold Schwarzenegger, Reg Park, Bill Pearl, Larry Scott, Mike Mentzer, Lou Ferrigno, Lee Haney, and many others.

Steve Reeves knew what he was talking about when it came to training, too. After all, you don't build a body like his by accident. Here's a sampling of his words.

STEVE REEVES ON GAINING 19 POUNDS OF MUSCLE IN LESS THAN A MONTH TO WIN THE MR. UNIVERSE TITLE

"I selected what I considered as being the best exercises for each part of the body. Only one for each muscle group. Then I performed each exercise for 10 reps of 10 sets. I worked out fast, going right from one exercise to another. Even then this routine took me three hours to complete. I also drank lots of water to replace that which I lost in sweat. I'd dress as warmly as possible during training to eliminate as much muscular stiff-ness as possible.

"I went to bed every evening at 8 p.m. and slept until 9 a.m. the following morning. I was careful to eat a well-balanced diet consisting of a large amount of high-protein food, huge green salads, baked potatoes, lots of beef—mainly steak. I ate raw eggs, honey, bananas, cheese, dried and fresh fruits, and other wholesome foods which gave me energy and muscular body weight."

STEVE REEVES ON MEASUREMENTS

"One of the things that today's bodybuilders do is take measurements after they're all pumped up. We would take our measure-ments first thing in the morning when we got up and before we exercised. When my arm stretched the tape to 18¼ inches, it was a cold measurement. In those days, the guys would let each other take the measurements. I'd measure George Eiferman's arm, Armand Tanny would measure mine, etc. We knew what we had. We knew we weren't conning anybody, and we knew it would be there tomorrow."

STEVE REEVES ON WORKOUT STRUCTURES

"I was able to develop muscle much faster and easier than the guys who trained six days a week. I'd work out three days a week for about two to two and a half hours per workout. I'd train my upper and lower body in one workout on alternate days (i.e., Monday, Wednesday, and Friday) and have four days off for rest and recovery. Rest is crucial to muscle recovery and growth. Because I had so much rest between workouts, I'd never take layoffs or feel overtrained. I always looked forward to my next workout."

STEVE REEVES ON HYDRATION AND TRAINING

"Bodybuilders must take in plenty of fluid when they exercise. Water actually helps to metabolize body fat. I would always drink a lot of water when I trained. I'd mix lemon and honey with my water, and that way I was able to replace all of my electrolytes that would be lost through perspiration. Biomechanically, I wasn't aware of what I was doing, but instinctively I knew it was the right thing. This was about 40 years before the sports electrolyte replacement drinks came out!"

STEVE REEVES ON HIS IDEAL PROPORTION FORMULA

"The ideal weight for an athlete or bodybuilder should be based upon their height. Let's say a person is six feet tall, he should weigh about 200 pounds. For each inch of height above six feet, add 15 pounds. Conversely, for every inch less than six feet, deduct 10 pounds. This formula worked really well for me."

Steve Reeves's Bodybuilding Titles

1946—Mr. California

1947—Mr. America

1948—Mr. Universe

1948—Mr. World

1950—Mr. Universe

BILL PEARL

The year was 1953, and a young man from Oregon would burst on the bodybuilding scene and change it forever. His name was Bill Pearl, and at the age of 22, Bill won the Mr. America and Mr. Universe titles in the same year.

Pearl had great physical prowess, and after joining the navy, he soon became a naval district wrestling champion (just like another man he admired, Sandow). Bill chose his inspirations wisely—Clancy Ross and John Grimek—and would go on to win the Mr. Universe title four times, winning his last one at the age of 41. In his final contest, Pearl beat "The Myth" Sergio Oliva, Reg Park, and Frank Zane. Bill Pearl had Herculean mass and knew just how to pose it, causing more than a roomful of fans' mouths to drop.

Pearl's knowledge was legendary, and after retiring from competition he went on to write bestselling books including such classics as *Keys to the Inner Universe* and *Getting Strong*. Here are a few morsels from the mind of Bill Pearl.

BILL PEARL ON BEING A REBEL

Bill believed he and Reg Park took size to new extremes. They got away from the old philosophies that were being used at that time. They started doing numerous sets and keeping the repetitions lower, and they changed the concepts of the sport.

Bill used Grimek as an example. He said that John Grimek had fantastic calves, and he could do 1 set of 50 reps on a particular exercise and everyone else followed his system. But then again, John probably would

(left to right) Bill Pearl, Bob Wolff, and John Grimek

have had fantastic calves if he had done 100 reps or none at all. Back then, many people just didn't break the mold.

Pearl felt that many of those guys back then were weight lifters, and the physiques they had were achieved by using the basic weight lifting movements like squats, bench presses, and standard exercises, and they didn't have a huge repertoire of exercises to pick from.

BILL PEARL ON BREAKING THE MOLD

Bill recounted that he and Reg used to call each other on the phone from England back to Sacramento and talk about training. They started doing inclines and flats and declines for chest, rather than just bench presses with a barbell. He and Reg would add numerous different movements to weight training that probably had not been done before.

As far as reps and sets went, they kept their reps low and did numerous sets, and they concentrated on it. They would train once a day, five or six days per week, for two or three hours at a time, and that, too, was an unheard of thing to do back then.

BILL PEARL'S RADICAL SETS

At the height of his training, Bill was averaging around 20 sets per body part three times per week. That would mean he was doing 60 sets per body part per week. But surprisingly, he didn't think they were over-trained because it produced the type of physique that caused him and Reg to become world champions. They ate lots of protein, kept the fats and carbs low, and they grew!

BILL PEARL ON WHY HE WAS A SUCCESS

Bill thought the secret of his success was to become totally dedicated to what he wanted to do and make it a total lifestyle. He didn't get in there for the quick fix. Bill said that Reg still trains today, and he himself has been training for more than 50 years. Talk about an inspiration!

Bill Pearl's Bodybuilding Titles

1953—Mr. Southern California

1953—Mr. America

1953—Mr. Universe (Amateur)

REG PARK

With a time of 10.3 seconds in the 100 meters, Reg Park could've been a world-class sprinter. But track wouldn't be his calling. Bodybuilding was. At the age of 21, Reg captured the Mr. Britain title at a body weight of 220 pounds. Park had the looks and physique to become a legend—even becoming the other star of Hercules movies. At 6'1" tall, Reg had slabs of muscle that included an amazing array of body parts including chest, calves, and arms.

Competition was in Park's blood, and in 1950, he went head-to-head with Steve Reeves at the Mr. Universe contest, which was Reg's only defeat that year. However, the next year, he came back to win it, and again in 1958. Then in 1965, Reg Park came back and won the Professional Mr. Universe title and became the first triple Mr. Universe winner in history.

In 1970, Reg competed once more, this time in the Mr. Universe contest against Arnold Schwarzenegger. While Arnold may have won the show, both of them won a strong friendship and a lifetime of mutual admiration.

After his competitive days were over, Reg Park became a highly successful entrepreneur and business and fitness consultant to people all over the world. To this day, when people look at photos of Park, they see incredible shape and symmetry, rugged mass, and a muscular quality that was uniquely his own. Here's a little sample of what Reg had to say.

REG PARK ON MUSCLE SIZE

Reg said that one of the best ways to keep the body growing and constantly off-guard is by using a variety of exercises. He would experiment and find groups of exercises that worked well for each body part. With literally dozens of exercises at his disposal, his workouts would always be fresh and productive. The result? His body was constantly guessing as to what kind of different exercise it was going to have to get accustomed to. This kind of surprise kept him constantly growing and stronger.

REG PARK'S "SPECIALIZE TO NORMALIZE" FORMULA

Reg had an interesting slogan, "Specialize to normalize." That meant using muscle priority and training a weak muscle section in order to put it back in line with the rest of the musculature. He would use many different variations to accomplish this. Sometimes he would simply add extra sets and reps to his regular workout regimen. Other times, he'd train the weak body part with 1 or 2 sets between sets of different body parts.

REG PARK ON CHEST BUILDING

Reg Park had an amazing chest, and to him, a massive chest is built by enlarging the rib cage, not through bulking up the pecs to disproportionate size. And it begins with a big and solid foundation. Reg believed that only when chest volume is first increased through pullover and stretching/dipping exercises can it accommodate massive pectorals.

REG PARK ON BUILDING AMAZING CALVES

Calves were another hallmark of the fantastic Park physique. Reg believed that for big calves, you must do high reps, high sets, full contractions, and muscle extensions. At times, heavy weight is important for packing on mass, however you must feel the calf burn to make it grow. Never sacrifice feeling the movement for the sake of just lifting heavy weight. Keeping the knees together and feet wide and varying toe position changes the angle the calf is worked. Putting the emphasis and stress over the big toe works the inner calf. Conversely, emphasis and stress over the little toe works the outer calf head. (Test it yourself. It really works!)

Reg Park's Bodybuilding Titles
1949—Mr. Britain
1951—Mr. Universe
1958—Mr. Universe
1965—Mr. Universe

THE PAST IS NEVER THE PAST

As many young and older bodybuilders are finding out, when it comes to training, what seems like such a new discovery is not really that new at all. Chances are that it's been around in one form or another for a long time. Many of the iron legends tell us there's really nothing new under the sun.

What is new is how many of today's intelligent bodybuilders are taking the training wisdom of the great legends and fine-tuning it to their own bodies and routines in order to reach their bodybuilding and fitness goals that much quicker.

The legends know what they're talking about. The results they were able to achieve—without the use of drugs—was incredible. Their knowledge will help you—but don't just take our word for it. Test it for yourself in the gym, the place where the truly great physiques in our sport were made.

Muscle Beach: The Golden Era of Bodybuilding

When we first started training, we used to hear people talk about the good old days of bodybuilding, the Muscle Beach days of bodybuilding in Venice and Santa Monica, California. To the older bodybuilders and strength athletes who told it, the period of the 1940s through the 1970s was the Golden Era and one in the history of the sport that will never be repeated.

After we moved to California, we had the chance to meet many of the great athletes who were part of that Golden Era of Muscle Beach and hear them tell story after story of the amazing people and the strength and physical ability feats that made them legendary. One man in particular, Bill Howard, was a fount of information. Here are some of the stories he and they shared.

WHO WAS A PART OF THIS MAGICAL TIME

Many of bodybuilding and powerlifting's great were a part of Muscle Beach. They included John Grimek, Steve Reeves, George Eiferman, Armand Tanny, Vic Tanny, Paul Anderson, Reg Park, Dick Dubois, Chuck Ahrens, Peanuts West, Pat Casey, Zabo Kozewski, Joe Gold, Isaac Berger, Pepper Gomez, Chuck Grayling, Gene Meyers, Pudgy Stockton (the first woman bodybuilder, and husband Les who did Adagio gymnastics), Dave Shepherd, Arnold Schwarzenegger, Franco Columbu, Dave Draper, Larry Scott, Danny Padilla, Chuck Sipes, Ken Waller, Robby Robinson, Serge Nubret, Sergio Oliva, and Frank Zane, just to name a few.

WHEN AND WHERE IT ALL BEGAN

The original Muscle Beach began in 1934 in Santa Monica, just south of the Santa

Monica Pier. Its heyday was during the 1940s and '50s. It remained open until 1959.

Muscle Beach was a sight to behold. Bill Howard was 14 years old when he saw it for the first time, and he recalled the first day he arrived. He was standing on the beach and saw famed bodybuilder George Eiferman. He remembered seeing George's pictures in the muscle magazines, but seeing him in person was beyond compare. It was the first time he had ever seen a real bodybuilder.

But it was the legendary Steve Reeves who made the biggest impression. Reeves was the man all of Muscle Beach was talking about. Howard was standing quite a distance away from the weight pen when Reeves started walking toward him. Reeves's physique was unlike any Howard had ever seen: big, wide shoulders, tiny waist, diamond-shaped calves, and a face like a Greek god. Everywhere Reeves walked, people would follow him and stare.

STRENGTH FEATS BEYOND COMPARE

Every weekend, thousands upon thousands of people and families would come to Muscle Beach to watch the gymnasts, the Adagio pairs, hand-balancers, weight lifters, and bodybuilders. And for most bodybuilders and weight lifters, their strength feat was the bench press.

Great crowds would gather around the pen (what the weight area was called) and wait anxiously for the next guy to bench some huge amount of weight. After he

benched the weight, he'd rack it and sit around for a long time talking to his buddies.

Bill remembered one Saturday when Franco Columbu came down to Muscle Beach, and he was watching some of the strength lifters do their bench pressing. Franco walked over to the pen, jumped the fence, lay down on the bench, and bench pressed 525 pounds for 3 reps—without a warm-up!

The audience cheered, and the strength men were shocked. The conventional wisdom back then was that bodybuilders weren't supposed to be that strong and lift that kind of weight—especially someone who weighed 175 or 180 pounds. It wasn't any time before they grabbed their belongings and took off. Bill thought Franco, with a 500-plus-pound bench press and more than 700-pound deadlift, was pound-for-pound the strongest bodybuilder he had ever seen.

SO WHO WERE THESE MUSCLE BEACH HEADS?

Many of the guys who came to Muscle Beach really had not too much in the way of formal education like college. Most of them didn't have a way of life or a means to support themselves. Bodybuilding was their calling, and many of them wanted to be in the movies like Steve Reeves.

Bill Howard said that back then on Muscle Beach there was a tremendous amount of camaraderie. They trained together, went out to eat together (that is, if they had the money), went to movies and dances, and hung out at each other's places and talked about two things: women and training.

It was true that back then, many of the guys who lived on Muscle Beach didn't have much money. Lots of them found work as extras in movies, building movie props, as light technicians, or working in the gym. The big goal was simply to find any kind of a job that would give them enough money to keep on living the Muscle Beach lifestyle.

There was a sense of community, and many of the guys looked to each other for support. Most of them had families in other cities or out of state. Most didn't have lots of friends, except those they met on Muscle Beach. And because there weren't many who looked like them, they made close friendships with the ones who did. It was like one big support group.

What was surprising, Bill said, was just how small a group of people they were. If they walked five blocks off the beach, people looked at them like they were freaks and would stare in disbelief. Except, that is, when they would go to one of their favorite weekend hangouts called the Muscle Inn for good food, laughs, and a few beers.

THE DIFFERENCES BETWEEN NOW AND THEN

Bill believed that in the old days, there seemed to be a genuine interest in health. Joe Weider was writing about health in his magazines, despite all the outsiders who called him crazy for doing so. To the bodybuilders and to Joe, bodybuilding was a lifestyle and philosophy whose message was health above anything else. People back then weren't obsessed with having the biggest body parts or looking the freakiest. They were into hard workouts—many of them lasting two or more hours—and eating lots of wholesome foods. They were into strength, and they quickly found that the heavier one lifted, the stronger and bigger one became.

The Muscle Beach lifestyle and creed was simple: live a very healthy life by taking care of yourself through working out, eating nutritiously, eliminating stress, and getting rid of any habits that kept you from becoming the best person you were capable of being.

OH, WHAT STRENGTH STORIES

Bill Howard had some great classic Muscle Beach strength stories. For example, during the transition period from the old Muscle Beach to the new Muscle Beach (just over two miles down the beach, north of the original location), he trained in the garage belonging to a powerlifter named Peanuts West. This was in 1963. Peanuts called his garage the Westside Barbell Club, and 10 guys who lifted there were world powerlifting champions.

When Howard started training with them, he was able to do a 350-pound squat, and he thought that was pretty good. However, one day when he was sitting in the Westside Barbell Club with Pat Casey, there was a barbell loaded with 350 pounds. Casey lay down on the bench, grabbed the 350-pound barbell, and started doing lying barbell triceps French presses! Howard said he couldn't believe it. Bill believed the guys who worked out back then were the ones who tore down all the barriers when it came to strength training for bodybuilding. They pushed Bill so hard that he went from doing a 350-pound squat to being able to squat 600 pounds in just 90 days.

Another story Bill told was of the late, great strong man Paul Anderson. Bill remembered Anderson squatting over 1,000 pounds and pressing 400 pounds—for reps. There were other guys like Chuck Ahrens and Steve Marjanian who could do 450- to 500-pound incline presses with ease. And George Friend, the world champion hammer thrower, who, at 242 pounds, could do 350-pound behind-the-neck presses for reps! Perhaps the most amazing thing about these feats of strength was that they were done without drugs or supplements. Just damn hard training, lots of rest, plenty of fun, and eating lots of good wholesome foods.

BODYBUILDING'S GREATEST LABORATORY

Bill Howard and everyone we have spoken to agree that the real roots of bodybuilding began at Muscle Beach. Back then, everyone shared knowledge about anything to do with training and nutrition. They prided themselves on being pioneers. They came up with all kinds of training ideas and then tested them in the gym.

Bill said that during the 1940s, doing 3 sets of 10 reps per body part, three days per week, was the rage. Then in the '50s, they worked out six days per week, three days on and one day off. They also did supersets and trisets.

In 1967, Bill worked with Joe Weider on something called crab sets, now known as giant set training, where they'd take four exercises per body part and do 4 or 5 giant sets for the part. Then came double split training, where they'd train one body part in the morning and one in the afternoon. Then came the four-day split, and so on.

Little may people today know it, but many people from the Muscle Beach days made big contributions to bodybuilding and fitness. For example, Vic Tanny started his fitness club empire with his first gym, known as the Dungeon Gym, located just a few blocks from the beach. This gym was a favorite training spot for many great body-builders, powerlifters, and strength athletes. A short time later, Vic began building a whole chain of health clubs across the United States. Jack LaLanne became a television star whose name and face were synonymous with fitness. Joe Gold opened a gym just so he and a few friends could have a place to train. Soon thereafter, Gold's Gym and World Gym were born, and now they're all over the world.

THE FAMOUS AUSTRIAN NAMED ARNOLD

Bill Howard believed it to be around September or October of 1968 when Arnold Schwarzenegger arrived on Muscle Beach. Franco Columbu arrived shortly thereafter. And it was during the Arnold era, the early to mid '70s, that the new Muscle Beach was in its heyday. On the weekends, over 250,000 people would come down to Muscle Beach.

As photos show and many others will agree, Arnold was awesome. Bill said that at that time, nobody in the iron game had Arnold's development: biceps, wide back, and big, thick pecs peaked like mountains. The former star of *Hercules*, Reg Park, was close, but Arnold was 6'2" and carried 235 pounds of muscle, and no one could touch that.

Bill recalled the first time he met Arnold. A group of bodybuilders were invited to a Christmas party at someone's house in Malibu, and when Bill walked inside, it looked like the Last Supper. Seated at the head of the table was Arnold, and everyone was seated around him, staring, and asking him all kinds of training questions like, What do you do for biceps? How'd your chest get so huge? What should I eat to gain mass? Bill said Arnold was holding court and loving every minute of it.

After Franco Columbu arrived in California, he started a bricklaying business. Bill used to work with Franco, and Arnold would help them whenever he was around and needed extra money. Many times when they'd go out to some exclusive neighbor-

The new royalty of muscle arrives (left to right): Ed Corney, Arnold Schwarzenegger, and Franco Columbu.

hood, like Pacific Palisades, and lay patio brick, they would cause a lot of commotion. For example, one day they'd go to someone's home and begin a job, then the next day when they came back there'd be a few women watching them through the window.

When Arnold would help them, there'd be about 15 women in the house watching! Those women didn't realize it, but the man who was laying brick on their patio would soon become the world's best bodybuilder. (Not to mention that he would one day be governor of California and a political powerhouse.)

But contrary to popular belief, Bill said Arnold didn't have it too easy when he arrived in America. He had his apartment and his writing and promotions deal with Joe Weider, but he wasn't getting rich by any means. Bill said at least a good 10 years went by before Arnold got some big breaks and began getting his foot in the door in Hollywood.

THEN THINGS CHANGED

Bill reminisced that after the Arnold era had passed in the mid '70s, Muscle Beach was quickly forgotten. Many of those in the bodybuilding community still knew what it was about and where it was, but bringing it back into prominence and to what it used to be was going to be a daunting task.

Then, in 1986, Bill's dream to perpetuate the legacy of Muscle Beach finally came true. After years of pleading his case, Bill got a petition together, formed an ad hoc committee, received a letter from Arnold, got approval for funding, and helped convince the City of Los Angeles to build a new building and weight training area and officially name the area Venice Muscle Beach.

Like others who were touched by it, Bill Howard believed that more people in America should know about Muscle Beach and its history. Bodybuilding really began on that southern California beach many years ago. Each year, countless numbers of people from all over the world come to Venice Beach, California, and see the new Muscle Beach. All of the foreign visitors have proven one thing beyond a doubt to Bill Howard: the words Muscle Beach are more well known in Europe than they are in America. If you're a bodybuilder visiting Europe, people will ask you if you've ever gone to Muscle Beach. We hope that this book, by introducing readers to some of the great athletes who were part of the Muscle Beach Era, will make bodybuilders in this country more aware of their heritage as well.

PART 2

Diet and Nutrition

3

Sliced and Diced: Dorian Yates's Tips for Lean Gigantic Mass

Perhaps the best person you could ask how to get your body in its absolute best-looking condition would be a Mr. Olympia. The degree of conditioning these guys must achieve for every show is beyond comprehension for most people. And when you think about all the years of that kind of body taken to the nth level of development and conditioning and that some of the pros are still able to beat their previous conditioning year after year, then it's safe to say they've not only found something that works for their bodies, but may have a few tips that would help you too.

Former Mr. Olympia Dorian Yates was one of those guys. Just when judges, fans, and his fellow pros thought that Yates had tapped his limits, boom! He came in bigger, harder, and more cut than the year before. Yates had a very smart approach to all aspects of his training and contest preparation, and this is what he shared on getting his body in peak condition.

Dorian looked at getting his body ready in two stages or phases. The first phase was carbohydrate depletion. The second phase was the carbohydrate loading cycle. Both were equally important to achieving that peaking condition. Here is how the first phase, the carbohydrate depletion phase, would work.

He liked to start depleting the body of carbohydrates six days before the show, and found that six days worked well for him. On the first three days, he would deplete the carbohydrates out of his system by decreasing his carbohydrate intake and doing high-rep and high-set training, which burns the glycogen from the muscle. The idea was that for three days you deplete the carbohydrate and glycogen stores in the muscle. When you still had glycogen in the muscle, that glycogen would still hold water inside the muscle, which gave it fullness.

Yates explained the theory was that you deplete the stores, and by reintroducing carbs in that depleted state, it caused the body to overcompensate and thereby made it hold a little bit more than it did in the first place. He said what you were doing was basically increasing your glycogen storage, which will make you bigger and harder, and he found that this worked pretty well for him.

He said that he found that he didn't need to drop his carbohydrate intake to a very low level to deplete carbs from his body. He might drop his carb intake down to maybe 50 percent of his normal intake when he was carbohydrate depleting, and he made sure that the calories he was losing by reducing his carb intake were replaced with protein and fat. He would usually use medium chain triglycerides (MCTs) as a fat source.

Dorian said one of the biggest mistakes he saw people making was dropping their carbs way down, which wasn't a good idea. And they didn't replace all of the calories that they'd lost. He explained that here they were, on very low calories and very low carbs at the same time. During those three days of depletion, they can lose a tremendous amount of weight, and a lot of that will be muscle tissue. This was a major mistake. In fact, he said he could deplete on 250 grams of carbs a day, whereas a lot of people were going down to 50 grams of carbs a day.

After the depletion stage of his peaking program was completed, Dorian was ready to go to the carbohydrate loading phase. The loading phase began on the last three days before the show. During the loading phase, he immediately wants to reintroduce carbohydrates into his body at a very high level. As everybody is different, he advised that people have to experiment here as to what works best for them.

When he was reintroducing carbs back into his body, Dorian wouldn't do it slowly. He liked going in very high and very quickly.

He believed that once the body was depleted, it was hungry for carbohydrates, and it was going to store them more efficiently on the first day as opposed to the second or third day.

For Dorian, it was all instinctive, and he let the mirror be his guide. He said that if he was starting to look full and really loaded up, he would start reducing his carb intake, because if he carried on too much at that point the body would start to hold water. On the first day of carb loading, he would go high. The second day he would go high but maybe not as high as the first day. Then on the third day, he might reduce it a bit more, and it all depended on how he looked.

When he was in the carb reintroduction phase, Dorian said he would eat about seven times a day, that would be seven small servings with two or three kinds of carbohydrates within one meal and also a very small amount of protein. He thought that was better than having too many carbs at once that would get into the system very quickly and could disrupt blood sugar levels more. Dorian believed that if the body got two or three different kinds of carbs, along with some protein, it might be absorbed slightly differently, along with helping to stabilize the blood sugar level, and he felt that was the better way to do it.

When it came to eating complex or simple carbs, Dorian said he would take in complex carbs. He ate very few simple carbohydrates anyway, even in the off-season, and that included eating very small amounts of fruit. On the last three days before a show, he liked to keep things pretty consistent and wouldn't eat strange foods like chocolate and cake that his system wasn't used to anyway.

When asked why he ate small amounts of fruit, Dorian said he just felt better when he didn't eat a lot of fruit. Through trial and error, he learned that whenever he would eat a lot of fruit, his digestion would not be as good. It was a bit acidic. Also, his blood sugar level seemed a lot more even and constant when he ate complex carbohydrates. He would get those complex carbs from such sources as fibrous carbs like broccoli and lettuce and the majority from starchy carbs like rice and potatoes.

When it came to protein, Dorian said he kept it fairly consistent to what it was in the off-season, which would be at least a gram of protein for each pound of body weight. During the precontest period, he would be taking more amino acids and getting a bit less protein from the foods he ate and more from the aminos.

His protein sources would come from chicken, turkey, tuna, and egg whites, and in the off-season he would eat red meat. In addition, he would get second-class protein from the vegetables he ate. His nutrient percentages were 60 percent carbs, 30 percent protein, and 10 percent fat. Dorian said he tried to keep the fat a little bit lower during the precontest period, however it was very hard to get the fat under 10 percent. Along with his macronutrients, Dorian said that as far as supplements went, he might cut down a bit on the amino intake for the last three days before the show just in case there was something there that might make him hold a bit more water.

Like many of us, Dorian would allow himself a junk food day in the off-season. He said that during that period, probably once a week he would go out and have a meal with whatever he wanted. Many times that meant having a steak and maybe some ice cream.

Even during precontest, once a week he would relax his diet a bit and not think of the calories. He explained that being on low calories all the time tended to slow the metabolism down, so he liked to vary it a bit. He said he wasn't afraid to eat pretty much what he wanted and take his calories up and have something that he was craving all week. He thought that doing that was beneficial both mentally and physically.

In regard to sodium and water, Dorian said that on the last three days before the show, he would really lower his sodium intake and would drink distilled water. He drank plenty of distilled water on the first two days, no limit, and then he would limit it slightly on the day before the contest. On the day of the contest, he would pretty much drink as much as he felt like having, but slightly limit it. Also on the day of the contest, he would add a little bit more sodium back into the diet.

As far as calories in the off-season and precontest went, Dorian said off-season, they could go as high as 6,000. Typically, they stayed in the 5,500 to 6,000 range in the off-season when he was training real heavy. During precontest, the calories would be anywhere from 3,500 to 4,500.

Dorian explained that every morning he would weigh all of his food portions for the whole day and that all of the carbs, protein, fat, and calories were calculated year-round and not just during precontest. He did that because he wanted to be precise and know exactly what he was taking in. If he was not gaining much size on 6,000 calories, then he knew that if he added 300, 400, or 500 extra calories he would gain more size. There was no hit or miss with Dorian. He knew and calculated his training and nutrition like few others.

Dorian said he would stop training three days before the show. He was only training during the carbohydrate depletion stage, and on the days that he was carb loading he would not do any training at all. However, he said he did do quite a bit of posing to keep the sweat going and flush the toxins out of his system. He felt that it was important that he didn't stagnate on those days that he wasn't training. He would do about a half-hour of posing in the morning and at least a half-hour at nightt.

When asked about how many weeks before a show he would begin preparations, Dorian said 12 months out of the year. However, he said as far as calorie reduction and things like that went, it would be something like 12 to 14 weeks from the show. Dorian said it was important to train for that show for a year, six months, or whatever period it was going to take to get into top shape for it.

While some guys can stay close to contest shape all year round, Dorian said he tried to keep his body reasonably close throughout the year, but didn't think that for a guy his size he could stay 10 to 15 pounds away from his contest weight. He liked to take in enough calories and to feel comfortable in the off-season, and those extra calories would probably put him 25 to 30 pounds over his contest weight. He said he would lose that extra weight slowly over 14 weeks before the show at an average of about 2 pounds a week. And since he didn't carry a lot of excess body fat, a lot of that extra weight would just be excess fluids.

4

The Supplement Lowdown: Advice from Shawn Ray, Eddie Robinson, Nasser El Sonbaty, Paul Dillett, and Porter Cottrell

In the world of bodybuilding nutrition, supplements come and go like the wind. One year, one supplement's the rage; and the next year, people couldn't be bothered with it. Companies that sell supplements saturate the magazines with ads for good reason: supplements can make them a fortune. Let's face it, many people are lazy and are always looking for that amazing new supplement that'll change their bodies quickly. Rarely does that ever happen.

Over the years we've talked to a lot of the pros about supplements. Some are big believers in them. Others think they're a huge waste of money. Some of the champs' supplement regimens are very precise and comprehensive, while others are very basic to nearly nonexistent. So which do you choose?

Keep in mind that the pros, if they're into supplements, typically will search for anything new that might give their bodies that extra edge, all the while staying with some tried-and-true favorites. The following is what some of these pros said were their favorites at the time.

SHAWN RAY

Shawn said he liked getting most of his nutrients from the foods he ate and not from pills or powders. However, he did say he took a vitamin/mineral supplement, such as vitamin B–complex, C, E, niacin, zinc, lecithin, and multiminerals.

Since Shawn liked to stay in great shape all year round, he kept his protein intake at the level to sustain his muscle mass, but not

any more than was needed to achieve that. The only other supplement he was taking at that time was a protein shake or two, and this was during precontest. The rest of his protein and carbs came from food.

EDDIE ROBINSON

Unlike Shawn Ray, Eddie Robinson believed plenty of supplements were key factors in his total training and conditioning game plan. He joked that at his home, there were three cupboards filled with supplements. Looking at his physique, he must've been on to something that was working.

Eddie said he liked L-glutamine since it helped replace muscle tissue after training and kept his body from becoming catabolic. The other benefit was that his muscle soreness decreased and energy level increased.

Eddie felt that when he kept his free-form amino acid intake very high (especially at night before he went to bed), along with taking OKG, it made a big difference in his training, recovery, and growth. To prove their effectiveness, Eddie said he could really tell a difference in his strength and recuperation when he stopped taking OKG and L-lutamine. Here was his supplement regimen at one time:

- L-carnitine, for fat loss: 6 grams per day—3 grams in the morning and 3 grams at night
- L-glutamine, for muscle recovery: 10 grams per day—2 grams before training, 3 grams after training, 5 grams at night

NASSER EL SONBATY

Nasser was a huge proponent of a high-protein diet, as in roughly 600 grams a day during precontest. That means eating lots of chicken breasts and meat as well as low-carb protein shakes. He said he liked whey protein because he thought the body used it more efficiently.

Nasser also admitted that during the off-season, he reduces his protein intake. When he was in precontest training and giving his body more frequent meals, his metabolism sped up, which made it crave more food.

In the off-season, he only ate when he was hungry, which comes out to about three or four meals a day along with two shakes. Nasser said that the biggest nutrient that changed his physique was extra protein.

- Creatine monohydrate, for muscle energy and recovery: 30 grams per day for the first five days, then 10 grams a day starting on the sixth day—5 grams after training and 5 grams with a meal about four hours later

- Protein powder, for muscle maintenance and growth: three drinks each day mixed with skim milk, taken between meals to ensure his protein level was high

- Branched chain amino acids, for muscle recovery: 15 capsules before and after each workout

- OKG, for muscle recuperation: the amount and the times he took it varied during the day based on body needs

PAUL DILLETT

Paul found that creatine worked best for him. He said creatine gave him plenty of energy and made him stronger. Because creatine helps keep muscles filled with water, Paul said he knew people put on as much as 10 pounds in less than 30 days simply by using it.

He said he found a great way to take it: five scoops a day for one week, then reducing that to three scoops a day. He took a scoop at five different times during the day, which was typically with his meals.

After his body had reached a saturation point with plenty of creatine stores—usually after a few weeks—he then tapered down the daily amount to two scoops or whenever he felt his body needed it.

Paul said he also liked protein powders. His recommendation was that bodybuilders eat 1.5 grams of protein per lean pound of body weight, not just total body weight. Paul said he used protein drinks that were high in protein and low in carbs, and he had three shakes a day—morning, midafternoon, and about an hour or so before bedtime.

He was also a believer in vitamins and minerals. Let's face it, we don't live in a perfect world where all of us get the right nutrients all the time. Add to that the stress of everyday living, eating processed foods, coffee, soda, and dehydration from not drinking enough water, and those things can rob the body of important vitamins and minerals it needs. Now factor in intense workouts, and you're asking the body to do a lot unless you nourish it properly. That's why Paul said he took a good multivitamin/mineral supplement twice a day, at breakfast and lunch or dinner.

PORTER COTTRELL

Porter was another pro that sang the praises of creatine. He said that after he started using it, he noticed an increase in strength, a better pump, and faster recovery. Here's how he used it:

- Take five teaspoons a day for five days. Each teaspoon is approximately 5 grams, and the daily total is 25 grams.
- After a few days of creatine loading, he reduced the daily intake to 15 grams or three teaspoons a day.

He found taking creatine with a small amount of fruit juice seemed to help his body absorb the creatine more efficiently. He always took one of his creatine servings right after a workout. At that time, the only side effect he said he found was that his body retained a little extra water, especially during the loading phase. Three or four weeks before a show, he stopped using creatine.

5

Hitting the Peak with Vince Taylor

If there was one pro who knew how to get dialed into incredible condition, it had to be Vince Taylor. Vince had a terrific proportion of symmetry, proportion, separation, and cuts, and he said that one of the reasons for his great condition was putting it all together nutritionally. Vince believed that while training was important, diet was critical to getting the body in top shape.

He said that in the past, he would start his peaking preparations about six weeks out from a show, and the way he did that was by keeping his body fat low throughout the year. However, after doing a little experimentation and testing how his body responded to having a bit more time to get dialed, Vince said he found success by taking 12 to 13 weeks out from the show.

Vince said that one of the biggest mistakes he made in the past was dieting down to look good. He said that he and Lee Haney talked about how Vince was losing too much muscle by dieting down too severely just so he could make a show deadline. As a result, his body looked drawn. What Vince did then was eat more, train harder, add cardio (which he admitted he didn't do before), and begin his preparations further out from the show. The result was that his physique was harder, fuller, healthier, bigger, and more polished. Vince said he believed adding the cardio into his training and preparations was the missing key to his training success.

Vince said that his training remained the same year-round. He did double-split training six days per week. He trained on Monday, Tuesday, and Wednesday, and it repeated Thursday, Friday, and Saturday, with Sunday as his day off. He said he typically did three or four exercises per body part for roughly 10 total sets of 6 to 12 reps.

He split his training up by doing two body parts in the morning and one in the afternoon. He also said he liked doing something called double sets. He explained that this was where he would do an exercise, like curls, do one set, put the weight down, act as if he had a training partner by waiting a few moments so the partner could finish a set,

then pick the weight up again and do another set. All of this would be considered one set. And while it looked like he was doing 10 sets, Vince viewed it as only doing five.

Vince said that during each workout his intensity would vary depending on his energy level. The reps would increase while he was on the dieting phase since he wasn't using the kinds of heavy weights he would in the off-season. As the competition neared, he'd pick up the pace by adding more reps, increasing his cardio, and decreasing rest time between sets. At this point, his goal was to carve the muscle for maximum cut and separation.

Nutritionally, Vince said that his foods during precontest rarely changed. In the morning about 7:30 a.m., he'd have either a bowl of oatmeal or grits with honey. This was his energy meal before he hit the gym at 8:30 or 9:00 a.m. After his morning workout, he had his second meal around 11:00 a.m., and it consisted of chicken, turkey, tuna, a potato, and a yam.

He said he wasn't a big fan of rice, so potatoes and yams were usually his primary carb sources. As he got closer to the competition, say from weeks 9 to 12, he got his protein from three sources: chicken, turkey, and tuna. Then during weeks 4 to 8, he'd drop the chicken and have turkey and tuna. During the last three weeks before the show, Vince said he dropped the turkey and would have tuna or some other kind of fish as his protein source. The goal at that point was to eliminate any foods that may have more fat than he needed.

Vince said his third meal was at four or five o'clock, and he had chicken, turkey, or tuna, along with a potato and a yam. At roughly three weeks out from the show, he dropped the carbs completely from the evening meal, since he was concerned about the foods that may hold or regulate water. Unlike many pros, Vince said he didn't believe in complete carb depletion. Instead, he would take in low carbs from this point all the way up until the contest.

He explained that he wanted his body to burn as much fuel as possible during the day, and when he went into the night, he wanted his fuel level cut way back. As a result, he said there was little to no storage of glycerin. Then when he woke up the next morning, it would be time to restore what his body needed and burn it off, without giving his body time to overcompensate and completely restore.

Vince said his last meal was at 8:00 p.m. and would consist of a salad with one of the three protein sources and maybe some light popcorn. He would even drink a Coke. Vince said he could have that kind of a meal up until about four weeks away from the show, and then he would make some changes by dropping the salad, popcorn, and Coke and going back to the tuna, potatoes, and yams.

What many may find surprising is that Vince didn't weigh his food portions or count calories. He said he knew what his body needed and for him, the critical stage of his precontest preparation was from four weeks out to the day of the show. This was the time where there was no more seeing what kind of foods he could get by with eating. That meant keeping his foods as clean and natural as possible. With only a few weeks away from the show, this was the time he also cut out green vegetables and stuck with the basics of fish, yams, potatoes, and water.

During the last week before the show, Vince would train all the way up to the day of the show. That could include light work-outs, practice posing, and perhaps some push-ups and crunches. This was also the time that he really watched his carb intake.

On the Thursday before the show, Vince said that he started increasing his carbs by adding a few more in-between meals of potatoes or some other dry carbohydrate that didn't require a lot of water to digest. He'd begin restricting his water intake on Thursday before the show and would reduce it from a gallon to a half gallon of water per day while keeping his protein intake unchanged.

On the morning of the show, he would have a normal meal like eggs and potatoes and found them to be good since they were drier than oatmeal. After the prejudging, he might have a carbohydrate drink, which was ideal for him since his body reacted very quickly to junk foods.

THE VINCE TAYLOR PEAK TRAINING SCHEDULE

For peak training, Vince Taylor trained his whole body twice per week on the following schedule.

Monday morning: triceps and shoulders

Monday afternoon: chest and abs

Tuesday morning: biceps, traps, and hamstrings

Tuesday afternoon: back, calves, and abs

Wednesday morning: quads

This schedule repeats Thursday, Friday, and Saturday; Sunday is a day off.

Taylor would do three or four exercises for 10 sets of 6 to 12 reps per body part. Cardio was done three times per week; for example, one workout could be 45 minutes on the bike or 20 minutes on the stair-stepper. He said this routine would be the same one he used in both the off-season and for precontest.

6

Taking the Body to Peak Condition with Sonny Schmidt

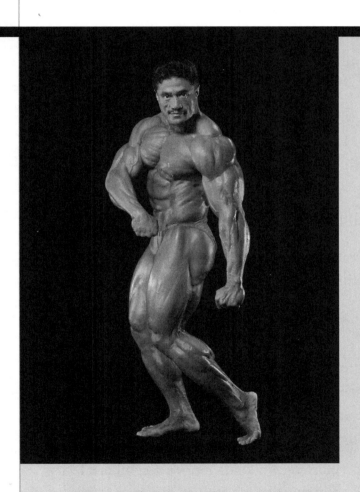

The late Sonny Schmidt was a fascinating pro bodybuilder, and sadly, he passed away much too soon. Sonny was a man of few words, but once you got to know the Australian, your heart was touched by his warmth and zest he had for life.

Sonny said he started training at the age of 23 but began boxing at the ripe old age of 5. Yet it took an injury for Sonny to head into the ring of weights. With the combination of good genetics and smart training, Schmidt's body grew very fast. And when it came time to get it in peak condition, Sonny found some powerfully simple ways. This is what he shared.

Sonny watched his diet all year round. Watching what he ate and keeping his body-fat level low throughout the year allowed him to start his contest preparation as little as six weeks before a show.

When he was in precontest preparation, Sonny's breakfast would consist of porridge with skim milk and Equal sweetener, 12 egg whites, whole wheat toast, black coffee, and water. About an hour later he headed to the gym for his first workout.

At six weeks out, Sonny trained twice a day. His morning workout was when he hit the heavy iron. His evening workout consisted of mainly aerobic work. He would train every day up until four days before the show, and he usually trained two body parts a day. For example, on Monday he might train chest and back. On Tuesday, he might hit quads, hamstrings, and calves. On Wednesday, the body parts could be shoulders and arms. He would repeat this routine again starting on Thursday.

Sonny said he liked doing four to seven exercises of 4 to 5 sets per body part, and his reps varied from 6 to 20. He liked changing the number of reps and the order of the exercises, and he felt doing such a thing helped keep his body off-guard and prevented it from getting stale.

For the precontest workout, Sonny described how he did chest and back. Starting with chest, Sonny said he liked warming up with flat or dumbbell bench presses, depending on how he felt. After a

set or two of warm-ups, he'd do 4 or 5 sets of 10–12 reps. From there, he'd go to incline presses for 4 or 5 sets of 10–12 reps. Dumbbell flat flyes were his third chest exercise, and he did 4 or 5 sets of 10–12 reps. Sonny's last chest exercise was weighted dips for 4 or 5 sets of 10–12 reps. Sonny advised that to hit the deep chest fibers, he did dips with his hands wide and with a deep stretch.

After a few minutes rest, Sonny was then ready to hit back, which was a body part he liked to train heavy all year round. His first back exercise was wide grip behind-the-neck pulldowns, and he did 4 or 5 sets of 10–15 reps. His next back exercise was front pulldowns with a medium to close grip. Sonny said he felt this exercise in the mid-back, and he did 4 or 5 sets of 15 reps.

After front pulldowns, Sonny said he did low cable rows for 4 or 5 sets of 12–15 reps. The next back exercise was bent-over barbell rows, and Sonny said he went as high as 400 pounds since he found heavy weight rows really made his back grow. He said he liked doing 4 or 5 sets of 6–8 reps. Sonny's final rowing movement was T-bar rows for 4 or 5 sets of 8–10 reps. Because Sonny's back had lots of thickness, he said he did hypers instead of deadlifts for 3 sets of 15–20 reps.

To refuel his body after such a grueling morning workout, Sonny's second meal was typically two big chicken breasts, 12 egg whites, various steamed vegetables, and plenty of natural water. He said he took plenty of vitamins and minerals, branched chain and free-form aminos, liver, and extra vitamin C and B with all of his meals. His protein came from chicken, egg whites, and turkey, and carbs came from vegetables such as potatoes, yams, beans, green leafy vegetables, oats, and rice. Sonny said he stayed away from fruit during his precontest peaking.

About three hours later Sonny would have his third meal, which included fish, a variety of steamed vegetables, branched chain aminos, and water. An hour later, Sonny was off to the gym for his second workout, which was cardio. His two-hour cardio workout would be treadmill for an hour followed by stationary bike for another hour.

Sonny said his last meal of the day was shortly after his evening workout and included more protein and fewer carbs than his other meals. He said when he ate too many carbs before he went to sleep, he was more apt to stay awake. He found that the extra protein for his last meal helped him to fall asleep better, and it gave his body the nutrients it needed to recover more quickly.

As Sonny reached the one week before show date, he said he went from training every day six weeks out from the contest to stopping training the Wednesday before the show. On Monday of the final week before a show, he began depleting his body of carbs. He would continue carb depleting from Monday until Wednesday. Sonny said he never counted carbs or calories when he depleted; he simply went by how he looked and felt.

On Wednesday night of the final week before a show, he started taking in carbs every two hours with foods like baked potatoes and rice, along with some protein. Sonny said he cut his protein intake down a bit during the carb loading phase because of all the carbs he was taking in. He'd continue in the same way, eating carbs and a little protein every two hours all day on Thursday and Friday. Then on the day of the show, Saturday, Sonny said he adjusted his carb intake depending on how he looked.

7

Refueling Your Muscle Tank

Make no mistake: nutrition is very important to your bodybuilding success. But good nutrition goes beyond eating small meals throughout the day. It also means getting the right kinds of fuel inside your body, at the right time and in the right amounts, to power you through workouts and the recovery period right after.

Some years ago I [Bob] was in Mexico training with a fitness celebrity, and after our workout he was tired, lethargic, and kind of out of it. So we went to a local market, and I got some fresh fruit juice and we drank a big jug of it. I'm telling you, it was less than 15 minutes and he was like a totally different person. The tiredness gone. The lethargy gone. His focus was sharp. He was back.

What he and all of us go through from time to time was low blood sugar, especially after an intense workout, when the body's energy reserves can be depleted very quickly. We've asked some of the pros over the years how they knew their blood sugar was low, and these were some of the things they said:

- They'd have loads of energy to train, and without warning, their body would start slowing down and get tired.
- Their eyesight could get a bit blurry, and they became uncoordinated with no reflexes.
- Their strength typically goes down slowly in the first few minutes and then drops quickly after that.
- Their endurance goes down, and their body wants to end the set sooner than normal.
- They find it tough to get and maintain a good muscle pump.

Bodybuilders also had varied responses when asked about the foods they ate before they trained:

- Some of them like a protein/carb drink combination.
- Some prefer having a piece of fruit within 50 minutes of their training.
- Some like to training an hour before meals, while others prefer having a good meal and then hitting the iron about 90 minutes later.

They gave a range of answers about how low carbs affected them while they were losing body fat:

- Many said the toughest part is the first week of dieting, since the body really wants the carbs. After that week, those cravings start going away.
- The first couple of weeks of reduced-carb dieting also affects energy levels. Instead of quick bursts of energy they might experience while full of carbs, the low-carb energy switch the body goes through produces steadier and longer energy.
- Many have tried all kinds of macronutrient combinations (high carbs/low fat, high protein/high carbs, and so on) and have found their bodies adjust to whatever diet they eat, provided they do it long enough.
- Some said their bodies were sensitive to too many or too few carbs. To make

adjustments for each, they would raise or lower their protein and fat percentages until they found the best ratio.

- Dennis Newman said that he liked having a shake after his workout. He liked the fact that he didn't have to cook a major meal after training, and if one used the right kind of protein with a good ratio of carbs to protein, then it was good and quick nutrition without the fat.
- Mike Matarazzo said he drank a protein shake for breakfast before he trained and would then have another right after the workout. He said he liked mixing different kinds of protein powders and would even double up on the protein whenever he felt his body needed it to make sure his body was getting enough nutrients for repair, recovery, and growth. Mike liked protein shakes because they are nutrient-dense, and he felt they helped him recover much quicker and gave his muscles a better pump.
- Dorian Yates said he might have a carbohydrate drink in between body parts when he trains. And after training, he would have it with branched chain amino acids. His post-workout meal might include 8 ounces of turkey, 5 ounces of rice,10 ounces of sweet potatoes, sweet corn, another vegetable, water, and two or three grams of peptide-bond amino acids and branched chain amino acids.

8

Ripped to the Bone: Advice from Kevin Levrone, Nasser El Sonbaty, and Michael Francois

Bodybuilders are a tough bunch to please. Think about it: On one hand, they want great size and strength. On the other, they want to be ripped and lean—all at the same time. People can spend much of their training lives just trying to figure out one. The trick is learning how to do both. Don't worry; help is on the way.

Over the years, we've talked to a number of pro bodybuilders about the subject, and their answers were as different as their physiques. You'd think a body is a body and it should respond similarly to training and diet, right? But you'd be wrong. Simply changing minute variables in training and nutrition can make all the difference between a flat or fabulous looking physique.

Three big dudes told how they got that way and how they leaned down to look amazing. Our advice is to read what they said and let it soak in for a few days or a week and then see which pieces of advice seem to make the most sense for you, your body, and your training goals. We'll start with Kevin Levrone.

KEVIN LEVRONE

Kevin said that he often got asked, what are the best foods for cutting up, and how much time does it take to do it? While the good ol' standbys of chicken and ground turkey make excellent protein sources, he found swordfish and flounder to be the best sources of protein, with broccoli and rice being great sources of carbs.

Levrone said he liked swordfish and flounder because they are very low in fat. He even experimented with using only flounder as his protein source, and his body still got ripped and shredded. While Kevin enjoyed steak, chicken, and turkey, he eliminated them about 12 weeks out from the target date he wanted to reach peak condition.

Like many pros, Kevin kept his protein intake very high (five or six pounds of fish each day, roughly 600 grams of protein), and he found this really helped him pack on the lean muscle mass. For some people, fish is not their first choice for most enjoyable protein, so Kevin advised to find protein that's clean, meaning high in protein and low in fat, such as ground turkey and chicken breast.

While a clean diet is crucial to a lean, muscular body, so is cardio. For Kevin, he said one of his biggest earlier problems was that he didn't do enough cardio training. He said he did cardio twice a day, which could be running two miles in the morning on an empty stomach and 40 minutes on the stair-stepper at night after his last meal. Kevin said running was a great cardio workout, but

cautioned to keep the protein intake high or else you'll lose muscle size.

Kevin thought a huge mistake that body-builders make is not listening to their bodies and not getting enough rest. They try to do too much, like getting ripped and getting big and strong at the same time, which, in Kevin's experience, were two very different things. The fallacy comes in thinking that they'll still be able to squat and bench press heavy as they get themselves in ripped condition. Kevin said he personally found that not to be the case, as his strength went down when he dieted.

Kevin advised to allow yourself about 12 weeks to get into peak condition. This means, for the average bodybuilder, doing it once a year is enough. Levrone also found that the body could hold this peak condition for about a week. Kevin said he tried holding it longer but found it very difficult because his body was so depleted of the foods and other nutrients it craved. However, when he slowly started adding more fat and a bit more sodium and sugar to his diet, everything just clicked.

After the peak conditioning period, Levrone started drinking juices and protein powders (low or nonfat) again. He found that a protein supplement was good for replacing much of the protein and calories he had gotten from the fish he ate during the dieting phase.

You may not realize this, but getting your body in ripped condition can have quite a few benefits:

- The heart rate goes down.
- The internal system is cleaned, and all the garbage is flushed out.
- The excess body fat is gone, and your body looks much better. Kevin said that even with him being 5′9″ and 248 pounds (at the time), he had a great deal of energy as he kept getting lean.

Another benefit bodybuilders will like to hear is that after you've gotten yourself in ripped condition and then go back on your regular diet, your metabolism speeds up. Kevin found that his body burned calories more quickly and efficiently and even put on body fat more slowly.

Even though dieting for 14 or so weeks before a major competition may have been grueling, Levrone liked the changes he saw each time he did it. He said the body changes after each time you do it. You start seeing more ridges and valleys and all kinds of cuts. Hey, that's welcome news to any bodybuilder!

NASSER EL SONBATY

Nasser was a big believer that in order to bring your body-fat level down, you must increase your protein and reduce the carbohydrates. He suggested that at least 50 percent of your diet should be protein, consisting of turkey, chicken, tuna, and protein drinks; 35 percent from complex

carbs from foods like dark green vegetables, cauliflower, broccoli, zucchini, and carrots; and 15 percent fat. Potatoes are good, but don't eat too many of them.

The big man found that when he ate too many carbs, his body didn't burn much fat. The muscles were using the carbs for energy instead of using fat as the fuel source. Nasser said he got great fat-burning results when he kept his carbs low for a few days, then increased them for a day, and then reduced them again.

Nasser was quick to confess that for years, losing body fat was difficult for him to do. He wanted to be big as a house, and he liked the feeling it gave him. Who could argue? Geez, the guy was strong and gigantic, however he was eating plenty of carbs but not doing much in the way of cardio training. He now sees that he was overtrained by doing too many workouts, too many reps and sets, using too much weight, and taking too many days off.

As far as mistakes went, Nasser made many of the classic ones, like eating too many carbs and eating those carbs too late in the evening. The more carbs he ate, the more he wanted. Sound familiar? He said he limited his carb eating times to no later than eight o'clock, and if he got hungry, he'd have a protein shake.

You can imagine that coming from a guy who was so big and strong, getting ripped might have been a real tough thing to do. After all, who wants to lose hard-earned muscle?

However, if bodybuilders do it right, what they'll lose right away is water. Then after the excess water is gone, the fat burning begins.

Nasser cautioned that the way to peak successfully is to diet slowly. This means taking 16 weeks and letting your body slowly lose the fat. Nasser said that a person only needs to do this once a year to see dramatic changes. Any more than that is extremely difficult for the body. And even if you know your body well, it won't always react the same to peaking and getting ripped.

He suggested starting your ripped cycle by gradually eliminating dairy products, white and wheat flour, and refined sugar from your diet, one at a time. Weeks 16 and 15, do cardio three times a week. Weeks 14 and 13, do cardio four times a week. Weeks 12 and 11, do cardio five times per week. Weeks 10 and 9, do cardio six times per week. From week 8 until you reach your ripped peak condition, do cardio seven times per week.

Nasser advised that after you've reached ripped condition, hold it for one or two weeks. He said most bodybuilders would find that their bodies will look fantastic, respond better to training, and it will be easier for them to achieve a ripped condition next time they want to do it. He also said most people will find their skin becoming thinner (which shows cuts and striations), and their bodies will become more muscular and vascular. And don't get frustrated if it takes a couple of times to get it right. It takes time, and people get better with practice.

Nasser said that someone who has peaked eight times would look much better than someone who has peaked only three would.

And as Kevin Levrone has observed, Nasser said that once you have stripped your body of the excess fat, your body may put the fat on again, but this time more slowly. This is a great benefit of getting ripped. As we all know, people in ripped condition can look much bigger than they actually are. Get those 10, 15, or 20 pounds off and prepare to be amazed.

MICHAEL FRANCOIS

Like Nasser and Kevin Levrone, Mike Francois said he kept his protein intake high—about 50 percent—and kept the carbs low when it was time to get in ripped condition. His protein came from chicken and turkey, and his carbs from potatoes and grits. However, Mike said that too many carbs caused his body to hold water and appear bloated.

Mike found that the body best burns fat on a low-carb diet, since it needs to go to other sources for energy. Bottom line: it uses fat for fuel. He also thought that too many bodybuilders eat meals that are too high in carbs and too low in protein. When you couple that with overtraining (which many do) and not eating enough of the right food, it's no wonder they're having problems getting hard and ripped while keeping maximum muscularity.

Mike said that one of the biggest mistakes he made was doing too much

training and keeping his body starved. It was crying out for more protein, and he wasn't listening. Finally, he did change things by upping his protein intake while keeping the training volume the same, and he said that within two weeks, his body began to transform itself.

He started losing fat. His muscles became harder, and he had plenty of power for training and was recuperating faster. Even though at first his energy level was down, after a few days his body balanced itself out, and he said he actually had more energy with the protein.

Mike also said that many bodybuilders make the mistake when cutting up of reducing their calories too much, yet they still keep the carbs high for energy. They also eat less protein than their bodies need to stay hard. For the first week or two, they may lose water and look harder, but this is only temporary since their muscles are burning themselves for energy because they are not getting enough protein. That's called catabolism, my friend.

You need to be patient about getting your body in ripped condition. Even for the pros, it takes weeks, and this is what these guys do for a profession! Mike said it was best to make dietary changes very gradually and let the body get used to those changes. He needed at least 12 or 13 weeks to get his body in great condition. Always remember that the more slowly you lose the body fat, the more muscle you will keep. If you're over 12 percent body fat, be sure to take a few weeks longer.

An interesting thing Mike said he did to keep his body off-guard was to change the ratio of protein and carbs in his diet each day. For example, one day his diet might be high protein/low carbs. The next day it could be moderate protein/moderate carbs. Mike said he found this also helped speed fat burning.

So how long does it take to see results if you follow his ripping advice? Mike said that in two or three weeks, you should start seeing some changes in your body. In four to five weeks, you will see some major changes going on. As the fat is melting off, you'll look

harder, more cut, and more symmetrical with nice lines.

Mike departs a bit from Nasser and Kevin in that instead of getting ripped only once per year, Mike said no more than twice a year. Whether you do it once or twice a year, the main thing is that getting yourself in ripped condition gets rid of the years of accumulated body fat. And if you get ripped at least once a year, then all you'll have is a year's worth of body fat to take off next time. Wait two or three years to do it, and you'll have two or three years of fat to get off. Mike suggested making it easy on yourself by doing it at least once a year.

Mike said he makes it a point to get really close to contest-like condition about two or three weeks prior to the date he targets for peak condition. He found that by doing that, losing those final few pounds wasn't so tough, and his body actually stayed harder that much longer. He said trying to hold the peak for only two or three days doesn't give the body enough time to settle in at that weight and condition. Mike also thought that the body would not look nearly as impressive as it could, compared to how it could look if it was in peak shape at least two weeks out. Mike suggested trying to stay in peak condition for two weeks. Any longer than that, he said, and the body begins to rebel.

Many people have found out that when it comes to training and gaining muscle, dieting and having low body fat can be really tough on the body. The reality is that to get bigger and stronger, you must put on some body fat in the off-season to gain the leverage to lift heavier weights.

Mike thought this was where a lot of people were missing the boat. Many bodybuilders will take a few weeks or a month off from training after a contest or after they've gotten themselves in peak condition, and he said he found this could be a huge mistake.

He said that the 30-day period right after a show was actually the time he gained the most and best quality of muscle. He explained that for 12 or so weeks, the body has been deprived of muscle-building calories and has had plenty of time to relax from the heavy training. Then when he started ingesting more calories, the body started to feel very full, the strength went up, and stimulating new muscle growth was very easy. This was the time the body would use those nutrients for growth and strength.

Mike shared an interesting observation on how his body changed after he started getting it in ripped condition on a regular basis. He found that the core composition of his body changed. That is, it took on a slightly different appearance. And each new time he dieted, he started at a better place than where he previously started, and as a result, his body kept looking better and better.

The hardest thing, most bodybuilders will find, is just getting the initial fat off. Again, Mike said that people need to take their time. Have fun learning about your body and how nutrition affects how it looks and feels. Perhaps the biggest motivating factor is that once you see your body changing, you'll have no problem doing it the next time. And the good thing about it, Mike says, is it gets easier each time you do it.

9

Eating for a Mr. Olympia: A Peek at the Training Table of Dorian Yates

Ever wonder what it's like to eat for a Mr. Olympia competition? Many bodybuilders have, and some years ago, Dorian Yates talked about what and how he ate for one of his earlier Mr. Olympia competitions.

Dorian said that his body strived for regularity and balance and responded best to being fed and trained at a certain time along with getting the proper amount of sleep each night. He said yo-yo dieting and taking things to extremes tended to throw the body off and actually did more harm than good, and that's why he believed the balanced approach worked best.

One of the goals for that year's competition was to bring his body in looking bigger and harder, and he did this by increasing his protein and cutting back on the carbs. He said that in the off-season, he took in more carbs, but he was always careful since too many carbs tend to hold water.

Dorian spoke of the importance of refinement and being flexible in his diet approach. His goal was to create the best physique Dorian Yates was capable of, and if that meant gaining or losing 5 or 10 pounds, he'd do it. Dorian said that what his body weighed wasn't nearly as important as how it looked on stage.

For this particular Mr. Olympia, Dorian took in 3,800 to 4,000 calories a day, and that included roughly 350 grams a day of protein, most of which came from turkey, tuna, lean meat, chicken, egg whites, and a high-quality protein powder. His carbs were in the 450 to 550 gram per day range, and they came from vegetables, whole grains, beans, rice, potatoes, yams, and pasta. His fat intake was kept low, yet high enough to give his body the required fatty acids it needed for normal function. Dorian said that when his fatty acid levels were too low,

his hair and skin would be very dry and brittle, and increasing the fat intake slightly corrected it.

Dorian was very instinctive when it came to his dietary intake and would rely on how he looked and felt as his guides. For example, he said that on some days, he found his body needed more food than other days, so he would slightly increase his calories. He also said his body responded well to six small meals a day spaced about three hours apart.

He described a typical food day as he prepared for this Mr. Olympia:

Meal 1: Oatmeal (approximately four ounces), 6 to 10 egg whites, two or three pieces of plain whole wheat toast

Meal 2: Liquid protein and carb meal taken 30 to 45 minutes before training

Meal 3: Turkey breast, rice, potatoes, and a mixture of other vegetables

Meal 4: Tuna, pasta (various varieties), and salad

Meal 5: Chicken, sweet potatoes, and a mixture of other vegetables

Meal 6: Oatmeal (approximately four ounces), 6 to 10 egg whites, and two or three pieces of whole wheat toast

All of Dorian's food for the entire day was weighed every morning before his first meal.

PART 3

Training and Workout Strategies

10

Nasser El Sonbaty's Tips for Growth

If you wanted a pro bodybuilder who could turn heads and drop jaws with his gigantic size, one need not look any further than Nasser El Sonbaty, the 5'11" 295-plus–pound behemoth. The progeny of an Egyptian father and a Yugoslavian mother, Nasser (his friends call him "Jimmy") spent a great deal of his childhood living in Egypt, Yugoslavia, and finally settling down in Germany.

When Jimmy got dialed into pro competition, he won the Houston Pro Invitational over the sensational Vince Taylor. He then went on to win the prestigious "Night of Champions"—the same show that launched the careers of Lee Haney, Dorian Yates, Kevin Levrone, and others.

Over the years, people have asked about Nasser's growth secrets. (Hey buddy, got any genetics you could spare?) And even though Nasser can speak seven languages, when he speaks the language of size and strength, everyone understands. Here is a little of what can be learned from him.

Nasser said his training and diet had remained consistent for a number of years. He found what worked best for him, and rarely did he deviate from it. He said he liked doing one or two basic exercises for each muscle group such as dips, squats, barbell curls, and bench presses.

To stay injury-free, he said it was very important to warm up before working out. That's why he typically stretched or rode the bike for 10 to 15 minutes before he worked out.

He said when he trained bigger muscle groups like legs, chest, lats, and shoulders, he'd do 10 to 15 sets of 6 to 20 reps. However, he liked doing higher reps for hamstrings and quads.

For smaller muscles like abs, calves, traps, biceps, triceps, and forearms, he'd do 8 to 10 sets of 6 to 10 reps. He said it was important to always concentrate on feeling the muscle burn and not just count reps when doing an exercise. Focusing his mind on the muscle he worked helped his body to grow very quickly.

In the off-season, Nasser said he would train three to four days, then take a day off. He also said he liked using such things as peak contractions, pyramiding, and other intensity techniques to keep his workouts fresh and his body growing.

Nasser preferred to train alone, having found in the past that many of his partners would come to the gym late or wouldn't even show up. Added to that, many of them didn't have the same goals about training that he did, so there was always a conflict. He said training alone allowed him to change his workouts whenever he wanted, and if he ever needed a spot for a heavy lift, there was always someone in the gym to help.

So what did such a big muscle machine eat? He said that in the off-season, he'd usually have between 5,000 to 6,000 calories a day. His carbs were high, the protein was moderate, and the fats were low. And yes, like most of us, he had an occasional junk food day when he might have ice cream, cake, and the like. He always made sure he drank plenty of water.

When it came time for precontest preparations, Nasser admitted he was fortunate that he had a good metabolism and believed this allowed him to start his precontest dieting about eight weeks away from a show. He said that as he got ready for a show, he would drop the calories down to 3,000 to 4,000 a day, cut out the dairy products and sweets, increase his cardio to 45 minutes a day, add 5 to 7 sets and reps per muscle group, and train 12 times per week (twice a day with Sunday as a day off).

Nasser had a good eating philosophy. He said that eating the foods he wanted, when he wanted them, helped him to enjoy life. He believed that sometimes it was too easy to get carried away by letting one's diet control one's life. To Nasser, that wasn't enjoyable.

He said many times he saw some body-builders spending their whole day doing nothing but thinking about bodybuilding and hanging around no one other than bodybuilders, something he found to be quite narrow-minded. Nasser said how could one make any progress in the other areas of life unless they put things into perspective and have the proper balance? He believed it was important to experience all of the other great things that life has to offer, and if you don't, there's always going to be something missing.

FIRST AND FOREMOST: THERE ARE NO SECRETS

Nasser quickly dispels the notion of "secret exercises" or supplements for growth. To him, bodybuilding growth and strength is based on a number of factors: genetics, mental approach, consistent high-intensity workouts cycled with lower intensity training, excellent workout form, plenty of sleep, and the right combination of nutrients.

At one time he said that the single biggest factor that caused his body to explode with new growth was gradually raising his protein intake from 100 grams to 600 grams per day!

However, when his protein intake was low, he said his muscles appeared flat and small. Then, as his protein intake increased, his muscles not only became big and full, but his training recovery time was cut by 50 percent.

NOT EVERYONE CAN EAT LIKE A PRO BODYBUILDER

Let's be really clear here. Most people don't train or eat like a pro bodybuilder. But there are some things we can learn that can make huge differences in our training. One of the things Nasser liked to do when he didn't have time to prepare and cook four to six meals a day was replace one or two of those meals with a high-quality whey, egg, or milk-and-egg protein drink.

Another thing was that each meal consisted of 65 percent carbohydrates (from potatoes, greens, and other vegetables, rice, whole grains, pasta, beans, lentils, fruit), 25 percent protein (from egg whites, lean beef, skinless chicken or turkey, protein powder), with the remaining 10 percent of the calories coming from fat, which was already in his diet from the foods he ate.

One of the things that surprised many people was just how few calories (relative to his size) Nasser ate in the off-season and in precontest. Off-season, when he weighed over 300 pounds, he ate an average of 5,000 calories a day. And in precontest, when his weight was a rock-hard 264 pounds, his daily calories would drop to 3,800.

BE CAREFUL OF TOO MUCH AEROBIC ACTIVITY

Nasser said that at one time he made the mistake that many of us have made of doing too much aerobic activity. He said he used to do 30 to 75 minutes of cardio training on an empty stomach, four to six times per week. And even though he believed he was burning fat, in reality he was burning muscle. Add to all of that, he was working out twice per day; doing one body part in the morning and another at night.

That's when he decided to change things around. Instead of training twice a day, now it was only once per day. He also did his cardio after his weight workouts and for never more than 40 minutes. The other thing he changed was training each body part only once per week, with the exception of calves and abs, which he trained every day.

Nasser found that these changes helped give his body more time for rest, recuperation, and growth. His energy level increased, and he had plenty of power for his workouts, which raised his workout intensity level big time. These simple but profound changes helped give Nasser a huge motivational boost (and he was already plenty motivated before these changes) and took his body and training to a higher level.

SEE IF YOU'RE MAKING THESE TRAINING MISTAKES

As you can imagine, someone doesn't get the size and strength of Nasser's caliber unless they've spent many hours in the gym and have made plenty of mistakes that they've quickly learned from to find what works and what doesn't. Nasser mentioned some of the most common he has seen:

- Many people waste their time in the gym by training too long and with low intensity. They're simply going through the motions and achieving little, if any results. They use too much weight and less than ideal form. The key is to use full range of motion and to feel every rep.
- You must train with the basic movements. Forget using machines. Neglecting basic movements and concentrating on machine work is a very big mistake.
- Stick with barbells and dumbbells, and do the basic movements like squats, presses, deadlifts, rows, and curls.

IT'S ALL ABOUT VARIETY

One of the things Nasser said he liked to do was constantly vary his workouts and not do the same exercise or same workout order two times in a row. For example, on Monday, he might work legs since his body had had a few days to recover from his last heavy workout. Then again, it could be his back. He said he liked mixing up his routines, exercises, sets, reps, rest times, and workout order.

One of Nasser's training schedules looked like this:

Monday: train
Tuesday: train
Wednesday: train
Thursday: day off
Friday: train

Saturday: alternating day off depending on recovery factors

Sunday: day off

WHAT ABOUT SETS AND REPS?

It's the age-old question, isn't it? "How many reps and sets should I do?" There's really not one universal answer. However, Nasser said he found some great body part/rep combinations:

Quads and hams: 8–20 reps

Calves: 30 reps

Chest: 6–12 reps

Back: 6–12 reps

Shoulders: 6–12 reps

Biceps: 6–12 reps

Triceps: 6–12 reps

He also found some excellent body part/ set combinations:

Calves: 4–6 sets

Hamstrings: 10 sets

Quads: 12–15 sets

Biceps: 8 sets

Triceps: 10 sets

Forearms: 4–6 sets

Shoulders: 8–12 sets

Chest: 8–10 sets

Back: 12–15 sets

WATCH YOUR ASSUMPTIONS AND ASK A LOT OF QUESTIONS

I've observed an interesting phenomenon when fans get a chance to be around their favorite champions. Besides amazement, many assume that guys like Nasser would be aloof and unapproachable, but they would be wrong.

Champs like Nasser all started where you are—as a beginner. But Nasser said he regularly sought the advice of those who were bigger and stronger than him. He had a thirst for knowledge, and not surprisingly, those he asked were more than happy to help.

But it helps to ask the right kinds of questions, like Nasser did, such as, "How much time must I spend in the gym each day in order to get the best results?" and, "What should I eat in order to maximize my size and minimize my fat?"

One of the likable things about Nasser was that he was a thinking person's bodybuilder. Not only could you talk to him about politics, religion, history, world affairs, and the like, but when it came to training, the more specific you got with the training questions you'd ask—such as, "With what percentage of intensity do you train in the off-season, precontest, and other times during the year?"—the better he'd like them.

Nasser liked giving people some good guidelines they can use as a starting point to find their own ideal training and nutritional strategies. He knew that another person's body type, genetics, goals, degree of training intensity, rest, recuperation, and nutritional factors may be very different than his. That's why he liked to say, take what I'm giving you and build on it.

11

Shirt-Sleeve-Bustin' Arms the Dorian Yates Way

One of the things that set Dorian Yates apart from so many of the other top-level pro bodybuilders was his incredible high-intensity heavy weight training. It was brutal, and for those who did venture into that territory, no one stayed as long as Yates.

A lot of things are needed to sustain such a training regimen. For one, a steel will and mind-set are crucial, as well as a well-thought-out game plan and honed image and goal of what the end result will be. You also need body parts that are damned strong.

Since arms and forearms are what grip those bars and hold those heavy weights, Yates needed and had them. His forearms made Popeye's look puny, and Dorian's arms were packed with rugged muscularity that not only allowed him great workouts but were good enough to pass the test of

Mr. Olympia. Here's what he said of how he trained them.

Let's quickly dispel any notions of him using lots of sets and reps. Dorian said he only did three exercises of 6 to 10 reps for a total of 8 to 10 sets for biceps and 10 sets of three exercises of 6 to 12 reps for triceps.

Dorian said it doesn't matter what body part people are working. If they're bustin' a gut and going balls to the wall, they're not gonna need a lot of sets to make their body grow. He spoke about how very early on in his training, he used to do set after set. Sure, he was growing, but not as fast as he wanted to. He said he decided to change some things around, and what he discovered made all the difference between him growing just a little or growing a lot.

In all of his exercises, he cut the number of his sets in half (for example, from 20 to 10), decreased his rest time, and began lifting as heavy as he could. The results he experienced were tremendous, such as deeper and denser muscle mass, greater strength, and more of a quality look to his physique. Dorian said that when people asked him what he did for his arms, they were amazed at what he said.

Dorian said in order to make the arms grow, you need to pick exercises that place the greatest demand on the biceps and triceps muscles—exercises that really make those muscles work hard. Dorian said he worked arms after chest. Working a big body part like chest and then following it with a smaller body part like arms left him plenty of energy to go all out in his training.

He said he began his arm workout with biceps because it allowed the triceps more time to recuperate from the heavy chest work. The pumped biceps also gave him a cushion/rebound effect when he began working the triceps.

He began with seated dumbbell concentration curls, warming up for 1 set and then going right into 2 heavy sets. He said his first heavy set was the heaviest, and he then dropped the poundage back a bit for his final heavy set.

He usually would warm up with 50-pounders for 10 reps. For his heaviest set, he would go to 75 to 80 pounds for 6 to 8 reps and then drop down to 60 to 70 pounds for his final set of 6 to 8 reps. Formwise, he said his arm was locked into the inside of his leg. Dorian said he had done them free-standing but felt the movement more when he was seated.

On the question of supination, Dorian said he didn't constantly think that he had to make sure he turned his wrist at the top of the movement. He just made sure he felt the muscle work during the exercise. As for sets and reps, Dorian said that in the past, all he ever did was heavy weight and low reps, however, he began experimenting with cycling his reps to 10s and 12s, and it was working very well.

Dorian's second biceps exercise was barbell curls. He did these with either a straight or EZ curl bar, and since his biceps were already warmed up, he'd jump right into his heaviest set. He said he liked going heavy on these, so on his first set he would take a medium grip and pick up a loaded 165- to 175-pound bar for 5 or 6 reps and then have a partner give him 1 or 2 forced reps. He would then drop the weight down a bit on the second set, say 145 to 150 pounds, and squeeze out another 5 or 6 reps, with his partner giving him 1 or 2 more forced reps. Dorian said he wasn't a big believer in using forced reps all the time because he thought it took away from making the muscle work and forcing it to become stronger. Forced reps are good if you use them occasionally and you're not doing them for too many sets.

His third and final biceps exercise was alternating dumbbell curls (also known as hammer curls) for the brachialis. Dorian said it was important to develop the brachialis muscle in order to have full and complete biceps. This exercise isolated the brachialis and worked it like no other.

Dorian liked to do this exercise standing. He would pick a pair of 70-pound dumbbells and began the movement with his thumbs pointed upward. As he approached the top of the movement, he would curl the weight out to his side and away from himself, supinating the dumbbell and contracting it at the top of the movement. He would this for 6 to 8 reps. On his second set of hammer curls, he'd drop the weight down to 60 or 65

pounds and do the same for another 6 to 8. That would be it for biceps.

As a rule, he didn't do any kind of direct forearm work. His forearms got a lot of heavy indirect work from the other exercises, such as holding a 200-pound dumbbell for sets of rows.

Triceps were next, and after a few minutes of rest, he was ready. Dorian said he thought it was very important to properly warm up the triceps tendon before working the triceps. The triceps tendon is vulnerable to injury, and if it isn't properly warmed, you're asking for trouble. He admitted that he used to be one of those guys who thought a quick warm-up set for the triceps was all he needed before he jumped into the heavy weights. It was only after much pain that he discovered that 2 or 3 warm-up sets of 10 to 12 reps is what it took to prepare his triceps for the intense workout that followed.

Dorian said his warm-up and first exercise was triceps pressdowns. He said he preferred using a curved bar, although he would vary hand positions by occasionally using a straight bar. After 2 or 3 warm-up sets of 10 to 12 reps, he would jump right up to his heaviest set. He said there were two styles he used on the triceps pressdown. With one style, he described leaning into the weight with the cable running down the side of his face and going close to his chest. Since he wasn't using such a strict style, he was able to handle heavier weight. For example, his first and heaviest set might be 250 pounds for 6 to 8 reps, and his second set could be 220 to 230 pounds for another 6 to 8 reps.

Dorian said that when he would do pressdowns in a more strict style, the weights would go down to 180 to 200 pounds for 6 to 8 reps, and he would always lock the movement out at the bottom and would bring the bar in line and no higher than the bottom of his chest.

His second triceps exercise was lying extensions with an EZ curl bar as it took the stress off of the wrist. Dorian described how he would take a close grip on the bar and lower the weight below his head. He would lock the bar out to full extension with his arms and the weight at a 45-degree angle, as this really hit the triceps.

He said he would do one warm-up set with 110 pounds, then would go to his heaviest set with 170 to 180 pounds for 6 to 8 reps. He would use slightly less weight on his next set, going down to 150 to 160 pounds for 6 to 8 reps . He said he liked to cycle his reps on this exercise by doing 6 to 8 reps one workout and 10 to 12 reps on another.

His third and final triceps exercise was dumbbell French presses or reverse one-arm cable pressdowns. As these were considered finishing exercises for the triceps, Dorian said he wasn't that concerned about how heavy he went as he was about using strict form. For one-arm dumbbell French presses, he said he would take a dumbbell, and with his arm straight upward from his shoulder,

he'd bring the weight down behind his head. He would then raise the weight to full lockout and hold the contraction at the top for one or two seconds.

For reverse cable pressdowns, Dorian said they were basically the same as regular pressdowns with the exception that he would do them with one hand and a reversed grip. He would take a reverse grip on a small bar connected to an overhead pulley and began the exercise with his hand at chest level. He would then press down and squeeze the flexed triceps muscle at the bottom and slowly bring the weight back up to chest level and repeat. Dorian said these movements isolated the triceps and worked well in bringing out the deep cuts in the muscle. He did 2 sets with moderately heavy weight and kept his reps in the 10 to 12 range.

All in all, Dorian said his arm routine was about 10 sets per body part, including the warm-ups, taking approximately 35 minutes. However, he said to get the most out of the routine, it was important to pay attention to a few details:

- Keep the reps as strict as possible and always under control.
- Feel the muscle work through the full range of movement.
- Slow the rep speed down—especially during the negative part of the movement. Dorian said this was where a lot of growth occurs, and those who do not pay attention to the negative part of

the rep were missing an important part of the movement.

Finally, Dorian had some good advice about avoiding common mistakes. He said one of the most common mistakes was overtraining. The biceps and triceps are relatively small muscles, and it is easy to overtrain them. Whenever you're doing pushing movements like chest and shoulder presses, your triceps are being worked. Whenever you're doing pulling movements like chins and rows, your biceps are being worked. Just remember that the biceps and triceps get a lot of indirect work from other exercises.

He also said to make sure you're doing every exercise and rep in as strict a form as possible. Dorian always paid careful attention to his form, even going as heavy as he did. Strict form helps isolate the muscle, reduces the chance for injury, and stimulates more muscle fibers for greater growth.

THE DORIAN YATES ARM WORKOUT

Biceps

- Dumbbell concentration curls: 2 sets of 6–8 reps warm-up; 1 set of 6–8 reps heavy; 1 set of 6–8 reps with 10 percent weight drop
- Barbell curls: 1 set of 6–8 reps heavy; 1 set of 6–8 reps with 10 percent weight drop
- Alternate dumbbell curls: same as concentration curls

Triceps

- Triceps pressdowns: 2 or 3 sets of 10–12 reps warm-up
- Lying EZ curl extensions: 1 set of 10 to 12 reps warm-up; 1 set of 6–8 reps heavy; 1 set of 6–8 reps with 10 percent weight drop
- One-arm dumbbell French press: 2 sets of 10–12 reps moderate to heavy
- One-arm reverse-grip pressdowns

12

Frank Hillebrand's Tips for Building Terrific Thighs

When you look at pictures of many of the pro bodybuilders, you'll see that although all of them are big and ripped, they have uniquely developed body parts. Yes, while a big arm is a big arm, the size and shape of one bodybuilder's biceps can look much different from another's.

Legs are another good example. Some guys can have Platz-like quads, and others can have more of the long, lean Arnold-looking thighs. In my book, one is not necessarily more desirable than another. It all depends on what you like.

One bodybuilder who had a nice set of "wheels" was Frank Hillebrand. While not freaky massive like Tom Platz or Victor Richards quads, they were symmetrical to Frank's physique and had nice lines. Lots of his fans liked them, too. This is how he built them.

Frank said that early on, he always had a problem with his legs because he was a boxer and ran a lot, and as a result, his legs were skinny. And yes, he heard all the comments about them, too, like his body looked like a Christmas tree with little legs. He said such comments only pushed him to train harder and harder until he really did have legs. How did he do it? He started listening to his body.

Frank said when he began training legs, he used to train like a crazy person, doing as many as 40 or 50 sets per body part. It was when he moved to California that he began to notice that other people didn't overly train, yet they were still growing. Observing this gave him the feedback that these people must've been doing something right, so he changed his thinking on training. For one thing, while many people were too concerned about overtraining, Frank discovered it was more important to think about undereating and undersleeping. A real wake-up call indeed.

He found that when it came to training thighs, it was very important to give every set and rep 100 percent effort, concentration, and strict form. Frank put his mind to the muscle, and this helped him train harder because he was training smarter.

Frank said he found training on a four-on and one-off routine worked great for him. It gave his body the rest it needed, and it allowed him to train his body very intensely.

He said he did legs on day three, with the morning workout doing hamstrings and in the evening doing quads. His workouts took anywhere from 45 to 60 minutes.

He began his thigh training by riding the stationary bike for 5 to 10 minutes to warm up, and then he would stretch out his legs. Frank said it was very important to warm the muscles and stretch them before doing any leg work as this helped avoid injury and also provided a fuller range of motion.

Frank's first exercise was squats, and he'd usually start the first set fairly light, with 135 pounds, and continue increasing the weight each set until he pyramided the weight up to his heaviest set. He liked to keep his feet about shoulder-width apart with the bar resting on the top of his shoulders across the traps. He would then lower the weight while keeping his back in a very erect upright position and would go to the parallel or slightly below. He did 4 sets of 10 to 12 reps.

He said proper breathing and good form were very important when doing squats. He would inhale deeply as he went down and would exhale as he started coming up. He kept his back in an upright position during the entire squat movement and found this helped keep the stress off of the lower back and concentrated the movement to the front of the legs.

Frank's next quad movement was either the leg press or hack squat. Sometimes, he said, he'd do both, but most of the time, he liked rotating the exercises each workout. For leg presses, he'd load up the heavy iron immediately since his thighs were already warmed up from the squats. He'd sit tightly in the seat and position his feet together since this hit the outer part of the thigh really well. Sometimes he would vary the foot positioning in order to feel the movement differently and found that toes pointed out wide hit the inner thigh and toes together hit the outer thigh. He would then lower the weight in a controlled manner as far as he could and press it back up to the starting position. He did 4 sets of 10 to 12 reps.

After leg presses, Frank did hack squats for 4 sets of 10 to 12 reps. He liked this movement because it gave his quads a nice sweep. He loaded enough plates on the hack squat to give his thighs the burn they needed. Frank said he liked keeping his feet close together since it helped give his quads a nice sweeping shape from hitting the outer thighs.

He would begin the exercise in a slow, deliberate fashion and take the weight down to slightly below parallel and then back up to the starting position. He said he would inhale deeply on the way down and exhale on the way up. He also cautioned to not bounce the weight off the bottom position on the way up, as this exercise puts a lot of stress on the knees and if not done correctly could leave one open to injury.

His last thigh exercise was leg extensions. He felt this was a good shaping movement, and it helped separate the quads really well. The goal on this one was to go for the burn, so weight wasn't that important. Feeling the movement was. Frank explained that as he did the movement, his legs were fully extended out in front of him. He would then squeeze and contract the quads as hard as he could and hold it for a count or two. He then slowly lowered the weight back down to the starting position and did this for 4 or 5 sets of 12 to 15 reps.

Frank said that when it came to building great quads, he was a big believer in good basic movements done with strict, controlled form. Over the years, he described how he saw many people not getting the results they wanted from their thigh training because of three big mistakes they're making.

The first was counting reps. Frank said it was important to feel the muscle and thoroughly work it first and to not quit too soon just because you did a certain amount of reps. Work the muscle thoroughly and make it grow.

He said the second mistake was by people paying too much attention to the weights. Weights are only a means to an end. His advice was to go as heavy as you could with good form, but never sacrifice form and feeling the muscle work just to lift heavy weights.

The third mistake, he said, was using bad form. Frank said to work the muscle through the entire range of its motion, and good form allows you to do that. His advice was that incomplete reps shortened the muscles. Perhaps most important, Frank believed the key to success was getting the mind into the muscle that you're working. That was a huge secret to making the quads grow.

THE FRANK HILLEBRAND ROUTINE FOR GREAT THIGHS

- Stationary bike warm-up for 5 to 10 minutes followed by complete leg stretch.
- Squats: 4 sets of 10–12 reps with weight pyramided and feet positioned in a moderate stance

- Leg press: 4 sets of 10–12 reps with feet positioned together
- Hack squats: 4 sets of 10–12 reps with feet positioned together
- Leg extensions: 4–5 sets of 12–15 reps with feet positions varied

13

Ageless Bodybuilding the Vince Taylor Way

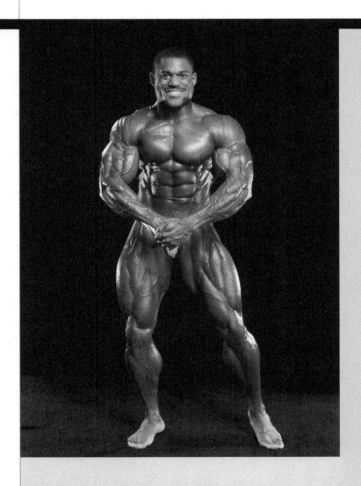

The old saw used to be that when one turned 40 years old, it wouldn't be long before the body went downhill. Today, we know that's no longer true. In fact, many people don't even start weight training until they're in their 50s or 60s, and they are surprised at just how quickly they gain strength and muscle tone and how fast the body can change how it looks and feels.

One guy who always amazed us was the eternally youthful Vince Taylor. Call it blessed with genetics, say the guy knows his body and how to train it, or just plain both, there's no denying that when people see Taylor, he turns heads. After Vince hit that 40 milestone, this is what he said about how he kept looking so good.

Vince kept his off-season and precontest body weight pretty close to each other, roughly about 10 pounds apart. He also said he was a big believer in cardio conditioning and not just sitting on a bike pedaling in the gym. Vince said he got up at 4:00 a.m. and did two miles of roadwork, just like a boxer. He found running was the thing that really stripped the body fat from his body (there wasn't a lot there to begin with). Taylor is serious about his running, too—as in running with heavy clothes and hood on in the hot Florida sun.

Taylor is a huge fan of instinctive training. He said that when he came back from a layoff, he came back in the gym not really knowing exactly what he would do, but rather kept his mind open to using all the things in the gym (cables, free weights, machines, and so on) to get his body's muscle memory back and start looking like a serious bodybuilder again.

What may surprise a lot of people is Vince said his diet (at the time) was somewhere in the neighborhood of 1,500 to 2,000 calories a day. As you've been reading, that's roughly half of what many of the other pros were eating. But when you look like Vince, who the heck can argue?

Vince said he trained seven days a week using the same routine he had done for years. For example, he said that Mondays and Thursdays, he trained chest, shoulders, and triceps. Tuesdays and Saturdays were back, biceps, leg biceps, traps, and ab days. Wednesdays and Sundays were leg days where he did 5-set series training—that was, three muscle groups and 5 sets of 12 to 15 reps per exercise. He also used what he called a high/low system, where he'd perform half of his training with heavy weights and the other half with lighter movements.

He said he believed in getting enough blood into the area that he was working, so he liked doing movements that he could feel, and he found cables to be excellent for that. Vince said he couldn't say what exercise he would use to train any muscle group until he got into the gym and saw how he felt. Vince trained instinctively and said that even if he were in the middle of a set, if he wasn't feeling the movement, he'd stop and go to something else.

Of all the great body parts Taylor has, his arms have to rank at the top. When asked what he did to build those fabulous guns, this is what he said:

- He used cables in lots of various angles.
- One of his favorite biceps exercises is a cable curl, and he did it like a salute to someone, whereby the arm was high and it came across the face with the cable coming down from a high pulley.
- Vince liked doing his cable arm work from a clock position, working the arms from all angles from 6 o'clock to 12 o'clock.

- He'd also change his body position. On one set, he might face the cable. On another set, he could have his back turned away from it.
- Vince said he rarely did heavy barbell curls. For him, they didn't work.
- He said his arms responded best to dumbbell hammer curls and cable curls.
- For triceps, Vince stayed away from leaning over and doing heavy triceps pressdowns. Instead, he focused on one-arm cable triceps work.
- One of his favorite triceps movements was one-arm cable push-outs. Vince did them with his back to the cable machine and pushed his arm out in front of him—just like a boxer would throw a punch.
- Vince found that turning his hands at all different kinds of angles created new and different feels for the biceps and triceps.
- Vince said that cables helped him to create an incredible mind-to-muscle link that produced great workouts and great results.

14

Chest Strategies of Porter Cottrell

Porter Cottrell was an inspiration to a lot of bodybuilders. Porter wasn't a giant by today's standards. He had a bone structure that put him more in the class of a Frank Zane than Sergio Oliva, but he knew how to take what he was given and turn it into something really good.

Porter was inspiring to the many, many bodybuilders who have never competed and do not intend to compete. He showed them just how excellent a physique can look if only one pays attention to symmetry and proportion and builds training around those two elements. Coming from a guy who weighed about 120 pounds when he first started training in the gym, how far Porter rose in the sport is a testament not only to his likable personality but to a physique that could turn heads.

One of Porter's best body parts was his chest, and on a number of occasions he spoke about training and how he developed complete pecs. In the years of developing his chest, Porter said he tried just about every kind of routine, angle, set, and rep range he could in order to make his chest grow, and after much trial and error, he found what worked.

Cottrell was a big believer in instinctive training. He didn't go by a prescribed number of sets, reps, or the same exercises. He constantly changed things around to keep his body shocked and stimulated for growth. For example, one chest workout may consist of 15 sets of four exercises, and his next workout might only be 8 sets with one or two exercises.

One of the other ways Porter used instinctive training was during the workout itself. This might be when he was in the middle of his 15-set workout, and on the eleventh set if he felt the blood dissipating from the muscle, he'd stop right there. The goal was to always end each workout with as much blood into the muscle as he possibly could.

Porter said the warm-up was very important, and he did it by using just the bar and doing a set or two of no weight incline barbell presses. Then, once he felt his body was warmed up, he'd go right into his first exercise, which was barbell incline press.

Porter used various angles on this exercise. For example, he might use a 45-degree angle one workout and a 30-degree angle the next. He was a big proponent of hitting the muscle from a variety of angles in order to work all the muscle fibers. Porter said he pyramided the weight to as high as 315 pounds (at the time) for a total of 3 or 4 sets of 6 to 20 reps.

His next exercise was incline dumbbell presses. However, before he did them, Porter did a warm-up set with that new exercise before he went up to the heavy weight. For this exercise, he'd do a warm-up set with 90 or 100 pounds, then pyramid up to 120 for a total of 3 or 4 sets of 6 to 15 reps.

Porter said he found the range of 6 to 20 reps per chest exercise worked well because he was able to train both slow and fast-twitch muscle fibers within the same workout. He also said he believed in taking every set to the absolute limit. He didn't stop just because he did 10 or 12 reps. If he could do more reps, he would. Porter believed that giving 110 percent effort to each set and rep is what made bodies grow.

For his third chest exercise, Porter would go to incline flyes. After the warm-up, Porter said he'd start pyramiding up to 80 pounds for 6 to 10 reps. He could stay there for a set or two or pyramid back down to 60 pounds and squeeze out 15 to 20 reps. He did 3 or 4 sets of 6 to 20 reps.

Porter's fourth and final chest movement was the cable crossover. Even though he considered this a shaping movement, Porter believed he could turn it into a mass builder if he used the correct form. Porter's goal on this movement was to pump as much blood into the muscle as possible. He pyramided the weight up for 3 or 4 sets and would go as high as 20 or 30 reps just to make sure he pumped as much blood into his chest muscle as possible.

Porter avoided doing any kind of flat bench pressing, since they overly stressed the rotator and didn't stimulate the kind of growth for complete chest development as he found inclines did.

THE PORTER COTTRELL CHEST WORKOUT

- Barbell incline press: 3 or 4 sets of 6–20 reps. He varied the angle to hit the entire chest. He took a medium grip and lowered the weight to where the neck joins the upper chest. Then, with elbows back, he pushed the weight up to where his arms are locked out, squeezing and tensing the chest. He then lowered the weight back down in a controlled manner and repeated.
- Dumbbell incline press: 3 or 4 sets of 6–15 reps. After a set of warm-ups, he pyramided up to his heaviest set. With a pair of dumbbells at his chest, he pushed the dumbbells up to full lock-out and tensed and contracted the muscle for a complete count, then he lowered the weight back down and repeated. The wrist was completely straight and the elbows were taken as far back as possible at the bottom of the movement.
- Dumbbell incline flyes: 3 or 4 sets of 6–20 reps. With a pair of dumbbells, he raised

his arms straight above his head and then slowly allowed the dumbbells to go as far as possible out to his sides while his arms were slightly bent. He then brought the weights back up (in a semi-arc position) to the finish position above his head, where he contracted the muscle, and then he repeated.

- Cable crossover: 3 or 4 sets of 20–30 reps. His final chest movement was a finishing movement deigned to pump as much blood into his chest as possible. Standing with a cable in each hand, he bent his body slightly forward and then squeezed his chest muscle as he crossed the cables in front of him. While keeping strict form, he then brought his arms up above his head to the starting position and repeated.

Porter's Weekly Workout Schedule

At the time, Porter said he was using a two-on/one-off workout schedule.

> Day 1: chest and shoulders
> Day 2: back and biceps
> Day 3: off
> Day 4: triceps and legs (quads and hamstrings)
> Day 5: chest and shoulders
> Day 6: off

Calves are worked every other day. Aerobics (in the off-season) consisted of approximately 30 minutes of stationary bike done in the morning.

15

Shawn Ray's Arsenal for Biceps and Triceps

One of the most admired pro bodybuilders, who was on the scene for year after year and would always come to shows looking awesome, was Shawn Ray. While many admired his confidence, which he had plenty of, Shawn was a smart bodybuilder and successful businessman. He was a guy you could depend on to show up in great shape and easily challenge any top pro for first place.

Ray had a physique that was well put together, and on that physique were an amazing pair of triceps and biceps. You will like his arm training approach.

Shawn said that well-balanced arm development was very important to a well-balanced physique. It was also a body part that was fun for Shawn to train. His success in making his arms grow was a combination of intensity of effort, consistency in not missing workouts, and finding the exercises that worked for him. And that, Shawn said, was the key. You need to find the exercises, number of sets and reps, angles, training pace, rest times, and so on that work for you.

Ray quickly dispelled any ideas of secret exercises for training arms. Shawn said he liked using basic exercises with slight variations that could be summed up as follows: basic movements, pyramiding as heavy weight as possible with good form, rare use of forced reps, 1 or 2 warm-up sets, then 3 heavy sets of 8 to 15 reps per exercise with three or four exercises per body part. On top of that, he said he liked changing the angles at which he worked his arms and felt it gave him a more complete muscle blast.

Shawn began his arm workouts with biceps, and his first exercise was dumbbell alternating curls. He did these either seated or standing and said they were his favorite biceps mass-building exercise.

He took a pair of moderately heavy dumbbells and did 1 or 2 warm-up sets of 10 reps, and he would then start pyramiding up the weight for 3 more heavy sets. He stood with the dumbbells next to his sides with his palms facing each other and then slowly curled one of the dumbbells up to about shoulder level and twisted his wrist at the top. His little finger was higher than his thumb in that position. He'd then hold the weight there for a count and squeeze and contract the biceps hard. Finally, he'd slowly lower the weight down and repeat the procedure with his other arm.

Shawn said his second biceps exercise was one-arm dumbbell concentration curls on a preacher bench. He liked this exercise since it isolated the biceps and gave it that peak. He cautioned that strict form was important. Weights were secondary as feeling the muscle work was what made them grow.

He would perform this movement by taking a dumbbell and having his entire arm hang off of a 90-degree angle bench. He slowly lowered the weight down and made sure he got a full stretch at the bottom. He would then bring the weight back up and fully squeeze and contract the biceps. He did this for 10 reps and then repeated it with the other arm for a total of 3 sets of 10 reps for each arm.

Shawn's last biceps exercise was standing dumbbell hammer curls to hit the biceps brachialis. He said that many bodybuilders neglected training the brachialis, and as a result, they had missed one of the most important elements to great arm development. Shawn said that because the brachialis sat underneath the biceps, when he worked it and it grew, so did the rest of his arms. He said how important it was to train the brachialis for complete arm development, and dumbbell hammer curls were an excellent way to do just that.

He began this exercise in much the same way he did dumbbell alternating curls. The big difference was at the top of the movement. Instead of turning his wrists at the top, he kept his wrist and thumb straight up and down. His palms faced each other throughout the entire exercise, and he found this to be one of the best ways to put the stress directly on the brachialis. After both dumbbells reached the top position, he slowly lowered them and repeated for 3 sets of 10 reps.

Shawn would rest for a few minutes after biceps and then move right into triceps. His typical triceps workout would involve two or three exercises and could include his favorites like standing cable pushdowns with a straight bar and one-arm seated dumbbell extensions.

He began with straight bar pushdowns. However, he always made sure he thoroughly warmed up the triceps tendon by doing 1 or 2 sets of light warm-ups with pushdowns. After the warm-up, he would start pyramiding the weight up for his next 3 sets.

Shawn would begin his pushdowns by taking a medium grip, about shoulder width, on a straight bar. He would keep his arms locked into his sides, and as he pushed the weight down, he would contract the triceps hard. From there, he'd slowly bring the weight back up to about chest level and repeat for anywhere from 8 to 15 reps.

He said it was important to keep the arms, especially the elbows, locked into the sides since it minimized cheating and placed more stress directly on the triceps. Shawn said he always did complete full-range movements and that many people did half-movements and as a result only got half the development.

Shawn's next triceps exercise was seated one-arm dumbbell extensions. Since his triceps were warmed up from 5 sets of the pushdowns, he'd go right up to the heavy weight. The way he did this was first taking a dumbbell and sitting on a flat bench. He kept his upper torso fully erect and then took the dumbbell and lowered it behind his head. He would then raise the dumbbell above his head until his arm was completely locked out. His upper arm didn't move while doing this exercise; only the hands and forearms. He said it was important to let the weight down as far as possible behind the head in order to get the maximum stretch on the triceps.

Shawn said he liked doing 4 sets of 8 to 15 reps on this exercise. He also said he found that the triceps responded well to slightly higher reps, with 8 to 15 being a good rep range. Another thing Shawn said he liked to do was change his exercises and routines often, as he believed it kept his muscles off-guard and growing.

While Shawn's forearms got plenty of work from holding the weights when he worked his other body parts, he said he might decide to do direct forearm work, usually with one or two good basic forearm exercises like barbell curls off of a preacher bench and standing reverse barbell curls. Shawn said the important thing to remember about the forearm is that it is a high-density muscle and it took high reps and the burn to make them grow.

That meant not stopping when the burn begins. Shawn said that the burn meant he was hitting those deep fibers, and those are the fibers that make forearms grow big. He said full range of wrist motion was important, as in letting the weight roll to the ends of the fingers and then curling the wrist toward the body as far as possible. He believed that just a few inches of added movement could make a big difference in how he felt the exercise. He did 3 sets of 8 to 15 reps per exercise for a total of 6 sets for forearms.

THE SHAWN RAY ARM WORKOUT

Biceps
- Dumbbell alternating curls: 1 or 2 warm-up sets of 10 reps, then 3 sets of 10 reps pyramided
- One-arm dumbbell concentration curls off 90-degree preacher bench: 3 sets of 10 reps
- Standing dumbbell hammer curls: 3 sets of 10 reps

Triceps
- Standing straight-bar cable pushdowns: 1 or 2 warm-up sets of 8–15 reps, then 3 sets of 8–15 reps pyramided
- Seated one-arm dumbbell extensions: 4 sets of 8–15 reps

Forearms
- Barbell curls on a preacher bench: 3 sets of 8–15 reps
- Standing barbell reverse curls: 3 sets of 8–15 reps

Nine Champs Talk About How to Make Better Gains While Avoiding Mistakes

How much would you pay to be able to sit down with your favorite body-building champs and have them tell you the mistakes you were making and how to avoid them? Besides saving untold wasted hours, perhaps even months, they could save you from being injured and wasting money on food and supplements you may not need.

Of the many champs we've talked with over the years, we've chosen nine to give you advice that just may make a big difference in your training and results.

RONNIE COLEMAN

Ronnie believed one of the most important things to bodybuilding success was not only training correctly, but making sure your diet, supplementation, and rest are all working. While lots of bodybuilders train hard, far too

many of them eat poorly, take too many supplements, and don't get enough rest.

The reality is, they've only got 50 percent of their bodybuilding success plan working, so how can they expect to get 100 percent results? They can't and are only deluding themselves. While there may be no secrets to bodybuilding greatness, if you're eating right, supplementing correctly, and getting plenty of rest, you'd be amazed at just how far and fast you can come.

JOHN MORANT

John counseled that no one could be the best because we are all the best, so just be yourself. The message here is to not desire size or strength because someone else wants you to or you feel you must prove something to someone. Who cares what other people think?

Working out is a personal thing, and if you desire strength and size, then achieve those things only because you want them. Give up the need to compare your body to anyone. John believed you are the only person on this earth who has your body, so take what you have, enjoy working out, and build it to be the very best it can be.

EDDIE ROBINSON

Eddie, like many champs, was a big visualizer. A huge motivating factor was how he could hold a vivid picture in his mind, seeing and feeling every detail—from the cuts and extra width in his back, to how his arms looked and felt in his clothing—even going as far as playing the preworkout in his mind

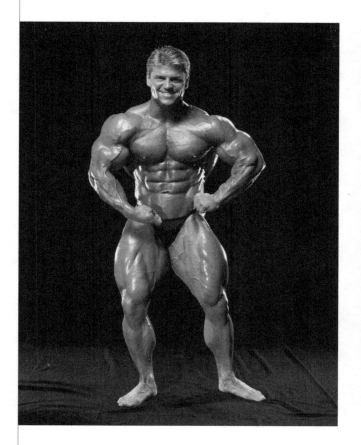

and how it felt to hold the weights and mentally doing the exercise, before he walked in the gym. All of these things became like a powerful magnet that gave his goals clarity and focus and helped him achieve excellent results.

RICH GASPARI

Sometimes, for all of us, it can be tough to always stay motivated. Rich Gaspari was no exception. He said he found that reading bodybuilding magazines and books and going to physique shows gave him added motivation to train and look his best.

Rich told of one period in his training life where his training interest dropped off.

However, after he cracked open the books and magazines again, seeing all the inspiring photos helped him get back on the road to great results. And here's a comforting thought: Rich said that even the most experienced bodybuilders are constantly learning and refining their approach. That's how they improve year after year. So always stay open to any and everything that can inspire you to become better.

DARREM CHARLES

An interesting thing Darrem said was that he believed that most bodybuilders weren't in tune with their bodies. They didn't pose enough or practice muscle control. This is

important since you need to fully control each muscle group so that you can isolate it and work it completely. Darrem also advised that excellent form and keeping your mind on the body part you're training were musts for best results.

CHRIS CORMIER

On the nutrition front, Chris told how the use of various protein sources and meal timing really helped his body grow. For example, he found that lean beef, chicken, turkey, fish, protein powder, and egg whites all affected his body differently depending on his training cycle. For instance, his body responded well to beef when he was training for size and power, but when it came

precontest time, fish and chicken breasts worked better.

When it came to meal timing, eating his meals every few hours gave his body lots of energy, as well as keeping it in a positive nitrogen balance. Forget those big gut-busting meals. Chris found that clean (not fried or filled with fat or sugar), small meals worked excellently.

MILOS SARCEV

Once bodybuilders build enough size and strength, it's easy to forget that it was heavy weights that brought them those great results. While Milos had plenty of size and strength, he never lost sight of the fact that the body still needs to be worked intensely

(even if it is just from time to time) to keep those great results coming.

Milos said that far too often, he saw people who would work out with only a fraction of the poundage they could. And many of them complained they weren't growing or getting stronger. One of the big reasons was because they weren't stimulating the deep muscle fibers.

The opposite was true for those who used big weights but terrible form. The key is to use a heavy enough weight, but not so heavy that it makes you use poor form. As your strength goes up, so can your weights, but never at the expense of working the muscle intensely with the best form possible.

NASSER EL SONBATY

Nasser was a giant, and one of the things he credited for his success was the use of barbell and dumbbell exercises as the foundation of his bodybuilding program. In other words, machines can be good for some things, but keep the majority of your training on free weights.

The other big factor was obviously nutrition, specifically changing his protein intake in both the off-season and precontest. He said that in the past he might eat about 100 grams of protein a day. However, when he raised his protein intake up significantly (in his case, some 600 grams a day!), the results he experienced were dramatic. He cautioned to not increase your protein too significantly or too quickly. Go slowly and see how little changes affect your body.

ROLAND CZIURLOK

If you think your body hasn't grown or gotten stronger in a long time, what Roland said could change everything for you. He said it took him about five years to realize that he was training too often and not thinking enough about his training. Like many of us, he'd go to the gym and work out hard, but his training wasn't focused. However, as soon as he got real specific about what he wanted to accomplish, his training intensity level rose dramatically and so did his results. Rest was a big factor to his success too. He believed that eight hours of sleep each night was crucial, and so were his few-minute naps each day.

17

Cory Everson on Stretching and Flexibility

Seems so much of what you read in the bodybuilding magazines and books talks about how to become bigger and stronger or leaner, but little is said about how to become more flexible. After all, what good are big, strong, or even lean muscles unless you've got the flexibility to use them to the fullest capabilities possible?

While Cory Everson may be known to her fans as a six-time Ms. Olympia, bestselling author, and TV show host, she also knows a thing or two about flexibility and stretching. For a refreshing change of pace, here is some great advice about those two things that Cory shared.

Cory said that for years she competed in many sports in school, and she quickly learned the importance of stretching and flexibility to her success as an athlete. For one, Cory said it helped her as an athlete because she was more agile, had more control over her body, knew her body better, and it gave her a greater range of motion. She said all of those things gave her an edge that not a lot of the other athletes had.

Years later when she hit the bodybuilding competition stage, Cory found another benefit: her flexibility helped her poses look more fluid and her routine more graceful. She said her goal was to show the audience and judges that with a greater range of motion in her poses, her transitions made her body look more elegant.

She also found another major benefit to stretching when she competed. Instead of experiencing nervousness, shakiness, and even muscle cramps before hitting the stage like some others did, she discovered that when she stretched before going out onstage, she would never experience muscle cramps or shakiness.

Cory said that on some occasions when she did a seminar, she might drop down to a full split or stand straight up and lift her leg unassisted behind her head just to shock people and show them what a bodybuilder was capable of, if they worked on their stretching and flexibility. And she had some great advice for anyone who wanted to be more flexible.

Cory said the first thing to do was to start out stretching very slowly. Remember, when you stretch, you're putting tension and stress on the muscle. You're pushing those muscles farther than they're used to, so start out slowly. She said that when she began stretching years ago, when she started martial arts, she pulled a muscle in her thigh because she pushed too hard too fast. Take it slow.

She advised to stretch for small gains on a daily basis versus large gains. Slow and progressive are the key words here. Cory said that if someone becomes impatient and goes for large gains, there was a good chance they would pull something and they wouldn't be able to stretch for weeks. People should make small increments their goal instead of wanting to increase their range of motion by five inches in a week.

Cory said it was important to stretch all the body parts with a good and thorough stretching program taking about 20 minutes. You could even do it at home while watching TV, she added.

She cautioned to never bounce or force a stretch. The way to do it, she said, was to get into a position where you can feel the muscle pull and hold it there for a count of five seconds. Relax, and then do it again. Then the next time you do a stretch, try going just a little bit farther. Do this three times per body part.

She said it was important to put extra time into the areas that require more flexibility. She used the example of a tennis player needing greater flexibility in the shoulders and hamstrings. Golfers need flexibility in their thighs, obliques, and shoulders. Volleyballers need it for legs and shoulders. And bodybuilders need it all over.

To make stretching a part of your overall training program, Cory said to find the best time of day to do your stretching and flexibility training. She stretched before and after a physical activity. If she stretched in the morning and then didn't work out until the afternoon, her stretching was not going to be nearly as effective as it would if she stretched out right before she trained. There would simply be too much time between stretching the muscle and actually working it.

Cory said set aside 20 minutes before the workout to stretch the muscles. She found stretching after a workout helped to decrease muscle soreness and that she got less sore if she stretched after a workout than if she didn't stretch at all.

All in all, she believed stretching was an excellent thing to do, since it warmed up the body, got the blood flowing, stretched out the ligaments and tendons, and prepared them for the workout.

18

A Quick Primer on the Training of Dennis Newman

Dennis Newman was one of the most promising up-and-coming bodybuilders we had seen. Not only did he have a terrific physique at 5'11" and more than 230 pounds, he also had magazine cover looks.

While Newman's star may not have ascended as high as his fans would have liked, he did make his mark and is still remembered fondly as the ocean-surfing California boy who made it big in the body-building world. Here are a few of the things he told us when it came to training and eating.

DENNIS NEWMAN ON THE ELEMENTS OF HIS TRAINING SUCCESS

Dennis explained that he trained hard, never missed a workout, and even though he didn't really count calories, he was very conscious of how his body appeared in the mirror, and if he detected fat anywhere, he'd make adjustments in his food intake as well as do more cardio, such as the bike.

A DENNIS NEWMAN SAMPLE WORKOUT PROGRAM

Newman trained on a three-day-on/one-day-off schedule, training his chest and arms on day one, his legs by themselves on day two, and his back and shoulders on day three. Calves were trained every other day, while abdominals were trained every training day. Here's one of his sample training programs.

Day 1: a.m.—chest; p.m.—biceps, triceps

Day 2: a.m.—quadriceps; p.m.—hamstrings

Day 3: a.m.—back; p.m.—shoulders

DAY 1: CHEST AND ARMS

Chest

- Incline dumbbell press: 4 sets of 8–12 reps
- Incline bench press: 4 or 5 sets of 8–12 reps
- Hammer chest machine press: 4 or 5 sets of 8–12 reps

- Cable flyes or dumbbell flyes: 4 or 5 sets of 8–12 reps

Biceps

- Preacher curls (barbell): 4 sets of 8–12 reps
- Preacher machine curls: 4 sets of 8–12 reps
- Dumbbell alternate curls: 4 sets of 8–12 reps

Triceps

- Lying French press: 4 sets of 10–12 reps
- Triceps pushdowns: 4 sets of 8–12 reps (heavy)
- Reverse extensions on lat machine (performed either one arm at a time or two arms simultaneously): 4 sets of 8–12 reps
- Bar dips: 3 sets of 10–15 reps (or until failure)

DAY 2: LEGS

Quads (a.m.)

- Leg extensions: 4 sets of 10–12 reps
- Leg presses: 4 sets of 10–12 reps
- Hack squats: 4 sets of 10–12 reps
- Squats: 4 sets of 10–12 reps (Dennis said he liked to do squats last because he didn't have to use so much weight, which could be tough on the joints, or

burn the back out before working the thighs.)

Hamstrings (p.m.)

- Lying leg curls: 4 sets of 10–15 reps
- Standing leg curl: 4 sets of 10–12 reps
- Stiff-legged dead lifts: 3 or 4 sets of 8–10 reps

Calves

- Seated calf raises: 4 or 5 sets of 10–12 reps
- Toe press on leg press machine: 4 sets of 10–15 reps
- Donkey machine calf raises: 4 sets of 10–12 reps

Abs

- Incline sit-ups: 4 sets of 35 reps
- Leg raises (on bench): 4 sets of 30 reps
- Crunches: 4 sets of 30 reps

DAY 3: BACK AND DELTS

Back

- Seated pulley rows: 4 sets of 8–12 reps
- T-bar rows: 4 sets of 8–12 reps
- One-arm dumbbell rows: 4 sets of 8–12 reps
- Bent-over barbell rows: 4 sets of 8–12 reps
- Chins: 3 sets of 10 reps (body weight)

Delts

- Behind-the-neck presses: 4 sets of 8–12 reps
- Side lateral raises (standing): 4 sets of 8–12 reps
- Bent-over lateral raises: 4 sets of 8–12 reps
- Dumbbell shrugs: 4 sets of 8–12 reps

DENNIS NEWMAN ON THE AEROBIC EFFECT ON THE BODY

One of the more interesting things Dennis revealed was how aerobics helped his body become more vascular. He found that training on a three-on/one-off split routine where he trained a large body part in the morning and a smaller one at night didn't really leave him much energy for aerobic work.

As many of his fellow competitors were saying that they were putting in two to three hours a day on aerobic work, he found with his system that all he had to do was ride the bike at a very low resistance setting at the end of both of his morning and evening workouts, for half an hour a shot, and he got super ripped.

DENNIS NEWMAN ON LESSONS LEARNED THROUGH TRIAL AND ERROR

Dennis spoke of the importance of learning how to train smart and not being too concerned about lifting a heavy weight that could hurt you. He observed that there are many people out there trying to lift to impress people. He said he meant the kind of person that uses spotters to help them with 1, 2, or 3 reps, which, in his opinion, wasn't going to build any muscle, and the kind of weight that would strain tendons, or worse, tear a muscle. Dennis believed that one needed to get at least 8 reps a set if they're interested in muscle growth.

Newman said that if people wanted muscle size, then they needed to eat for it. He believed that as much as 70 percent of bodybuilding success was due to diet and only 30 percent was due to the actual training.

19

A Chest Above the Rest: The Dorian Yates Brief but Intense Way to Build It

They say that those who have giant muscular chests all have one thing in common: they used heavy weights. Over the years we've met some pros (and amateurs too) who were genetically endowed in the chest department and actually made theirs grow with only moderate poundages. But when it comes to building a massive chest for most of us, it all comes down to using the great exercises in the best form and wisely using the kinds of weights that'll make it grow.

Dorian Yates was one of those guys. While there is no question Yates had the right gene pool, he also had the right attitude and intelligent approach to all facets of his training. And while he might have been able to use the kind of heavy iron to build that chest that most people will only dream of, it was the way he did it that was also critically important. When asked how he built his chest, this was what he said.

Dorian liked to do plenty of warm-ups and stretching before he hit his chest. Those warm-ups could include light dumbbell work like incline presses to get his chest, shoulders, and triceps ready for the chest workout. He said that after he was completely warmed up, he would go to his first exercise, which was the flat bench press. On this exercise, he would take a medium to slightly wide grip on the bar and try to lower the bar in a controlled manner and really pull his elbows back to where he would get a full stretch.

He would do 3 progressively heavier sets of 10 reps to warm up, then would put on as much weight as he could do for 6 to 8 reps. All of this would be considered his first set. On his second set, he would decrease the weight by about 10 percent and do another 6 to 8 reps, and that would be it for his first chest exercise.

His second chest movement was the incline dumbbell press. He found he got a much better stretch and movement from doing the dumbbell inclines than from doing barbell inclines. On the dumbbell inclines, Dorian explained he would usually do just one warm-up set before going to his heaviest set. Since he was already warmed up from the previous exercise, he wanted to get in there and really move some heavy iron. After the warm-up, he would do 2 heavy sets. The first set would be the heaviest, and the second set would be about 10 percent lighter.

Dorian's third chest movement would be flyes, and he felt they were good—especially the incline flye—to hit the upper area of the chest and fill in the clavicles. However, each workout he would change the angle of the incline since he felt this helped hit the pecs more completely. Also on flyes, Dorian explained that he might triple drop descending sets as well. This is where he would do a set to failure, then drop the weight down for another 6 to 8 reps, then drop the weight down one more time for another 6 to 8 reps. All of that would be considered one set. Be warned: this is intense stuff. Dorian said that for those with stubborn body parts, doing triple drops every so often may be the key to getting them to grow.

If he doesn't do flyes, Dorian said he might do cable crossovers with a similar set, rep, and weight protocol: one warm-up set, then straight into his heavy set for 6 to 8 reps. The second set dropped the poundage down about 10 percent, and he'd go for another 6 to 8 reps. He said that squeezing the pecs hard when the hands are in front of the body and getting the arms back as far as possible was the key to getting the most out of this movement.

He might also do triple drop sets on cable crossovers, as he believed that varying the angles and exercises helped hit the chest completely. Same with the importance of getting the full stretch of the movement and going as heavy as he possibly could (in good form) for 6 to 8 reps. Dorian said that if he included the warm-ups and heavy sets, he was doing about 20 sets for chest and that was it.

Dorian Yates was a big believer in regularly monitoring his progress, and if a body part needed a bit of work, he would attack it until it came up, and he would do that for every body part until they were all in proper proportion.

Besides great exercises and all-out intensity, Dorian said he also liked using a training partner. From time to time, different people would pop in and train with him, and he enjoyed that. Perhaps it was his competitive nature, but he said whenever someone wanted to train with him, he would go out and try and bury them. As in, try and keep up with me. Interestingly, that was one of the things Dorian said was missing in so many of the gyms—that kind of bustin' a gut or training hard mentality and not a complacency or lack of drive.

For Dorian, the mental aspect was hugely important. He said bodybuilding gave him the kind of challenge that tested his limits both mentally and physically, and he thought it to be almost more of a mental exercise than a physical one. Pitting himself and challenging himself all of the time really appealed to him.

It was refreshing that whether Dorian was training for a contest or training in the off-season, he only trained once a day. He explained that he found if he was hitting his body parts with all the intensity that he could, training once a day was plenty to stimulate growth. The body grew by working it hard and making sure it got enough rest so it would recuperate and be ready for the next workout.

Dorian said he saw a lot of bodybuilders who trained every day, but they didn't train that intensely. Because they were not training intensely, they were not depleting their bodies and they were not stimulating growth. The mistake they were making, he said, was thinking that because they were not growing, then they needed to train more. However, that wasn't the answer.

He said it was important to train hard and find out what worked best for your body. For Dorian, he found what worked best for his was training three out of five days in the off-season while doing aerobics for cardiovascular fitness on the days he wasn't training any body parts. For precontest, he would pick up the pace and train every day along with adding aerobics every day to help keep the body-fat level as low as possible.

THE DORIAN YATES WEEKLY WORKOUT

Day 1: chest, triceps, and biceps

Day 2: legs

Day 3: day off

Day 4: back and deltoids

Day 5: day off

THE DORIAN YATES CHEST ROUTINE

- Flat bench press: 3 progressive heavy sets of 10 for warm-up. Then 2 heavy sets of 6 to 8 reps. Drop 10 percent in weight for the second set for 6 to 8 reps.

- Incline dumbbell press: One warm-up set of 10 reps. Then 2 heavy sets of 6–8 reps. Drop 10 percent in weight on the second set for 6–8 reps.

- Incline flyes: Same reps and sets as the incline dumbbell press. He said he would vary the angle on flyes to hit the pecs more completely.

- Cable crossovers: Sometimes a substitute movement for flyes. Same rep and sets that he would do for flyes. The key is to squeeze and contract the pecs hard when the hands are crossed in front of the body. Make sure to let the arms back as far as possible to get the full stretch of the movement.

20

One Day Inside the World of Achim Albrecht

Ever wonder what it would be like to have the life of a pro body-builder? Many do. Think of it: your job and profession would be to work out, get big and strong, eat, rest, diet, compete, travel, make money, meet great people, and see the world.

Well, some of the pros do have lives like that. Others are still working on it. And while there may be many pro bodybuilders, they all have different lives, routines, and schedules.

To give a glimpse into the lives of one of these pros, consider the very popular pro Achim Albrecht, who was gracious enough to open the doors to his world—if only for a day—so that you could see what it was like to be the German giant.

Achim said he usually got up around 7:00 a.m. and would prepare his food for the rest of the day. He said he found it much easier to prepare everything in advance so he didn't have to cook every time he wanted to eat—especially after a hard workout. After his food was prepared, he had breakfast, usually at 7:30 a.m. For breakfast, Achim liked four to six ounces of oatmeal along with 10 egg whites and plenty of water. After breakfast, he would rest for two or three hours by either watching TV or reading the latest bodybuilding magazine, and he would then be ready for meal number two.

At 10:00 a.m., Achim had his second meal of the day. Since his first workout was coming up, he wanted to give his body enough protein and carbs and did so by having chicken, potatoes, salad, and water. He hit the gym about 45 minutes after the second meal.

He said his workouts in the off-season were four days on and one day off and that he trained twice a day. He liked the basic movements and might do four basic exercises for a muscle like the chest, 4 or 5 sets of 6 to 16 reps per exercise. After his weight workout was completed, he said he might ride the bike for 20 to 30 minutes.

Achim said he'd have his third meal shortly after he got home from his first workout, which would be about 1:30 p.m. For that meal, he'd have rice, vegetables, fish, and water, along with some extra aminos. Because he trained very hard, he needed quite a bit of rest, and after the meal he might take a nap or lie out, relax, and work on his tan.

About 4:00 p.m., Achim would have his fourth meal, which was similar to his second meal and consisted of potatoes, chicken, and water. The goal was to make sure his body had plenty of carbohydrates and protein for his second and final workout of the day that took place at 5:00 p.m. If he worked chest for the first workout, he said he might do shoulders for the second one. Again, he used the good basic movements for 4 or 5 sets of 6 to 15 reps.

Achim's fifth and final meal was at 8:00 p.m. and would include four to six ounces of oatmeal, ten egg whites, and water with some extra aminos. He said he was a big believer in getting plenty of fluids and would drink as much as six to eight liters of water a day.

To relax, he liked going to the movies or renting a video and relaxing at home. Sometimes he took long walks at the mall and went shopping. However, the thing he really enjoyed was going out for dinner.

He liked Chinese, Greek, and Italian food. What he really enjoyed was going to a nice restaurant with a good atmosphere such as one that had outdoor dining in a quiet garden or secluded patio. Like many Europeans, Achim savored his dining experiences and didn't like to rush when he ate, sometimes taking two or three hours eating and talking to good friends.

Unlike some of the pros, Achim's life was laid-back, as he truly enjoyed peace and quiet. He said he enjoyed reading and classic old cars. And while his typical day may sound a little too structured for some people, Achim also had those "special days," as he called them (only in the off-season), when he ate what he wanted and went to bed and got up whenever he wanted.

Coming from Europe, Achim said it took some time for him to adjust to the Los Angeles lifestyle—especially in Venice, California. Achim said he was used to training in Germany where the gym atmosphere and the people are more serious, and that was really the kind of atmosphere he liked.

Even though living and training in California took some adjustment, Achim found the ways to do it that suited him best. When one looks back at all his fans and the years of success he had, it's hard to argue with the results.

21

Creating the V-Shaped Torso: Milos Sarcev's Symmetrical Delt Workout

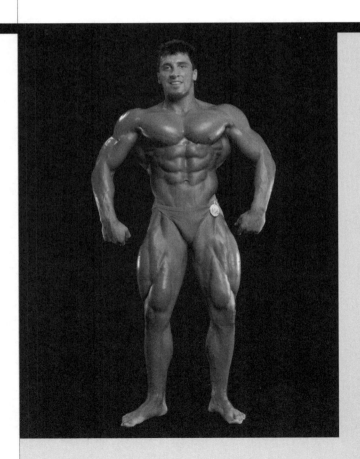

It has been said that a man with big shoulders is to be admired. It is also safe to say that a bodybuilder with great symmetry will always be remembered. From Steve Reeves to Frank Zane to Bob Paris, all of these guys are still at the top of many people's minds when the talk turns to who had great symmetry.

Another guy who should be on that list is Milos Sarcev. While Milos will never be known for his gargantuan mass, he doesn't need to be. He had one heck of a symmetrical physique, with great shoulders to boot.

And you know, great shoulders are truly important to that much-sought-after V-taper.

To help you in your quest for that symmetrical body, you can't go wrong by starting to build great shoulders. Here's what Milos did to build his.

Milos said that to some people, his training methods may seem a bit unorthodox, but for him, they worked. For example, he said there have been times that he would train up to 100 days in a row without a day off. However, he always went by how his body felt, and if it needed a day or two off, he'd take it.

At the time we spoke, Milos said he broke his training up by working his body parts over a four-day period and would then repeat the routine. Also, every other time he worked his body, he'd change the exercises, sets, reps, intensity level, rest time, and other factors that can affect growth and strength. Here was his routine:

Day 1: chest, front/side delts, calves
Day 2: quads and abs
Day 3: back, rear delts, traps, calves
Day 4: hamstrings, arms, abs
Repeat cycle with alternate workouts.

For delts, Milos said he liked breaking his training up because it allowed him to focus more intensely on each delt head he was working. He explained if he did all his delt and trap training in one day, he'd probably end up doing something like 45 sets. However, when he breaks it up, it only ends up being 22 sets for front and side delts on day one and 23 sets for rear delts and traps on day three. This allowed him plenty of time to recuperate between workouts.

Milos admitted that while he realized many bodybuilders don't have the time nor desire to do 45 sets of delt and trap training, they didn't have to to get good results. All that was needed were a few good exercises that hit the delts and traps from all angles. He found keeping the reps in the 4 to 20 range and the sets in the 3 to 8 range per exercise worked great for the delts and traps. Here's the routine he shared that will put size on those delts:

- Seated dumbbell press (front/side delts): 5 sets of 4–20 reps
- Upright one-arm cable laterals (side delts): 5 sets of 8–15 reps
- Bent-over two-arm cable laterals (rear delts): 5 sets of 12–20 reps
- Seated dumbbell shrugs (traps): 5 sets of 8–15 reps plus burns
- Cable upright rows (traps): 5 sets of 12–20 reps

He began with seated dumbbell presses for the front and side delts. He liked doing this movement two different ways: palms facing forward and palms facing his head. He felt these movements in different areas of the front and side delts, and he would alternate each exercise by doing one of the movements one workout and the other movement on the next workout. Regardless of which movement he picked, he always made sure to do 1 or 2 sets of warm-ups before pyramiding up to the heavier weights, as this helped warm up the shoulder area and prevent injuries.

Milos said that when he did the exercise with palms facing forward on the seated dumbbell press, he would sit down with a pair of dumbbells and raise them up to the starting position at shoulder level. He would then press both of the dumbbells up to near lock-out in an arc or semicircular motion and found this kept continuous tension on the delts.

Doing the seated dumbbell press with his palms facing his head was a bit different. He said he would begin with the dumbbells at shoulder level with palms facing his head. As he pressed the weight up and got closer to the top of the movement, he would turn his wrists away from his head to where his palms were facing forward. The upward motion on this is more of a straight-up overhead movement. He didn't fully lock the arms out at the top, so that he could keep continuous tension on the delts. He said he'd do 5 sets of 4 to 20 reps of one of these movements per workout.

His next delt exercise was upright one-arm cable laterals for the side delts. Milos said he felt this exercise right in the belly of the side delt head. He described how he did it by taking a cable and pulling it across the front of his body and raising it to about shoulder level and holding it there for a count or two, and then brought it back down

to the starting position and repeated. Milos cautioned to not to raise the arms higher than shoulder level, as any higher tends to work the traps more than the delts. He did 5 sets of 8 to 15 reps.

Milos would move to his third movement, which was bent-over two-arm cable laterals for the rear delts, and found the exercise to work wonders to bring out the rear delt head. He would begin by taking hold of two opposite cables and would bend over in a near parallel position, and he would then pull his arms straight out to his sides and hold them there for a count or two. He would slowly lower the weight to where the cable handles were in front of him and do it again.

One thing Milos said really helped his delts was to keep continuous tension on the muscle when he did bent-over or side cable raises, as this helped bring out the muscle and gave it an incredibly intense burn. He said he would do 5 sets of 12 to 20 reps on bent-over cable laterals.

After shoulders were finished, Milos would move to traps, with his first exercise being seated dumbbell shrugs. Milos pointed out that most people did these standing, however, he found doing them seated really worked well. He said that while he couldn't use as much weight as he could standing, doing them with full and complete stretches and using partial-movement burn reps really worked well. He would do 5 sets of 8 to 15 reps plus a few burn reps.

His final trap movement was cable upright rows. He said doing this movement immediately after seated dumbbell shrugs fried the traps. He did them by taking a straight bar attached to a low pulley and raising the bar in front of him to about nose level and holding it there for a count, then lowering it and repeating. A little trick he found was to keep the bar moving and not let it rest at the bottom. He said this kind of nonstop continuous tension really made the traps and delts grow. He would do 5 sets of 12 to 20 reps of cable upright rows. Milos said that anyone could split delt and trap training up on different days like he did or do the routine all on one day. Either way, if you do it right, you will have some big shoulders.

22

Mountains of Mass from Switzerland's Jean-Pierre Fux

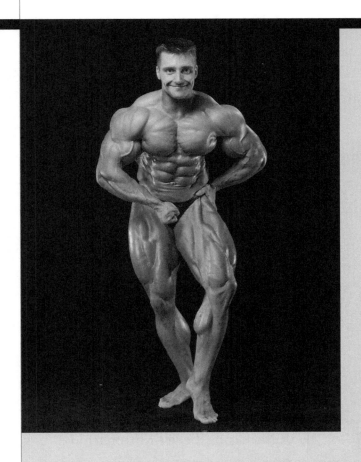

A few years back, there was an amazing amateur bodybuilder who lived in a little mountain village near Matterhorn, Switzerland. His size and symmetry were phenomenal, and to all those who saw him, the word was, here was a guy who could do serious damage as a pro. His name was Jean-Pierre Fux.

Jean-Pierre had a lot to say about training. Here was a guy who became so strong so fast, he literally had to beg gym owners to buy more weights. He started when he was 16 and weighed 143 pounds. Compare that to when we spoke, weighing in at 295 pounds in the off-season and 270 pounds in contest condition and standing 6' tall.

Jean said that when he first started training, he was very impressed by the size of one guy's arms and knew he wanted to have arms just like them. That guy even became his training partner, and he immediately began training like a serious bodybuilder. That meant heavy barbells and dumbbells, with cable work kept to a minimum.

Of course, such unbridled passion for size and strength can lead easily into overtraining and that's just what happened to Jean-Pierre. With a beginner routine of 15 sets of 12 reps per body part, it's easy to see why.

Thankfully, such an experience wises us up quickly, and Jean-Pierre honed his training approach and successfully mastered what all the great bodybuilders must: give their bodies just enough stimulation for growth and never any more. Here's what he did:

After a 10- to 15-minute warm-up and 1 or 2 light sets, he begins with the heaviest weight he can use for 6 reps.

On each succeeding set, he'll reduce the weight and add more reps.

He'll do 2 heavy sets for every muscle group.

His training days (at the time) were Monday, Tuesday, Thursday, and Saturday.

Jean-Pierre said that to avoid injury and burnout, he liked to cycle his training by doing 12 weeks of heavy training followed by four weeks of lighter circuit training. And he'll follow this program even when his size and strength are increasing. Here is a guy who listens to his body and makes it do what he wants, and not the other way around. Whenever his body felt tired, he'd simply take a few days off, then start again with lighter weights for a good muscle pump.

So what does the Swiss giant do for size and strength? His workout looked like this:

Monday: calves and quads

Tuesday: hamstrings, chest, front delts

Wednesday: off

Thursday: back, traps, rear delts, calves

Friday: off

Saturday: arms, calves (1 or 2 sets depending on how he feels)

Sunday: off

He didn't do ab work. The heavy weights used in his exercises along with his diet kept them razor-sharp.

Here's what he did and how he did it.

DAY 1: QUADS AND CALVES

Jean-Pierre said he liked to do calves at the beginning of his workout. Starting with calves, he'd do 3 or 4 sets with heavy weights of one exercise of either seated calf raise, machine donkeys, or standing calf raise. Then, after a good warm-up, he'll jump to his heaviest weight for 20 reps, and each set thereafter, the weight decreases and the reps increase until they reach 80. It's those high reps that make the calves burn big time.

He was also a big believer in stretching the calves. He found stretching helps increase range of motion, promotes better blood flow, and helps the calves grow bigger and faster. For a great calf stretch, he used a machine with heavy weight.

For quads, Jean-Pierre said he liked to train by feeling. This meant that he decided what kinds of exercise, set, rep, and weight combinations to use after he got into the gym. One workout might have him prefatiguing the quads with leg extensions first, then leg press, then squats. Another might be a simple workout of 5 sets of squats. Another could be using various combinations of low-to-high reps and light-to-heavy weight in the same workout.

Here are a few favorite quad workouts he liked doing:

- Leg press: 2 sets very heavy, at least 6 reps
- Squats : 1 set very heavy followed by 1 set with lighter weight and a few more reps
- Leg extension: 1 set, at least 10 reps

Jean-Pierre will do a total of 5 or 6 sets for legs using heavy weights. One of those sets will be a stripped set consisting of three descending sets of 6 reps each. For example, for leg press, Jean-Pierre may do a set of 6 reps with 1,000 pounds. Then, while holding the weight at the top of the movement, he'll have two partners take a few plates off and do another 6 reps. He'll bring the weight up again and fully extend his legs, the spotters will take off a few more plates, and he'll do a final set of 6 reps. Jean-Pierre would also do a brutal preexhaust for quads that consisted of one set of leg extensions for 50 reps and then go right to the following workout:

- 45-degree leg press: 2 sets of 6–12 reps using up to 1,400 pounds
- Squats: 1 set of 4–8 reps with up to 700 pounds
- Stripping set of squats: 3 strip sets of 6 reps starting with 600 pounds, then 510, then 420 pounds

DAY 2: CHEST, DELTS (FRONT AND SIDE), AND HAMSTRINGS

On this workout day, Jean-Pierre will start with hamstrings. Strict form and heavy weights are a prerequisite. As a result, he said his hamstrings didn't need lots of exercises or sets. Jean-Pierre's tried-and-true exercises were lying or standing leg curls done with one heavy set of 6 to 12 reps, followed by one stripped set.

Chest is next, and the first exercise was incline dumbbell press for the upper chest. However, Jean-Pierre did these differently than other bodybuilders. For example, as he pressed the weights up, he rotated his wrists until his palms were facing each other at the top. He said he felt deeper contraction doing them this way.

He followed these with a set of dumbbell pullovers across a flat bench (at that time, with 140 pounds). This really stretched his rib cage. Jean-Pierre would then do another set of dumbbell incline presses and finish with a final set of dumbbell pullovers. His last chest exercise was one set of narrow-grip bench presses—hands about four to eight inches apart—on the Smith machine to hit the inner chest.

DELTS

For Jean-Pierre, delts were a tricky muscle to grow, but he found the secret: Prefatigue the delts with high-rep laterals to failure before doing any pressing.

Here's one of his delt-growing prefatigue workouts:

- One set of dumbbell side laterals for 50 reps.
- Immediately followed by 2 heavy sets of seated dumbbell presses (at the time, with 140 pounds).
- One set of cheated heavy side laterals with one arm (at the time, using up to 80 pounds).
- At the end of the set of side laterals, he'd hold the weight for 20 to 30 seconds out to his sides and away from his body. As he held the weights out, he'd then resist as his strength decreased and the weight came down. He found this resistance to hit those remaining deep muscle fibers that may not have been worked during the workout.

BACK

Jean-Pierre believed the back was a big muscle that needed to be worked with a variety of exercises. And in his book, rowing was one of the best movements for building a big, thick back. He also liked hitting the traps with heavy weights—even doing (at the time) barbell shrugs with 400 pounds for a full range of motion.

He also liked finishing every back workout with 1 set of 2 reps of deadlifts, provided that he didn't already do heavy deadlifts with higher reps in the workout. Jean-Pierre would always change things around, with some workouts using lighter weights and high reps and pyramiding up to heavy weight and low reps or the reverse.

Typically, after a few warm-up sets, he'd do one heavy set of lat pulldowns to the chest for 8 to 12 reps. He'd follow that exercise with one set of bent-over rows on the Smith machine for 6 to 8 reps. Jean-Pierre said he liked the Smith machine because the weight moved in a perfect groove which helped him feel the movement more.

After Smith machine rows, he'd then quickly do one stripped set of standing rows with a reverse grip and another set of the same exercise using straight sets and heavy weight. Form was crucial, and he kept his upper body at a 60- to 70-degree angle. He also found that a barbell worked best for reverse-grip rows.

His next back exercise was the seated rowing machine. The key is to make the lats stretch, and he did this by fully extending his arms at the start of the exercise and then pulling the arms back and arching the back at the finish for a maximum contraction.

Whenever Jean-Pierre did deadlifts with his back workout, he'd do 1 set of deadlifts for 8 to 12 reps (at the time, using 600 pounds). He'd then do one more set using heavier weight for 2 to 4 reps or a single max rep using a heavier weight (at the time, about 750 pounds).

REAR DELTS

Jean-Pierre found that his rear delts responded really well if he worked them right after back. One of his favorite rear delt workouts was simply doing 1 stripped set of dumbbell bent-over laterals followed by 1 set of cable bent-over laterals for 20 reps. Who said you need to get complicated to build great shoulders?

DAY 4: CALVES AND ARMS

On the fourth day, he began his workout with calves and would use a training approach similar to the one he used on his leg-day workout. Once calves were worked, Jean-Pierre would move to biceps.

It seems that most bodybuilders want big arms, and Jean-Pierre found a way to make them grow. They need to be pumped. He also found that partial-range reps—roughly three-quarter movements—gave him great results. Jean-Pierre said he felt that partial-range reps kept the biceps under constant tension and forced them to work harder. He also liked changing up the exercises and order.

One of the best biceps workouts he found was this:

- Supinated dumbbell curls: 2 sets of 6–8 reps
- Cable curl: 2 sets of 6–10 reps
- Preacher curl: 2 sets of 6–8 reps

Triceps followed biceps, and here again, Jean-Pierre was a big fan of prefatiguing the triceps with a moderate weight and higher reps before doing his heavier weight movements. For example, he might do pressdowns before jumping right into heavy weight dumbbell French presses. Prefatiguing also gave him another benefit: warming up the elbow area to reduce chances of injury and allowing him to get a deeper stretch.

In fact, Jean-Pierre was a big advocate of warming the triceps up thoroughly and pyramiding up slowly, in order to avoid injury. The elbow area is vulnerable to injury if it's stressed with too much weight too quickly. That's why he took his time and did a few sets of light- to moderate-weight pressdowns before moving to the heavier weighted movements. He believed this was a big reason he stayed injury-free.

After the triceps were warmed up, Jean-Pierre would get right into one of the best triceps mass builders he found, the dumbbell French press. He'd typically pyramid up to his heaviest weight (at the time 140 pounds) and do 2 sets of 6 to 8 reps.

His next exercise was the lying EZ bar French press, which he did for 2 sets of 6 to 20 reps. He might finish his triceps workout with machine pressdowns, either a straight or curved bar or a rope, for 2 sets of 6 to 12 reps.

Over the years, some have asked me what Jean-Pierre did for cardio. His answer was surprising. He flexed and held the muscular contraction. He also posed (both on- and off-season), but it was flexing that gave him a terrific cardio effect.

He said that as an amateur, he did all kinds of cardio, and what he noticed was that he was wasting a lot of muscle tissue and that all that cardio made his body look and feel soft. He then began experimenting and found when he posed, tensed, and fiercely contracted the muscle, his body began changing. But not just posing and tensing one muscle, but as many muscles as he possibly could at once. And if you think that's not tough, just try doing what Jean-Pierre did: posing for one hour, nonstop.

MORE TRAINING TIPS FROM JEAN-PIERRE FUX

- The number of sets per body part always stays the same. What changes are the exercises, weight, and reps.
- He always changed his workouts to keep things fun and his body growing.
- For big muscles like legs, chest, and back, he liked doing four to six exercises of 2 heavy sets each per body part.
- For smaller muscles like delts, traps, and arms, he liked doing 2 or 3 exercises of 2 heavy sets each per body part.
- For calves, he liked doing three or four exercises of 2 heavy sets each per body part.
- Each workout took about 60 minutes.
- For low set/heavy weight training to be productive, he believed that you must warm

up each muscle group very thoroughly before going to your heaviest weight.

- Far too many bodybuilders are injured by going too heavy too quickly and pushing their bodies too hard too often.
- Get in tune with your body. Forget using heavy weight until you can feel every rep work each muscle with a maximum contraction.
- One of the reasons some bodybuilders can get great results from low sets is because they've learned to feel the exercise. For others, it takes many sets to accomplish the same result.

JEAN-PIERRE'S SIZE-BUILDING EXERCISES

- Squats for quads
- Incline dumbbell press for chest with hands turning and palms facing each other at the top
- Dumbbell pullover for the chest and rib cage
- Side laterals with heavy weight and limited range of motion for the delts
- Seated dumbbell press for delts with heavy weights
- Reverse-grip barbell row for back
- Deadlift and stiff-legged deadlift for hamstrings and lower back

23

Arms like Steel from Norway's Geir Borgan Paulsen

It's easy to think of Arnold or Mike Mentzer or Larry Scott when you think of great body-building arms. Sure, there are scores of others, but for some reason, these legends always seem to make it to the top of any bodybuilding fan's list when the question of "Which bodybuilder do you think had great arms?" is put to them.

Perhaps in the not-as-famous category, but certainly noteworthy, were the arms of Norwegian Geir Borgan Paulsen. Originally, he began his weight training and quickly worked his way up to becoming an Olympic-level weight lifter, however, he became a bodybuilder and went on to win many world-class honors.

At 6' and 240 pounds, Geir had a mighty impressive physique, but he also had a big heart and never forgot those who helped him. Geir also had something else: a pair of terrific arms. To give you a different perspec-

tive on how he built his big guns with Olympic training and then with bodybuilding, here is what he said about his training.

Geir said that for years, he trained as an Olympic lifter and did lots of presses, cleans, jerks, and snatches. Lifting heavy with good form gave him quite a bit of mass. So much mass that he hardly did any direct shoulder work due to years of doing presses brutally hard. However, he said, arms were a different story. An Olympic lifter doesn't do a lot of curling movements, so he had to find a way to bring his biceps up to par with his triceps.

One of those ways was by doing basic movements. He said he didn't need to do five exercises for biceps and five for triceps to make his arms grow. Three exercises for each body part did the trick.

Geir would usually begin his arm workout with biceps, and one of his favorite exercises was standing barbell curls. He would take a medium grip on a barbell with his arms locked into his sides and then do a warm-up set of 6 to 12 reps. From there, he would load the bar to 145 pounds and do another set of 6 to 12. On his second set, he would go past 160 pounds and do 2 or 3 sets until failure, which usually happened somewhere in the 6 to 10 rep range.

When he was going heavy, it might be difficult keeping his upper body completely erect, so he would use a modified cheating principle whereby he'd use his upper body momentum to help get the weight started. Then, after he curled the weight to the top, he'd slowly lower it to really make the biceps burn. He did 4 sets of 6 to 12 reps.

His second biceps exercise was alternate dumbbell curls, and he would do these either standing or seated. Geir said that since his biceps were already warmed up from the heavy barbell curls, he'd go right up to the heavy weights. He would start the movement with his arms fully stretched out with his palms facing his legs. From there, he would curl the dumbbells to the top of his shoulders. As he approached the top of the shoulders, he would then twist his wrist and supinate the dumbbell away from his body to fully contract the biceps. He would hold the peak contraction for a second or two and then slowly lower the weight back down to the starting position. He'd do 4 sets of 8 to 12 reps.

Geir's third biceps exercise was cable curls. He believed cable curls worked the biceps in a different way from other biceps exercises because they isolated the biceps, while other movements used the shoulders and the back to help the biceps complete the movement. He said if cable curls are done correctly, they are a pure biceps exercise and can really bring out biceps hardness, definition, and peak. Here's how he did them.

He would stand either parallel to or facing the weight stack and then grab the handle and very rhythmically curl the weight up in a steady continuous motion. By doing it like this, Geir said the biceps never had a chance to recover within the set, as it was constantly under continuous tension and stress. He also said he used this exercise to finish his biceps workout and would typically do 4 sets of 10 to 12 reps. However, he explained these were continuous nonstop reps, with strict form, and done with very little rest between sets. On the heavy movements, he would rest about 45 seconds to one minute, and for the last exercise, he'd rest for less than 30 seconds between sets. After his last exercise of biceps, he would rest for a few minutes before hitting triceps.

Geir's triceps exercise was lying French press. He might do these with dumbbells, barbells, or an EZ curl bar. He preferred the EZ curl bar. He began by using a moderate weight and doing a set or two of warm-ups. He would lie on a bench with his arms slightly angled above his head, and then he would bring the bar down to just about the top of his head and then back up to the lock-out position.

He said he liked to go heavy, however he never sacrificed good form just to lift heavy weights. He stressed the importance of warming up and that only after he had done a few warm-up sets would he then work his way up to his heaviest set. He tried to stay as heavy as possible for 4 sets of 6 to 12 reps.

For his second triceps exercise, Geir liked triceps pushdowns for bringing out the horseshoe in the triceps. He liked changing the exercise a bit by using different bars (straight, curved, angled) or even a rope. And since his triceps were already warmed up from his first triceps exercise, he went right up to the heavier weights for all of his sets.

Geir described that as he did pushdowns, his arms would be locked into his sides and he would push the bar down to full lock-out and extension and then bring it up to where it stops at about chest level and would do a total of 4 sets of 8 to 12 reps. He explained that many people will bend over, not lock the weight out, do partial reps, and let their hands come above their head, and he thought that was bad form and prevented them from getting the most our of the exercise.

His last triceps exercise was overhead dumbbell triceps extensions. He said he might do these with one arm or both and that doing the movement with one arm made it more of a finishing movement and two arms made it more of a mass movement since he could use heavier weights.

Geir said that if he did it with one arm, he'd take a dumbbell with his arm above his head and lower it below his head as far as he could. After the triceps was stretched at the bottom of the movement, he'd then bring the weight back up above his head and lock the triceps out to contract it. He did this for 4 sets of 10 to 12 reps.

He said that as he did the exercise, the position of his working arm didn't move, as it essentially stayed in a straight line with his body. The only thing that did move was the elbows. He believed this exercise worked especially well if he lowered the weight below his head as far as he could and then brought the weight to the top and locked it out for a count of three.

Geir said he would do anywhere from 8 to 12 sets for smaller muscle groups and 12 to 25 sets for the larger ones. He learned that his body adapted very quickly to whatever demands he placed upon it, and it took more than just lifting big heavy weights to keep it growing. That's why he said he always liked to vary the sets, exercises, order, reps, rest, and anything else in the workout that would keep his body off-guard and constantly growing.

THE GEIR BORGAN PAULSEN ARM WORKOUT

Biceps

- Barbell curls: 4 sets of 6–12 reps
- Alternate dumbbell curls: 4 sets of 8–12 reps
- Cable curls: 4 sets of 10–12 reps

Triceps

- Lying French press: 4 sets of 6–12 reps
- Triceps pushdowns: 4 sets of 8–12 reps
- Overhead dumbbell extensions: 4 sets of 10–12 reps

The Geir Borgan Paulsen Weekly Workout (off-season)

Day 1: back and chest

Day 2: legs and calves

Day 3: arms

24

Building Awesome Legs the Tom Platz Way

The day the *Tom Platz Leg Training Manual* arrived in the mail the photos were unbelievable. The freakiest and most awesome legs ever. Here was this guy who had quads that busted seams out of gym shorts. Hamstrings that looked like bundles of steel cords. And diamond-shaped calves cut and separated like the finest gemstone. And they all belonged to one man—Tom Platz.

Platz was a giant inspiration to many top bodybuilders. Tom took his training far beyond what many of us would call "sick" (in a good way, mind you). He was a visionary who used the power of visualization coupled with incredibly intense workouts—with weights, sets, and reps that would have even the best of them heaving—

and it took leg development to a level unheard of before he came on the scene.

Even today, his heyday leg pictures are untouchable. That's how far ahead of the pack he was. In an interview, Tom talked about how he trained legs and his training philosophy. While *his* personal workouts were brutal, yours don't have to be to get great results. But there are some things you must do if you truly want them.

Make no mistake, Tom Platz loved squats. They became almost like a special sport to him. He enjoyed the camaraderie. Guys standing around the squat rack in the corner of some old dungeon of a gym and people getting crazy using heavy weights, bars bending, the old rusty plates jingling. It's a zone where few people today want to tread.

Platz began his training adventures back in Michigan when he was 9 years old, and he became so good so fast, he was competing as a powerlifter at age 14. But the surprising thing was, Platz didn't squat when he first started training. Yet as soon as he began powerlifting, he did start squatting, and his muscle size and strength exploded.

YOU JUST GOTTA SQUAT

We all have heard the excuses for not squatting: bad for your knees and back and they'll make your glutes too big, and so on. Tom heard them too, but didn't listen. His own experience and the experiences of others proved to him just how terrific this exercise was at building incredible legs and overall muscularity.

Tom's body was built for hard workouts and responded very fast in size and strength. How fast? He said that on his first squat workout, he was able to do a tough set of 8 reps with 95 pounds. However, it didn't take long to get up to 225 pounds. Soon after that, Platz was venturing into the three, four, five, six, seven, and eight plates (on each side) neighborhood. Think about that: eight 45-pound barbell plates on each side!

Another thing squats did was help Tom break through mental barriers. It became the exercise that inspired him to great things in other areas of his life. And he had good reason to feel excited. In 1984, just one month before the Mr. Olympia, he squatted 635 pounds for 15 below-parallel reps, touching his glutes to his ankles and without knee wraps. In fact, Tom said that he used knee wraps only once in his life, and he didn't like them. He said wraps gave him a feeling that the work emphasis went to his glutes and lower back and that they became too much like a lever. Suffice it to say that Platz built his legs without wraps and encouraged all who would listen to do the same.

Now, if you think 635 for 15 below-parallel reps with knees unwrapped is quite a feat, just wait. Try doing 525 pounds for 24 reps. Or how about squatting your body weight (for Platz that was about 225 pounds) for 10 minutes—nonstop! We're talking reps in the hundreds, and that was with 225 pounds!

Some say that Tom Platz had all the makings of great legs with superior genetics, but he'd tell you differently. What took Platz to the top in the leg world was laserlike focus, intensity, and not being content to be stay in one place. That is, always going beyond what his mind and body was used to so that he could reach new heights.

TO BE THAT BIG AND BE FLEXIBLE

One of the amazing things about Platz's development was his physical flexibility. The guy could do the splits with thighs the size of truck tires! When asked about his flexibility, he had some interesting things to say.

For one, it's just a plain old myth when people say you can't be big and flexible too. To Platz, flexibility was important to squatting performance. He believed it helped him avoid injuries and allowed him to train heavier and do more reps.

So how did he become flexible? Simply by doing 5 to 10 minutes of various stretches prior to a leg workout and mentally picturing himself as having great leg mobility and flexibility. Again, he was a big visualizer.

A COOL TRICK FOR BETTER RESULTS

If you're a bodybuilder worth your salt in the gym, you want to know any and everything that can help get great results. There are some little-known things that Tom did that helped give him an edge. Get ready for this one . . .

He said that when he worked legs, he wore high socks. Seriously. But for a reason you may find surprising. Wearing long shorts with high socks made his legs look shorter.

And because they looked shorter, that visualized image gave his brain the message that he didn't have to squat down as far. And he said because of that, the weight felt lighter. He also said he wore a tight shirt, which gave him more support and helped him spring up from the bottom position like a piston.

Tom also had a few Platzisms that people who want great legs would do well to make their own:

- Never work legs more than twice per week.
- Don't think about how much you can do or how often you can do it. Instead, think about how well you can do it.
- Use full-range reps. Chances are you don't do half curls or bench presses. So don't do half leg movements. Go all the way down and all the way back up. Keep the stress on the muscle.
- Don't bother doing split leg training by working quads one day and hamstrings the next. The results are minimal at best. Do all your leg work on one day and one workout.

THE BIG THREE

Tom Platz had a simple philosophy about leg training success, and it all came down to three principles:

1. **Instinct.** In Platz's book, this was the biggest. It all comes down to doing what feels right. We all know which exercises

our body responds best to and those that do them can overcome a lack of genetics and technical knowledge to achieve great success.

2. **Genetics.** Of course, one can only go as far as genetics will allow. However, most people have no idea what their true genetic potential is and stop far short of what they might be capable of achieving.

3. **Education.** No, this doesn't just mean book smarts. It's empirical, real-world, in-the-gym knowledge that teaches you how variations in training, exercises, weights, sets, reps, and the like make your muscles work harder and grow. By applying that knowledge to your leg workouts, the faster you'll reach your goals.

AVOIDING THE MISTAKES

Hey, we all make mistakes, so relax. Tom Platz has seen his share of them too, by lots of bodybuilders. Be it too many exercises and too many sets, to training too often, there are still many bodybuilders who believe that the more leg exercises they do and the more often they do them, the more they'll grow. Wrong!

Tom found that doing one leg workout heavy and one leg workout light during the week brought great results. In fact, he said that if someone works legs more than that, they're doing too much. And at the time of our interview, he said he was only working legs once a week and doing squats two times

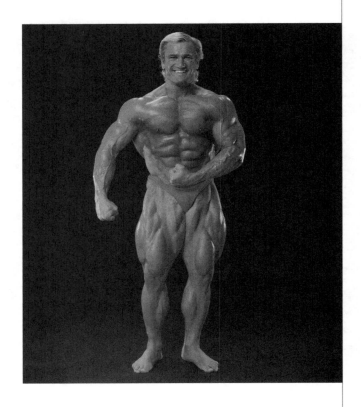

a month and the results he was getting were amazing.

LET'S TALK EXERCISES

So what exercises did Tom Platz do to get such great results? Nothing fancy. He said his leg routine is so basic that it was still the same one he used ever since he started training. Here it is:

SQUATS

Platz said the squat was the single most important leg exercise for his leg growth and strength. But you need to do them correctly:

- Wear a special squat shoe that allows the heels to be elevated. Hiking boots are fine. However, sometimes Tom would squat in regular athletic shoes just for variation.

- Keep the bar high on the traps.
- Place your feet at about shoulder-width apart and turn them slightly outward.
- Descend in a controlled manner to at least parallel or below parallel position.

HACK SQUAT MACHINE

For hitting the inner, outer, and middle thigh and hamstrings, the hack squat machine can't be beat. The trick is changing foot, leg, and body positions. Tom said he liked the old hack squat machines—with the 45-degree angles—much better than the newer hack squat machines with 35-degree angles, which in his opinion work too much glute and hamstring. Tom liked doing them like this:

- Try keeping the heels up and back and knees way out over the feet to hit the lower quad.
- Try keeping the hips and glutes off the back pad to hit the upper quad.
- Try turning the toes outward to hit the inner quad.
- Try keeping only the upper back and shoulders resting against the back pad and heels up and knees over the feet to hit hamstrings.
- Experiment with various body and foot positions and see which ones hit different parts of your quads and hamstrings best.

VARIED LEG POSITION LEG EXTENSIONS

Here is one exercise that Tom liked to do that allowed him to use forced reps, negative reps, and static contractions. Tom said he would typically have a spotter help him up with a forced rep, have the spotter push the weight down for only a few inches, and then he would hold it, and then have the spotter force it down for a couple more inches and do the same thing. Talk about full-range muscle exhaustion!

Tom also liked to turn his legs outward and lean back on the machine, as he found that doing so really helped hit his inner and upper quads. Tom believed that while he couldn't change the shape of a muscle, he could selectively develop one muscle head more than another simply by varying his leg and upper-body position while doing the exercise. It was by using this technique that Tom developed his famed vastus lateralis so much that it gave the illusion that his legs were monstrous.

LYING LEG CURL

Tom liked doing leg curls right after squats and hack squats. He said that his first set would be a high-rep set of 50 to 60 reps, but with a lighter weight. For his next set, he'd jump right up to the heaviest weight on the stack and then have a spotter give him forced reps, negatives, and static contractions.

STANDING CALF RAISE ON MACHINE

Much to many people's surprise, Tom's calves grew from this exercise not by how much weight he used, but by changing exercise form and body position. For example, Tom would hold the weight in the top peak contracted position for a few seconds on every rep. He also was fond of using an exaggerated kind of motion, whereby he would go all the way as high as he could and then all the way down as low as he could.

But he wouldn't stop there. Platz went beyond the point of failure by doing partial reps and bending his knees and thrusting his body toward the machine to get even more rep movement. At the point when he reached rep motion failure, he'd then hold the weight in a fixed position for as long as he possibly could. Talk about a burn.

ROUTINES FOR BEGINNER, INTERMEDIATE, AND ADVANCED

Okay, so now you know the exercises that Tom Platz used. What about putting them in workouts for the beginner, intermediate, and advanced? Say no more. Here's how he said to structure them:

FOR THE BEGINNER

Start with the basics and work legs twice per week. Keep your form excellent and find the best exercise groove.

Beginner Routine

- Stretch for 10 minutes
- Squats: 3 sets of 10 reps
- Leg curl: 2 or 3 sets of 10–15 reps
- Machine standing calf raise: 2 or 3 sets of 10–15 reps

FOR THE INTERMEDIATE

As you're getting stronger, you're now able to handle more volume and intensity in your training, which will become the two main variables you'll adjust for each workout. Tom suggested that intermediates alternate their workouts by doing heavy weights/low reps for one workout and lighter weights/higher reps for the next workout.

Intermediate Routine

- Stretch for 10 minutes
- Squats: 3 sets of 6–15 reps
- Leg extensions: 3 sets of 12–20 reps
- Leg curls: 3 sets of 10–60 reps
- Machine standing calf raise: 3 sets of 6–60 reps

FOR THE ADVANCED

The more advanced you become, the quicker you can create exercise intensity, meaning it'll take less work in order to get results. However, Tom advised that if you do less work for too long, you will reach the point where you have to add work volume and intensity again.

As an advanced bodybuilder, you'll also have to balance doing just the right amount of work to not overtrain. For that reason, Tom believed it a wise idea to vary your advanced workouts with beginner and intermediate periods of training. In fact, Tom said he did it and plans to do it for as long as he'll be training. We're never too old or too experienced to be a beginner again. Your advanced routine will look like this:

- Stretch for 10 minutes
- Squats: 4 sets of 6–25 reps
- Hack squat machine: 4 sets of 8–20 reps
- Leg extension: 4 sets of 10–30 reps
- Leg curl: 4 sets of 8–60 reps
- Machine standing calf raise: 4 sets of 8–60 reps

25

Rich Gaspari's Advice for a Lifetime of Learning

During the Lee Haney/Lee Labrada competitive years, one of the bodybuilders who was immensely popular among his fans was Rich Gaspari. Gaspari touched a nerve in people who could relate to what he was all about. He wasn't tall or freaky muscular, but he was well put together, and if he came to a show in razor-sharp condition, he was a force to be reckoned with—even winning the celebrated Arnold Classic.

Rich was likable. He was a guy who was street smart and took his observations of others and the lessons he learned the hard way and turned it all into a successful bodybuilding career. Here's a little of what he shared.

Rich was always a seeker of information and answers. To Rich, it didn't matter how old or young a person was. There was always something new and different waiting to be learned. Such a philosophy helped Rich quickly reach his bodybuilding goals.

Rich was also a businessman and turned his dream of owning a gym into a reality. And it was there, in the gym, that Rich observed some interesting things that you may find helpful. One of them is that old members can learn a lot from new members. Sure, the older member may be stronger and have more muscle or be in better shape; however, new members bring many of the mental and physical qualities that old members may have forgotten they shared, including the following:

- **Fresh attitude.** Building a great body is exciting, and seeing your body change is powerful at helping change how you see yourself. The gym is the place where bodies and lives are changed, and this fresh attitude starts positively affecting the members' workouts, job, relationships, and other areas of their life. All of this helps them become positive thinkers since they're experiencing firsthand many, many positive rewards both in and out of the gym.

- **A strong belief.** Experiencing such positive results only stokes the fire of desire for more results, and this is exciting stuff. People all around you begin to see changes in attitude and body taking place, and you realize that something amazing is going on here. People treat you with more respect, which reinforces the self-image and inspires you to set even more goals to achieve. You're not just going through the motions anymore. Everything you do now has more purpose, and that purpose fits into the big picture of your life.

- **Goal achieving.** As your life has become more defined with purpose and a reason for you to train, you begin to fine-tune and hone your training so that your actions will take you to your goals in the most efficient ways possible. And before one goal is achieved, the next one is set so that you become a goal-seeking and achieving person.

- **Grow, grow, grow.** As your muscles get bigger and stronger, your body and life take on a new look and feel. You also realize that it is your efforts and hard work that are making these changes. It isn't some fuzzy idea, but something real you can feel and see in the mirror right now. Such an experience is hugely exciting, and that excitement spills over to all other areas of your life.

- **They are excited.** How can you not be excited about all the changes you're seeing and feeling? As people love being around other people who are enthusiastic, it's hard to hide your excitement. Now, instead of just going to the gym to work out, everything you do in the gym—from the exercises, sets, reps, and weights—takes on a whole new meaning.

Now, sit back for a moment and try to remember when you first started training and how many of those same qualities you experienced. Probably a lot, if not all of them. Rich said he saw it in his members at his gym. Bringing back into your training and time in the gym those same qualities can pull you out of the training rut so many get into from time to time.

Look at the new members' enthusiasm and remember that you were once like that too. Look at their attitude and listen to their dreams and goals and remember that you had a head full of them not too long ago too. Look at their passion for asking lots of questions and trying new exercises and workouts and remember that you did that too.

Learn an important lesson from Rich: be open to any and everything that can help you grow and reach your goals. It could be just the perfect time to bring back the old exciting you, the one that inspired you to build the body that the gym showed you that you could have.

26

Best Butt: Four Women with Great Ones Reveal Their Secrets

Did you ever wonder why it is that the males who work out are usually interested in having a big upper body like arms, chest, back, and shoulders, and women who work out want nice legs and, of course, great buns? Okay, glutes, buns, butt, bum, tush, whatever they call it, they still want it to be firm, tight, have nice shape, and look awesome.

While some guys may not be into an overly muscular woman's physique, most of them do like a nice-looking butt. So the age-old fitness question for women is, how do I get it? Following are a few great suggestions by some of the women who have what so many women want.

MIA FINNEGAN

Mia said that the body weight–only reverse lunge was one of her favorites. She said that lunges make the body recruit more muscle fiber than any machine exercise. While machines may allow you to work the muscle in the full range, you're not having to recruit those additional muscle fibers for balance. Lunges hit the whole glute instead of just a section of it. Here's how she did them:

- She started with her feet together and then took a step backward to where her front and back knees are both at 90-degree angles. She did not let the knee touch the ground.
- Once she was at the bottom position, she pushed up, but not off of the back foot. She used the front foot to lift.

MELISSA COATES

Melissa said she really liked low-pulley cable kickbacks, saying that it was the one glute isolation movement that she could really focus on. At one time she used to do a lot of squats, lunges, and other types of glute exercises and found that while those movements hit the glutes, they hit a lot of other muscles too. As a result, she really wasn't able to focus on the glutes like she wanted to.

Melissa believed that kickbacks are ideal because they work nothing but pure glutes and allow her to burn them for great results. She likes to use triple drop sets—doing a heavy set, then decreasing the weight and doing another set, then decreasing the weight one more time for a third and final set—on this exercise. Here's how she did them:

- On the low pulley on a cable crossover station, she attached an ankle strap to each leg. She attached the cable to one leg and then stood in front of the weight stack and, with both hands, held on to the vertical steel columns for support.
- With her upper body fairly upright with just a slight lean forward, she kicked her leg straight back behind her. She didn't use full-range reps. Instead, she kept the movement short and in the peak tension range.
- She kept her knee slightly bent and also varied her foot position. On some sets, her toes were pointing back and away, and on other sets they were pointing forward and down.

- She did 3 sets of 10–20 reps. The first set was for 20 reps, 15 reps on the second, and 10 on the third.
- She did lunges four days per week. Lunges were done first in her workout, before hamstrings and calves. The lunges not only hit the glutes hard, but the quads as well.

To get the most from lunges, it's important to really concentrate on the glutes and not on the quads. Most people make the mistake of lifting with the quads and not the glutes. Always push off of the front foot, and you'll get great results.

- She did 5 sets of kickbacks, with her last sets being triple drops. Her 3 straight sets had a rep range from 15 to 30. Her triple drop sets were 60 pounds for 10 to 12 reps, 40 pounds for 12 to 15 reps, and 20 pounds for 15 to 20 reps. She did go heavier (at the time, about 60 pounds) because she believed that, within reason, slightly more muscular glutes look better.
- The exercise was performed at the end of her leg routine and was done once every five days.

PENNY PRICE

Penny said that heavy barbell lunges were the best. She said she tried every glute exercise and every variation of lunge (dumbbell, Smith machine, and so on) and the only one that ever made her sore was the barbell lunge. She said her routine was simple: 4 sets of 8 to 10 reps, 2 or 3 times per week, with 45 seconds of rest between sets. Here's how Penny did them:

- She took the barbell out of the squat rack, stepped back and lunged forward, and alternated left to right.
- Penny said she made sure the knee didn't go over the toe when she was at the bottom position.
- She kept her head up and shoulders back and focused on getting a lot of power from the thrust. She didn't lean forward, but rather took long strides and focused on keeping her midsection tight during the exercise.

Penny had one more piece of advice for those who want a great butt, but for whatever reason (knee problems, etc.) may not be able to do lunges. She suggested using the Smith machine, but in a uniquely different way:

- Lower the bar slightly above your body.
- Position your body so that you're on all fours under the bar like a dog.
- Put one foot under the bar and kick (raise) it up.
- Really focus and feel the glutes working.

CAROL SEMPLE

If you have noticed, each of these women has found her own unique way of working her butt, and who can argue with the amazing results they were able to achieve? Here's another one of those ways.

Carol Semple said hyperextensions were one of her favorite glute exercises. She said she felt they were the only exercise that totally isolated the upper hamstring/gluteal tie-in. After only a few sets of hypers, her glutes and hamstrings were exhausted big time. She found a terrific way to do them that isolated her hamstrings and glutes and not her lower back:

- When she was in the fully stretched position—that is, with her upper torso bent over and hanging down—she started contracting her glutes and hamstrings.
- As soon as she started contracting them, her upper body would come up in a

- She concentrated on keeping her hamstrings and glutes contracted first and always kept the back rounded in order to totally isolate her hamstrings and glutes.
- For the first 10 to 15 reps, she went real slow and really squeezed the glutes and hamstrings.
- At the top of the rep, she held the contraction for one or two seconds and slowly lowered her body.
- For the last 5 reps, she just went up and down without stopping.
- She said she liked to do 4 sets of 15 to 20 reps. In the off-season, she did hypers three or four days a week and did them either with abs or legs.

hollow-rounded position (head down and chin tucked, arms crossed in front of chest, shoulders forward and rounded) as opposed to doing them with a flat back, which she said she found to work more of the lower back.

- She focused on keeping the small of her back toward the ceiling and pressed her hips toward the floor.
- She would come up no higher than where the small of her back was at parallel or slightly under.
- Carol kept her feet turned outward under the heel support pad. She felt the movement better with her feet in this position.

27

Dorian Yates on Building Meaty Shoulders

Dorian Yates was a guy who, many say, took the physique to a whole new level of development and conditioning. This was a guy who trained brutally hard in his dungeon-like Temple Gym in England, and each year he competed, he showed up bigger and better than he was the year before. At that level of development, that's not an easy thing to do.

Yates had many body parts that people awed over, from that amazing back to quads and calves that just seemed otherworldly. One of those body parts was his shoulders. Guys like big meaty shoulders, and Dorian had them in spades. Here's what he did to build them.

Dorian said that building wide and massive shoulders wasn't as hard as people might think, and it didn't take 20 sets to do it. He also said he found many of the reasons why people may not be getting the kind of shoulder-building results they've been searching for.

They set too high goals too quickly, as in wanting four inches on their shoulders now. He said this kind of thinking just doesn't work. He advised to break things down into small steps and shoot for smaller, easily achievable goals and build step-by-step from there, the result being that before they know it, they will have reached their ultimate goal.

Another problem is that people are over-trained in sets and reps and undertrained in intensity. They do too many sets too often and this leads to burnout, stagnation, and little, if any, growth.

So what did Dorian recommend as a way to overcome these obstacles and train shoulders for great results? He said his approach to bodybuilding was simple: train with 100 percent intensity; use a variety of exercises and angles always in strict form; do 1 or 2 sets per exercise; and allow enough time for recuperation. Done correctly, he said, that's all the training a body and shoulders need to pack on some serious size.

Because the shoulder joint is a vulnerable area for injury, Dorian said he thoroughly warmed it up before he went into his routine. He did a few sets of light presses to make sure the shoulder area was warmed and full of blood. From there, he would go to his first exercise, which was the seated dumbbell press.

Dorian said he liked seated dumbbell presses for building complete shoulder mass and thickness. He varied this movement by doing it either with his back against a vertical bench or simply seated on a regular bench. He said that doing dumbbell presses on the vertical bench is a very strict move-ment, and some may find that they're not able to do as much weight as they might be able to if they did presses without the back support.

His first 2 sets of presses were basically warm-ups with a moderate weight, as he wanted to get the shoulder area ready for the heavy weight that follows. Dorian said he did two warm-ups of 8 to 10 reps per set, and he then would jump right up to the heaviest weight that he could do in strict form for 6 to 10 reps. For Dorian, it had to be all-out 100 percent intensity or the muscle wasn't going to grow.

Dorian said he would do one more set after that and then drop the weight down a bit so he could get another 6 to 10 reps. He rested just long enough to let his partner get his set in. The total work done on shoulder press was 2 warm-up sets and 2 all-out heavy sets for 6 to 10 reps.

His second shoulder exercise was alter-nate front dumbbell raises, and he did these either standing or seated. Dorian said this was a terrific front-delt developer, and even though the front delts got quite a bit of work from the chest workout, he found working the front delt directly by doing alternating front dumbbell raises helped put that thick muscular cap on the front of the delt head.

Dorian cautioned that if someone already had well-developed front delts, to be careful not to overdo things on this movement. If taken to extremes, it had a tendency to give one a rounded look. Balance on all three delt heads was the key. He found that keeping the delts constantly moving with little, if any, rest was the way to make them grow. And since his delts were already warmed from the shoulder presses, he'd go right up to the heaviest weight he could do in strict form for 2 sets of 6 to 10 reps.

Dorian's third exercise for shoulders was dumbbell side laterals, and he might do these standing or seated. He said he liked doing them standing because he could use more weight and he felt the movement better. He said good form was important, and when he did these, he kept his arms out to his sides and his palms facing the floor with his little finger turned up slightly higher than his thumb. He said that far too many people did the movement incorrectly by raising their arms higher than their shoulders, which worked more of the traps.

Dorian said that if someone wanted wide shoulders, then this movement would do it, provided they did it correctly. That meant strict form, keeping the delt constantly working with little or no rest, 100 percent intensity, and going as heavy as possible. He made his grow by doing only 2 all-out screamin' burning sets of 6 to 10 reps.

His fourth and final delt exercise was rear dumbbell laterals leaning forward on an incline bench. Dorian said there were a number of ways to work the rear delt (bent-over cable laterals, reverse pec dec laterals, standing dumbbell bent-over laterals, and so on) and they all worked well, however, one of the best ways he found to work the rear delt was to do rear laterals lying facedown on an incline bench.

Again, Dorian said that strict form was important: his palms were always facing the floor and his little finger at the top of the movement was higher than his thumb. He said he also tried keeping his arms straight out to his side with just a slight bend to them. The goal of the exercise was to bring his arms back as far as he could at the top of the movement and keep the delts moving, with little or no rest between reps. He said he did 2 sets of 6 to 10 reps.

In summary, all Dorian did for shoulders was 2 warm-up sets and 8 regular sets. But let me add, it's how Dorian did those 8 sets that made all the difference!

THE DORIAN YATES SHOULDER EXERCISES

Seated Dumbbell Press

Dorian took a pair of dumbbells and raised them to the tops of his shoulders. He then pressed them to near full lock-out above his head and lowered them in a controlled manner and back up again, always keeping the delt working through the exercise. He said he focused on keeping his back straight during the entire movement, as the work from the exercise needed to be concentrated on the entire delt head and no other muscle.

Alternate Dumbbell Front Raises

Dorian said on this one, he would take two dumbbells in front of him and then raise one dumbbell to head level, and as the weight came down, he would alternately raise the other side to the same position. He said he didn't go any higher than head level because by doing so, the stress is taken off the front delt and put on the traps. Dorian kept the weights moving, however, but not at the expense of swinging the weight up.

Dumbbell Side Laterals

While he could do these seated, Dorian said he liked doing them standing. He explained that with two dumbbells to his sides or slightly in front of him, he'd raise the weights out to his sides and hold the weight at shoulder level momentarily. He then lowered the weight back down to the starting position and repeated. At the top of the movement, his little finger on each hand was higher than his thumb, and his palms were always facing the floor. Dorian said he liked going as heavy as possible with strict form and keeping the weight moving, and he went for the burn, which he said helped put that cap and width on his shoulders.

Rear Dumbbell Laterals Leaning Forward on an Incline Bench

Dorian said he would do these lying with his stomach on an incline bench. He would take two dumbbells in front of him and raise the weights out to his side. He said that to really hit the rear delt, it's important to keep the arms as straight out to the sides as possible and bring them back as far as you can with your palms facing the floor. Dorian said he held the weight at the top for a moment and then lowered it back down and repeated the movement.

The Dorian Yates Workout
Day 1: chest and triceps
Day 2: biceps and legs
Day 3: off
Day 4: back and deltoids
Day 5: off

28

Ken Lain: Secrets of a 700-Plus-Pound Bench Presser

They say they grow 'em big down in Texas, and when it came to bench pressing, one of the biggest and strongest of the bunch was Ken Lain. How does more than 700 pounds grab ya? Well, if you were Ken Lain, you could certainly grab it and then bench press it. That's what a lot of bodybuilders wish they could do—perhaps not bench press 700 or more pounds like Ken, but just have a bigger, better bench. As a guy who set world records and could easily do 20 reps with 405 pounds, Lain knew how to make anyone stronger on the bench press.

It was surprising just how big this guy was. He had a body that looked more like a pro bodybuilder than a powerlifter, and he was huge. He was 5'11" and weighed anywhere from 280 to 320 pounds. He had

21-inch arms, a 58-inch chest, 31-inch legs, 20-inch calves and a 36-inch waist. So what was Ken's training philosophy for his success?

Ken said he liked using basic movements in his training. We're talking squats, bench presses, seated rows, straight barbell curls, chins, pulldowns, close-grip bench presses, and those kinds of things. He said he found success by cycling his training and believed that it helped him gain size and strength and prevented injury and burnout. He liked to keep his sets in the 9 to 12 range for each body part.

Ken said there was a time when he wanted to set world records that he allowed his body weight to climb to over 300 pounds, and did it by eating any and everything he could. Sure, he was strong as a horse, but he also felt uncomfortable. Soon thereafter, he went back to eating healthy again with foods like chicken, fish, vegetables, whole grains, and fruit. He said he was a big believer in supplements and took, at that time, his own brand of supplements that included amino acids, protein powders, weight-gain powders, energizer drinks, and vitamin packs. He believed the supplements allowed him to eat the junky calories and use and burn them more efficiently.

While strength was important to Ken, it was never at the expense of good health. That meant cardio workouts such as riding the bike. Ken said he found cardio helped him sleep and feel better, as well as helping him live longer.

Like so many of the world's best athletes, Ken used the power of visualization to help him reach deep inside his potential and break the barrier to a world record lift. One of the ways he did that was to visualize himself completing the lift very vividly. He would visualize the bar, the crowd, the weights, the bench, the spotters, and everything else. He would visualize coming down with the bar, stopping it, driving it back up, holding it at the top, and racking it. From start to finish, everything in Ken's mind was crystal clear and very vivid.

But he also might have had a little unseen help, too, from a more powerful force called his spiritual connection. Ken said he gave all of his success to God. He was fortunate to not have any serious injuries, and he thanked God for that. God was a major source of his inspiration and motivation, and he believed any athlete who had a good relationship with the Lord was going to do better.

So how should people train if they want a bigger and better bench press? Ken said that if there was some magical formula for his success, it would have to be the percentage system he used for his lifts. Here's how he used it:

- The first thing he did was choose a projected maximum lift that he wanted to do, and he then gave himself 10 weeks to train for it.
- He explained that if someone wanted to bench 550 pounds and the person's best

bench at the time was is 500 pounds, he'd have them structure their training like this:

- Week 10 they'd do 55 percent of the projected maximum, or 3 sets of 10 reps at 300 pounds.
- Week 9 they'd do 60 percent of the projected maximum, or 3 sets of 9 reps with 330 pounds.
- Week 8 do 65 percent of the projected maximum, or 3 sets of 8 reps with 355 pounds.
- Each week the person would continue to do the 3 sets but would increase the weight by 5 percent and decrease the reps by one until the projected maximum weight was reached.
- He cautioned people who used this system to only do this type of chest routine once a week. The other chest day should be only 80 percent of what they did on their previous chest workout.
- Recovery and proper rest are very important, and Ken said he found it could take his body up to three weeks to recover from a maximum lift.

Whether it was in his gym or at seminars, Ken always got asked lots of questions from those eager and hungry bodybuilders and power athletes who were searching for more size and strength. Ken said one of the biggest mistakes people made was overtraining. Lots of beginners were doing 18 to 20 sets per body part when they could do really well with as few as 9 sets. Especially for chest: 3 sets of heavy bench presses, 3 sets of heavy inclines, and 3 sets of heavy flyes— Ken said that was all you need to put on some good mass.

Of course, guys want big arms, and Ken had plenty to say about that. He found that in order to gain one inch on the arms, you've got to gain 10 to 15 pounds in body weight. That meant that if a guy weighed 120 pounds and had a 12-inch arm and wanted a 20-incher, then he had better expect to put on roughly another 100 pounds in body weight, and Ken wasn't talking about gaining fat.

Ken was one of the most motivating guys you'd ever want to meet, and he had a few things he thought could help anyone who wanted to reach their best. They were:

- Don't put any limits on yourself. He said he had no idea what his maximum bench press was because he never put any limits on himself.
- Don't think about the negative consequences of what might happen. That will definitely keep you from excelling.
- Be sure to have role models who inspire you.
- Don't tell yourself that you can't do something. If you put a limit on yourself, that's exactly as far as you will ever go.
- Be patient, and the results will come. Just believe in yourself, and you will do it.

29

Rut Blasters: Workout Routines and Strategies to Keep You Growing

Here's something you can bank on: if you work out, if you are getting bigger and stronger, you can bet that at some point in your training, you'll hit a rut in your training road. If you don't know how to deal with it, such an experience can be frustrating. If you do know how to make the right changes in your training, then that rut will only be a little bump, a pothole if you will, that you'll be able to travel over quickly and without any problems. Just remember that your body is not a machine. Many have found they look forward to and like their workouts better if they change things on a regular basis.

One of the quickest ways to achieve success is to copy the things that successful people do. For getting out of training ruts, it helps to look at what those who make bodybuilding their life do so they can continue training week after week, month after month, year after year. With that in mind, here are some of the "rut-blasting" strategies that some pros have shared.

PAUL DILLETT

If one guy had the reputation for instinctive trainer, it would be Paul Dillett. Paul liked to train instinctively because his body never got used to training one way for too long. Here's an example. One workout he might do arms (phenomenal arms, by the way) and then not train them for another two weeks. Or he might train arms every day for six or seven days in a row. Everything he did in the gym was instinctive. There might be a great

work, now you'll have a huge pool of training information to pick from whenever and wherever you need it.

KEVIN LEVRONE

Kevin said that far too many bodybuilders go to extremes when trying to get out of a training rut when the truth is, it doesn't take something drastic for the body to grow. He liked the logical and simple approach.

Levrone used those inevitable rut periods as times to learn. It became like his own classroom whereby he'd look at his total training approach. And then he'd ask ques-

workout he had planned for days, and then once he actually got to the gym and began his workout, he'd change everything on the spot.

Paul even took this instinctive training a step further. For example, let's say he was in the middle of doing an exercise, and the exercise wasn't giving his muscles the pump and feel he was wanting. He'd stop right in the middle of the exercise and go to another one that would give him those results.

Dillett was a big believer in listening to his body and would constantly experiment to find the best exercises, sets, reps, weight, and rest times for him. It might take a little time to find these things, but the rewards are worth it. Instead of guessing what might

tions: Is his diet as good as it could be? Was he ingesting enough protein and carbs? Was he well rested, or was he experiencing more stress than normal? Did he take off enough days between workouts so that his body could completely recuperate? Was he using the workouts, angles, weights, reps, and sets that were giving him excellent results? By asking such questions and then listening to the answers, he'd return to the gym refreshed and ready.

One of the things he believed was that people fall into training ruts by training large muscle groups too close together. Like training chest followed by back or legs. Kevin found that his body became depleted quickly after a tough back workout, and if he would come in the next day and do chest or legs, the workouts would suffer and so would his chances to recuperate completely.

CHRIS DUFFY

Chris listened closely when his body hit a rut and sticking point by taking a few days off and then backing down on the volume and intensity of his workouts. Once he got back in the gym, he'd typically do only one exercise for each body part. For his chest, it might be dumbbell or barbell inclines. For back, it might be chins or rows. For quads, it might be squats. For delts, it might be presses. For arms, it might be barbell or dumbbell curls for biceps, and dumbbell French press or lying EZ curl extensions for triceps.

Chris said that one of the greatest rut busters he found was to do just one exercise, but for 10 sets of 10 reps. Such shock treatment literally forces the body to grow. Choose any body part that just doesn't seem to grow. Stop training it for a few days. When you hit the iron again, only do one exercise for 10 sets of 10 reps.

Such a training regimen will so thoroughly blast the deep fibers of the muscle that after the fifth or sixth set, that muscle will be screaming for you to stop. The key is to follow this routine for no more than six weeks. After that, choose a different routine until you hit the next plateau, and just keep repeating the process.

Porter said he'd typically do this rut-busting routine for four weeks in a row, and then he'd do the routine once every two to three weeks. Doing this workout twice every eight days gave him good results.

NASSER EL SONBATY

While Porter blasted his body with high reps and heavy/light supersets, Nasser took a different approach by training very heavy and keeping the reps in the 4 to 10 range. He also used combinations of different exercises done back-to-back for the same body part. Here's an example:

- After a good chest warm-up (2 or 3 sets), Nasser would jump up in weight and go as heavy as possible on barbell inclines for his first exercise.

PORTER COTTRELL

Porter had an interesting take on how to bust out of a rut: Do 60- to 70-rep leg presses supersetted to 30- to 40-rep leg extensions. He said it worked amazingly well, and here's how he did it:

- He loaded just enough weight on the leg press so that he could barely do 60 to 70 reps.
- After the last rep on the leg press, he quickly moved to the leg extension, and using a light weight—say 20 or 30 pounds—Porter would do 30 to 40 reps.
- He repeated this for 5 supersets.

- After doing 4 to 8 reps, he'd then rack the weight and go to heavy decline presses for one set of 4 to 8 reps.
- After declines, he would then go to incline dumbbell flyes and do 6 to 10 reps as heavy as he possibly could, but with good form.
- The last exercise would be the standing cable crossover, and he'd do 6 to 10 reps.
- All of these exercises would be done immediately after each other for one giant set.
- For his next giant set, Nasser would do the same exercises, but in reverse order (cable crossovers, then incline dumbbell flyes, then decline presses, then barbell inclines).
- He'd also use the same specific rep range for each exercise.
- His third and final set of exercises would be two or three of the best exercises from the four exercises he performed in the giant set. The criteria was simple: choose only those exercises that gave him the best muscle pump and fatigue.

30

Manfred Hoeberl's World's Largest Arms Tips

Some years ago, John and I (Bob) cowrote a book called *10 Minutes to Massive Arms* that featured the European strength phenomenon Manfred Hoeberl. Manfred was a former winner of the World's Strongest Man title. But what mesmerized anyone who saw him was the size of his arms. At over 25 inches each, Manfred's arms were bigger than most people's legs.

Manfred had a unique approach to arm training and found that brief workouts that used specific exercises, done in specific ways, along with key arm stretches helped his arms grow gigantic. Here is a taste of some of Manfred's arm training philosophy:

- Remember: you work your arms nearly every workout. Triceps are worked when you do chest, and shoulders and biceps are worked when you do back. That's

why it's very important that you give your arms plenty of time to recover after every workout. Proper rest is crucial if you want the biggest arms possible.

- If you really want to build unbelievable arms, you must experiment and find a stable of exercises that work great for you. The problem with most bodybuilders is that they want someone to tell them what exercises to do, how many reps and sets and how much weight they should use.

- To have gigantic arms, you must be meticulous and precise—like a scientist or engineer—and find the best angles, weights, exercises, reps, and rest that work for you. Following are some fantastic biceps exercises that worked extremely well for Manfred

STANDING DUMBBELL ALTERNATE CURL

Manfred used this movement off and on for many years, however, he didn't consider it to be a great mass builder because of the limiting body mechanical factor of heavy weights. The natural tendency when using heavy weights is to turn the body sideways, thereby putting extra stress on the lower back and spine.

The most important point in doing this movement is to use perfect form and make sure the biceps are maximally working. Manfred rarely used more than 65 pounds for this exercise. Here are a few points in getting the most from this movement:

- Take a pair of dumbbells and stand with your feet about shoulder-width apart.
- With your arms straight and your palms facing your legs, curl your right arm up to about shoulder level.
- As your arm is coming up to shoulder level, turn (supinate) the curling wrist outward and away from the shoulder. This will increase tension on the biceps, making it work harder.
- Hold the dumbbell in the peak contracted position for two seconds, then slowly lower the weight back down to the starting position.
- As the right curling hand is coming down, start curling the left hand up and follow the same procedure.

DUMBBELL CONCENTRATION CURL

If you want incredible peak in your biceps, then this is the movement for you! It's one of the very best biceps shaping movements, bar none. The secret in getting phenomenal results from this exercise is in the form you use and not the weight. You have to do fairly high reps (12 to 20) in order to smoke those biceps. Visualize the size and shape you want your biceps to be. See it clearly, and you'll be amazed at the results! Here's how to do the dumbbell concentration curl:

Seated

- Seated on a bench with a dumbbell in hand, place your upper arm against your inner thigh with your arm fully extended.
- Curl the dumbbell up, and turn your wrist outward (supinate) and away from the shoulder at the top of the movement.
- Hold the peak contraction for a one to two count, then slowly lower the weight back down to the starting position.
- Be sure to get a full stretch at the bottom and a tight contraction at the top of the movement.
- Always make sure that your curling arm stays firmly positioned against your inner thigh. Only your elbow should move. Make your biceps do all the work.

Free-Standing

- With a dumbbell in one hand and your curling arm hanging straight down, curl the dumbbell up to shoulder level.
- At the top of the movement, turn your wrist out (supinate) and away from your shoulder.
- Hold the dumbbell in the fully flexed and peak contracted position for a one to two count.

- Slowly lower the weight back down to the starting position.

Manfred used 55 to 75 pounds for this movement.

The free-standing dumbbell concentration curl allows you more freedom to move your arm so that you find the best position to attack your biceps. Manfred preferred doing his concentration curls seated, but each of us is different, so choose whichever one you like best.

DUMBBELL ONE-ARM PREACHER CURL

This is one of Manfred's favorite biceps exercises. He liked to perform this exercise on an incline bench that has a 60-degree angle. He used 65 pounds for this exercise. Here's how he did it:

- With a dumbbell in one hand, fully extend and lay your arm over the 60-degree angled incline bench.
- At this bottom position, your palm is facing upward and is actually turned a little to the outside and away from the bench.
- Then curl the weight up until your biceps is fully flexed and peak contracted. Never let the biceps relax by curling the weight too far toward your shoulder.
- Hold the weight at the top for a two count and then slowly lower the weight back down.
- Always lower the weight down slowly in order to prevent any injury from overex-

tending your elbow at the bottom position.

- Manfred did anywhere from 6 reps to total failure.

REVERSE-GRIP CLOSE-HAND CHIN-UP

Manfred did this exercise a lot when he first started to train, and it packed on biceps muscle mass like you wouldn't believe! The great thing about this biceps mass builder is that you can do it anywhere there is a straight bar you can hang from. Here's how to do it:

- Take an underhand grip (reverse grip) with your hands shoulder-width apart.
- Pull your body up until the bar is right under your chin.
- Hold yourself there for a quick one count, and slowly lower yourself and repeat.
- Be sure to fully extend your arms at the bottom to give your biceps a good stretch.
- Don't swing or jerk yourself up. Make the biceps do the work. Think biceps, biceps, biceps!
- Go to failure on every set, and never count reps.

DUMBBELL HAMMER CURL

This is a terrific mass builder for the biceps and biceps brachialis. Manfred regularly used 150-pound dumbbells for this exercise! The brachialis—the muscle that sits under the biceps—is neglected by most bodybuilders because they can't see it. Don't make that

mistake! If you want huge, unbelievable arms, you must train the biceps brachialis, and this exercise will do the job. Here's how to do it:

- With one arm and your body in a slightly bent-over position, hold onto an incline bench in order to counterbalance the heavy weight that you will curl with your other arm. With your other hand, pick up a dumbbell.
- Before you curl the weight up, your curling arm should be completely straight and fully extended. You then curl the weight up, making sure that your thumb is up during the entire movement.
- This is how to activate and make the brachialis fully contract: make sure you bring the weight up as high as you can go. This is important in order to get a total biceps maximal contraction. Slowly lower the weight and repeat.
- Manfred did 6 to 10 reps.

SEATED DUMBBELL TRICEPS FRENCH PRESS

This is a good triceps mass builder. You can do it with one or two hands. Manfred preferred using both hands because he was able to intensely work both triceps at the same time. He also liked using two arms because it gives more stability and he was able to use heavy weight.

You can either do this movement standing up or seated. Manfred preferred doing it seated with a backrest. The backrest should be straight up and down and not at an angle. This allows for greater stability when performing the movement with heavy weights.

REVERSE-GRIP STANDING EZ BAR FRENCH PRESS

Manfred did this exercise differently than most people. He gripped the EZ curl with an underhand grip—like he was going to do a barbell curl. You won't believe the results you'll experience doing the exercise like this!

Using a reverse grip makes the triceps work in a way that they're not accustomed to. Not only that, a reverse grip takes the stress and strain off of the wrists and elbows and allows you to train the triceps more completely. Here's how to do it:

- Take a reverse grip on a moderately heavy EZ bar.
- Raise the weight above your head with your arms completely locked out.
- Keeping your arms close to the sides of your head, lower the bar down as far as possible behind your head. This is very important in order to get the fullest triceps stretch possible!
- Bring the weight up above your head and lock your arms out completely. Hold the weight there for a one-two count and really squeeze and contract your triceps hard.

You have to be the one to decide which exercises work best for you. Find those exercises and create your own 10-minute workout.

GROWING THE LARGEST ARMS AND THE CRUCIAL IMPORTANCE OF STRETCHING

It is important to really understand how important stretching is if you want to build the biggest arms possible. Stretching is a very important part of training. This includes every body part and not just arms. You must stretch your muscles before and after training. There are absolutely no exceptions to this rule!

People experience many unnecessary injuries because they didn't take the time to stretch or they didn't stretch properly. Even Manfred experienced some injuries early on in his training until he learned how to stretch.

Manfred suggested that you stretch 15 minutes before you work out and 15 minutes after your workout. You will find that this 30 minutes of stretching will give you results like you never dreamed possible. Once you see the results, you'll never look back. But then again, you probably will look back and wonder why you didn't do it years ago!

In order to get the very best results from stretching, you must do it every time you work out. You won't benefit if you do it one workout and then don't do it for another week or two. This will only slow down your progress and frustrate you because you won't be seeing the kinds of results you want. Consistency is the key.

Stretching gives you flexibility. Most people are not very flexible. Many bodybuilders have big arms but are so inflexible that they really have problems getting their arms in their shirtsleeves and being able to touch their hands behind their back or over their head to their traps or upper back. To me, this is sad and spoils the great feeling of being big and being able to move freely in all directions. Think about this: what good is having incredibly huge arms if you can't freely move them wherever you want?

People who don't stretch are highly prone to injury. One of the most common injuries in the Strongman competitions is the snapping of the biceps. This can happen for many reasons, including muscles not being warmed up properly and the inflexibility of a muscle from not stretching.

Many of the strength feats weight lifters perform call for total muscular contraction at once. Imagine squatting down and picking up one end of a car and walking with it—with the engine still in it! Talk about using 100 percent of your muscles at once!

Here are some pointers you can use to immediately get started stretching so you can experience some incredible results!

STRETCHING THE BICEPS

Find yourself a partner or simply a wall you can push against.

Open up one hand and twist your wrist to the inside until you feel a slight pull in your forearm. Stretch only one arm at a time.

Press your hand against your partner or the wall and hold this position. Before a workout, stretch in this position for 8 seconds. After a workout, stretch in this position for 24 seconds.

Do 3 sets of stretching before and 3 sets of stretching after the workout.

Do not use a pulsing or bouncing movement when you stretch. Always stretch with controlled and constant tension. If you feel any pain, immediately stop!

STRETCHING THE TRICEPS

Raise your right arm above your head and bend it like you wanted to scratch the back of your head. Stretch only one arm at a time.

Take your left hand and place it on the elbow of your right hand and slowly start pushing the right elbow back. Slowly and steadily keep applying pressure on the right elbow in order to fully stretch the triceps.

Before a workout, stretch in this position for 8 seconds. After a workout, stretch in this position for 24 seconds.

Do 3 sets of stretching before and 3 sets of stretching after the workout.

If you feel any pain, immediately stop!

THE IMPORTANCE OF CARDIOVASCULAR TRAINING

Another important part of having big arms and a healthy, muscular body is the far-too-often neglected aspect of cardiovascular training—doing some type of aerobic exercise that will elevate your heart rate for a certain period of time in order to get the aerobic effect.

Manfred liked brisk walking, working out on the heavy bag, riding a stationary bike, or using a treadmill. His Strongman sport demanded that he not only be strong, but have the endurance to perform difficult feats of strength for long periods of time. It has to be all show and all go!

Manfred suggested that you begin your cardio workout by doing it three times per week. He liked doing 20 to 30 minutes of cardio work each workout before the weight workout. This helped stretch his muscles—remember how we talked about the importance of stretching in order to grow!—and it also raises the body's core temperature and got him warmed and ready for the weights to come.

He suggested doing a warm-up for the first 5 minutes, then exercising in your target heart range for 15 to 20 minutes and then cooling down for the last 5 minutes. To find your target heart range, do this:

- Take the number 220 and subtract your age.
- Multiply that number by 60 to 70 percent and you'll have your target heart-range number.

Almost immediately, you'll begin to feel better and more energetic after your first few cardiovascular workouts. Not only that, you'll notice your body fat decreasing, and regular cardio work will help you live longer.

THE ROAD TO SUCCESS

Let's face it. Each of us has different dreams and goals. That's what helps make us so unique. It allows us plenty of room to do our own thing. When you start to plan your career and your life, it's good to follow some basic rules that have helped Manfred grow not only physically, but mentally and spiritually as well. He advises you to apply these ideals to every facet of your training.

MANFRED'S RULE NUMBER 1: HONESTY

Be honest with yourself. Manfred said he often talks to people who live in a dream world. They fantasize about achieving something they haven't and go around telling people that they have. While it's good to think about what you'd like to accomplish in the future, don't lie to yourself and other people by believing and telling others that you have achieved something you haven't. Be honest, and others will greatly respect you for it.

MANFRED'S RULE NUMBER 2: DETERMINATION

Bodybuilding is one of the most difficult sports and lifestyles there is. You cannot just do bodybuilding. You must live it in and out of the gym. You have to train like a bodybuilder and eat like a bodybuilder to achieve a bodybuilder's results.

You'll find times in your life and training where the road to success may seem like a long one. You can't ever give up! Hang in there. We all go through problems in life. That's only natural. Those who reach the top in bodybuilding and in other areas of life are those who had the guts to hang in there and never stop despite all the obstacles and setbacks. You must be the same!

MANFRED'S RULE NUMBER 3: POSITIVE THINKING

Surround yourself with positive people. We live in a world filled with negative people who will try to steal your dream or pull you down to their level. Don't you dare let them. Think only positive, happy, and healthy thoughts. Surround yourself with only those who do the same.

MANFRED'S RULE NUMBER 4: LIVE YOUR OWN LIFE

Only you can give yourself the kind of life you want. Only you can make yourself truly happy. Don't get caught up in the material world. Manfred said he would never do something just for the sake of money. He only gets involved in projects because he likes the project. He knows that if the project is done well, he will be rewarded financially. The financial reward is only the effect of his action and never the cause.

You will only reach your true potential and become totally happy if you do what you love to do. Decide to live your own life the way you want it to be. Family and friends may give you advice and have your best interests at heart, but only you know what you must do to be totally fulfilled, happy, and content. Accept nothing less!

31

Lee Haney's Delt Blast

Even by today's standards, Lee Haney had a body—especially upper torso—that was phenomenal. That classic photo of Lee standing on a street in jeans and no top spreading those wide cobra-like lats still ranks as one of the best physique shots ever snapped.

As awesome as Lee's lats were, for the upper body to be a complete package, he also had to have the arms, chest, abs, and of course, wide-as-a-barn-door shoulders to tie it all together.

Lee spoke many times about his training, and for those who ever wanted to know just how he built those amazing shoulders, this is what he said.

Lee said that while good genetics and bone structure are big plusses to how big one's shoulders can be, with the right kinds of delt training a bodybuilder could put as much as five inches on his shoulder-width without a problem. However, Lee advised that for that to happen, you need knowledge and a good game plan.

First, to knowledge. Lee pointed out that the deltoid's function is to move the upper arm in a variety of directions. And because each head of the deltoid works in different degrees, proper training of each head is important to ensure complete deltoid development. For example, the frontal head of the delt is called the anterior head, and it contracts to move the upper arm forward and upward. It can also contract to move the arm out to the side when the palm is facing upward.

Lee said that the best anterior delt exercises were overhead presses and front lateral raises with a barbell, two dumbbells, or a single dumbbell. He also added that most chest movements, particularly bench presses, incline presses, and parallel bar dips, strongly stress the anterior delts.

Lee explained that the medial deltoid (also known as the side delt head) contracts to move the humerus directly out to your side when the palm is facing the floor. The best medial delt movements, he said, were side lateral raises (with dumbbells or pulleys) and wide upright rows. Keep in mind that to a certain degree, all overhead pressing exercises can also stress the medial deltoid heads.

The last delt head Lee talked about was rear or posterior delt, and its job is to contract and move the upper arm to the rear. Lee said the best posterior delt movements were bent lateral raises with a dumbbell or pulleys and rear lateral movement performed on a pec dec machine. He also said that most lat exercises (especially barbell and dumbbell bent rows, seated pulley rows, and T-bar rows) also work the rear delts. Finally, Lee spoke about the traps. Two of the best trap movements he found were shrugs and upright rows. So with all that in mind, how did Lee work those delts and traps? How about only twice a week? Yup, and here's how he did it.

Lee said he began by warming up his delts to prevent injury. One of his favorite delt warm-ups was supersetting 10 to 15 reps of upright rows with 10 to 15 reps of standing presses behind the neck. He used roughly 40 percent of his normal workout weight and did 2 or 3 nonstop warm-up supersets.

From there, his first heavy deltoid exercise and mass builder was seated dumbbell presses, a movement in which he liked to pyramid his weights. He began by taking a pair of moderately heavy dumbbells and would sit with his back against a 90-degree angled seat. He would bring the dumbbells up to shoulder level and push them directly upward in a semicircular arc, until they were at arm's length above his shoulders. From there, he would bring them back down in a deliberately controlled motion to shoulder level. He repeated for 4 sets of 5 to 7 reps.

Lee's next delt exercise was the dumbbell side lateral. He took two moderately heavy dumbbells and would stand erect with his feet about shoulder-width apart. With his palms facing each other, he pressed the dumbbells together a few inches in front of his hips. While keeping his arms slightly bent, Lee slowly raised the dumbbells in semicircular arcs directly out to his sides and upward until his hands were just a little above shoulder level. From there, he would slowly lower the dumbbells back to the starting position and repeat the movement for 3 sets of 8 to 10 reps. He said it was very important to keep the palms always facing the floor when doing side laterals, as this helped keep the work directly on the side delt muscle.

His third exercise was dumbbell bent-over laterals for the rear delts. Lee explained that he'd take a pair of moderately heavy dumbbells, set his feet a little wider than shoulder-width apart, straighten his legs, and bend over until his torso was parallel to the floor. Keeping his arms slightly bent, Lee slowly raised the weights directly out to his sides and upward in semicircular arcs until they were above the level of his shoulders. He then lowered the weights back down to the starting position and repeated for 3 sets of 8 to 10 reps.

For traps and for his fourth exercise, Lee liked doing high pulls, or what is known as upright rows. Lee said he might do uprights with either a cable or barbell. He explained that while some people like to work traps with back, he preferred to work traps with shoulders.

He began the movement by taking a straight bar attached to a low pulley or a barbell and would stand erect and hold the bar in the lowered position in front of his legs. He would then raise the bar until it was about chin level and squeeze and contract his traps for a one or two count. He would then slowly lower the bar until his arms were completely stretched out at the bottom position. Lee said he liked to use an exaggerated stretching motion, stretching his traps as completely as possible by sagging his shoulders as far down as they would go. He did this for 3 sets of 12 to 15 reps and always used a controlled motion to make sure he felt the trap work through the full range of the exercise.

Lee Haney's delt workout was simple and very effective, especially if you just keep these key points in mind:

- Thoroughly warm up and pyramid the weight poundages up to prevent injury.
- Use excellent form with controlled movements and work the muscle through the entire range of motion of the exercise.
- Use progressively heavier weights, but never at the expense of poor form.

- Work out consistently since that's how you get good results.
- Train, eat, and supplement wisely.
- Get plenty of rest

THE LEE HANEY DELT WORKOUT

- Seated dumbbell press: 4 sets of 5–7 reps
- Dumbbell side laterals: 3 sets of 8–10 reps
- Dumbbell bent-over laterals: 3 sets of 8–10 reps
- Barbell upright rows/cable high pulls: 3 sets of 12–15 reps

32

The Power of 10: Great Training Tips from the Pros

How do you think it would be if you could sit down in a room with, say, 10 of your favorite bodybuilding stars, and for the next hour, they gave you some of their tips for bodybuilding and workout success? You think you might be able to learn a thing or two? Here are a few of those valuable tidbits gleaned from some of the pros over the years.

that were terrific, as his quads and hamstrings quickly got up to par with his upper body.

Robby also said he made sure he got a full and complete stretch from the muscle group he worked. While he didn't stretch after each set, he did stretch the muscle completely after it was worked.

FRANCIS BENFATTO

Francis said he liked to get into the muscle and make it work intensely as quickly as possible and not start off slowly, like so many do, and do 2, 3, or 4 sets before they start feeling the muscle working. Here are two ways he got the muscle working quickly.

When he begins a workout, he could immediately do 1 or 2 supersets or even a set of very high reps just so he can get into the

ROBBY ROBINSON

Robby liked to do two things during his workouts that he said contributed to his size and overall muscle quality. First, he liked putting as much effort, enthusiasm, and energy into his workout as possible. He said that the greater amount of work that he could squeeze into a shorter period of time, the greater the impact and improvement it had on his physique.

As an example, Robby said his upper body had always been complete, but felt his legs lagged behind. Then he changed things. He said that since his legs were his weakest body part, he started training legs when his energy level was the highest. We're talking intense workouts too— sets of 50 to 75 reps on the squats with minimal rest in between. Robby said the results he got from doing just

muscle quickly. He said he liked doing compound sets, whereby he would do a superset for the same body part. If he was training arms, he might begin with barbell curls for 6 to 8 reps and then immediately do standing dumbbell alternating curls for 10 to 12 reps.

The other thing he said he liked doing was randomly picking someone in the gym and then following him in his routine. Francis said that by doing so there was a good chance he'd do some things completely different than what he'd normally do, and that kept him excited about the workout.

RICH GASPARI

Rich said one of the things that worked well for him was stretching and flexing his muscles between sets. For example, after

each set of chins or pulldowns, he'd stretch each side of his back by holding onto a stationary bar or machine. The important thing was to really stretch the lat. He said if you're doing it right, you would feel the lat stretch from near the waist at the bottom to near the shoulder at the top. Rich said he found this helped increase his muscle feel and control.

Rich said he also did lat spreads after every set and found that doing a combination of stretching and flexing the lat helped spread open the clavicle and would help the back get used to coming out even wider than it was.

LEE LABRADA

Lee said he could see a big difference in his physique when he added a sixth meal to his diet. He said he thought the extra protein kept his body in a positive nitrogen balance and helped keep it full of the right nutrients for recovery and growth.

Here's how he explained it. Let's say that someone was having problems gaining muscle mass and was eating five meals a day. Let's also say that each meal was roughly 600 calories. That would be 3,000 calories in a day. If that person were to add a sixth meal, that would now be 3,600 calories a day.

In a week's time, just adding that extra meal a day would give the body an extra 4,200 calories of protein and carbs it could use for growth and recovery, as well as stoking the metabolism. The interesting

wanted big legs, or big any other kind of body parts, then they needed to do full and complete reps.

He also used forced reps and found them to be effective. The way he did them was when he was no longer able to do full-range reps on his own, he would have his training partner give him just enough help so he could squeeze an additional 2 or 3 reps out. Achim cautioned that because forced reps were very intense, it was best to only do them occasionally, in order to prevent overtraining.

DORIAN YATES

Dorian had laserlike focus, and he said his secret to bodybuilding success was total commitment and dedication to every aspect of anything that could help him improve his physique. That meant giving everything he did 100 percent focus and effort—even searching for things (information, ideas, etc.) outside the gym that could help him improve his physique.

thing about all of this was that Lee said he had already been a bodybuilder for a number of years before he tried the sixth meal addition, and the difference it made to his physique was amazing, proving one is never too old or experienced to learn.

ACHIM ALBRECHT

Achim said that full-range movements were very important. No half movements. No half squats. From the beginning of the movement to the end, everything has to be in the full range of motion. He said he would hear people complaining that their legs just won't grow, and he would watch them, and lo and behold, they would be doing only half movements, and it was no surprise why they didn't grow. Achim believed that incomplete reps build incomplete body parts, and if one

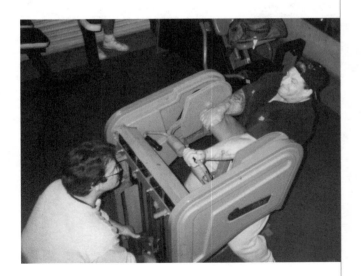

Needless to say, inside the gym, Dorian gave the physical aspect of his training 100 percent total concentration. He said that meant using a variety of exercises and training as heavy as possible while keeping good form. He constantly tried doing more reps with heavier weight to keep his workouts at the intensity level for growth and strength.

While some are content to stay with a certain weight or rep range for their exercises, Dorian was always pushing the limits and stressed the importance of constantly striving to go heavier and heavier each workout. He said this kind of intensity forced his muscles to adapt to the added demand placed upon them by growing. However, he also said that it was very important to concentrate on feeling the muscle being worked during each rep and set and to keep your mind positively focused on how you want your body to look.

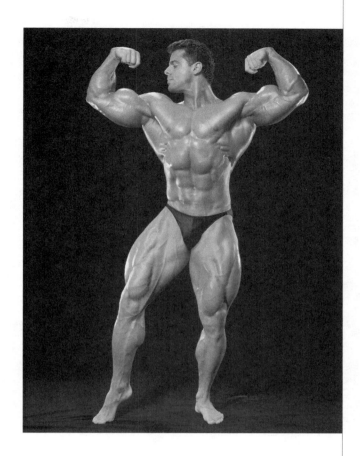

to only do the exercises that your body feels, and that meant experimenting and finding which exercises were best for you.

FRANK HILLEBRAND

Frank spoke about the importance of being consistent and steady. That meant in one's diet, training, rest, supplementation, and every other aspect related to bodybuilding success. Another important part of that success, Frank said, was doing only the exercises that worked. He said that many times, bodybuilders did exercises that did not work for them, yet they continued doing them just because someone told them to or they read that it was the best exercise for building a body part. He said that it was very important

SHAWN RAY

Shawn said he really liked variety in his workouts and would not do the same thing twice for each body part. He constantly varied the exercises, sets, reps, and the angles he worked his muscles and said doing this never allowed his muscles to get used to the stress he was placing on them. Here's how he did it.

If he did four exercises for chest one workout, then on the next chest workout, he would do four completely different exercises and maybe even do them at a different gym.

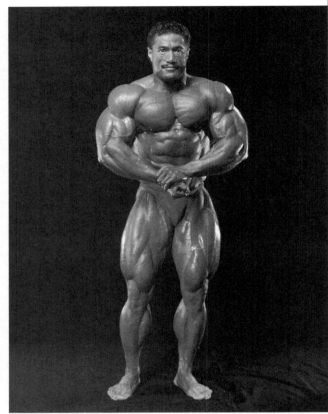

Shawn said that bodybuilding can become mundane and routine if one is doing the same thing day in and day out. He found the way to keep it interesting for him was to have variety in his workouts; whether that meant the exercises, reps, weights, or even different gyms.

SONNY SCHMIDT

Sonny said he thought longevity was key to bodybuilding success. That meant being able to train over a long period of time without injury. For that reason, Sonny said he always warmed up thoroughly before he began his workouts. He found that

stretching the muscle before, during, and after the workout was very important in preventing injury and promoting growth. He believed a stretched muscle was able to contract more fully, thereby allowing it to be worked to a greater degree, with the result being a fuller and more completely developed muscle.

He said that pyramiding his training also helped him avoid injuries. Sonny would pyramid all his weights for every muscle group. For example, if he was working delts, he would start off with a set or two of light to moderate behind-the-neck barbell presses for 8 to 10 reps, and then after his delts were warmed up, he'd go up to a heavier weight for 4 or 5 sets of 8 to 10 reps. After that, he might decide to do dumbbell seated presses, side laterals, bent-over laterals, barbell uprights, or dumbbell shrugs. He said he liked doing 4 or 5 sets of 8 to 10 reps for each movement, but always make sure, he cautioned, that the muscle is warmed and ready before heading into heavy weight territory.

J. J. MARSH

J.J. said he liked doing peak contractions in between exercises. As an example, if J.J. was working arms, like triceps, he would finish his set of presses or pushdowns and then immediately stand in front of a mirror and squeeze the arm and hold it to get the peak contraction in the triceps. The key, he said, was to make sure he kept constant tension on the muscle through the complete range of the movement, and he did this for every

muscle group he worked. He said that by doing peak contractions, his muscles became much more dense and vascular, and it improved the overall quality of his physique.

PART 4

Go Ahead and Ask: 20 Questions with Some Greats

During the 1980s and 1990s, some of the brightest stars in the bodybuilding firmament came to light. Some were just starting their careers; others (such as Robby Robinson and the late Mike Mentzer) were still sending shock waves through the industry with their advanced level of development and radical (but rational) approach to bodybuilding exercise. What follows are those interviews, and the introductory context in which they were conducted, in their entirety, allowing the reader to step back in time and to experience the thrill of conversing with these bodybuilding immortals firsthand. Such encounters revealed more than just the "sets and reps" of bodybuilding, giving the authors—and now the reader—an opportunity to get to know the human beings behind the muscles; to learn about their lives, their likes, their dislikes, their philosophies of life, and why bodybuilding was so important to them at this point in their lives.

33

Eddie Robinson

Without a doubt, one bodybuilder's name that was on the lips of all the top cognoscenti within the sport is Eddie Robinson. A natural in the purest sense of the term, Robinson won his first bodybuilding contest, the Mr. Largo (Florida), at the tender age of 18, without ever having touched a weight.

Robinson signified to many the return to mass—a time when size ruled the sport of bodybuilding—but to classify Robinson as merely a mass-freak would be a glaring injustice. Robinson has perhaps the finest lines in the sport's history, tremendous symmetry, and definition—and none of it at the expense of the bodybuilder's most prized possession: muscle mass!

At age 24, Robinson routinely benched 600 pounds and squatted well over 800 pounds in his training and sported arms that, in these times of inflated measurements by top champions, legitimately stretched the tape to over the 20-inch mark and thighs that, at a height of 5′6½″ and a body weight of 213 pounds, exceeded 29 inches.

Robinson worked closely with Nautilus Sports/Medical Industries and with Weider Health and Fitness and devised a training system that reflected his work with both institutions. Needless to say, Robinson and his training system collaborated very well, resulting in his total domination at the NPC USA. As a result, the titan from the "Citrus State" had more endorsement offers than he knew what to do with, appearing regularly on "Muscle Magazine," a bodybuilding show on TV, as well as endorsements. Here's what he said in answer to "20 Questions."

Q: What first drew you to bodybuilding?

EDDIE: I just liked lifting weights. All through school I lifted weights for football and boxing [he was a former Golden Gloves champion in Ohio], and when I left school, it was something that I kept an interest in and, fortunately, was able to turn into a profession.

Q: What has been your proudest moment as a bodybuilder?

EDDIE: I'll tell you, it's changed my life a lot! I'm now suddenly in demand for everything; I've got the Giorgio cologne and a lot of other things that are looking my way. But I'm going to try and target everything toward the modeling and acting aspects of the sport of bodybuilding. I've been taking acting classes, and that's what I'm trying to target it to because, you know, nowadays you've got all those movies directed toward

[laughs] the "muscle-head" type of scene! Everybody wants the "freaky physique" in those films, and I can act and speak properly and, of course, the TV work I'm doing helps out tremendously.

Q: On the other side of the coin, what's been your lowest moment?

EDDIE: There really hasn't been any "lowest" moment, not yet anyway. It's the same old thing, you know, I've been just training hard and keeping on a good diet all the time. The hardest thing, I guess, has been trying to coordinate all of these guest appearances, it seems that I'm so booked up that I'm turning people away. I hate to do that, because the money's really good, and you get to a point where [laughs] you sort of have people bidding on you. It gets hectic because you obviously want to make the best money you can, but at the same time you hate to cut people off because someone else has bid higher for your services. The business aspect of it is the roughest part.

Q: To keep your body in such a fat-free condition, do you perform a lot of supplemental aerobic activity?

EDDIE: I do a lot of cycling, basically, I also believe in hitting the body bag and speed bags a lot. That's a carryover from my boxing days, but it is also an excellent aerobic exercise, and I'll use between 30 and 45 minutes on the heavy bag.

Q: How important do you think genetics are to the bodybuilder?

EDDIE: *Genetics are everything. You have to have the genetics to really succeed in the sport. I don't think you need to have genetics to improve; a lot of bodybuilders have proved that simply by getting ripped. However, I think for the "total package," to be both ripped and massive, you've got to have the total genetic package. Not everybody can be a professional bodybuilder, you know, a lot of people are blocky waisted, some can't get peaks on their biceps, and some just can't get certain areas to grow properly. I think that the person who has the genetic advantages to present the "total package" is the one who's going to do damage in the sport.*

Q: You worked closely with Nautilus for a while. How did you like that experience?

EDDIE: *It was very educational. I learned a lot about different ways of training; you know, basically a lot of slow, continuous tension, firing the muscle fibers in every inch of muscle throughout its range of motion and not to relax the muscle between reps. It's basically just like the Weider Principles in a way, with slight variations. Nautilus believed in training the full body all the time, and I don't believe in that. I believe that if you train the full body all the time, you're just not going to grow. They believe in training three times a week for only half an hour to 40 min-*

utes a shot, the full body, and I think that's ridiculous.

Q: If you don't subscribe to the high-intensity theory, what routine do you find to be the most effective for you?

EDDIE: *Well, I believe that a three-day-on/one-day-off is the best, where you hit each body part twice a week. It lets me concentrate much better on the body parts that I'm training. For instance, I usually train back and biceps, then chest, shoulders, triceps, and then a leg day. I do a split with that in which I hit the smaller body parts at night. On my leg day I would do my quads and hamstrings in the morning and my calves at night, at which point I would also just stretch out my hamstrings. On chest, shoulders, and tris, I would do my chest and shoulders in the morning and then my tris real hard at night and also concentrate on the rear deltoid as well. I like to divide them up and split everything!*

Q: Let's not stop here! What do you do in terms of sets, reps, and exercises?

EDDIE: *I usually do 4 or 5 sets of 10 to 15 reps on a lot of exercises. I like to superset, doing 4 sets of supersets, which would be like doing 30 reps. You'd go, like, 200 pounds, to 150, to 100 for 10 reps a shot, just dropping the weight each set. This really pushes the blood to the muscle, really pumps it up. I believe in getting a lot of really good gains off of that.*

Q: What exercises do you use?

EDDIE: *For chest, I basically do a lot of dumbbell exercises. I concentrate on strict form and don't use a lot of barbell exercises, maybe the odd set of inclines, but I don't do the bench press. I prefer dumbbells because I can concentrate more on the stretching and really get into the muscle. With shoulders, I use barbells for behind-the-neck presses, and then I go into a machine exercise for my rear delts, and then dumbbell presses and lateral raises, again, for 4 sets of 10 to 15 reps. On my leg day, I'll go up to 15 to 18 sets, depending on the body part.*

Q: Do you ever find yourself overtrained on this system?

EDDIE: *I don't. I can feel like I'm overtrained, but my body can take a lot of punishment. A lot of people could only do half of that and be overtrained, but I feel that my metabolism helps me out a lot in this respect because if I do any less, I don't get anywhere.*

Q: What about for those who may not want to compete, but who're looking for a routine that will give them more massive muscles? What would you recommend for them?

EDDIE: *I'd advise them to go down to lower reps and heavier weights, basically a power-lifting type of program to really shock that muscle and break it down in order to build it up again. Basically, you want to get that muscle up there, and once you have the size you want, then start into toning and shaping it. But to get the size, stay with the power lifts, your basic lifts: heavy dumbbell work, heavy bench pressing, and work on getting your 8 reps per set. I'd say a four-day-a-week training routine for the beginner, so that he learns how to work out each muscle group properly. Then, once you get the size you need, I think it takes a lot more repetitions and longer workouts to get the lines out on the muscles. For the beginner though, I'd recommend from 8 to 12 sets per body part.*

Q: What bodybuilders inspired you in your training?

EDDIE: *I really had no inspirations in bodybuilding overall. There were certain bodybuilders that I liked for the development of different body parts. You know, take a look at Boyer Coe's biceps, which I think are phenomenal! For legs, you have to look at a guy like Tom Platz, who's got the craziest legs that I've ever seen! But I'm looking for someone with the "total package," I've never really seen anyone who has had the most incredible, freaky legs, arms, chest, back, and shoulders all in one! There's a lot of well-balanced physiques out there that look good, but not freaky and devastating.*

Q: What are your thoughts on the recent move by the IFBB to implement drug testing to the professional men's contests in bodybuilding?

EDDIE: *I'm for that 100 percent! I think it's the best thing to happen to bodybuilding, to be totally honest with you. I think if it cleans up the sport, there'll be a lot more recognition out there and gain a lot more spectators. The respect factor will increase, and we'll receive a lot more TV coverage and, hopefully, one day have it as an Olympic sport.*

Q: Given what you term your "metabolism," how many days do you think the average person, those not so metabolically blessed, can train without overtraining?

EDDIE: *It's tough to say because everybody is so different. You can't judge all body-builders the same; some people can do very little training and still make unbeliev-able gains, and other people have to do a lot. It's hard to say, but I would say that the best routine for the average bodybuilder would be the three-days-on/one-day-off, which is what everybody is doing and gives you one day off before you hit everything again.*

Q: Leaving the realm of bodybuilding aside for a moment in order to find out more about your belief system, what philosophy of life do you subscribe to?

EDDIE: *I believe that I was put on this earth to do one thing, and that's to dominate the sport of bodybuilding! To be the "total package." And that's what I'm doing, and that's what keeps going through my head, and that's what I'm going to do. That's what*

my life's about. I want to set a good example of what a bodybuilder is all about, I want the respect from all my peers, and I want to make this sport a well-known sport and respectable and set an image of the bodybuilder as a nice guy as opposed to a "muscle-head" jerk-off, which a lot of them are. I want to help people out and to be well respected.

Q: Given your busy schedule, what do you do these days to relax?

EDDIE: *I like to take my girlfriend down to the beach and throw a line in the water and maybe do some fishing. And maybe after that I'd grab a bottle of wine, hit the beach, and watch some stars fall. That's relaxing for me [laughs].*

Q: What books have influenced your training the most?

EDDIE: *I'd have to say the Weider books influenced me the most. Those and the articles that appear in the mags are great for learning about training and nutrition.*

Q: Given that you're making a good living from the sport, what tips on investing could you offer fellow bodybuilders?

EDDIE: *Just not to be stupid with the money that they do make from the sport. Invest it into loans or real estate. A lot of body-builders when they make some money, go out and buy a flashy car or zebra-skin boots or something like that. That's great, but you've got to watch your p's and q's as* well because you could break your leg the next day, and then you're out of commission for a while, those checks stop coming in and those guest appearances are cancelled. You need to be a good investor.

Q: How do you think we can improve our sport of bodybuilding?

EDDIE: I don't know how we can really improve it. I think the drug tests are a step in the right direction. Publishing articles on positive bodybuilders, like Mike Christian, he's a real friendly type of guy, and not concentrate so much on the hard-assed, "get out of my way, I lift weights" type of guys. That's one thing that I hate about the sport; that there's still a lot of guys out there like that. Bodybuilding is an individual sport and yeah, we all compete together and we all want to win, but, hey, we're human too and we're like a team; we all want to improve ourselves, and doing so raises all of us up to higher levels of physical development and self-improvement.

Q: What sort of diet do you follow to "rip up"?

EDDIE: I basically keep my fats low; I eat a lot of chicken and egg whites. I eat very little fish because of the oils, and I eat a lot of vegetables. It's just a basic diet. I'm not big on counting calories, but I make sure my protein intake is adequate.

34

Ian Harrison

Imust admit that I'd never heard of Ian Harrison until a friend mentioned his name. I felt quite sheepish, as I normally pride myself on being up on most bodybuilding happenings, training systems, and, yes, even competitors.

This time, however, I really hadn't a clue. However, what I subsequently learned about Ian Harrison could fill a book. He was only 21 years of age, but at a height of 6' even and a body weight of 260 pounds, observers thought this infantile Hercules could well be the man to wrest the Mr. Olympia crown away from the rapacious Lee Haney.

"Believe and Achieve" was Harrison's motto, and this lad wasn't wanting for confidence in his ability. He was big, he was industrious, and was going places in the sport of bodybuilding. Here are Ian Harrison's answers to "20 Questions."

Q: Ian, what first drew you to the sport of bodybuilding?

IAN: I've always been interested in it. I liked the Marvel comics when I was younger, and I've always admired power and everything. I started doing judo when I was

8 years old. In fact my father taught judo for 18 years. By the time I got to age 10, I was getting really good at judo, but I was finding that the guys who were, like, 16 years old could just pick me up and put me where they wanted to. So I started doing push-ups and stuff like that, and then, at age 14, I saw Pumping Iron. *I saw Arnold and was totally inspired. I couldn't believe that people could actually look like that! Then six months later, I got my first muscle magazine,* Muscle and Fitness, *that had Scott Wilson and Shelly Gruwell on the cover. Then, when I turned 16, as Christmas coincided with my birthday, which is on January 3, I got my first barbell/dumbbell set. Then me and my father cleaned our garage out, and I started in training at six days a week.*

Q: What did you weigh when you started training?

IAN: I weighed 9 stone, or 9 times 14 pounds [126 pounds]. I entered my first contest at 16 years of age as well, which was the Under 17 Mr. Yorkshire. At this time I weighed 12 stone [168 pounds], but for my next show, some three months later, I weighed 14 stone [196 pounds], and I got beat in that one because I was too fat. Then I took some time out and entered the Under 17 Mr. North East, and then I started dieting down for the Under 21 Mr. U.K., which was my first under 21 contest. I got really bad knee injuries at this point from squatting too heavy too young. I was

squatting 620 pounds for 12 reps at 16 years old.

Q: So are you saying that you were an infantile Hercules and just genetically strong?

IAN: Well, I was really strong on squats until I had to go off to the hospital for a month to have surgery, mega-surgery, on both knees, and I had to go on crutches for two months after that.

Q: How has that affected your leg training at this juncture of your career?

IAN: I don't squat at all now, and yet my legs just grow! I just have to look at my legs for them to grow. I'm very lucky with my legs that way. I've got to try and concentrate less on my legs. I think what I've been trying to do is overcompensate from the injuries that I've got by training my legs even harder if anything. I always thought of them as a weak body part, but now they're overpowering the rest of my physique and I've got to bring them back into line with the rest of it.

Q: What is your current training routine?

IAN: I'm currently training four-days-on/one-day-off. My first workout is chest and triceps, my next workout is shoulders and calves, my third workout is back and biceps, and my last workout is legs and calves.

Q: How many sets would you average per body part? What would your workouts break down into in terms of sets and reps?

IAN: *Say, for back I'd average about 15 or 16 sets, chest about 14 sets, shoulders about 12 sets, both biceps and triceps between 8 and 10 sets, and for legs I'd do about 20 sets in total for front and rear thigh, and calves about 10 sets.*

Q: What exercises do you favor?

IAN: *I favor basic movements. I don't like using any machines at all if I can help it. I rarely even use cables unless I'm preparing for a precontest routine. I normally use bent-over rows and pulldowns for back. My leg training is a little different because I have to train a lot lighter, but I do a hell of a lot of reps! I do between 20 and 30 reps per set, every set, and I always preexhaust on leg extensions and then go into hack squats, and then finish off with some light sissy squats, and the rest of my workout philosophy is to train very heavy, do a hell of a lot of forced reps and try to keep my sets as low as I can. I find that if I put my sets too high, I overtrain quite easily.*

Q: What's your big biceps routine consist of?

IAN: *For biceps, I usually start off with basic barbell curls and then finish off with either some dumbbell concentration curls or some preacher curls. It's all basic stuff, it's just the intensity that I put into it! I mean me and my training partner, they think we're crazy back home! We put so much into it, we just lock into that set and, like Arnold said, "A bomb could go off around me and I won't notice that it had*

gone off," I just go crazy! On the basic curl, I would do 5 straight sets, and then when I go into the preachers I tend to do double dropping or descending sets to add a little bit of intensity. I gauge it by how I feel when I walk into the gym.

Q: Do you do a lot of aerobics in your precontest phase?

IAN: *Precontest yes, off-season never! I find I lose weight much too easily. When I start dieting for a show, like when I was dieting for the British championships when I got my pro card, I started dieting some 26 weeks out from the show to knock off fat. I find that if I drop my calories off too much, I just lose it too fast. So what I do now is just keep my calories the same and come in really, really slow down for the show and just increase my aerobics slightly.*

Q: What sort of aerobics do you do?

IAN: *I use the stationary bike and fast walking. I can't run anymore because of my knees. They're in a real state still, I still feel some pain—especially in the cold weather. That's why I'm going to move out here [California].*

Q: Ian, what has been your proudest moment as a bodybuilder so far?

IAN: *Well I've had two really; my first major accomplishment was winning the NABBA Mr. Britain in May 1988, which was a really renowned show. The second was the British Championships in October of 1989.*

What I loved about that show was I was the only man on stage that had a full-time job. In my first year as a "Mister," I'd just come out of the junior class, and I'd come over from NABBA to the IFBB, but I felt like politics was against me because I was the youngest and had gone over to a new federation. So the odds were all stacked against me, but I won and proved them all wrong. Ha!

Q: What are your thoughts on genetics' role in bodybuilding?

IAN: *I think that the main thing is the mental intensity and the drive that someone's got to get to the top. If you've got the genetics to go with that, then I think that you'll go all the way. Hopefully, I'm going to go all the way. I want it so bad that I'm not ever going to stop in my drive to be the best!*

Q: How do you find the training in the States as opposed to back home in England?

IAN: *It's a bit more down-to-earth back home. It seems to be much more glamorized—especially in a place like Gold's. When I see a lot of the guys, the pros, and you read about what tremendous weights they use and how intense they're training, to tell you the truth, I don't see them training that intensely. When I train, I train intensely. I've seen a few guys, like Mike Quinn, and he trains intensely! But I haven't really seen anyone else train intensely, but that's not taking anything*

away from them, because they're still getting the results, and that's what counts. It's very much the basics at home. The equipment is not quite as good, which can hold you back a little bit; the atmosphere in terms of the weather isn't quite as good back home. And the attitude of the general public back in England is not quite the same as what it is over here. They're not at all supportive in England. In fact, you're considered a "freak" in England still if you've got muscles. It's like going back to the Stone Age in that sense. I'll be making my home in Phoenix, Arizona, and working with Lance Dreher. He's such a wealth of information, I know he's going to help me a lot.

Q: Given that most people who work out aren't competitors, but want to put on more muscle size, what routine would you recommend for their benefit?

IAN: *Basically, a three-day-a-week routine, splitting the body into two halves: chest, back, and biceps; and legs, shoulders, and triceps. You know, two splits, doing each workout alternately, say, on Monday, Wednesday, and Friday. This will give each body part a long rest in between workouts. I'd also recommend that they eat good food, small meals, six times a day. They should also have 30 to 40 grams of good protein with each meal, a decent amount of good complex carbs. All clean food, plenty of rest, and you'll grow. It's the intensity that you put into things as far as I'm* concerned. *If you want something badly enough, you'll get there.*

Q: Given that intensity is a prime factor, could they train with as many sets as, say, you do, or would that be overtraining?

IAN: No, not at first. I made that same mistake, as I'm sure most bodybuilders have done, where you train according to Arnold Schwarzenegger's arm routine, which says "to get big arms, do 20 sets for your biceps," and then you wonder why you're not growing. I think that bodybuilding has progressed a lot in terms of just going in and thinking "more is better." People now realize that it's the intensity that counts. Say somebody starts bodybuilding, they still want to put in the same intensity that I put into each set but less total sets because they're obviously not accustomed to the training that I've been doing for the last six years. It's all common sense, really. It's like what I was saying about believing in yourself, there's a saying back in the gyms back home: "Believe and achieve." When I won the British Championships, my training partner came backstage, and I just shouted across the room, "Paul, believe and achieve!" It's exactly how I felt at the time, if you believe something badly enough, and you want something badly enough, you'll achieve it.

Q: What do you do to relax? It seems that with your training and dedication to bodybuilding, you wouldn't have a lot of spare time.

IAN: To tell you the truth, before these last two to three months, when I was at home, I didn't have time to relax. I've been working full time for the Electricity Board, which was a very manual job. I'd be digging eight hours a day, and then I would come home and train, so I've only really been able to relax these last couple of months. I just go to the pictures. I don't like nightclubs or the pubs, I'm not really into that scene. I never drank, I've never smoked or anything like that. Basically, [begins to laugh] I've been a recluse in a gym for the last six years of my life.

Q: What philosophy of life do you subscribe to?

IAN: "Believe and achieve" is my main philosophy, but there's another one that I love as well. It was in the film The Highlander *with Sean Connery. There's a scene where he's going out of a church and he turns around and says, "I've got something to say: it's better to burn out than fade away." And that's exactly what I think. If you're gonna go, go with a bang!*

Q: Are there any books or individuals who have influenced your life?

IAN: In bodybuilding it's weird because I was never really brought up with Arnold as a competitive bodybuilder. I've been brought up with Arnold as a film star, so Arnold has never been a really great inspiration to me. I'd say Lee Haney. Haney's a real inspiration to me. He's actually a tall bodybuilder, and his physique is really incredible. I mean the ultimate thing that I wish to get, which I will get, is a taller version of Labrada with Lee Haney's density.

Q: What are your thoughts on the IFBB's recent decision to implement drug testing at the pro level?

IAN: I love it. I'm laughing because as far as I'm concerned, the guys who really do put in the hours in the gym, and who really do train hard, are going to come out on top eventually. I mean that suits me down to the ground because from what I've seen of a lot of the guys, they don't train hard. I think some of the guys, I won't say they rely on the drugs, but some of them have gotten a big advantage from the drugs compared to someone like myself. I think it's a great idea!

Q: At this point, Ian, I'd like you to select one body part and tell our readers exactly what you do to train it.

IAN: I guess we'll go with legs. I start off with 4 sets of leg extensions. I do 2 warm-up sets and on my third and fourth sets, I'll do 2 forced reps each to preexhaust my thighs. Then I'm off to hack squats, where I do 5 sets with a rep range of 25 to 30 reps, and I'll go to probably 400 pounds on those. Then I'll finish off the front thighs

with 3 sets of really light front squats for 25 to 30 reps or 3 sets of sissy squats for about 20 reps a set. We take what we call a "coffee break," where we rest before going into leg biceps. We usually have two workouts for leg biceps; the first one is 3 sets of stiff-legged dead lifts and 4 sets of leg curls—straight sets. Then, the next workout, what we do is 5 or 6 sets of leg curls, but we double drop each set. It's like doing a set with, say, 80 kilos for as many reps as we can with 2 forced reps, dropping the weight immediately to 40 kilos and going straight into our next set. Just burning and burning. We do 5 or 6 sets of that, and that's it for our leg workout.

Q: Thanks for talking with me today.

IAN: Thank you. I'd also like to thank my family, my mother and father and my brother especially; we've had our ups and downs, but they've always been there when I've needed them. And you asked earlier about people that I've admired in body-building. The person that I've really admired in bodybuilding was my grand-dad, who died when I was 13 of cancer. I mean, physically he was strong, but mentally he was so strong as well. I admired that, and it really spurred me on. Every time I win a contest I just look up into the sky and say, "That's for you, Granddad!"

35

Patrick Nichols

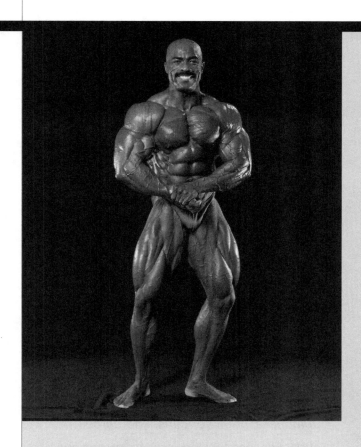

One of the most exciting body-builders to explode onto the competitive scene in years was London's Patrick Nichols. Nichols was not only a major physique, he was also a very articulate individual with an unpretentious outlook on life and, more important, a man with a clear vision of his future in the sport.

In the following "20 Questions" interview, Nichols tells all about his training methods, his personal philosophy, his influences, and his battle plans for the future.

Q: Patrick, what first drew you to the sport of bodybuilding?

PATRICK: *Well I started to do bodybuilding as an assistance for my athletics. It wasn't really "bodybuilding" when I started, it was just training with weights. I did it to improve my strength and also to put a bit of weight on.*

Q: How long ago would that have been?

PATRICK: *That would have been 15 years ago. I weighed about 145 pounds then,* and now, 15 years later, mind you, I'm 233 pounds.

Q: How many titles have you won now?

PATRICK: *I've won Mr. Barbados seven times, I've won the Mr. Caribbean and Mr. Central America seven times, I've won the Amateur British Grand Prix, and I've been both second and third in the IFBB World Championships.*

Q: Where do you live at present?

PATRICK: *Right now I'm living in London, England, and believe me it's great here.*

Q: What is your current training routine?

PATRICK: *Right now I'm in my off-season phase or my pre-precontest phase. I'm trying to build up a bit more size, build up some areas and define a few more areas, and I'm training four days a week. I'll train two body parts a session, or sometimes, what I call "two and a half," which might be chest and back, which might be two majors, and then biceps or leg and shoulders plus triceps.*

Q: What would a breakdown of a typical week of training look like?

PATRICK: *On Sunday, I would train chest, back, and biceps. I'll rest Monday, then on Tuesday I would train legs—and that would be the entire leg: quads, hamstring, and calves and abdominals. Wednesday I would train shoulders and arms, rest Thursday, and then Friday I would come back and*

repeat *what I'd done on Sunday and then rest Saturday.*

Q: What sort of exercises, sets, and reps would you do on those training days?

PATRICK: *I would mainly concentrate on basics. For example, in my leg training, I would concentrate mostly on squats [full squats], leg presses, hack squats, and standing leg curls and lying leg curls. For calves I would do seated calf raises, standing calf raises, and calf extensions on the leg press machine. For chest I would do the bench press, either barbell or dumbbell—I never do both, it's one or the other—as the basic movement on either a flat or an incline bench. Then I would do flyes and parallel dips. For shoulders, I would do presses with dumbbells or press behind the neck with barbell. I'll also do upright rowing, side laterals, and rear delts on the rear deltoid machine. For biceps, I'll do alternate concentration curls with dumbbells, preacher curls, and barbell curls. For triceps, I'll do triceps extensions and bench dips, wherein you put your feet up on one bench and your hands behind your back on another one with a weight across your legs. From there I'll go to triceps extensions on the pulley, and I'll finish off with one-arm reverse extensions.*

Q: What about your back routine? Your lats are huge!

PATRICK: *For my back I'd do chins—lots of chins; maybe 5 to 8 sets of them! Then I'll* do T-bar rows or barbell rows or seated long pulley rows as my basic movement. Then I'll do pulldowns to the back and one-arm pulley rows, seated on the bench.

Q: What kind of sets and reps do you do?

PATRICK: I go from 3 to 5 sets, depending on how I feel that particular day and how much my muscles are pumping up. I go very much by instinct and feel; if I start to do an exercise and I'm getting a really good pump on the first set—I can get warmed up properly and really up the weight quickly—then I can finish up with just 4 sets. Sometimes, again it depends on the weather, you can do 4 or 5 sets before you get right into the heavy stuff, but it's basically between 3 and 5 sets per exercise. I'd average between 15 and 20 sets per body part.

Q: What are your thoughts on genetics and bodybuilding?

PATRICK: Genetics is very important but, having said that, if you've got really good genetics but you haven't really tapped your potential to the maximum, then it makes no sense. If you've got a little bit of genetics but you really go all out to exploit it to the maximum, it will be the little guy with little genetics who exploits it to the maximum who's going to come out ahead of the guy with the superior genetics who doesn't train as hard.

Q: And how would you "exploit it to the maximum"?

PATRICK: First, it would take you about two to three years to find out how your body will react to various types of dieting and training. But once you've got it worked out—it's not something that happens in a matter of months—but once you've got it worked out then you should adapt a routine with the proper principles in it to adapt to your body type.

Q: Do you include aerobics in your training?

PATRICK: Not very often, because close to competition time, the way I train and the pace that I use, it's close to an aerobic type of training. I would do more or less the same amount of work that I would do in the off-season, only in a shorter space of time.

Q: Do you train any differently before a contest?

PATRICK: A little bit; I just change movements. Instead of just doing heavy basic movements, I'll do more shaping movements. I'll also step up my four-day-a-week program to five days a week, and maybe in the last week or so I'll step it up to six days a week.

Q: You've mentioned that you don't change your training all that much to get ripped up for a contest, but what about your diet? Do you count calories?

PATRICK: No, because all year round I try to stick to a good eating pattern that doesn't allow my body to gain too much weight. I eat about 60 percent carbs, 30 percent protein, and about 10 percent fat. During this period, my off-season, I would eat a lot more than my precontest phase. Precontest is just cutting the fats down really low and reducing the amount of portions of my meals rather than shifting it down too drastically.

Q: What has been your most productive training routine in terms of really having packed on the most size?

PATRICK: Basics. Heavy basic movements combined with six medium-sized meals a day. It was only a four-day-a-week program with sets in the range of about 15 per body part.

Q: What are your thoughts about the IFBB's move to bring drug testing into the men's pro ranks?

PATRICK: I think it's a good idea to bring it around, but only if they can totally eradicate it. If you still get guys who are ducking around and cutting corners and getting under the rules, then I don't think it's very good. What needs to be done is to educate people as to the good and bad sides of the issue. I'm not sure that it's possible to totally wipe out drug use at this stage in time.

Q: Who were your bodybuilding heroes when you were first starting out?

PATRICK: Sergio Olivia, and Frank Zane. I know they're at polar ends of the

bodybuilding scale, but the reason is that I like the aesthetic type of physique of Frank Zane; it's pleasing to the eye as a near to natural person that's still very muscular. And then the awesome, unbelievable size of Sergio Olivia!

Q: What philosophy of life do you subscribe to?

PATRICK: Well, I've always believed that you shouldn't expect too much, too soon, and you should always keep your focus.

Q: Could you recommend a bodybuilding routine for those who aren't competitive bodybuilders, but who still want to pack on some additional muscle mass?

PATRICK: Sure, that's no problem. First it depends on the person's metabolism but, generally speaking, stick to the basics and keep your carbohydrates high. Get some very good supplementation into your system, extra amino acids and stuff, and then lots of heavy training and lots of rest! I should also mention that the most common mistake made by bodybuilders just starting out is when they pick up one of the magazines and read about some of the top bodybuilders who have these very advanced routines and they try to follow the routine of one of the champions. A lot of the upcoming bodybuilders are really badly overtrained because they try to do this sort of routine. They expect too much too soon; they want to look like an Arnold or a Lee Haney in a matter of months, and it just doesn't work that way. They've got to be prepared to put down a serious foundation first before eventually moving on to a more advanced routine. If someone starting out followed my routine they'd overtrain, unless, of course, they ate enough food to overcome that. If you're doing too many sets, too many reps, and you're undereating, you're going to burn out. But if you can get a really good balance between the amount of sets and reps you do, the amount of hours spent in the gym, and the amount of food that you consume on a daily basis, then you'll be on the right track.

36

Geir Borgan Paulsen

He was huge. He towered over all of his foes with shoulders broader than the sky and forearms gorged and swollen from years of muscular work. The other Giants that opposed him cowered under his might and his triumphant grin was clearly visible underneath his wildly flowing red beard whenever he saw an opponent approaching as he relished a good fight.

—from *Tales of Thor* by Jonathon Haines Ross

When Jonathon Ross penned those words about the Norse god of thunder, Thor, he (save for the red beard) could well have been describing Norwegian bodybuilder Geir Borgan Paulsen.

Certainly, Paulsen has been one of the biggest bodybuilders competing on the scene, with shoulders reminiscent of Pete Grymkowski's when in his prime. Paulsen doesn't just walk upon the stage to pose, he strides out proudly, his feet sounding like claps of thunder every time they hit the rostrum.

And when he flexes! His body seems to explode into millions of tiny splinters of striated muscle tissue! Although he lost out to mammoth Britisher Dorian Yates in the New York Night of the Champions, Paulsen nevertheless impressed both the judges and those in attendance with his dazzling muscularity and gargantuan proportions.

However, apart from the obvious fact that this man was huge, ripped, and ready to cause some problems for some of our more complacent champions on the competitive circuit, precious little was known about this man and his training methods. With this in mind, it didn't take long for me to track him down, with tape recorder in hand, to ask him "20 Questions."

Q: What first drew you to the sport of bodybuilding?

GEIR: *I'd been involved in competitive weight lifting for quite a number of years, and I really enjoyed the feeling of hoisting* *around really heavy chunks of iron. Well, weight lifting isn't really the safest sport in the world, so in time I developed some problems with both my back and my knees that became serious enough that I was told to "cut it out." Fortunately at this point in time, a friend of mine told me that I had the talent and genetics to do quite well in the sport of bodybuilding. That's when I first switched over to bodybuilding as opposed to weight lifting.*

Q: Was it "love at first sight"?

GEIR: *[laughing] No, actually it was quite the opposite. I didn't like bodybuilding at first. I can't in retrospect really remember why, apart from the fact that I didn't know much about it and envisioned bodybuilders as "fancy guys" who just thought about themselves all day long.*

Q: What made you change your mind and take the big leap into such a "fancy guy" sport?

GEIR: *I trained in bodybuilding initially just to help rehabilitate my injuries that I incurred from weight lifting. The bodybuilding movements seemed to free me from my pain, and my original intention was to just train with the bodybuilding movements for a while and then switch back to weight lifting. In fact, I did go back to weight lifting for a while, but I found that I was in more pain again, so I switched back to bodybuilding. After a while, some friends told me that I should compete, and*

I did—and I won! From that point on I just loved the sport.

Q: Were you a quick gainer in terms of muscle mass when you first started training, or did the gains come slowly?

GEIR: *They came very slowly. I was never what could be termed a fast gainer. I'm just gaining slowly, but steadily every year.*

Q: What has been the most productive training routine that you've ever utilized?

GEIR: *My most productive routs have been ones that were basic, heavy, and employed the "pyramid principle." For chest, I favor heavy benches, for legs it has to be squats, back is covered very thoroughly with barbell rows and deadlifts. I just used the basic exercises with maybe one or two isolation movements and trained as heavy as I could on any given training day.*

Q: You mentioned your preference for using basic exercises and heavy weights—what's your top weight in the bench press?

GEIR: *[smiles] My top weight in the bench? Let me see. My best bench press weight would be 230 kilograms, which would translate into roughly 500 pounds.*

Q: That's pretty damn impressive! What does your current training routine consist of?

GEIR: *In the off-season, I train two days on/one day off. I'll train like this for maybe two months and then go to a four-day-on/one-day-off system. And then, six weeks* *out from a contest, I'll switch again, this time to a three-days-on/one-day-off program. The off-season is when I build the most of my mass, though, and I should mention that I train two days on/one day off, then one day on and one day off—this allows for more recuperation and greater muscle growth.*

Q: On this system of training, the two-on/one-off, one-on/one-off, what is the sequence of body parts that you train?

GEIR: *I train my chest, triceps, then my back and biceps, and then my legs—in that order.*

Q: Aha! You've neglected to mention your "mammoth shoulder training day"!

GEIR: *I omitted that intentionally because I don't train my shoulders at all in the off-season.*

Q: Why's that?

GEIR: *My shoulders are already as big as I want them to be, so there would be no point in trying to make them any bigger during the off-season. So doing would just throw my symmetry out of line. In fact, some have said that my arms appear small because of the size of my shoulders, so I have to try and aim toward a balanced physique and not just one big lumpy appearance.*

Q: So you don't train your shoulders at all during the off-season. However, at one point in your career you must have trained

them—and trained them rather hard by the looks of them—what routine did you at one time employ to make your shoulders Buick-sized?

GEIR: *[laughs] I didn't know they were that big! Well, I believe in training basic. Shoulder presses, dumbbell presses—both alternate and simultaneous although not both in the same workout—shrugs, upright rows, and lateral raises. In terms of sets, I will do maybe 3 sets of each for a total of maybe 9 or 10 sets per workout.*

Q: I didn't hear any direct exercises in your routine for the rear deltoids. Do you train them at all?

GEIR: *For those I would just do bent-over lateral raises, and I'd substitute that exercise for one of the ones that I've just listed and perform 3 sets of it.*

Q: That's your shoulder routine. Let's run through your whole routine, body part by body part, starting with your chest and triceps training?

GEIR: *For my chest I would again do the basics: bench press, incline barbell presses, and pullovers. I'd do these for my first chest workout, but then for my next one I might do flat bench dumbbell presses, incline flyes, and dumbbell flyes, again for 3 sets of each exercise and pyramiding the weights each set.*

Q: You seem to train with a lot less sets than most pro bodybuilders, and yet you're still getting great results from it. Do you train with high intensity each and every set to get the most out of it?

GEIR: *Yes, I train really intensely each and every set. You have to if you want to progress in this sport. Your body has to adapt to stress, which is what weight lifting is, so you have to put it under greater and greater levels of stress for it to continue to respond with muscle growth.*

Q: That takes care of your chest training, what about your triceps?

GEIR: *Again, I should back up a minute and say that for my chest, when I said I only did 3 sets of each exercise, I should say that I do a total of 12 to 15 sets for my chest. It's only my shoulders that I train with 9 to 10 sets because they're already so well developed. But back to your question, I train my triceps typically with pushdowns, seated French presses, and that's it, for about 4 sets each for a grand total of 8 sets. Maybe 10, if I'm feeling energetic, but typically that's it in the off-season. Before a contest, my sets might go up to 12 sets and the reps would fall into the 10 to 16 range. My reps for triceps in the off-season would be 6 to 10.*

Q: Day two finds you training back and biceps. What's your routine here?

GEIR: *I again like to use the basics. I'll start typically with pulldowns, then move on to chin-ups, bent-over barbell rows, seated cable rows, and deadlifts. Again, my sets*

vary depending on how close it is to a contest, but generally they stay in the 3 or 4 sets each range. For biceps my routine is equally as simple; I'll start with 3 sets of alternate dumbbell curls and finish with 3 sets of Scott curls on the preacher bench. And, again, this will change the next time I train. For instance I might do standing barbell curls for 4 sets, followed by 4 sets of concentration curls.

Q: Is there any particular technique that you use in your training such as "continuous tension" or the "cheat method" or any such technique, or do you use mainly straight setting?

GEIR: *I use just about everything going. Again, it all depends on how I'm feeling on any particular training day. If I think that putting a few extra pounds on the bar and cheating it up will stimulate more muscle growth on a given day, then that's what I'll do. Or, if I'm not into heaving heavy weights around and feel that just a straight pump will benefit me more, then that's what I'll do that particular day. It all depends on how I'm feeling physically.*

Q: Do you have any advice that you could offer to young bodybuilders who are coming up the ladder and want to get as massive as possible?

GEIR: *I've been training for 20 years, 7 of those in bodybuilding, so my advice would be to stick with it and train heavy and basic and you'll succeed. The biggest draw-*

back to bodybuilding success today is over-training, which they have to be especially guarded against. I hear people saying "Oh, it's impossible to overtrain," but I'm here to tell you that they're wrong. It is possible, and it happens far too frequently. For young bodybuilders, there's no reason for you to train more than three or four times per week. If you can't gain on that, you're not going to! They should train with the basics and also use the pyramid principle to warm up their muscles properly.

Q: Do you include aerobics in your precontest preparations in order to get more ripped?

GEIR: *Yes, I do. I usually use a stationary bicycle, which I'll ride for half an hour, two or three times a week. I find that getting ripped is mainly a matter of diet though. I eat 3,500 calories a day when I'm just beginning my diet, and I'll drop that by*

maybe 1,000 calories for approximately eight weeks. I'm in good shape all year round.

Q: Geir, we've covered your chest and triceps, your back and biceps, and even your shoulder training, which you seldom train—but we've yet to cover your leg training. What is your leg routine?

GEIR: *For my legs, I train basic: squats, leg presses, leg curls, seated leg curls, and stiff-legged deadlifts. In terms of sets, I generally do between 12 and 20 sets. I also feel that your legs need a few more reps than your torso muscles. In the leg press, for example, I'll train with 900 pounds for 30 reps. For calves I'll do standing calf raises on the machine and then seated calf raises and then calf raises on the leg press machine for a total of 8 to 12 sets.*

37

John Sherman

When Texas native John Sherman walked out onto that stage in Santa Monica to compete in the light heavyweight division of the NPC USA contest, the audience drew a collective gasp.

After all, the man they were now witnessing was as big as a house, with proportions that were simply flawless. When Sherman posed, things appeared to explode and splinter under his skin, and when he hit one of his patented leg shots—man! you could hear the confidence leaking out of his fellow competitors' contest hopes like air from an old worn tire.

The man, at 5'5" and 185 pounds of granite-hewn muscle, was nothing short of awesome. Even the eventual overall USA champion, the phenomenal Flex Wheeler, would admit to this author that he felt "real nervous about Sherman." I think it's time for "20 Questions."

Q: What first drew you to bodybuilding?

> **JOHN:** *I was always pretty athletic, and I really liked big muscles. I loved the way it*

made me feel when I trained and how it changed the way I looked. I just loved it!

Q: How long have you been involved in body-building now?

JOHN: On October 31st, it will have been eight years.

Q: Who were your early influences in the sport?

JOHN: I guess in the beginning it was a Texas bodybuilder by the name of Rick Wilson. He'd won Mr. Texas in 1987, and ever since I came out of elementary school I really looked up to him. Fortunately, he put me on a program from day one, and I've been on the same one ever since. Rick had his own gym, it was called Bodymasters of Texas. I joined that the day I graduated from high school, and he put me on a program, and that was it; I was hooked from that point on.

Q: What was the program?

JOHN: It was a push/pull system. You know, back and biceps one day; chest, shoulders, and triceps the next; and legs by themselves on day three. It was actually a six-days-straight program, wherein you'd repeat the body part sequence again starting on day four and then take Sundays off. In terms of sets and reps, I was averaging about 4 sets per exercise for 10 reps each. I'll say this, though, after six months on this program I entered my first contest, called Today's Physique. I

placed second at that contest, but I was only 18 years old at the time, and for only six months of training that was pretty good.

Q: What contests have you won since then?

JOHN: I won the Teenage Texas in 1987, I won the Texas Lightweight class in 1988, the middleweight and overall Collegiate Nationals in 1988, the middleweight USA in 1989. I placed fourth at the 1990 Nationals in the light heavyweight division, fifth at that same contest in 1991, and now I've finally won the light heavyweight division at the USAs in 1992.

Q: Let's talk training now. What is your training program, and how did you get into the kind of condition you did at the USAs this year?

JOHN: I'm still training six days a week. I'm training chest and biceps on the first day, back and shoulders on the second day, and triceps and legs on the third day, and then I repeat the cycle over again. For my chest training, I'll start with either incline barbell or incline dumbbell presses. If I use a barbell, I'll work up to 315 pounds. If it's dumbbells, I'll go up to 120 pounds. I'll do roughly 6 sets in working up to my top weight and perform between 12 and 15 reps a set. After inclines, I'll go to bench presses to the neck. I'll do about 4 sets here, working up to 315 pounds for 12 reps a set. I try to really get the feel in the muscle with this one. After the neck presses, it's on to flat bench flyes or incline flyes—I'll pick which one once it comes time to perform it. I don't have a really set workout, preferring to train by feel. Some days, I'll start with inclines, while other days I'll end with them. It helps to keep the muscles confused. I don't go real heavy on the flyes, maybe 70- to 80-pound dumb-bells, and again, I just concentrate on getting the squeeze in the muscle over 3 or 4 sets. In terms of reps, when I'm getting ready for a show I'll do 12 to 15. In the off-season though, I'll up the dumbbells to 110 pounds and keep my reps in the 8 to 10 range. To finish off, I'll do dumbbell pullovers across a bench, and the weight on this movement doesn't really matter. Again, I just concentrate on squeezing my upper chest when I'm lifting the weight. My reps are never under 15 on this exercise.

Q: You seem to prefer higher reps in your training. Why is this?

JOHN: *Well, a while back in my training I started to incur a lot of injuries from going heavy all the time, so I had to back off a little bit and give my injuries a chance to recuperate. I'll go back to the heavier weights in time because I miss those heavy weights. Right now, I don't need the heavy weights because I've got pretty much all the mass I need and want at this time.*

Q: Do you train your biceps right away after having finished training your chest, or do you come back later in the day to train them?

JOHN: *No, I do them right away, as soon as I've finished training my chest. I have to go to work, and I work from noon until 10 p.m. at night at the Harris County Sheriff's Department. I work at the "boot camp" out there. For biceps, my training is never the same. I might start out with alternate dumbbell curls, maybe going up the rack from 50s to 70s and then working my way back down. My reps here are anywhere from 12 to 15. Then I go to the EZ curl bar and put 110 pounds on, again for roughly 4 sets of 12 to 15 reps. From there, it's on to concentration dumbbell curls on the preacher bench. I'll use between 40- and 50-pound dumbbells on this exercise, and I never count my sets on this one; I just train until I get tired.*

Q: What about your forearms?

JOHN: *I hardly ever work my forearms. I might train them once a month, if that. And that's only before a show, like two months out before a show, I'll start working them a little bit. Maybe just reverse curls. That's it. They tend to get really pumped up just from all the gripping and holding I do on my other exercises.*

Q: So what happens on day two?

JOHN: *Day two is reserved for back and shoulders. I'll start off my back workout with chins to the front with a wide grip. The reps on this one don't really matter to me as I'm just using it to stretch out a bit. My actual workout starts with lat pulldowns to* the front, and the reps are maybe 10 to 12 on that one. From there, it's on to close-grip pulldowns for the same number of reps. In terms of weights, I'll use whatever the stack is. Even for my wide-grip pulldowns, whatever the stack is, that's what I work my way up to. From there, it's on to bent-over rows, either with free weights or the Smith machine. I like the Smith machine better, so that's what I'll use exclusively two months out before a contest. Before that, though, I was using barbell rows all the time. So much so, in fact, that I got burned out using them. In terms of the amount of weight I use, on the Smith machine it doesn't really matter, maybe 225 pounds at the most, but on the barbell rows, I'd really jack it up to, say, maybe 315 pounds. After that, I'd move on to one-arm dumbbell rows and one-arm cable rows. On the dumbbell rows, I'll use the heaviest dumbbells we have in the gym, which is around 135 pounds. I'll do 10 reps per set for roughly 4 sets and then jump right into the one-arm cable rows for another 4 sets of 10 reps, and I'll finish off my back work with some hyperextensions for 4 or 5 sets of 15 reps. I think the hypers have been one of the most signifi-cant factors in creating the inordinate thickness in my lower back. Mind you, I'll also do good mornings, but I don't go too heavy on the good mornings. I pulled a muscle back there one day a while back, and it always scares me to go too heavy on that exercise ever since then. Hypers,*

though, don't bother me at all. I'll use a 45-pound plate for 15 reps on that.

Q: So that takes care of your back, and then it's right away into your shoulder program?

JOHN: That's right, straight into shoulder training. I'll do side laterals first in my routine. I'm not into hoisting a lot of real heavy weight on this exercise because I once hurt my shoulder doing that and had to back off. I'm using 40s and 45s and trying to get 12 reps per set and trying to get that burn deep inside the muscle. Next I move on to dumbbell bent—laterals, and I don't go too heavy on that either, maybe, 40s or 45s again. I used to use 80s but I wasn't doing the exercise correctly. I was cheating and falsely believing that some-thing was happening, but I wasn't growing at all. So I backed off on the heavy weights and the rear delts started to really come out. From there, I'll move on to military presses behind the neck, and I'll go up to 225 pounds for 10 reps over 4 or 5 sets.

Q: We notice that you tend to do all of your isolation movements first in your routine and then move on to the compound move-ments, why is this?

JOHN: Well, I got burned out on doing mili-tary presses first in my routine many years ago, and I didn't get anything out of it. However, when I started doing side laterals and bent laterals first, I was already starting to get a pretty good burn going, so I didn't have to go real heavy by the time I got to military presses. And when it came time to do military presses, I could feel them right away, unlike before. And that's my shoulder routine.

Q: So now we come to day three. What's your program for this day?

JOHN: Legs and triceps. I'll start with triceps. My first exercise is triceps press-downs on a lat machine. The weight here really doesn't matter, I'm just going for a burn here. Again, it's 4 or 5 sets at 12 to 15 reps a crack. From there, it's on to rope extensions on the lat machine, and I make sure to flare my hands out laterally at the bottom of the movement to really get those striations in the back of my triceps. I just keep going till it burns! My next exercise is lying triceps extensions with an EZ curl bar, also known as "skull crushers." I'll jerk that weight up pretty high, using 160 pounds worth of plates, plus whatever the bar weighs. I'll go for 4 or 5 sets of 10 reps on this, as it is my primary mass exercise. After the skull crushers, I'll move on to dumbbell kickbacks and just use maybe 20-pound dumbbells on this one for 12 to 15 reps and 4 or 5 sets per arm, just going for the burn.

Q: And that takes care of your triceps training for day three, which brings us to those tree-trunks you have for legs. What's your routine for those monsters?

JOHN: Squats. I just squat until I don't want to squat no more. Squats and leg presses

are my chief leg exercises. I go rock bottom on my squats and, off-season, I may go up to 550 pounds, and getting ready for a contest, I'll stay around 405. For reps, I'll work up to 405 pounds using sets of 12 reps. For leg presses, I don't even count the weight, I just stack it on, while my reps are usually in the range of 20-plus. I just keep going. All of my leg exercises are performed in a straight-sets style. I don't superset. After 4 or 5 sets each of squats and leg presses, I'll move on to leg extensions to just burn out my quads. I don't use really heavy weights here, maybe 150 pounds for no less than 15 reps. That's it for my quadriceps.*

Q: You've got the most incredible vastus medialis development in the sport. That "teardrop" muscle looks more like the hubcap of a Cadillac than a teardrop. How did you build that? Is it genetic or what?

JOHN: I would say that it's largely genetic. I've always had a pretty good degree of development in that area. I just use the basic stuff, nothing fancy or special. As long as everything keeps working, I don't see any reason to change.

Q: We've covered your quad training, but what about your hamstrings?

JOHN: My hamstring training is even more simple. It's just standing leg curls on the machine and stiff-leg deadlifts. On the deadlifts, I'm going up to only 225 pounds over 4 or 5 sets. My rep range is between

15 and 20, and I'm not going all the way down and touching the ground with the bar. I prefer to just go to a point touching my knees and then back up again. I keep my back straight. On the one-legged curls, I'll use maybe 80 pounds per leg and try for 15 to 20 reps over 4 or 5 sets. And that's it for my hamstrings.

Q: How about your calves?

JOHN: I train my calves about four days a week, and I'll just pick one exercise and do about 8 sets of it. The exercise will vary each day that I train them. I'll do either seated calf raises or standing calf raises in which I'm constantly moving that selector pin. I go really high in terms of reps for my calves and carry the exercise to the point where I can't walk around anymore.

Q: The only body part we haven't yet covered is your abdominal training. What's your training methods for this body part?

JOHN: I train my abs every training day, six days a week. I do rope crunches first in my routine, and I'll superset them with regular crunches. After those two, I'll come back and do knee-ups with those straps that you place under your triceps and attach to a chinning bar. In terms of reps, I'll do 20 to 25 reps per set and roughly 5 sets per exercise. So it's 5 supersets of 20 to 25 reps of rope crunches and regular crunches. And then 5 more sets of 20 to 25 reps of hanging knee-ups.

Q: What's next for you?

JOHN: I'll be gunning for the Nationals title in October.

Q: After the Nationals, what do you want to do?

JOHN: Turn pro, man! That's the ultimate! Competing with the big boys, and hopefully I'll be able to do well in that class of competition!

38

Flex Wheeler

As soon as Ken "Flex" Wheeler strode out on stage to do battle for the 1992 NPC USA bodybuilding title, it became obvious to all in attendance (including the judges) that we had just seen our winner.

Sure, there were other great bodybuilders in attendance that day, some (such as Light Heavyweight champion John Sherman) could even be classified as exceptional. Nevertheless, that day, nobody looked better than Flex Wheeler.

The man had it all, from huge rippling muscle mass, tapering down into a wasp-thin waist, and proportions that would have made Shawn Ray envious. In fact, it's doubtful that any of the current crop of Mr. Olympia hopefuls could have stood next to Flex on this day, so awesome did he appear!

Needless to say, Flex won the show hands-down. It was his second attempt at the USA title, having placed second the year before. The fact that he wowed all in attendance with his superior conditioning is a testament to his talent in our sport. Wheeler

is a supreme bodybuilder, without question, but he's also an articulate individual, soft-spoken and purposeful and yet, in his own way, quite shy and unassuming. The complete opposite, really, of what you might expect from a 225-pound slab of grade A muscle that also happens to be an accomplished martial artist to boot!

When I caught up with Flex after his tour de force at the USAs, I found him to be very congenial, knowledgeable, and, more important, willing to answer these "20 Questions."

Q: Flex, you've just won the most important contest of your career to date, and you seemed to exude confidence on stage this time around. Was this really the case?

FLEX: I was really confident this time around, but I still didn't know everyone who was going to be at this show, which means that some guy could pop in who could look really great. However, I was confident with myself and knew that I was looking the best that I ever had while weighing more than I ever had, so I felt that whoever it was that thought they were going to give me a battle, they had a battle in store for them.

Q: You mentioned that you weighed more for this show. What exactly did you weigh, and what's your height?

FLEX: I'm 5'9", and I weighed in at 223.5 pounds for the USAs.

Q: How many years had you been gunning for the USA title?

FLEX: This was my third attempt at a National title. I tried in 1991, and I took second place, and then I tried at the end of the year at the Nationals and I took second once again, so this was my third attempt and, fortunately, it was successful this time.

Q: What's next now that you've got a national title?

FLEX: Right now I'm talking with Joe Weider, and he's really interested in having me go into the Mr. Olympia contest this year, but he has to talk with a few more people from the IFBB first, so I'm waiting to hear about that. Other than that, I'll just pick out one of the shows next year and go and make my pro debut in it and try and collect some money this time around for all my hard work in the gym.

Q: Let's say the Olympia doesn't materialize for you this year, what other pro show are you leaning toward?

FLEX: Well, prematurely, right now I'm thinking about the Iron Man Invitational and using that as a warm-up for the Arnold Classic in Columbus.

Q: Well, you certainly looked good enough to compete in the Mr. Olympia contest regardless. What did you do to get into such good shape?

FLEX: I've been working with Neil Spruce since 1991, and that was the first time, at my first USA show, that we ever worked together. Then, we really didn't know my body that well, and neither did he. The second time we worked together was at the Nationals, and I noticed that things were coming together a little bit better for that show, although we still had some distance to go. I'd been finding and hearing that I had a problem with my water retention and getting as dry as possible, so of course I used Neil again for my nutrition analysis. I even incorporated another guy by the name of Joe McNeil this time around who specialized in helping bodybuilders get as dry as possible for contests. He lives in Florida, and I incorporated him to help me get as dry as

possible. Still, I was able to come in eight months later at 10 pounds heavier than I had ever previously competed at.

Q: That's great. Let's get into the training routine that helped to put on the mass that you displayed on the USA stage this year. What kind of a training program did you follow?

FLEX: It's a four-on/one-off program. Normally the first day will see me train chest and biceps; the second day will be legs, and I'll train hamstrings in the morning and quadriceps at night. The third day consists of shoulders and triceps, and the last day consists of back only. Me and my other two training partners really feel that, as a professional, you need to have a "professional" back, and too many athletes don't put enough into their back training—and it shows on the day of the contest. We attack back! That's why we train on a four-on/one-off and leave that fourth day for back only.

Q: Do you use the four-on/one-off all year round?

FLEX: Yes I do, both off-season and precontest. I find it best for overall recovery and growth.

Q: Can you take us through, step-by-step, this four-day split routine?

FLEX: Sure, on Monday it's chest and triceps, so I'll start with chest. My first exercise is incline barbell presses, where I'll usually go up to 455 pounds. After that we'll go to the dumbbell press, where we'll go up either 170 or 180 pounds. I should mention that once we get to that type of weight, the heaviest that we can go, we'll still try and manage 5, 6, or 7 reps, the last few with a spot. Anywhere going up to that number, even up to 315 pounds on the incline presses, and we'll still do 10 good reps per set with it. I'm not really sure how many sets we'll do all told in working up to that weight because we really don't pay that close attention to anything other than our own individual set at that moment, the reason being that our in-the-gym philosophy is that if you have the energy on that particular day to go for more, you should. We don't look at a number to stop at. If one of us has 400 pounds on the bench and we rep that out pretty easily, then we're going to yell at that person to go for more because he hasn't even begun to put out yet. In any event, after the dumbbell presses, we'll go to flat bench presses with a barbell, and we'll go up to maybe 385 to 400 pounds because we feel that there's a lot of stress on the pectorals with this exercise at this point in the workout. It's also this point in the workout that most people get the majority of their pec tears, so we're really scared of going too heavy here. Instead we just do more repetitions. After flat bench, we'll go to cable crossovers and then maybe finish up on the pec dec.

Q: You seem to have a real "hard-core" approach to training with back-busting weights and blitzing training methods. What's your reasoning behind it?

FLEX: *I just feel that if you have the energy, you might as well go for it. If, some days, we go into the gym and we don't have the energy to lift super heavy, then we just put out whatever we can. To our bodies it's still a maximum amount at that time. If we feel good, though, the three of us can normally generate a lot of energy toward each other, so we're normally able to put out really high-intensity workouts all the time.*

Q: So after chest is biceps. What's your routine for those monsters?

FLEX: *Well I'll start off with standing barbell curls, using the "21" method, doing 7 half reps, 7 half reps from the top only, and then 7 full reps. We'll work up to maybe 135 pounds on this one because we're still just trying to warm up, and with 21 repetitions on such a small muscle, it gets an extreme burn so there's not really any need to go that heavy with it. My other two training partners go heavier than that, but I don't because I feel that my biceps, and my arms period, are kind of overwhelming and I don't want to make them much bigger because my biggest thing I have going for me is my symmetry, and if I have these two things that look like legs coming out of my shoulders without shoulders to match them it's not going to help me one* bit. After "21s" I'll go on to alternating dumbbell curls and mess around with anywhere from 75- to 90-pounders. If we're competing against each other, we'll go into the 90 range but, other than that, we'll stay around 50 or so and just make it burn. That, actually, is about where I quit. I may go to one of the preacher curl machines and do some nice, slow concentration movements, but I'll usually stop at that time because I don't want to get any more of a pump or anything. I just want to do maybe three or four exercises for my biceps. Again, I don't really count sets here, I go by how I feel. However, saying this, we have to at least do 10 sets for biceps. That's day one's training.

Q: What about forearms, do you do those on day one as well?

FLEX: Well, those come into play a lot with the curls and so on, so I don't do all that much direct work for them as a rule. However, when it's precontest and I have a lot more time on my hands I may do a couple of sets, but they really do come up well with just the curls alone.

Q: So what happens on day two?

FLEX: Day two consists of hamstrings in the a.m., and I'll start with leg curls on the lying down leg curl machine. My repetitions will be anywhere from 15 to 25, and we normally start with 70 pounds and then work our way up to whatever the stack holds, whether it's 130 or 150 pounds.

We'll do 4 or 5 sets of those, and the next exercise will be the 45-degree angle leg curl on the Flex machine, which is set up to train your hamstrings one leg at a time. We'll once again do anywhere from 15 to 25 reps, and one of our partners will spot me at the end of the set, so that I can really contract that muscle and then we'll let it down slowly. We'll go up to about 75 or 80 pounds on that one, and from there move on to stiff-legged deadlifts to stretch the muscle back out, and basically that's it for hamstrings. On stiff-legged deadlifts I'll go up anywhere from 405 pounds to 430 pounds. However, because of that I've got a severe back injury, so now I try not to go over 180 pounds, but normally, we'd go heavier. We start from the hamstring and squeeze all the way into the high glute muscle. After hamstrings, we take a break and then come back later that evening and start training our quadriceps. I'll start with leg extensions, doing anywhere from 40 to 50 repetitions, single leg, alternating legs one at a time, and we'll use anywhere from 30 to 50 pounds on that. We'll do about 7 sets of that to really get the blood flowing to our quads, and then it's on to hack squats. We'll do 5 sets of these, and we'll start off with 2 plates and then move up to 6 to 10 plates on each side of the hack machine. We have to do 15 reps—that's our rule—no matter what the weight is we have on there. So if you need a spot to get those last few reps, you've got it, but you can't get out until you've done your 15.

After the hack squats we go to the leg press, and this is when they really go crazy! I'll go to approximately 10 plates on each side of the press, and that's about all my back can handle because of my injury, but they'll go up to 15 to 17 plates per side! And one of my training partners, Chris Cormier, will do up to 50 reps with that weight! That's really their exercise, they just go crazy on that, so I'll just take the back seat on that. There's no way they can talk me into trying that once I get to the point where I'm hurting or am on the verge of hurting myself, I'll tell them to screw off. It's like a golden rule, I can't tell them that until it's really that point and then, because they'll cuss you out in front of the gym if they think you're dogging it, they back off. After that, we'll go over to the leg extension machine again, or the Eagle machine, and we'll put 17 on, which is 170 pounds, and we'll rep 20 repetitions out for 4 more sets. And that's it for day two.

Q: What happens on day three?

FLEX: *Day three is shoulders and triceps, and we'll come in and start with rear delts on the pec machine where you can work your rear delts. There's two types of rear delt machine; one has pads and the other has handles, and we use the one with handles and we face the rear of that and we work our rear delts, doing 7 sets and working up to 130 pounds. From there we'll go on to a 90-degree angle bench, and we'll work our rear delts again with*

dumbbells. We'll use anywhere from 25 to 40 pounds for 4 sets of 10 to 15 reps. From there we'll go on to dumbbell side laterals, and we'll either do them bilaterally or simultaneously. We'll use anywhere from 25 to 30 pounds, or sometimes we'll go the "death way" and do 60 repetitions with the 25s and do 4 sets of 60. I hate it when my training partners call this exercise out. It really makes me want to cry, and I end up, literally, on the floor, and they call everybody over and start making fun of me. I mean, I tell them, "Guys, you want me to give it all I've got, and when I do I'm tired and you make fun of me!" [laughs] Anyway, after that, we'll go to the cable machine and do side laterals again from a different angle, and that's basically all we do for deltoids.

Q: Do you then take time off and return later to hit triceps?

FLEX: *No, we hit triceps immediately after deltoids because it's such a small muscle. We'll start off with triceps extensions with a close grip, and we'll use a bar hooked up to the overhead pulley and do 4 to 6 sets. From there it's on to the skull crushers or lying triceps extensions with an EZ curl bar. I used to go up to two 45-pound plates on each side for this movement until I really started destroying my tendons and my elbows, and so now I'll only go to two 35-pound plates on each side. We make sure we do 10 reps per set with this. From there it's off to the seated machine where you do* a sort of reverse push-up and extend your arms for 4 sets. Then it's cable extensions with a rope because we feel we get a better contraction with the rope for 4 sets. We use high reps on this last movement because it's the last exercise, so we'll go from 15 to 25 reps.

Q: That brings us to day four in your training—back day. What's the routine?

FLEX: I always start off my back workout with pull-ups to the front for 4 sets. Then it's on to pulldowns to the rear for another 4 sets. And then pulldowns to the front where we'll do about 7 to 8 sets of this because all of us want to enlarge our V-taper from the front. Then I'll go on to deadlifts because I like to try and work my lower back. With my small waist, the training gives the illusion of no lower back, so I'm trying to correct that by training my lumbar area with deadlifts. They'll go to the cable bent-over row machine, which I can't do because of my back problems. Then we'll meet again and finish off with close-grip pulldowns to the front, and we'll end our back training with that movement.

Q: When you do pull-ups or "chins," what kind of reps are you looking at?

FLEX: I can get 10 on my own, but normally I'll just get somebody to spot me and I'll just forget about the number and just go to failure. Each time I go to failure, which I would say would be 20 to 25 reps because 10 to 15 is pretty easy.

Q: What about direct trap work?

FLEX: No, because I used to go really crazy with my traps before. You know, going up to 700-pound shrugs. There are pictures of that published in the magazines, but I stopped doing them because they started to get so well developed that it started making my pecs look flatter from the top because my traps were getting so high. Now, because of all the side laterals we do for our shoulders, the traps come into play quite a bit so they're burning just as bad as my shoulders when I train my delts, so now I don't pay any special attention to them.

Q: At what point of your career did you notice the most progress? Was it a low set, heavy weight routine or a high set, light weight routine that really triggered the growth?

FLEX: It was a high repetitions with heavy weight program that really made the difference for me. Since 1988, when I've been competing, I've averaged an increase of 10 pounds of muscle with every appearance on stage. And it's been more of a dense type of weight in the last two years since I've been training with higher reps and heavier weights. I owe a lot of it to my two training partners, Chris and Rico. Without them pushing me in the gym I doubt that I would have been able to train as hard as I needed to in order to make such rapid progress. It's basic—high-intensity workouts always cause more muscle growth. When you put a muscle under strain, then the muscle has to deal with it, so it goes back and tries to recuperate itself and grow so that you can't strain it that way again. It tries to deal with the stress by growing; I mean, it has to grow to deal with it. So you have to strain it again with high-intensity workouts.

Q: What about overtraining? You'd think that with so many brutal workouts in a row you'd run the risk of overtraining.

FLEX: Well, there's two theories to that. One is that if you're always eating correctly and having a proper caloric intake, then you'll never overtrain. I feel that's true with regard to the body because the body can do whatever you want it to. We don't have the brain power to tap fully into what the body can do, so that right there let's us know that you can never overtrain physically, but mentally you can get burned out. And there are some days when we go into the gym and we're mentally burned out and the body is stressed at this time, and we just back off. We'll go as heavy as we can at that time, which to the body still registers as going to the max because that's all it can register at that time. We won't look at the weight and say, "Oh no, we can't do the same amount"; we'll just go as heavy as we can, that our bodies allow us at that time, and we'll just call it a day. We all know that you can't train all out every day, but we do try to be as intense as possible when we train.

39

Achim Albrecht

A friend called me. "Look," he said, "I just got back from the IFBB World Championships in Kuala Lumpur, Malaysia, and this guy Achim Albrecht looked incredible. You should find out more about this guy."

After scouting around for the number, I found it, and a soft-spoken voice with a German accent answered the telephone. It was the mighty German himself, Achim Albrecht. After introducing myself and telling him the purpose of my call, Achim opened up and proved to be a most congenial interviewee. "I've just signed a contract with Joe Weider, and I'm very excited," he began. "It's every bodybuilder's dream to sign a deal with Joe Weider!"

Indeed, along with Achim's win in Malaysia and his deal with Weider, he's received numerous exhibition and seminar requests, he's appeared on ESPN's "Muscle Magazine" television show in the United States, and he has received numerous business offers to start up various health clubs, and that's after only winning the World Championships!

Imagine what will befall this mountain of muscle if he should win the Olympia this year. But who is he? Where in Germany is he from? What are his thoughts on training? And, most important, how did he pack that 244 pounds of rock-solid muscle on to his 6' frame? Read on, as we put these and other questions to Achim Albrecht.

Q: Achim, what first drew you to the sport of bodybuilding?

ACHIM: *I've always liked muscles and strength. Before I started bodybuilding, I was into all kinds of sports such as rowing and boxing. I really liked boxing, actually. In fact, I might have been a good boxer, but I think I started too late. I was 17 or 18, and I think that was leaving it a bit too late to become a boxer. but with bodybuilding, there doesn't seem to be that cutoff age. I mean, look at Al Beckles!*

Q: Where do you hail from, Achim?

ACHIM: *I come from Germany, in a little town near Cologne.*

Q: You recently won a very major competition in the form of the World Championships, which were held in Malaysia. How did it feel to win such a prestigious contest?

ACHIM: *[laughs] Really good! This might sound a little bit arrogant, but I wasn't all that surprised to win it. The reason was not that I was thinking, "Oh, I'm the best!" but rather that I'd trained all year to win the World Championships. I trained every day for four to five hours at a stretch! I really wanted it badly! I had victory so fixed in my head that I knew I had to place high enough to win.*

Q: You've touched on your training, which seems a perfect segue to my next question. How do you train to build up such great muscle mass during the off-season?

ACHIM: *In the off-season I train four days on, one day off. On the first day I'll train chest in the morning and then shoulders in the evening. On the second day, I'll train back in the morning, and in the evening triceps. Then, on the third day, I'll train thighs in the morning and hamstrings in the evening, and on the fourth day, I'll train biceps and forearms.*

Q: What sort of sets and reps do you use?

ACHIM: *In the off-season, I use about 4 sets per exercise and about four to five exercises per body part. For legs, for example, I'll do leg extensions, then leg presses, squats, and, when training hamstrings, leg curls and stiff-legged deadlifts. For chest, I might do bench presses, incline presses,*

and dumbbell flyes and, before a contest, cable crossovers. My back training consists largely of basic exercises such as T-bar rows, barbell rows, chins, and cable rows, while shoulders might consist of military presses, dumbbell laterals, and cable laterals.

Q: How does your precontest routine differ from this one?

ACHIM: *Not really all that much. I normally just add a set or two of a finishing movement such as crossovers, hack squats, cable curls, laterals, or other movement and, of course, I also include more aerobic activity to help burn up the fat.*

Q: How important do you think genetics are in determining a championship physique?

ACHIM: *I think that if you were to put the attributes together that would make up a champion bodybuilder they would be genetics, diet, and then training, in that order. I always say in my seminars how important nutrition is. People think, "Well, if I do the bench press or some such exercise, like some champion does, I'll get a physique like him." It's not that simplistic. Training is only one part of the equation, and believe me, proper nutrition and genetics make up a bigger piece of the pie.*

Q: How would you define "proper" nutrition?

ACHIM: *I would say that it's healthy eating—eating a balanced diet and staying* away from junk foods. That's what I have to do, anyway. If I eat a lot of sugar, it's good-bye definition! Eat a balanced diet from the four basic food groups, and supplement it if you need to with vitamins and minerals and protein.

Q: What did you weigh when you won the World Championships in Malaysia?

ACHIM: I weighed 244 pounds for that contest.

Q: And how tall a man are you?

ACHIM: I'm 6' even. I'm not as tall as Lee Haney, I'm closer in height to Gary Strydom.

Q: Who were your bodybuilding "idols" when you were growing up?

ACHIM: I never had any idols, but there were plenty of bodybuilders who served to inspire when I was growing up. Casey Viator was one; he was so big! Other body-builders of a more recent vintage would be guys like Gary Strydom, whom I trained with for a while. We worked out well together as training partners. I also liked the physique of Matt Mendenhall and that newcomer, Eddie Robinson. I like his physique! I like the big guys; the ones with the really outrageous muscle mass. They really inspired me to train.

Q: What are your thoughts on the IFBB's recent move to implement drug testing to the men's pro ranks?

ACHIM: It's a difficult question to answer, I'm thinking with regard to whether or not it's a good thing. Whenever I'm at a seminar, somebody will invariably ask, "Hey, do you take drugs?" And if you say, "No, I've never taken drugs," they just laugh at you. And if you say, "I take drugs," then you are the black sheep. I think it's OK to test the women and the amateurs, but I find it a bit different for the professional level. Amateur bodybuilding and professional bodybuilding are two completely different types of sports. They're different, and I don't think it's a good idea to make it mandatory to test the professional ranks. I mean, you're playing around with people's livelihoods here; it's how we make our money. It's not fun, it's not a hobby, it's really hard work and it's our way of life.

Q: Given that most people who train are noncompetitive bodybuilders but may be looking to pack on some muscle mass, what routine would you recommend for them to do that?

ACHIM: I think that they should train three to four times a week. I think it's better, even for beginners, to split their body parts up. You read all the time about training the whole body three times a week, but I don't think that's so good. Beginners can and should do a split routine. The first day could be chest, shoulders, and triceps, the second day could be legs, back, and biceps, then, on the third day, repeat the first day's program, and then rest on the fourth day and then just alternate the routines. The first week, certain body parts are trained twice and the other body parts are only trained once. Then the next week you alternate it again.

Q: How many sets would you recommend they do?

ACHIM: I think, for bigger body parts, two exercises would suffice, and for the smaller body parts, only one exercise. And only use the basics and only for 4 or 5 sets and a rep range of 6 to 12.

Q: Why don't you think the three-day-per-week routine is that efficient?

ACHIM: I started on this routine, and I've also worked for a long time as a personal trainer at different gyms, and I used this routine, the one I've just described, with the people I've trained, and I can see that they get better results than with a whole-body program.

Q: Who would you classify as the top 10 physiques of all time?

ACHIM: I would place in first place, Arnold Schwarzenegger, then Lee Haney, Gary Strydom, Casey Viator, Mike Mentzer, Matt Mendenhall, Robby Robinson, Berry DeMey, Sergio Oliva, and Mike Christian.

Q: How do you live your life these days, now that you're a successful bodybuilder?

ACHIM: I live bodybuilding 24 hours a day. Even during my rest time, I'm thinking about bodybuilding. I hope someday to open a bodybuilding business, so, as you can see, bodybuilding is very important to me—at least at this stage of my life.

Q: What's next for Achim Albrecht?

ACHIM: The Mr. Olympia contest in September. I won't be in any contest before that because my opinion is that it will allow me more time to prepare my body in the off-season; to pack on more mass and diet in the definition so that when I enter that contest, I will come in five pounds heavier than I was in the World Championships.

Q: What can we do, if anything, to improve our sport of bodybuilding?

ACHIM: It's different, depending on whether you're talking about female or male body-building. In male bodybuilding, I think we are on the right track, but we must make more headway into other media such as television. In America, it's not too bad, but in Europe, Germany in particular, you never see a bodybuilder on television, apart from on Eurosport. It's becoming more and more popular in Europe, but the important people in television don't seem to be paying attention because lots of people like bodybuilding but it just doesn't get the coverage that it does in the States.

Q: What's been your most productive training routine, the one that has packed on the most muscle mass that you've ever experienced?

ACHIM: Unquestionably the four-day-on/one-day-off system. It's not important to do a ton of sets. It is important to feel the movement and really work the muscle group you're training. Keep your repetitions moderate, approximately 10 to 12, use good form, eat well, rest up, and you'll really build big muscles.

40

Chris Duffy

When Juno Beach, Florida, native Chris Duffy stepped on stage for this year's NPC USA heavyweight class competition, audible gasps were heard throughout the auditorium. The man was massive in the purest sense of the term, and even then, that term seems woefully inadequate in trying to capture the impact with which he hit that Santa Monica crowd. His delts, at one time a weak point in the Duffy arsenal, were round, pronounced, meaty cannonballs that rippled and twitched with every pose he hit. Ditto for his pecs and lats—and don't even mention the redwoods this man had for legs!

The amazing thing about it all was the fact that Duffy, while always big, had never looked fuller or more complete in his career. The judges also took note of his conditioning and awarded him second place, just behind Flex Wheeler, who himself happened to be in the best shape of his amateur career. And while Wheeler would be the one to win the heavyweight and overall USA title, it was

Duffy that was being talked about long after the curtain had come down on the proceedings. Here's what he said in answer to the infamous "20 Questions."

Q: You improved so much for the USAs, most notably in your deltoid region. Can you tell us exactly what you did in terms of sets, reps, exercises, and poundages, which we hear are nothing short of monstrous, in your workouts?

CHRIS: *Okay, it's really weird, it's really different. I tried everything for shoulders, and I'd asked and bothered the best pros because I'd had the opportunity of being out here where they are, and they were earnest in trying to help me, but I just got no closer to getting it. Last year before I left for Florida, I saw Mike Matarazzo and Jim Quinn training side laterals, and they were using these really huge dumbbells. They were doing them sitting down, but if you ever see somebody that has an outstanding body part do an exercise, it's almost like magic; it's like a swoop. You see it most easily in curls, or I would even say the way I used to squat when I used to work legs. If somebody's got one body part it's almost like genetic, it's almost like it just knows how to be worked. So when I saw that, I made some sort of a connection, so when I got training again, I just didn't listen to anybody and I just started using heavier and heavier weights. My style's a little loose, but it's surprisingly strict for the weights I use. Chris Lund*

called me after the contest to shoot some photos, and I really wanted to use some heavy weights to impress Chris, but I was more tired than I thought after the show. I routinely go up to 105-pound lateral raises. I mean, they're slung up pretty good, but the form is incredibly tight.

Q: What would your shoulder routine be? Let's walk through it.

CHRIS: *I start off with 5 warm-up sets with super-light weights. I'll start out with 5 pounds, then go to the 10s, and I always use straps when I do my laterals. I find that I use a lot less. I could really concentrate on my delts more. Then my first real set is with the 60s for a set of 10 reps. Then it's on to the 80s for 3 sets of 10, try and do 90s for another 3 sets of 10, and then I'll always push a little and try and push as far as I can. So I'll do about 15 to 20 sets of laterals.*

Q: You seem to be averaging about 3 sets per weight increase. Why is this?

CHRIS: *Well, about 3 sets, but it's more on feel. If I'm feeling real strong, I'll fly up faster. I'll go real slow, too. If I'm tired between sets, I'll think nothing of taking a five-minute rest.*

Q: Where do you get the energy to hoist up dumbbells weighing 105 pounds after doing 3 sets of 10 reps with 90s? You'd think that kind of poundage would have left your delts just fried!

CHRIS: *Yeah, but it just works. I don't know. Maybe it's the long rest. I eat an amazing amount of calories in the off-season through protein drinks and such, and I spend most of my day in quiet time, thinking about my job of bodybuilding, and that's my game. I'm a worker in the gym.*

Q: You've mentioned that you don't mind taking an extended rest in between sets. What kind of a rest are we talking about?

CHRIS: *Average is probably no more than three minutes, but on delts it usually doesn't get longer than that but on heavy exercises . . . if I'm doing deadlifts, like I'll go over 700 pounds on deadlifts, or bent-over rows, I might take a five-minute rest before I'll approach a heavy set.*

Q: You've done 20 sets for your delts, just to start off. Is that your delt routine, or do you include other exercises?

CHRIS: *Well, I'll average between 15 and 20 sets of lateral raises using both arms, and then I'll usually do one-arm laterals, which I'll stick with a 100-pounder. I'll lean on the rack and tilt my body a little forward, which seems to get the back part of the lateral head, the further back portion, because with laterals, you end up using a lot of front delt and your front delts get blasted so much from all the chest work you do, so doing the movement this way gives you a nice, round, fuller look. And, until this contest, my delts were [laughs] fairly pathetic. I mean, I had nothing. My arms*

and delts were a pretty wide-open point for people to make fun of if they ever cared to talk about such a physique. To me, it worked amazingly, and the background for my doing the laterals first in my routine is because if I do my presses first, I use so much triceps that my triceps fatigue before my delts do. So by the time I get to the presses, I'm still using some pretty heavy poundages, but I prefer to use machines because my stabilizers are pretty fried by then. Anyway, on the one-arm laterals I wouldn't do too many sets, maybe 5, and then it would be on to Smith machine presses for maybe 5 again, and only 3 of those would be really heavy. I'd max out around 315 pounds for sets of 10. I pretty much always do sets of 10 because I'm on a base 10 system [laughs], the Dewey decimal system. Then I'll do some kind of machine press that's really guided. You know, where there's no bar to hit my head. The one I use is like a Bodymasters machine, just something where your arms can come beside your head so you don't have to lean back, and it gets more specifically lateral head this way. Whereas on the Smith machine, because you have to make room, you're going to work a little more front delts. I don't have the flexibility to go behind my neck on anything, and I think it's probably a little too tough on your rotator cuff. By the time I get to the guided machine presses I'm pretty much fried, so I'll do maybe 3 sets of maybe 20 reps with the stack. For rear delts, I'll do 7 sets of bent-over laterals with nothing much, maybe 60s. I'd keep the same weight pretty much for the entire 7 sets. I do them bent over so I'm not afraid to put a little "oomph" into it. And that's pretty much my delt routine. I don't vary it much, I might switch the machines around sometimes, but as long as I can dump my load on the laterals and get them done, I mean I don't save anything ever, but the last thing I care about is how much I'm going to press or anything. Laterals are my big exercise. I only do presses because I'm afraid to drop them. After those laterals, I'm not sure they do anything at that point anyway.

Q: What exactly is your training system, and when does your delt routine come into play?

CHRIS: *For the first time ever before the USAs, I started working my whole body over six days and working each body part twice a week, and it worked great. After this show, I'm training for the Nationals, so I'll do just stretch out training my whole body over five days. I'll do that for about three weeks just to rest and heal up some, but it's a lot harder work and, previous to doing it, I never would have thought I'd have the recuperative power to handle it. Even on a five-day stretched out, with a day off, I never really seemed to heal. I didn't get worse, though. In fact, I'd almost venture to say that it got better when I switched to working out more often. I'd*

train three days on and then three days on again and take Sundays off.

Q: What is the body part breakdown on this system?

CHRIS: *Well, for one thing, I wasn't working legs at all on this system because my legs were always too heavy. On my first day I'd come in and do back, and with back I'd do traps and deadlifts. Day two would be chest and triceps, even though I much prefer and think there are biomechanical advantages to working biceps and triceps together, after training for so long and coming from being so weak, I was starting to have joint pains, so I would do triceps after chest only because they were so warmed up. Now that I'm healthier, I'll go back to working the arms through supersetting biceps and triceps, which made a tremendous difference in my arm development. Day three would be delts and biceps.*

Q: And you wouldn't work legs?

CHRIS: *No, I'd do some leg curls on one of those days, like once a week, and calves I worked with whatever the least workload would be. And for abs I'd do that Legendary Abs system, which takes like eight minutes a week. I'd do it twice a week for four minutes a workout.*

Q: Let's go through your routine now. We have your delt routine down, but for the sake of continuity, we'd better get the rest of it, starting with back and traps and lower back. What are we doing here?

CHRIS: *That's fun because I love to train back. I guess it's because I still have this phobia about my legs being too big. I mean, I wasn't known for legs and I really hate being known for a body part. I want to be known as a bodybuilder, as a total physique, so I set out to get wider. To accomplish this I'd do about 12 to 15 sets of pulldowns, real heavy, and then I'd go to bent-over rows and do 7 sets real heavy.*

Q: What's "real heavy" on these two exercises?

CHRIS: *Well they have the stack, which is just 250 pounds, on the pulldowns, so I usually put a 45 on and do a good 8 sets like that. And then I'll go over to bent-over rows, and I didn't get as heavy as I wanted to this year because I was watching my form because my back would be tired after all the deadlift stuff I did also. I like to go to 365 for each workout, and for the Nationals I'm really going to be pushing it and I'll make sure I get into the 400s in pretty decent form. I'll use momentum once I'm in the working belly of the muscle, but I won't initiate the movement and start off with momentum so that I'm swinging it. That's how I define a cheater. If I've got to jerk my body and use support muscles to initiate the movement, that's cheating. If I get a grind and then use a*

little explosion, that's how I work out! After the rows, I'll go to the cable rows—which I only found out how to do properly one month before the show! I used to watch how all the guys did this, and it occurred to me one day, "Why does everyone with the best backs cheat on this movement?" And it's not really "cheating," I guess, but it is a real flowing motion. I had gotten screwed up because of this macho thing. There was a story printed, and it might have been in FLEX, about Joe Gold sticking his knee in Gaspari's back or something, and, for some reason, that image seems to have surfaced around, and whenever you train back and use that exercise you'll invariably hear someone say, "Someone should be able to have their knee in their back"—I think not! I mean, that's great if all you want to work is your lat bellies on the outside, and that's the easiest part of your lat to work! It's that center column, with those traps and the rhomboids; those are from rotating those shoulders back around the thorax, like. Pulling back. So you do lean a little more, and it is a flowing motion. Again, not with momentum but a good, strong pull, and the stack went to 300 pounds and I'd stick on as many plates as I could to get it up to 345 or 390 pounds on there. Usually that still wasn't heavy enough, so I'd do sets of 15 reps. That would be about it for lats. Sometimes after my bent-over rows, if I'm all screwed up from doing them, you know those assisted pulldown machines?

I'll do some of them. If I'm on low calories I won't because I think it looks silly and is wasting recuperative power, but it does help me get a little more of a contraction back there. If I'm feeling good, I might do some of those. Then I'm on to traps and shrugs. I'll use about five plates on each side for 5 sets of 10 reps. Then I'm on to deadlifts. Until I switched to training twice a week I had been doing deadlifts as a regular and central part of my back routine. I'd worked up to a best weight of 725 pounds for sets of 6 reps, but I was considerably more fatigued by the end of that workout. I generally did my deadlifts before my trap work. In those days, I normally wouldn't go over 600 or 650 pounds and incorporated it into my work-outs. Toward the end I started to get plagued by injuries, so I think it compromised the thickness of my back. I got really pissed off at myself! So I would only go up to 500 pounds on the deadlifts or just do them every other workout, but I'll never do that again. Now that I go to a chiropractor three times a week, a guy named Mitch who's a great guy, he fixes me up, and now I'm, like, bulletproof. So I'm going to keep deadlifting right up to the show.

Q: That takes care of day one. On day two you're back in the gym working chest and triceps. What's this break down to?

CHRIS: *Again, before the chiropractic sessions, I thought I had a rotator cuff problem, but it wasn't. It was just some ribs out of place, so I had to quit my benching just when it was getting good. It's always been my goal to be doing sets of 10 reps with 405 pounds. And I'd just gotten up to sets of 8 with 405, but my shoulder was killing me! I mean, I'd be spending up to 30 sets trying to warm up and get through it, and it was just chronic, I couldn't sleep at night! So I got away from those and went to dumbbells, but the dumbbells only went up to 150 pounds, which are much too light. So I used a vertical press machine, made by Polaris, and used the stack along with one of my partners, who weighs about 250 pounds, standing on top of the stack, and I just went nuts! Like 3 warm-up sets and just go crazy! Just lose your mind because there's nothing to worry about in terms of balancing the weight or losing control—you just push. As soon as you know you're not going to get hurt, after your warm-up, you just go crazy! And at that point, I was fatigued enough to go over to the 150 pound dumbbells and try and do 4 sets of 15 and dwindle the reps down to 8 or 10. Then I'd go crazy on another assisted machine, like the Hammer ones, they're guided and you can put like six or seven plates on either side and just go nuts. I love certain pieces of Hammer equipment, while some of it I find too easy to get swinging. They really used some thought in their design, though, which is refreshing. And then I'll do some incline stuff. I think it's really, really important to do your lower* chest work before you get into your upper chest work, because if you just try and do your upper first, your lower assists too much and you can't stimulate it to the degree that you need to. So if the lower's fatigued to the point where it can't help, then your upper's going to be isolated and you can fry it! So I went to the Smith machine using about three plates per side and whatever the slide weighs so we would do some real heavy sets, about 5, on that, and that would be about it. Injuries were plaguing me on some of those movements, so I would do some cable flyes, using an incline bench between the cables. But just before the show, and I always get strongest before the show, I was doing incline flyes really strict—and I mean I was stretching right out—with 105s! And I'm going to go back to working on that movement. I want to be doing flyes with ISOs for the Nationals.

Q: And then you'd go into triceps training. What was that all about?

CHRIS: Fortunately I would always start with an easy exercise, and I'm basically a lazy guy. Triceps pushdowns, real heavy, say, 200 pounds, followed by those "skull crushers" with an EZ curl bar. Before my elbows started hurting I was up to 275 pounds on that one, and that was working great. I guess for the USAs my chest wasn't quite as thick as it could have been because of the shoulder injury. My back wasn't quite as thick as it could have been

because of the general discontinuity of my structure before I went to get chiropractic help. And then my elbow also, which is just a soft tissue thing. So those three things, I know it sounds like I'm copping out, but now with the fortification I'll be keeping it on with the heavy weights and the basic exercises for longer, all the way into the show. With triceps, and for me they used to be a huge, huge weak point, then somebody just said to me in passing, "Well, that portion of your triceps needs to be worked by doing overhead stuff." I'd never, ever done any overhead stuff, nor had I ever heard or listened to a comment of someone's suggesting it to me—and it really made a big difference! Ideally, I like to have my back against a preacher bench and use a barbell for French presses, and after all the heavy stuff that had gone on before, I'd sometimes just use a pulley with a bar attached to it, and that was nice. I wouldn't do a lot of sets, maybe 3 or 4 really hard sets of pushdowns, 3 or 4 hard sets of skull crushers, and then 3 sets of French presses. And that would conclude my triceps work.

Q: We've got your delt routine, so that would leave biceps.

CHRIS: Biceps, I've got a real specific way of training those puppies. Again, it was fostered by the shoulder injury, which was kind of unstable; I say it was in "hydra-drive" because it was only supported by fluid. And my arms were previously weak because for your arms to grow you have to keep them in to your body or your brachialis, which is a small but a very tough muscle, will take over. Your weights and poundages might go up, but your brachialis will only grow a little because it's a dense muscle, like a calf or something, so you're not going to get the gratuitous biceps growth. So, for me, I found the best way is to do all biceps exercises supported. I'll start off with straight bar preacher curls on the steep side of the preacher bench, using a false grip to force my hands to supinate. In fact, it supinates them just as much as you can with a dumbbell. Then I'll go to a cable curl on a 45-degree preacher bench with an EZ curl bar, using a full range of motion and a full stretch, and then I'll do a funny little one, and Chris Lund shot me doing it, too. I find it very comfortable on the ends of a 45-degree, regular old adjustable incline bench. I just lean over the end and make it into a preacher bench. It's kind of like a concentration/preacher curl. You have to keep the elbow supported so that I can force it into my body and keep all the angles lined up and still get some pretty freaky intensity angles. It seems to take me a long time to learn how to do what seem to me to be unnatural movements under the amount of effort I'm engaging in.*

Q: How many sets are you doing on the preacher bench?

CHRIS: *Not many. Maybe 3 or 4 depending on energy levels.*

Q: What about your forearms? How do you train them?

CHRIS: *For forearms during the off-season . . . my upper arms aren't really 90 kajillion inches, so I don't really train them that hard, slender forearms are more to my liking anyway. Not "slender," I guess, but I just do some funky version of a hammer curl that I've got. It's more slanted toward my brachialis and the top of my forearm. I curl the weight up and across my body. It feels right that way. I'll do 5 sets of those, and then I'm out of there.*

Q: What kind of a trainer are you?

CHRIS: *Oh, I'd say an obnoxious one. I really wouldn't want to train in a gym that had too many guys like me training in them. I really scream a lot, and I get so tired in between my sets. I really don't have time for posturing, I usually just slump around. I look like a big sloth or something. If I'm not lying on the floor sweating and making reservoirs of perspiration, I'm usually just sucking wind.*

Q: You mentioned that you no longer train your legs much anymore because you felt you were getting a rap about being out of proportion. Still, they're huge, so you must be doing something or have done something that would account for such development. What's the deal?

CHRIS: *Right now they're just a little over 30 inches. The first time I was weighing over 300 pounds for my first contest, they were 36 inches. And they were just disgusting! I looked like a Tyrannosaurus rex! So the deadlifts really help to keep my hamstrings in line, and I did work my calves hard because calves are pretty prevalent now, more so than they were five years ago when I started competing. My calves were smaller before, and people thought they were a hot item, and now they're just that much bigger. As for quads, I felt bad toward the end and started doing some extensions, but I don't really train quads anymore.*

Q: What do you do for your calves?

CHRIS: *I usually like to do the gambit. I do some standing calf raises and typically do higher reps, maybe sets of 15, and then I'll go to one of those donkey machines with maybe somebody sitting on top and then finish off with some seated calf raises—but always with as much weight as I can use. They're pretty strong.*

Q: Do you feel that your thighs are the way they are due to genetics, or is it the result of heavy training done when you were younger?

CHRIS: *When I was a little kid I was supposed to be a football player, so I read a book by Dick Butkus, and my mom had a 1972 Riviera, which is a real big car, and I used to drive it to parking lots and just push it around, doing sprints trying to push this car. I also used to run on the beach with combat boots and several pairs of leg weights on my ankles, so I think it's just tenacity. Certainly there is some genetic component—I mean my mother's legs are shaped just like mine but they're just much skinnier! Certainly I was drawn to bodybuilding like a duck to water. For me it was a case of you crawl, you walk, you lift weights.*

41

Gary Strydom

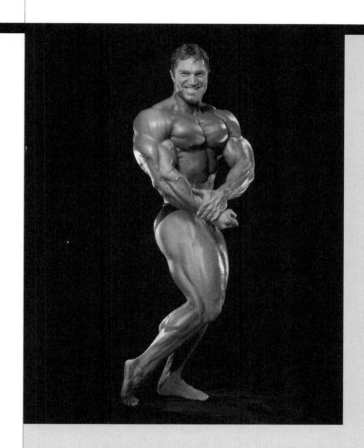

At this past year's Mr. Olympia, it was expected that Lee Haney would once again win the title handily. This opinion prevailed until competitor number 17 appeared on stage. Gary Strydom was in the best shape of his career and had a good many people convinced that they were then looking at the physique that would indeed topple Haney from his Mr. Olympia perch.

History would record that Gary Strydom did not defeat the Peach State Colossus that evening. In fact, Gary would place a very debatable fifth in the 1988 Mr. Olympia. However, while his overall placing in the competition may be subject to debate, the fact that his physique had improved markedly was indisputable. What had brought about this sudden transformation?

How had Strydom gone from being just another large (well, let's be accurate, "phenomenally large") bodybuilder who had won a few major titles to suddenly being the one physique that could wrest the Mr. Olympia title from Lee Haney? What were his training methods? What was the diet that

allowed him to become so ripped? And what really made Gary Strydom tick—his influences, inspirations, and ambitions? In order to obtain these answers, I decided that it was time to ask Gary Strydom "20 Questions."

Q: First of all, Gary, your physical condition for the 1988 Mr. Olympia contest was phenomenal. How did you improve yourself in preparation for this contest?

GARY: Well, to be honest, I have learned to train less and rest more. My body type overtrains and depletes much faster than others. This is mainly due to the fact that I have such a fast metabolism. My most productive training routine is training four days on and one day off out of every five days. In other words, I train my whole body once in every four days. I then rest a day and then start the whole routine again. On day one I train legs, on day two I train

arms, on day three it's chest and shoulders, and on day four I train back. I used this routine right up until two weeks before the contest, at which time I trained with weights every other day and did bike riding on the other days to rip up. In terms of sets, I would ordinarily perform 20 for my legs, 18 for my lats, 5 for my traps, 15 for my chest, 10 for my deltoids, 8 for biceps, 12 for triceps, 10 for my abdominals, 12 for calves, and that's it. I don't do any direct forearm work.

Q: You've touched upon what training method you use and your general set and rep scheme, but our readers need more data! What are your exercises during your five-day split routine?

GARY: Well, on my leg training day, I would start out with my quadriceps and really train them hard with basic exercises like squats, leg presses, and hack squats. Occasionally I'll throw in some exercises for separation such as lunges and leg extensions—but in any event, my total leg training seldom exceeds 18 to 20 sets, and in some instances, if I'm training with super high intensity, I might even go as low as 5 total sets, but then, when you use 1,200 pounds in leg presses for upwards of 20 reps—you really don't need more than 5 sets! For hamstrings, I seldom do more than 9 sets, but again before a contest I may go as high as 12 sets, incorporating exercises such as lying and standing leg curls and a really good basic movement such as stiff-legged deadlifts. That would complete my leg training day. I should also add that I generally train my hamstrings apart from my quadriceps as my things get so pumped and tight, I really can't do justice to my hamstrings in the same session. So, generally, I'll train my quads in the morning or early afternoon and then come back in the evening to train my leg biceps.

Q: Alright, that informs us what your leg training is all about. Now the money muscle—the arms! How did you build those howitzers?

GARY: My arm training usually falls on the day after I train my legs, so that there's adequate rest between muscle groups. I'm not a big believer that heavy barbell exercises are necessarily the best way to develop my arms—although I will use barbells in my arm training. Consequently, I use heavy dumbbell concentration curls, either barbell or dumbbell preacher curls with maybe a standard barbell curl workout thrown in approximately every two to three weeks. All of my arm exercises are done for 4 sets each for 8 to 10 reps per set. Before a contest, in addition to the 4 sets of preacher curls and 4 sets of concentration curls, I might add a set or two of cable curls as a finishing movement with the reps, again, falling between 8 and 12. Unlike my legs, I will train the arms' antag-

onistic muscle groups together in the same workout, as I really enjoy pumping as much blood into them as I can and feeling the skin around them draw tighter and tighter. For my triceps, I start out with the standard compound movement, close-grip bench press. I then move to lying triceps extensions and from there to cable pushdowns on the lat machine. Again, each exercise is done for 4 sets with the reps falling in the 8 to 12 range. Before a contest, I'll also include 1 to 2 sets of cable kickbacks. I still go back to the gym in the evening after my arm training in order to train my abs and calves. For calves I do 4 to 5 sets of standing calf raises, donkey calf raises, and seated calf raises, while for abs I'll do machine crunches and decline sit-ups. My third workout day is chest and shoulders. I start with chest and begin with bench presses for 4 sets of 6 to 8 reps and from there I proceed to incline machine bench presses for another 4 sets of 6 to 8 reps—these really fill in my upper pecs! Then I do dumbbell bench presses for another 4 sets and conclude with 4 sets of flat bench dumbbell flyes. Occasionally I'll throw in 2 or 3 sets of cable crossovers, but again, this is generally just before a contest. In the evenings, again, I will return to the gym and train my shoulders with 4 sets each of heavy behind-the-neck presses, dumbbell lateral raises, and bent-over cable raises for the rear head of the deltoid. The reps on shoulders are generally in the 8 to 10 range. On my fourth and final training day in the cycle I will focus all of my energies upon my back. I start in the morning with 6 to 8 sets of fairly heavy deadlifts—an exercise that really works the entire body! I'll usually work up to 500 pounds or so on this one. That usually wipes me out for the morning session, so I leave the gym only to return later in the evening after I've recovered somewhat to train my lats and upper back. I do chins to the front of my neck and then behind the neck. I'll follow these with seated cable rows, dumbbell rows as heavy as possible! And then pullovers—believe me after a back workout like that, I need the next day off! I use 3 to 4 sets per exercise for my back. And that, my friend, is my workout.

Q: What are your thoughts on the "intensity versus duration" issue in bodybuilding today?

GARY: Intensity produces a mature-looking physique whereas duration—long, boring workouts—sometimes have to be used in conjunction with periods of high-intensity work in order to achieve a more complete look. I use both in my training, alternating between periods of high intensity and high volume. I think that this leads to a more refined looking physique.

Q: Is it possible for an aspiring trainee to make impressive muscular gains by training three days per week, on alternate days, or are more or less training days required?

GARY: Yes, it is possible, but not on a pro level.

Q: At what point, in terms of effort and duration, is the overtraining threshold reached?

GARY: When you consistently train to failure and don't have enough days off to recuperate between workouts.

Q: What role does aerobics play in your precontest preparation?

GARY: Aerobics are part of my precontest preparation. I ride stationary bike for aerobics—real easy bike-riding—in other words, "easy tension" for about 20 to 35 minutes three times a week. I ride at an easy tension because my objective is just to burn body fat, and if I used a high level of tension, I would be breaking down muscle tissue—which I don't need to do when I'm not in the gym!

Q: What routine would you recommend for those of our readers who are trying to gain solid muscular size?

GARY: I would recommend that they use my routine. How do you think I built my physique!?

Q: Do you favor compound or isolation exercises for this task?

GARY: Compound mainly, with maybe one or two isolation exercises. I've never really strayed from the basics myself. In fact, as a rule, I don't generally add in isolation exercises except before a contest.

Q: How many calories do you limit yourself to in attempting to "rip up" for a contest?

GARY: *I generally take in 4,000 to 5,000 calories—minimum. I have a very active metabolism, so I have to take in a large amount of calories, plus my training on top of that only adds to my caloric deficit.*

Q: For how long would you adhere to this regimen?

GARY: *For seven to eight weeks before a show. At this point I would tend to eat even more throughout the day. Smaller sized meals, of course, with an emphasis on reducing both my calories and fat intake, but I still try to keep my protein intake as high as possible to maintain my existing muscle mass.*

Q: How would this differ from your off-season diet?

GARY: *In the off-season I generally eat 5,000 to 6,500 calories per day. When "ripping up" I prefer a low-fat diet and tend to eat more carbohydrates and proteins. In fact, I ingest probably twice as much protein as most bodybuilders. It's not unusual for me to eat up to 14 chicken breasts a day in addition to over two dozen egg whites, and then my carbs on top of that. With my training, however, I need massive amounts of protein. The standard maxim about 2 grams of protein per pound of body weight wouldn't work for me, and I usually take in upwards of 650 grams of protein per day.*

Q: What diet would you recommend for someone trying to pack on muscular size?

GARY: *It depends on what they look like. It would depend on their metabolism—whether it's fast or slow—I would definitely recommend a low-fat, high-carbohydrate diet, but in terms of calories, they're determined solely by what kind of frame the individual in question has, and consequently, it's difficult to assess. As a rule of thumb, however, I would recommend a balanced diet composed of 60 percent carbohydrates, 25 percent proteins, and 15 percent fats, and I would recommend that you take your meals at various times throughout the day—like have six or seven daily feedings as opposed to only two or three. To add weight, increase your daily need of calories by 10 to 20 percent or so, and, of course, don't overtrain.*

Q: Who were, or are, your greatest influences both inside and outside of bodybuilding?

GARY: *In bodybuilding, I would have to say both Tom Platz and Joe Weider. Outside of bodybuilding, it would be God and Michael Jackson.*

Q: What philosophy of life do you subscribe to?

GARY: *My philosophy of life would be that of persistence; what I cannot do today, I'll do tomorrow! Never do I give up on anything I set out to do.*

Q: What gives you happiness in this world?

GARY: Jesus Christ is my number one happiness, and my wife is number two. After that, it's up to me to make myself happy. I never dwell on the negative because ultimately it proves futile and never benefits those who do.

Q: Do you think the drug issue (steroids) in bodybuilding has been overdramatized by the magazines, or is it really a legitimate issue?

GARY: It is a legitimate issue, but we need to face it and make the steroids safe. Nobody is going to use something that is bad for them if there is an alternative that is safe and 100 percent more effective. Magazines should be searching for and dramatizing that aspect. If you dwell or expose anything negative for long enough it attracts people to explore these negative things because they think it's a shortcut, but again, nothing comes easy.

Q: What impact has your success in bodybuilding had on your personal life?

GARY: My personal life is the same. I don't live bodybuilding 24 hours a day. When my bodybuilding career comes to an end my personal life will be the same. Life on earth is short when you compare it to eternity, and my bodybuilding career is short when compared to life.

Q: What, if you could quantify them, would be the three most important things in your life and why?

GARY: God, because without God I have no hope in life. Family, because of their love and support. Helping others, because I already have so much.

Q: How can we improve our art/sport/science of bodybuilding? Or does it need improvement?

GARY: It needs improvement, alright, and we can improve it by making our sport more appealing to the general public. Everyone involved in this sport; the athletes, promoters, authors and magazines, etc., are ambassadors and should project the sport in a positive manner.

42

Steve Brisbois

It's a shame that Steve Brisbois has not placed higher in some of his more recent contests, and it's not because he has flaws in his physique, either! Brisbois has what in bodybuilding circles has become known as the small man's curse. In other words, Brisbois is often (although you'll never hear the judges admit to it) marked down due to his lack of height.

Standing a height of only 5'3", Steve would never give Ralph Moeller any fits in a Tall Man competition, but if Steve is compared body part to body part, he'd not only leave Moeller in the dust, but would shake the confidence of other top bodybuilders competing today.

With his awesome mass, excellent proportions, terrific symmetry, and dazzling muscularity, Brisbois is always a fan favorite whenever he competes. He has also amassed a considerable collection of trophies, many from his native Canada—including the Novice Ontario Championships back in '83 and the Northern Ontario Championship in '84. Steve then won the lightweight and overall titles in the Canadian Championships prior to becoming Canada's first World Champion since Roy Callender pulled it off as a middleweight back in '76. Steve has also won several professional championships since signing up with the IFBB and is one of the most sought-after professionals competing today, due to both his tremendous physique and his professional and enlightened seminars.

He's also an animal when it comes to hoisting mammoth training poundages in the gym. At a body weight of 170 pounds in the off-season, Steve can bench press 325 pounds for 10 reps and squat with 500 pounds for 10 reps as well! How the heck did he get so damn massive? What routine does the Canadian Colossus utilize? It's time for "20 Questions."

Q: Steve, what first drew you to the sport of bodybuilding?

STEVE: I came from a place that had so many bars and pubs that you wouldn't believe it! I used to drink and smoke too much. All we did was party at home in Timmins, Ontario. At 20 years old, I just got fed up with it. I grew to hate that lifestyle; I drank beer like there was nothing else to drink, and I smoked cigarettes, and I got fed up and felt like I needed a change. I went to the gym one day with a friend, and I've never looked back. In fact, it has been just over nine years now since I started training.

Q: When did you first start training exactly?

STEVE: It was back in 1982 on Memorial Day weekend.

Q: What has been your proudest moment so far as a professional?

STEVE: I really like competing. I guess everybody likes to compete who can compete, but I think what motivates me the most is talking to the judges, talking to people in the audience, and just being approachable. It's flattering when the people let you know how good or how bad you are because you can just get yourself motivated from that.

Q: Alright then, what, on the other side of the coin, has been your lowest moment as a professional?

STEVE: That's tough. There have been a lot of low moments here and there because, I guess you realize, when you go through bodybuilding, there's always stressful moments. You know, I can be open about this, for instance: I went through a shady divorce and shady business deals where I've lost a lot of money, and, through my bodybuilding career, these would have to rate as my lowest points or worst times. They brought me down a lot, but you've got to pick yourself back up.

Q: Steve, you're renowned for your "lines" and your symmetry. Do you attribute a lot of that to genetics, or do you gear your training specifically to accomplish this?

STEVE: I believe in genetics a lot, I really do. But I also believe in proper training tech-

nique. If you had seen my dad, then you'd know why I've been able to do so well in bodybuilding. My dad has a physique like a brick shithouse! And everybody's always talking about my "huge" forearms, but my forearms are small compared to my dad's. This guy has got the most awesome forearms that I've ever seen, I mean, they are huge! So I definitely attribute a lot of my success to genetics, unquestionably they play a big role. There's no denying that you've still got to put your training and nutrition together.

Q: How do you compare the bodybuilding scene in Canada with other countries?

STEVE: Do you know what? Canada is beginning to be a very big bodybuilding country. You know, bodybuilding in Canada was at one time a pretty conservative sport; somebody would always stereotype us as "big and dumb." It's understandable in a sense because nobody then understood the sport. But now it's beginning to become a really big sport up there, and now, with the drug testing in a lot of shows, I think there's even more credibility added to it, so it's becoming a far more popular thing in Canada.

Q: What are your thoughts on the drug testing issue in bodybuilding?

STEVE: I'm for it! I believe that it's going to be a good thing. There are a lot of guys out there who believe that it's bad and it's going to make the promoters lose money

because people aren't going to want to come and pay money to see natural athletes—but I don't believe that. The reason I like the test is because I'm scared to take the drugs! I've taken them before and I've had problems with them! And because there's so much garbage going on in the world today and so much garbage that's out there, I don't want to take a chance on taking shit out there when I don't know what I'm taking. You cannot believe anybody who says "This stuff is real" anymore. But saying that, let's face facts: drugs do work. They do help and they do make a difference, but we don't know what is out there anymore, and I'm just too scared to put those things in my physique now.

Q: Steve, you're renowned for your definition as well. What sort of aerobics program do you follow before a contest?

STEVE: I use biking, or else my girlfriend and I walk a lot. We walk every night because it's relaxing for us, and aerobics, I believe, helps a lot too—although doing too much can do you more harm than good. I remember when I was doing too much aerobics, I would be biking twice a day in the morning and night and then also walking at night, and it just took too much out of me.

Q: What sort of a walking program would you recommend, then?

STEVE: We just go for a nightly brisk walk. We like to walk at night and just walk a nice little fast walk, my girlfriend and I, and it just makes us feel more relaxed and we sleep better at night that way. I'm not a sleeper at the best of times, so it's just relaxing and, for me at least, quite beneficial.

Q: Given that the bulk of people working out are noncompetitive, what training program would you recommend for them to increase their size and strength?

STEVE: *You know, everybody is different. I think the biggest problem, and I've been to a lot of different gyms around the world, is that 90 to 95 percent of the people I see, in my opinion, don't know how to train properly. It's not their fault, I think they just weren't taught how to perform the movements correctly. They're not educated, and they're not provided the proper gym service of teaching them the right techniques and way to use the muscle! I think that if everybody learned how to use the muscles right and concentrated on the muscle group they're training, and trained properly, they could make better gains! It doesn't necessarily mean that you have to do this exercise or that exercise, I don't believe in that. I just believe in training right.*

Q: Alright, Steve, what then is training right?

STEVE: *It's knowing how to use the muscle you're training properly, not using these half motions here, or half reps and "cheating reps" and so on. I don't believe in that! A muscle needs to be extended*

and contracted to its fullest in order for it to do the work right. And going through that motion in a proper way so that you're focused on what you're doing and you know that that muscle is doing the work that it should be doing.

Q: But surely you must have a training system that's worked well for you, a certain series of exercises that you use and can rely on to stimulate your muscles to grow?

STEVE: *I just train right [laughs]. I train just like everybody else who's competing today, but I do not like to have my training monotonous. I do different exercises every time I walk into the gym, but my main point, like I made earlier, is just to focus on what I'm doing. I like to make sure that I'm feeling it pulling. I like to be able to really feel my muscles functioning. I don't like to go through any given movement fast because I do not feel that it works the muscles. Slow, controlled movements, and just focus on what you're doing.*

Q: Before a contest do you up your training to three on, one off the way that other bodybuilders do?

STEVE: *No, I train every day—especially before a contest.*

Q: Don't you find yourself overtrained by training every day?

STEVE: *No, I don't believe in overtraining. Not if you eat enough. I mean, there are some days when I'll only be training a* small body part like shoulders or just biceps on that day—but I'll also be doing something else like biking. If I don't bike, I'll walk, but of course close to a contest I'll be biking a lot, but I'm active every day. I like to keep myself active, and I can't remember a day where I've been completely inactive and just rested for the whole day.

Q: What have you found to be your most effective training routine? If you get the idea that I'm pushing you for one—it's true!

STEVE: *[laughs] My routine is nothing spectacular; I just train like everyone else! I train normal. When I walk into a gym, I just want to make sure that I know how to use that muscle group that I'm going to train that day. I'll do, for example, chest and triceps—either together that same workout, depending on how I feel, or I'll just go in the morning and do chest and then come back later and do triceps. The next day I might do back and biceps together, or, again, depending on how I feel, I might do back alone and biceps later on—perhaps along with calves. The day after that I'd train my legs and try to split up my hams and quads if I can, and if I feel that I can do the whole workout in one shot, I'll do it. And I'll come back in the evening and do shoulders with my hamstrings if I haven't done them in the morning. I go by how I feel. If I feel that I can do the whole workout in one shot, then I'll do it. If not, if*

I'm not energetic enough, I'll come back later and do it. In fact, closer to a contest that's what I do, I try and split it up to include my aerobics and my posing throughout the day with the routine.

Q: Do you have any set and rep scheme you follow with this system?

STEVE: *Not really. On the average, I'd stick to about 15 to 16 sets for my bigger body parts such as back, chest, and legs. For biceps and triceps I'll only go as high as 10 to 12 sets. I'll never, or at least rarely, go beyond 12 sets for contest preparation. In the off-season I'll bring those sets down just a little bit. In terms of reps, I'm always using a minimum of 12 for every body part except for legs, which I use 20, 25 and up because they're a big muscle. I don't believe that they can be stimulated by 10, 12, or 15 reps. Because it's such a big muscle, how are you going to hit those deep fibers with the same amount of reps that you use to train your biceps? I just don't believe that it can be done without using those higher reps.*

Q: What is the difference in your training in the off-season and in your precontest phase?

STEVE: *There isn't really a big difference, I just use less sets. The thing is, I've only been training for nine years, and I'm still learning about my physique. It's amazing, but I could still train like this for the next three or four months and not be satisfied* *and change everything around, or I might just end up doing something different as early as next week or a month from now. I'm learning. I've been doing different things for the past eight years, but basically I've been sticking around the same sets and reps scheme.*

Q: Given your nine years of training and what you have studied and learned, how long do you feel the average person can train without running the risk of overtraining?

STEVE: *It's very hard to say because everybody's different. A big problem is nutrition. I don't believe that you can overtrain a muscle if you are eating right, eating enough, and eating good quality foods. You can't overtrain, but you can underfeed a muscle; that's my theory. I've been training for my last contest for eight or nine months, and I can't remember a day that I've taken off. If I have it's been for five or six days in the last eight months. I keep myself paced properly, and I watch not only what I eat, but how I eat. I believe that by doing that you can continue training without overtraining. But then again, there were times when I felt that I should not have been training, and instead of going to the gym and training, I've just done some aerobics, went for a walk, did a little bit of posing just to keep myself active. I'm just such a highly strung guy that I can't relax and I've got to keep going. I've got to keep doing something.*

Q: Well, outside of the gym, what philosophy of life do you subscribe to? What's your worldview?

STEVE: *[laughs] This is a great question! You know what? I don't know if you've noticed this, but if you meet a lot of the pros, okay, we do diet for a contest, and some of us get irritable and moody and so forth, but I've always felt that you should be able to leave that at home. If you can't leave that kind of attitude at home, then why are you out here? I mean, you're out here meeting the public, you're meeting people. I get stopped on the street everywhere I go! I used to think that the only place where people knew me was in Canada, and they'd stop me at various places, like in a mall or shopping center, and say, "Hey, Steve Brisbois!" Man, in this business you have to be focused and keep a positive mental attitude. If you spend a couple of minutes talking to these people and you're nice to them, when they go out and talk to people and your name comes up, they'll say nice things about you too. If you keep a positive mental attitude, you'll do okay, but if you don't use your mind enough, then nobody's going to be able to help you with that.*

Q: Steve, you're not getting out of here until you give us your "magic arm routine!" What do you do, in terms of exercises, sets, and reps for those bloody great guns of yours?

STEVE: [laughs] Alright! For biceps, I'll do three exercises. I'll start with incline dumbbell curls, preacher curls, and standing one-arm dumbbell curls, and I'll do about 4 sets of each, which would consist of one little warm-up and then 3 good sets. I'll stick to about 12 reps for those exercises as well. Then, the next time I go into the gym, I'll do three different exercises again. I have to change around those exercises because that's the only way that I feel you're going to get quality all round. And I don't believe that heavy weights are necessarily the answer to bodybuilding success. How can you build muscle with heavy weight when a muscle will only respond to reps, and then at a high-rep level? To stimulate growth in a muscle—

and alright, I've only been training nine years, I'm still learning a lot, but I still believe that a muscle will only respond with higher reps. I can't remember a time when I've done below 10. In my off-season right now, I might go down to 10 reps, but even then I try to keep them at between 10 and 12 reps. I can't believe that a muscle will be stimulated to grow by doing fewer reps, by just doing "power" movements. If you can focus on slow, controlled movements and you can get through that exercise with 10 good reps, that's the only way a muscle is going to respond! I mean, 6, 7, 8 reps—I can't believe that that is going to help. All heavy training does is give you sore joints and tendons. Who needs that?

43

Brian Buchanan

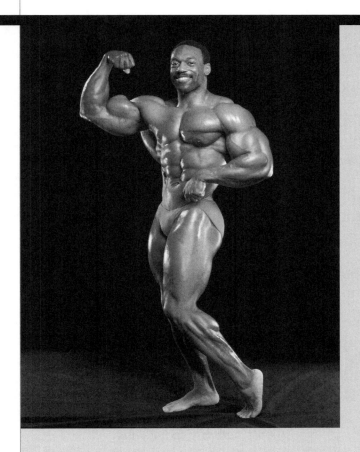

I had never met the massive Britisher Brian Buchanan before, but many others told me that he was one of nicest guys in bodybuilding and would be a great person to talk to. With that in mind, I wanted to find out how he built that fabulous body of his (his arms and that unbelievable V-taper), and to find out what he ate to assist him in building it. In other words, it was time to ask Brian Buchanan "20 Questions."

Q: In what way do you think that you have improved yourself?

> **BRIAN:** *I'm harder and bigger, and that is mainly due to diet.*

Q: Have you done anything different in your training?

> **BRIAN:** *I tore my rotator cuff six months ago in America, just after the Columbus show. So, training-wise, I had to change my training in that I had to train lighter; more sets and more reps because I couldn't train heavy. You see, I normally train heavier. And, for some reason, it's given me*

a look of more "quality," I suppose. My cuts are deeper. So in a way the injury was a blessing in disguise.

Q: Generally, how many sets would you do for each body part?

BRIAN: *Well, generally, I'd only do about 10 to 12 in the off-season, but come contest time that would increase to 16 to 20, but that would be mainly supersets. Constant work: 16 to 20 sets. To do a body part won't take me more than 15 to 20 minutes for about 20 sets.*

Q: What are your thoughts on the intensity/duration issue in bodybuilding today? Some authorities maintain that you should lift heavier weights and consequently don't do as many sets, and then you have the other schools such as the Schwarzenegger school saying that you have to do 20 sets, six days a week for two hours at a crack, twice a day.

BRIAN: *Nah. I tried training as the "Schwarzenegger School" suggests, and the only thing it does for me is overtrains me, and I get smaller. A lot smaller. I get "scraggy" [a Buchananism]. I've trained the other school, the 4 sets a body part school, and you don't get the "quality." So I believe that the muscle cell [laughs], we're going into physiology here, has got to be hit with different sorts of training methods all the time. It can't be straight heavy, heavy, heavy all the time if you want to get overall development. So I believe in like a*

medium or a cross between the two systems, especially before a contest.

Q: Do you think it's possible for a young bodybuilder starting out to make substantial gains on what traditionally is referred to as the three-day-per-week program?

BRIAN: *That's how I started, and I made huge gains on a three-day-a-week program. I'm a great believer in the traditional methods. I mean they work, that's why people stuck with them, and that's why they're "traditional."*

Q: Do you remember your initial routine when you did the three-day-per-week program?

BRIAN: *It was pure basics. It wasn't all that dissimilar to what I'm doing now. It was bench presses, flyes, squats, and leg extensions, chins and rows, just the basic stuff which isn't [laughing] really all that different from what I do now. I've just modified the basics and changed it in the way I string it together. Now I do basic movements before I do finishing movements. That's in the off-season. But now I train for shows, and as I said before, I do a lot of supersets. That means pre-exhaust supersets.*

Q: How do you like the technique of preexhaust?

BRIAN: *I like doing it before a show! It increases the intensity. I believe that when you train for a show you can keep at maximum intensity, training-wise, for about* *six weeks. Six days a week for six weeks. Diet-wise, maximum intensity for no more than three weeks. So the hardest part of my diet is for three weeks, and when I diet, I mean diet! I diet hard.*

Q: You'd have to, to get into the kind of condition that you're obviously in. At what point, in terms of effort and duration, would the overtraining threshold be reached?

BRIAN: Well, it changes from individual to individual. Me, personally, I'm comfortable takin' a hell of a lot of bashin' before my body breaks down. The only time I really break down is when I'm training for a show and I'm restricting my food intake. So I haven't any nutrients to allow me to recuperate. It does change from individual to individual, but I do feel that 10 to 12 sets is the maximum when you're seasoned. I don't do any more than 20 sets, even when training for a show.

Q: What role does aerobics play in your precontest preparation?

BRIAN: Quite a large role. Every day I do half an hour to an hour's biking depending on my condition. Plus it helps to stop your metabolism from slowing down. Your body's got a self-defense mechanism; if you're going to be restricting your calories for a long time, your body wants to stay alive and stay healthy, so it's going to slow its metabolism down in response to it. Doing aerobics keeps your metabolism up. I do aerobics all year round, so I stay in good

condition. I'm always in shape for guest spots.

Q: On that note, do you have any products that you'd like to plug? Any courses or books, because I know that you have a lot of fans who would like to know the answer to this question.

BRIAN: Yes, I'm bringing out [pauses and laughs] . . . everybody seems to be making comments about my waistline! I look in the mirror sometimes and I think, "Gee, it is a bit on the freaky side!" [we both laugh] Just a little bit, so I'm going to bring out a line of posters and they're going to be . . . something different. Just a humorous and sexy line of posters concentrating on my waistline. Then I'm going to bring out some courses on how I actually train my waist to get it as it is today.

Q: A final training question. What routine would you recommend for people who want to build up to a respectable size?

BRIAN: Stick to basics. You've got to remember, when you read a magazine and you're seeing somebody's precontest routine, that this guy's been training 10 to 20 years. He's reached the point where he's adding "polish" to his physique, and he's not building his physique any more. Stick to basics, and the only thing I can say is not to do too much. Don't do too many sets, under 10 to 12 sets, and do basics first and then shaping movements last. So you'd do bench presses and incline presses, followed with flyes for example.

Q: Would you recommend that on a three-day-a-week program such as you initially used?

> **BRIAN:** *I would recommend that on a three-day-a-week. That sort of training.*

Q: How many calories would you limit yourself to in attempting to rip up for a contest?

> **BRIAN:** *I never count calories. What I do is I count energy factors in my food, since it's mainly energy factors that will make you fat. By energy factors I mean carbohydrates and fat are the ones that your body uses for energy. If there's an excess of those it's going to store it as fat. Protein is normally used to rebuild lean tissue. So what I do is keep my protein as high as I possibly can. I don't keep any restriction at all on my protein; I eat a lot of protein—up to five pounds of fish a day before a contest to maintain my lean body mass. Also, to force my body to burn or use the internal fat it's got on it, I keep my energy factors in my diet low, so I'm forcing my body to obtain energy from its own stores. So my fats are low, my carbohydrates go from high to moderate to low, depending on how far I am out from the show. So all year round it's a low-fat diet, high protein, high carb—until like 12 weeks out, moderate carb—6 weeks out, moderate to low—3 weeks out, and then low. Very low. My low period lasts no longer than three*

weeks. That's my low, low period. I'd eat fish and vegetables and some fruit. And my carbohydrate intake would be from 60 to 80 carbohydrate grams per day for three weeks. And then I carb up two days before; I'd have 400 to 500 grams two days before.

Q: In the off-season, I'm guessing you'd eat a little bit more than that.

> **BRIAN:** *In the off-season, I'd have my carbohydrate intake at about 250 to 300. I want training energy, and that keeps me lean—I don't want to get fat. Another thing, as we were talking about how I had improved myself, for the past two years now I haven't "bulked up," and that has helped a lot! It's helped me get into better condition every time I compete. I don't have much to reduce for a contest. Months and months of training and there's no fatty tissue being built up in between the cells that you have to get rid of, so you just—it's like a slab of beef; you cut through a slab of beef and you'll see marbled fat—that's what a body without quality looks like. When you've got a slab of beef and you cut through it and you see nothing but lean, hard beef—I've reached that stage now because I'm dieting all the time.*

Q: What diet would you recommend for your readers who are going to follow the routine that you've outlined?

> **BRIAN:** *Once again, carbohydrates are extremely important for bodybuilders and*

for normal people as well. Low blood sugar is quite a common problem in society in general and not just bodybuilding. So always keep your carbohydrates up to a good level and keep your proteins high. So a good diet for me, meal by meal, would be as follows:

Breakfast: *I would start the day with pancakes with jam that has no sugar. You know, pure fruit jam. And with that we'd have some skim milk [turning to his girlfriend], wouldn't we, darlin'? [motioning toward his girlfriend] This is the chef here, she's the "inventor" of all these things [laughs]! Skim milk, and for protein, we'd have some egg whites and some . . . [laughs] what the hell do I have for protein in the morning? Ha! Maybe some white meats and some turkey or chicken. And then a few hours later . . .*

Lunch: *Some turkey and rice. I eat a lot of turkey and rice. A few hours later after that I'd have maybe some chicken and rice, and a few hours later . . . some more turkey and rice.*

Dinner: *[laughing] A few hours after that, some more chicken or turkey and rice or potatoes. You know, it's not a complicated diet, it's mainly foods that come from turkey, chicken, fish, rice, potatoes, fruits and vegetables.*

Q: An extra couple of training questions. What's your back routine?

BRIAN: *For years, it's remained roughly the same: I start out with chins, and I work up to doing 150-pound chins for 5 reps. This* was during my "building years." Then I do pulldowns and I work up to doing the stack plus plates and so forth. Then I would go into the long-range pulley, and then I would go into barbell rows. Each exercise would be for 3 or 4 sets. More likely 3—3 heavy ones after warming up; and the rep range would be 6 of each.

Q: What is the ratio of your chest to waist? And how tall are you?

BRIAN: *I have never weighed myself. Yesterday was the first time I have weighed myself in six years. I weighed 210, and I would have thought myself closer to 220, actually. Because I'm sure there were some mistakes with the weighing because there's no way that Peter Hensel weighs 240 pounds! There's no way Lee Haney weighs 230! Peter Hensel weighs 30 pounds more than me? No way! I won the Junior Britain weighing 200 pounds, and now I only weigh 210? I'm 5'9" or 5'10". So I mean there was some discrepancy there with the weight scales, so that's why I never bother looking at the scales, I know I look 20 to 30 pounds heavier than I actually am, and that's all that really matters to me. But there must be at least a 25-inch difference between my waist and my chest. At least, I mean bare minimum.*

Q: On a closing note, give me your "magic arm routine."

BRIAN: *[laughing]. Ah, the "secret," the "magic arm routine." Barbell curl, preacher* *curl, seated dumbbell 45s, and concentration curls. I've done that routine, and that's a bread-and-butter routine that I've done for years and it's worked so well for me. It's the same thing again, 3 or 4 sets of 6 reps per exercise. And it's worked well for me over the past 10 years.*

Q: And for triceps?

BRIAN: *Pushdowns, which I mix around with French press more or less 50-50. So it would be pushdowns, French press, dumbbell stretch, and one-arm cable. And that's another bread-and-butter routine that's worked so well for me. But readers shouldn't think I've been following that routine set for set, exercise for exercise, for the past 10 years without changing. They have to realize that that is my bread-and-butter routine that I've done for the majority of the time. We always change the exercises around regularly. You know, substitute that exercise for that exercise.*

44

Berry DeMey

At the 1988 Mr. Olympia, Berry DeMey caused quite a sensation. Not only did he place third overall in the contest, but his condition, already phenomenal, had markedly improved! There was talk that Lee Haney himself had been heard to worry out loud about the condition of the Dutchman, and certainly DeMey had the full support of the California crowd.

I [John] had seen DeMey compete once before, and that was at the 1986 Mr. Olympia competition, and I was impressed with his presentation and peak athletic condition, so naturally, I was pleased when I got the chance to interview him.

When I finally caught up with him, it was in the lobby of the Registry Hotel in Los Angeles. Berry was relaxing on the couch in the front foyer, looking through some clothing archetypes that he planned to introduce to the bodybuilding public at a later date. When I approached DeMey, he was poring over his clothing designs and looking actively for a cup of coffee. I introduced myself, complimented him on the improvement he so obviously made in his condition over the past year, told him of my journalistic intentions, and disclosed where the coffee machine could be located.

This last bit of information seemed to improve DeMey the most, and he agreed that if I would fetch for him a cup of the magic steaming liquid, he would gladly comply with my request for an interview and answer any and all questions I might have. Although he hadn't known it at the time, he had just signed himself up for "20 Questions."

Q: Your lumbar area looked incredible at the Olympia! How did you achieve this look?

BERRY: *Well that's also part of the fat percentage. Sometimes you don't see the details that you already have because it is still covered up with some fat. At the '88 Olympia, I was really low on body fat. Another thing that I did in order to look a little more, I won't say slim, but to achieve a more aesthetic look was to lose even more weight from around my midsection. Even my belt was smaller this year. To achieve this, diet played a big part, but also my training was different. For example, in my leg workouts, I trained my* legs really hard. I don't think I've ever trained my legs so hard! Very intensive. I didn't do very heavy squats, but I did "strip-offs" with really high intensity and a lot of sets and reps. ["Strip-offs" are when Berry strips weight off the bar when he reaches failure. He then continues with the exercise using this reduced poundage.] Normally I would do those kinds of things in two leg sessions, but here I did it in one session without stopping. Normally I would leave it at that and not do any aerobics on my day of leg training, but this time, I'd move to the stairs right away after a leg workout and run up the stairs. I think that the stairs are really hard on the legs, and it's even more of an anabolic exercise than squats. Plus it really gives you good definition in your legs, and I know that my body really slimmed down from running the stairs.

Q: What has been your most result-producing training routine? The four-day-a-week? Three-day-a-week?

BERRY: I always train three days on, one day off. The only change that I do is perform some aerobic activity on one of my off days. Aerobic things like running, calves, and abs, etc. I'm always training to some degree on every day of the week for the last two months before a contest. On the first day I would do chest and arms, on the second day I would do legs so that my upper body can totally rest, and the third day I would do back and shoulders. Then I

have a day off so that my upper body has a rest again, and then I start the cycle over again.

Q: Did you do this routine for the Olympia?

BERRY: Yes. Actually I never change it. The only thing that I change about my training before a contest is the intensity! I still train heavy, even in the off-season I train heavy, but I also do a lot of reps. A lot of guys cut back on reps, but I still do a lot of reps and sets in the off-season because in body-building, people think that the limit to building mass in terms of repetitions is about 8—I don't think so! If you do real "giant sets" with strip-offs and even go up to 20 reps in one set—there's no way that that can be construed as a catabolic exercise. It's an anabolic exercise; as long as you have time enough to recover. However, I can't do my strip-off sets if I haven't made the muscle tired beforehand. So I need to do a kind of "preexhaustion" system. What I do for that is to start with, for example, chest, and start to train that muscle group with a basic exercise and heavy weight and then perform 6, 8, or at the most 10 reps—using this movement as a kind of preexhaustion. After that, I continue the movement with more sets and reps, thereby pushing the set further than I would have otherwise.

Q: How many sets would you perform for each body part?

BERRY: *That's difficult to say. Sometimes I would go crazy with sets, but it usually varies between 10 and 20 sets. It depends on whether it's the first day in the week or the second day in the week.*

Q: What are your thoughts on intensity versus duration? For example, some bodybuilders say that you have to do a lot of sets, whereas other bodybuilders say that you shouldn't do a lot of sets.

BERRY: *I think that for me at least, it's definitely a combination. Like I said, I need it if I start to do that strip-off technique with a lot of sets from the beginning of my training, I can go on for hours. So I really need the heavy training with less reps and short sets. In the beginning for the prefatigue. It's a really important part of it.*

Q: You mentioned that before a contest you include a lot of aerobics in your training. What role do aerobics play in your precontest preparation?

BERRY: *I diet for a long time, but I never like to go below 3,500 calories. That means that in order to get ripped I would rather do more training than eat less. Therefore I need to do aerobics such as the stairs or riding the bike. I love to do running, but I think that my body weight is too heavy. I don't feel really comfortable when I run, and I think that the chance of incurring an injury is greater for a person my size. So I prefer to either bike or do the stairs, for 20 minutes, three times a week.*

Q: What routine would you recommend for the readers of this magazine who want to increase their muscle mass?

BERRY: *Well I'd look at diet, number one. I'd have them figure out how many calories they'd burn in one day, and then if they want to gain weight they should increase that number and, conversely, if they want to lose weight they should drop their calorie intake somewhat and make sure that they cut out all the fat and have a split-up of 60 to 70 percent carbs and the rest protein. They should train using the basics. I've never really strayed from the basics myself. Only the intensity has become higher in all my years of training. I would have them start with basic things and don't overtrain. If somebody who's even been training for two or three years tried to train the way that I do now, they'd end up overtrained. I'm sure about that. Keep the sets down low, and definitely don't train more than four days per week.*

Q: How many calories do you limit yourself to in attempting to "rip up" for a contest?

BERRY: *The lowest I go is 3,500. For about four months I've been between 3,500 and 4,000. In the off-season I wouldn't be much higher, maybe about 5,000. Well, actually I went up again for the Olympia because I reached my peak early. So what*

I did was to go down for a little while, but then I was just playing with the calories and went up again. I was just maintaining. I mean, I had the fat percentage at the point that I wanted it at to enter the contest, so all that I had to do was to maintain my weight.

Q: When you're "ripping up" for a contest, do you prefer the low-calorie, low-carbohydrate, or low-fat diet?

BERRY: *What do those guys who drop all carbohydrates from their diet do? [laughing] Especially if they want to keep up their calorie intake—what are they going to eat, 3,500 calories of protein? I mean Brian Buchanan does it. If I were to do it—well, it makes no sense at all. First of all, your body has a limited need for protein, and anything over that amount will be transformed into glycogen, and faster than we all thought years ago. So it's just harder for the body to break down protein into sugar to fuel your workouts, when you could save your body the extra labor by feeding yourself an adequate supply of carbohydrate to begin with. It's better to figure out how much protein your body needs every day. In my case, I take in about 260 grams of protein from my foods, plus my amino acids, while the rest of my calorie intake is mainly complex carbs.*

Q: What are your future goals both inside and outside of bodybuilding?

BERRY: *Well, this past competition was really something for me. Aside from being just another Olympia again—as it was my fourth Olympia, and all those other four times I've always been in the top six—this time I really want the title. I mean really want it! If I don't get it this year, then I'm really going to ask myself some questions. Right now, with the results from the 1988 Olympia, it's possible to make some decisions, and one of the decisions is to continue. I see where I can improve—I still haven't reached my full potential yet. I mean, even after all these years of training, I improved to such a marked degree this past year that I know how to do it again—beyond even my condition at this past contest. So I want to continue to improve and go for the Mr. Olympia next year. That's my primary future goal for bodybuilding.*

Q: Who have been your greatest influences?

BERRY: *The fellow who's influenced me the most is Rich Gaspari. Particularly before the '88 Olympia because we trained in the same gym and had a lot of talks. Actually, I discovered from this that in the last two weeks, I've done a lot of the same things that he was doing training-wise and held a lot of the same theories behind it all. Even yesterday, [the day of the 1988 Mr. Olympia contest] we were beside each other in the lineup as we had been at all the Grand Prix contests last year. We were pumping up together yesterday. So he* *really inspires me! And then yesterday at the Olympia the top three called out were Lee Haney, Rich Gaspari, and myself [this was also the final placing of the contest] during the prejudging and I thought to myself, "I've already won my personal contest"—to be called out to compare with that class of bodybuilder proved to me that I'd already won a victory of sorts and certainly testified to the improvement that I'd made this past year.*

Q: What philosophy of life do you subscribe to?

BERRY: *For me it would be to have something in my life that gives my life satisfaction, no matter what it is. If you're satisfied with it and can be happy with it, that's all that matters. Not everybody has to be a doctor or a lawyer in order to be successful in life. If somebody has his own little shop and he doesn't make a lot of money but he's happy with it, and he has his family— that's what it's all about! It depends on the individual in question, as every individual demands something else to be happy. For example, I'm really satisfied with my way of life right now. I don't feel there are any rules to follow—just be happy. That's all. And what's "happiness" again is just personal satisfaction, and that's something you'll have to arrange for yourself. I always say that "whatever it takes, be happy." If it takes a 20-inch arm to be happy, well then, make sure you get the 20-inch arm. If it takes getting a big car—then get the big car.*

Q: Well, speaking of felicity, what brings you happiness in this world? Bodybuilding?

BERRY: *Well, not bodybuilding in particular. To have success brings me happiness. I put so much time and effort into training, and sometimes it really impinges on my private life, so I wouldn't say that bodybuilding, per se, really brings me a lot of happiness. At least I want to have success. I don't want to end up frustrated after years and years of competing and end up placing lower and lower. This year was the first time that I placed in the final of the Olympia, so it's enough for me to continue. I would really be wasting my life if I was, for example, in this shape and ended up in, say, eighth place or something, and it's not a point of giving up or being a coward or anything. It takes even more courage to make the decision. They write in the magazines all the time things like "Ah, he's got guts, he goes on all the time, he's not a loser despite his consistently low placings, etc." But sometimes a competitor can carry on a bit too long, and I think it becomes stupid. I mean, why do it at all? For what? If you don't have the genetics to become Mr. Olympia, why kill yourself with the strict dieting and brutal training and so many other things? Don't misunderstand me, I will do bodybuilding all of my life. That's my lifestyle—I can't live without it! [laughs] I'm a bodybuilding junkie! Really, it's not that you have to do it at that level your whole life. If you can't—and I'm not talking about* *myself because I've got a good idea of my potential in this sport—then don't frustrate yourself. Be objective and realize your limitations.*

Q: What do you think are the ingredients of a successful relationship, either emotional or financial?

BERRY: *You've mentioned two things that have two very different ingredients to be successful. For example, the "business" me is the fake me. However, I like doing it, so it's a part of me, but it's not how I am when I'm at home. I'm a totally different person. Again, I guess I really can't say "fake," but I am different. At home I'm really quiet. Sometimes I like to be alone. But the ingredients for a successful emotional relationship are totally different than they would be for a successful business relationship. For example, my girlfriend; in the first place, we love each other very much, she's really into it and she really wants to be a part of everything I do. She's really into the lifestyle. Actually, we're like a company in a way. Whenever I prepare to enter a competition, we both take part in it. I do the workouts and show the results, but we both are part of the final result. Aside from all the romantic stuff—which of course is really important, but you can't build an emotional house just on that as your sole foundation. The most important thing for a couple to be in a relationship is friends. If I go out to a movie or a party, I like to do it with my girlfriend*

because she is a friend. That's really important.

Q: What are your thoughts on the drug issue in bodybuilding today? Are steroids a real, legitimate threat, or has the press sensationalized their significance?

BERRY: *I think that the use or abuse—whatever you want to call it—of anabolic steroids are as bad, or good, or large scale or small scale, or positive or negative in bodybuilding as they are in every other sport. Only bodybuilding has the "name." If somebody is watching television and sees the Tour de France—the European cycling tour—they think it's normal that the guy they're watching can ride like that; that many hours straight and cover that kind of distance. In fact, his doing that is just as abnormal as my arm! So because we as bodybuilders show it in a way that people cannot imagine that it could be natural, so they think it has to be "magic" or that we have to take stuff. They don't realize that we've had to work for whatever gains we have—however abnormal they may appear! These people can't experience what it's like. How it really is. To go through those four months of training and dieting. I love it, because even after a competition I feel kind of "down" because there's an emptiness for a while. I'm glad when I can prepare for a contest, although it is often difficult. I like it.*

Q: What effect has your success in bodybuilding had on your personal life?

BERRY: *Well, I've been doing exhibitions since 1983, when I came in second behind Bob Paris, so I've gotten used to it for a while now. Particularly when I won the World title in 1985, it started, which has been three years now. I think people like me because I always try to be myself.*

Q: Except when the fake you is conducting business practices . . .

BERRY: *[laughs] I like to say things as they are and I enjoy what I'm doing. But I'm recognized far more now due to my body-building pursuits than I ever was before I became a bodybuilder—which is great!*

Q: What would be the three most important things in your life right now, and why would they be?

BERRY: *That's a really good question that you've asked. Three most important things in my life? My happiness. Again, everybody works on that for themselves every day, even though they don't realize it. Again, to do something either indirectly or directly that makes you feel comfortable mentally and physically is, by my definition, happiness. The other two components would be things that would lead to the creation of happiness. Last year, of course, I was thinking about the Mr. Olympia and placements and everything, but the one thing that most people don't realize and that inspires me the most for training so hard this year was the moment right after the last Mr. Olympia, when I came backstage with my clothes on and my bag on my shoulder and I saw some friends of mine and they said, "Hello, how are you doing?" It wasn't like yesterday's reaction at all, when they said, "Oh man! you improved!!" So when people start noticing things like that, it really inspires me to train even harder! And even though I didn't win the contest, it still inspires me to train hard!*

Q: Do you think there's room for improvement in this sport and, if so, at what level do you think it should be improved?

BERRY: *The professional level still has a lot of room for improvement. I mean, they're really doing a great job; people like Ben and Joe Weider and of course Wayne Demilia, but still, if you compare it with any other sport, there's no other major sport that's so well organized just on one side.*

45

Rich Gaspari

If there is one bodybuilder who is responsible for ushering in the "ripped" era of bodybuilding, that one body-builder would be Rich Gaspari. Until Gaspari, bodybuilders were either massive with a moderate definition or quite defined with moderate muscle mass. But then Rich Gaspari came along with muscle mass to rival that of a bull elephant and a level of vascularity and definition heretofore unseen but on skinned cadavers in university anatomy classes.

Gaspari brought with him from his native New Jersey a brand-new level and standard of physique by which bodybuilding contests are still being judged! At this year's Mr. Olympia, Gaspari's muscle mass was up considerably from the year before in Rimini, Italy, and his famed definition was still light-years ahead of his closest competitor.

Nevertheless, history will record that Rich Gaspari placed fifth in this year's Olympia, losing out to the lines of Shawn Ray, the flair in posing and symmetry of physique of Lee Labrada, and the Legend Maker himself, Lee Haney. Despite the low placing, the fact that

Gaspari had made marked improvements in his physique was at once palpable and impressive. He's organized his own contest in his home state of New York, he's in the midst of opening his own gym, he's the physique that has brought the sport of bodybuilding into the 1990s, he's Rich Gaspari—and he speaks of all these things in "20 Questions."

Q: Rich, after placing second to Lee Haney all those years in the Olympia contest, how did you handle last year's fourth-place finish in that contest?

RICH: Well, after last year's contest I was devastated because I was always, like you said, second in the Olympia. I entered that competition, I thought, in top shape and fully expected to win, so coming in fourth was really a big disappointment. However, I realized from the photographs, looking at it and being analytical, that I wasn't in the "Gaspari" shape I should have been in. I though afterwards that I probably should have been in third place, but it really doesn't matter. The point was I came in fourth, and I said, it's time to do my homework, that's over with and it's time for me to go for next year's Mr. Olympia.

Q: It was "business as usual" after the setback?

RICH: Absolutely! The entire year I set my goals for what I felt I needed to come into the '90 Olympia. One of the big factors was that, because of the drug testing, I did want to structure my training so that I could recuperate more as I would be off the drugs, yet come into the contest just as big as Rich Gaspari is known for. I didn't want any changes in my physique in terms of loss of size.

Q: What about modifications or improvements to your physique for this year's contest?

RICH: I did want to make improvements to my physique and bring up certain areas that some of the critics have said that I didn't have. One of the points that I really wanted to work on was the width and inner thickness of my back. I really worked on building up both the thickness and the width of my back to give the illusion of looking even wider than I normally do. In addition, I also concentrated throughout the year on increasing arm size and decreasing waist size.

Q: How did you accomplish all of these things?

RICH: Well, I knew I had to concentrate really hard on all of these things. For my back, I put in the muscle priority principle; I trained my back first in my routine when I was full of energy and cycled my methodology. The first three months I concentrated on the basics: heavy deadlifts, heavy barbell rows, and those types of exercises that build the thickness into the middle of the back. I also concentrated on performing a lot of width exercises: the chins, the pulldowns, and again, just working that muscle group first to get the muscle to grow better and by concentrating on it as I trained it. It's important also to remember that I just didn't heave heavy weight; you have to concentrate on the muscle being worked and the form of the lift itself. It really worked! The more I concentrated on the form, I also concentrated not only on low reps but high reps; I'd go from 8 reps to 18 reps. I'd traditionally always done low repetitions, but I've never gotten results as good as when I switched over to high reps. It not only thickened my back but also gave me that intricate detail that I needed and that a lot of my fellow competitors had, and I felt that I could have too, if only I'd make the correct training adjustments.

Q: How did you increase the size of your arms?

RICH: *You know, I'd always overtrained my arms in the past. I've always done between 12 and 16 sets because I'd read in all the books that was how Arnold and everyone trained their arms. But I found out this year, that I have trained my arms a lot less—especially when it came down to dieting for the contest. I went down to as low as 8 sets for arms, and that was it. I trained them with very high intensity, however, say 3 sets of a different exercise and then one more exercise for another 2 sets, and that was enough for me to not only maintain my existing mass, but also to increase the size of my arms.*

Q: You also mentioned that you were able to somehow decrease the size of your waist, an area that some critics have said was too blocky or asymmetrical. How did you do this?

RICH: *For my waist training, I'd always been leery about using weights because I'd been afraid that if you work muscles with weights, you'll make them grow—which I didn't want to do with my waist! Then I read another theory that if you "overwork" a muscle it will become stringier and eventually come down to a smaller size. So what I did after last year's Olympia was to start training abs every other day and then 20 weeks out from this year's contest, I started training them every day. Now every day I would do 25 to 30 reps of leg raises, side crunches, crunches—everything I could think of to do for abs, and I'd do it after my workout every day. I'd do 3 or 4 sets of each exercise, or a total of about 15 to 16 sets for abs every day. All my training partners hated me because I'd make them do abs with me every day! But it paid off because I've always had trouble getting detail into my intercostal area, and I had it this year, and the increased training really made my waist streamlined. A lot of other factors helped me too, not the least of which was the absence of drugs because drugs tend to retain water, which can make your waist look bloated. However, the heavy training that I did in the off-season allowed me to keep my mass, and the overtraining* that I did for my abs before the contest allowed me to make my waist streamlined.

Q: You also mentioned that because of the drug test, you had to space your workouts out more to allow for fuller recuperation. What system did you use?

RICH: I trained on a four-day split. Usually I would be on a three-on/one-off all year round, but this time around I trained only once a day during the off-season on a four-on/one-off system. So I worked my entire body over four days and then took a day off and then trained for another four days again, and it worked tremendously. It gave me more recuperation for each body part that I was training. I then moved back on to the three-on/one-off—but only the last 16 weeks out when I trained with another bodybuilder who was getting ready for a competition. I wanted to get into "contest training" a bit earlier than a lot of other competitors, but it seemed to work, as it got me harder a lot quicker. What I did was pace my workouts; when I got into three-on/one-off, twice-a-day training, if I seemed to "lean out" too much, I'd cut back on the sets. I didn't want any changes in my physique in terms of loss of size.

Q: How about aerobics? Did you perform much of these during your contest training?

RICH: Yes I did, usually in the form of either the Stairmaster or by riding the bike. I even did this in the off-season for about three or four times a week, and when I wanted to get even leaner, I'd up it to every day. And when I started to look too lean, and I was looking this way about six weeks out from the contest, I'd started cutting out the cycling completely because I knew that it would only burn into my muscle mass, and from there, I've got to say that the last two weeks before the 1990 Mr. Olympia I just basically glided in. I was ready, so I just did fewer sets with more crunching, more squeezing, lighter weight, and more quality training, and my physique improved to the point where it was far better than it's ever been and, if you know Rich Gaspari, you know he comes to a show only to win!

Q: So if you could condense what you've learned from all of this, what would it be?

RICH: That when I cut back on my sets, I got bigger, and also that I had to cut back on my total training. When I was training twice a day every day it was too much for my body, whereas training once a day and cutting back on sets allowed my body to recuperate better. I also didn't pig out or eat anything bad since April, when I had to guest pose at my own show, the Rich Gaspari Classic. I ate only good food, lots of complex carbs. I ate five times a day; every three hours I'd eat moderate protein, only one gram per pound of body weight and no fat, and it really worked.

Q: Could you elaborate on your diet a bit more?

RICH: *Sure. The carbs gave me a lot of energy. I took a lot of amino acids before each meal to replenish my body. Usually branched chain amino acids, before and after, to replenish my muscles. I took a lot of different supplements to give more energy to further my training and, with this year's Mr. Olympia, the bodybuilders are becoming more knowledgeable about nutrition. The thing about steroids is that they make you lazy. You don't have to know as much about nutrition and training methods with steroids, but believe me, you can still make gains without them.*

Q: What were your thoughts when the IFBB decided to implement steroid testing in the men's pro ranks?

RICH: *I was generally pleased that they decided to do it. It certainly didn't bother me. I just changed my methods of training and, you know, just do what you have to do. I still think that a lot of the guys are going to be good up there, but I think there's going to be a lot of changes up there on that same stage, especially in those guys who didn't do their homework! A lot of people asked me before this contest, "Are you as hard or sharp without the drugs?" I'm just as hard and looking better than I've ever looked—a lot of it, though, is dependent on diet.*

Q: Do you count calories before a contest in an attempt to "rip up"?

RICH: *Oh definitely. I do count calories. I have a book that tells me all of the caloric contents of various foods so that I know exactly the nutritional value of each and every type of food that I eat. From the last 20 weeks out from a contest is when I really clamp down on my calories. The rest of the year I just more or less guess what I'm consuming, but I write down everything from protein, carbs, and fat. In the off-season I take in about 3,500 to 4,000 calories a day, but closer to the show, I'll reduce that to no less than 2,600 to 3,500 calories a day. Right now [the day before the Olympia], I'm taking in about 3,200 to 3,500 because my body fat went down and for me to maintain my muscle, I had to increase my calorie intake.*

Q: What about the Rich Gaspari Classic. How did that come about?

RICH: *Well, I lived In New Jersey all my life, and I wanted to put something back into the sport because I've gotten a lot out of it. New Jersey helped me out, so I wanted to put on my own show there for the people, and the turnout was fantastic for a first-time show! The caliber of people was incredible, and I had over 70 competitors coming out—which is a really large number for a bodybuilding show—to compete. I hope to make the Rich Gaspari Classic an annual affair.*

Q: And you've also plans afoot to open your own gym, isn't this true?

RICH: *Hey, I see you've been doing your homework! Yeah, that's right, I'll be opening my own gym on October 6 in Ocean Township, New Jersey, so I'm pretty excited about that.*

Q: Rich, your muscle mass to body-fat ratio is legendary in the sport. What's your training routine?

RICH: *Well, I train in the off-season on a four-on/one-off system, and I use predominantly basic exercises. Chins, barbell rows, heavy deadlifts, T-bar rows, these are the core of my back routine; then behind-the-neck pulldowns and seated cable rows round out the rest of my back routine. I also sometimes did hyperextensions, but I always changed the workout. This routine would be what I used on a heavy day. Then on another day's back workout I'd start out with 4 to 5 sets, then I would do bench rows, where I would lie on the bench with a bent bar doing more strict form for 12 to 15 reps and pull the bar up until it touched the bottom of the bench. From there I would do cable rows with a two-handled grip, which allows me to fully contract my back better—I'd do about 3 to 4 sets of these exercises and then, say, pullovers for about 4 sets. But I would always strive to change my workouts—the heavy day would include deadlifts, the other workout would be lighter but would*

allow me to work on more detail. From there I would start on chest training, which would include exercises like incline bench press with dumbbells for 4 or 5 sets and incline flyes for 3 or 4 sets, and then I would use a vertical bench press machine, which really builds up the fullness in your chest! I didn't really bench press that much. For dumbbell bench press I'd do maybe 3 or 4 sets of 8 to 10 reps, and then maybe pec dec and 2 to 3 sets of decline flyes, and that was my chest workout.

Q: What about those "guns" of yours? What did you do to build your arms up to such an impressive degree?

RICH: *On arm training, I did maybe 8 to 10 sets total for either biceps or triceps. For biceps, I'd do 3 or 4 sets of incline curls, 3 sets of preacher curls, and 2 or 3 sets of what I call "outside" curls, which are done by sitting on a preacher bench with your back resting against the padding so that your elbows are on the preacher bench, and you would curl your arms up into what would resemble a double biceps pose. Curling this way I feel really made my biceps fuller on the double biceps pose. I hit on this exercise when I was trying to figure out a way to get the inner head of the biceps to stand out more when I was doing a double biceps pose. My arms looked good when they were at my side, but I wanted them to look good when they were in a double biceps pose, and doing* this exercise, when my elbows were stationary on the preacher bench, really hit that area for me. For triceps I'd do overhead extensions, which is a great movement for thickness and overall size in the triceps muscle. Then I would go to triceps rope pushdowns for 3 or 4 sets of each, and that would be my triceps routine.

Q: What about your shoulder routine?

RICH: For shoulders I'd try and work out harder, but I always try to change this workout around too. I'd start out with, say, "Arnold presses" [an exercise wherein you pick up a pair of dumbbells and press them overhead while rotating your wrists so that your palms go from a position where they're facing each other at your shoulders, to a point where your knuckles face each other at a point above your head] and then superset those with side laterals for 4 supersets each, going back and forth. Then, I would go on to another side lateral movement, this time on an incline bench, doing 2 sets of 8 to 12 reps. All my rep ranges are between 8, 10, and 12, except precontest, when I'll go as high as 15 reps. Anyway, from there, I would go on to bent laterals, but I'd also do these on an incline bench so that my chest was stationary and my arms were overhanging and do reps that way because I feel that I can do my reps a lot more strict. Then I would do a cable lateral or rear delt machine for the rear delts for 3 sets each, and that would be my shoulder workout.

My trap workout would include shrugs, and how I do them is to sit on a bench with a bent bar, which I feel is stricter, and you can come straight up with it instead of having the bar in front of you, which requires that you pull it up and out in front of you. I'd do this for 3 or 4 sets.

Q: You and your glutes, quads, calves, and hamstrings are renowned in the sport. Do you do anything special to develop your lower body?

RICH: For legs, I always start out with leg extensions for 4 to 6 sets, going up in weight and keeping my reps between 10 to 12. I'd go up in weight until I'd get to the heaviest weight that I could do where I could still get 12 reps, and then I would decrease the weight by doing descending sets from 8 to 10 reps. From here I would go to a heavy exercise such as front squats or leg presses for 4 or 5 sets for 12 to 15 reps. I would always use a moderate weight and increase the weight slowly. I would often use the front squat machine, which removes the stress you would normally feel in your lower back and places it all on your legs. I'd use that for about 3 sets, and that would be it for leg training. So I only do 4 to 6 sets of leg extensions, 5 sets of either leg presses or front squats. As far as calves go, I'd train them every other day. I would do 5 sets of donkey calf raises and 5 sets of seated calf raises. I would do the 5 sets of donkeys on the machine and do 12 to 15 reps on my first set, which is a warm-up, and then increase the weight until it's my heaviest weight and do maybe 15 reps, and then do drop sets. I always do drop sets on my last 4 sets. My training partners always suffer when they do calves with me! From there, I'd go on to seated calf raises for 5 sets and increase the weight for all of those sets until I get to the heaviest weight.

Q: What do you think are the important factors in successful bodybuilding?

RICH: There are several factors. I can't just say that "intensity" or "4 sets to failure" is the best way to work a body part. I feel that I have to work a muscle in parts, like the back. The back is a very intricate muscle group; you've got the upper back, the lower back, the inner thickness, the outer thickness, so you have to work on that muscle from all different angles. Saying that, it's also important to work out with intensity in working that muscle from all different angles. The biceps are like that also. You can't just work one head; you have to work both the inner and the outer head. I believe partly in what Mike Mentzer used to say about intensity, but I don't believe it fully because I feel you have to work that muscle from different angles and also work that muscle with intensity.

Q: Rich, as you know, most of the people in gyms are noncompetitive but still want to pack on the muscle mass. Is there any advice you could give them in their quest?

RICH: Well, whenever I wanted to put on mass and size, I always stuck to the basic exercises. A big mistake I see all the time is people in the gym trying to do the training of a professional during his precontest phase. Stick to the basics. For the back, try and build the thickness by sticking to the deadlifts, the bent barbell rows, pulldowns, pullovers—just the heavy basic exercises. For the chest, heavy inclines, the heavy benches, the heavy flyes. Stay away from the cable crossovers and other "precontest" types of exercises. For shoulders, basic behind-the-neck presses, dumbbell presses, side laterals, bent-over laterals, and for biceps, stick to the basic barbell and dumbbell curls. Keep your sets lower, get to the point where you're not only doing the basics, but it's also very important not just to heave heavy weight, but to do it in good form and control the muscle that you're training. If you don't control the muscle you're not going to be able to train it correctly. Train on a four-day split, like I do in the off-season, working your entire body over four days, take a day off, and then work your entire body again over four more days. Such a system of training allows for better recuperation and, let's face it, you have to recover fully between training sessions for each muscle group, or there's no way you're going to grow. The four-

on/one-off split I've found to be great for packing on the mass, but if you don't feel recovered on this system, you should maybe switch to a four-on, two-off system, which will give you a bit more recovery time. Here's how I divide up my routine: day one would be shoulders and abs; day two would be legs and calves; day three would be back, abs, and calves; day four would be arms, forearms, and/or calves; and day five I would take off. And keep your sets to 8 to 12 for each muscle group; don't be afraid to cut down to 6 to 8 sets if you become overtrained.

Don't give yourself limitations. I was told by critics that I never had what it took to win a major contest. I've won every major contest there is with the exception of the Mr. Olympia, and I've placed second in that contest so many times I've lost count. Train hard, believe in yourself, and you will eventually succeed!

46

Lee Haney

Those in attendance at the 1990 Mr. Olympia contest in Chicago witnessed a changing of the old order. Arnold Schwarzenegger's record of six straight Mr. Olympia titles was not only broken—but the title of "the greatest body-builder of all time" changed hands. Now that title belongs to Lee Haney.

The man from Georgia won his seventh straight Mr. Olympia title in front of a packed auditorium of 5,000-plus fans (and millions more watching on cable television throughout the world). And he did it in convincing style and, as always, with a lot of class.

Haney is a rarity in the sport of bodybuilding: not only does he have (in the opinion of many fans) the greatest physique in the sport's history, but he's also a gentleman in the purest sense of the term.

The year 1990 was quite a year for Haney. Not only did he set the record for consecutive Mr. Olympia wins, but he also started to franchise his Animal Kingdom gym chain; he came out with a brand-new line of home and commercial equipment; he had a day named in his honor in his home city of Atlanta; he trained the new heavyweight boxing champion of the world, Evander Holyfield, for his successful title fight against Buster Douglas; and then, to top it off, Haney became a father for the second time when his wife Shirley gave birth to a beautiful baby girl named, appropriately enough, Olympia. It seemed only natural to ask one of the greatest bodybuilders of all time "20 Questions."

Q: Lee, you've achieved what seemed the impossible—won an unprecedented seventh straight Mr. Olympia title. How did you prepare for such an accomplishment?

LEE: Well, this time I trained in Texas because I needed more concentration and I wanted to come in with some really sharp combinations. It took going that extra distance to bring about what we were looking for in my appearance at the Mr. Olympia. At home in Atlanta there were just too many things going on to distract me, but Texas worked out just fine.

Q: This was the first Mr. Olympia to be drug tested and, according to Dr. Bob Goldman, head of the IFBB Doping Committee, you had the "clearest sample" of all the competitors, so obviously you found the right training mode. What exactly was your training routine this year?

LEE: Well, it consisted of training twice a day and eating a lot of good food and getting a lot of rest. That's something I

wasn't able to do while living in Atlanta and having a lot of business to take care of, so my training partner and I went to Houston. We used a regimen similar to the three-on/one-off routine. In fact, sometimes it was three-on/one-off and sometimes three-on/two-off, so we more or less trained instinctively. We used a different sort of approach to our training although we still trained twice a day, once in the morning and once in the evening. After the morning workout, we'd get back and have a meal, take a nap, wake up, have another meal, relax a little, have another snack, watch some TV, work on some posing or whatever. Then we'd go back to the club in the evening for our second workout, then get back and have a meal and then have a snack at the end of that day. In terms of training, we did some giant set routines, superset routines and also a basic ballistic type of routine to keep the mass up because that's very, very important. I found that ballistic workouts as you're training down for a contest are very important to keep that mass in the muscle. A lot of athletes make the mistake of going on these diets and then going into a high-rep mode. But the white muscle cells are no longer being worked, and they just lie there, getting smaller and smaller. As a result, you lose muscle size. So I made sure that in our routine we maintained the ballistic training to give proper stimulus to the white muscle cells and, at the same time, by doing the rhythmic sort of move-

ments, we also stimulated the red muscle cells.

Q: What's the breakdown of the body parts that you trained with this system?

LEE: We would do biceps, calves, abs, and bicycle in the morning; then that evening, we'd do chest, triceps, and some more aerobics, and that would be our Monday routine. Tuesday would be frontal thighs in the morning; in the evening it would be hamstrings, calves, and abs. Wednesday might be back, abs, and a little aerobics in the morning; in the evening, shoulders, calves, and some more aerobics. Thursday would be a day of relaxation! During that time we might do some sprinting or light aerobic activity, then go to a movie, relax, and just rest the mind and the body.

Q: Did you do anything different this time?

LEE: Well, we changed the workouts. Of course when you do giant sets, you're going to do fewer sets because giant sets really blast the muscle and get the blood in there. When I was training my arms with giant sets, I would average around 12 sets, which is low compared to some routines, but it's a killer! Then we'd do a superset, from which it doesn't take as long to recover as it does from a giant set. Then you have your basic training, which is more or less a ballistic form of training and which requires the least amount of recovery, but you've got to be careful of your joints.

Q: By ballistic, you're referring to quickly executed, explosive movements?

LEE: Right. Heavy benches, heavy squats, heavy shoulder presses, heavy barbell curls, things like that.

Q: We'll get back to training in a moment. Now that you've had time to assess the experience, how does it feel to know that you've broken Arnold's consecutive Mr. Olympia wins record?

LEE: Man, it feels great! I guess it's sort of sunk in now, but you know, it's still not over. I'm the kind of person who when he does something says, "Well, seven in a row—great!" But still it's only seven overall. I want eight. When I do eight, I'll say, "Okay, this job is finished, let's go Yee-hi! and Yahoo!" Right now it's like some unfinished business with me!

Q: Not only did you train yourself, but you also trained Evander Holyfield, the new heavyweight champion of the world. What was the program you put him on?

LEE: What we did was mix camps with Evander. I had one of my assistant personal trainers, Charles Jordin, and one of my own personal training partners, Fred Richards, who's a retired Marine, keeping tabs on him. Evander has over 17 years of military experience, so I was surrounded by some really tough, disciplined people. I don't like half-steppers. In the training routine for Evander and myself, we used a combination of ballistic and rhythmic that gave us both mass and quality. We didn't set out to make him a bodybuilder or anything, we just kept him at two exercises for a body part with the exception of legs, where we had him doing leg extensions, leg curls, and squats. He trained two body parts each workout and trained four days a week. We trained him with basic movements, benches for chest, barbell curls for arms, squats for legs, overhead presses for the shoulders. But once you give a fighter strength, you have to turn it into explosive strength. That's where other things came in, like drills and plyometrics. Fred Hatfield played a vital role in that, and he's the best in the world in exercise physiology.

Q: You were also at the fight itself. What was your reaction?

LEE: *It happened just the way I thought it would, but I didn't think it would happen so quick! I expected Evander to at least work up a sweat! But Buster Douglas was so fat! A lot of the media were negative toward Evander using weight training. They felt that it would make him stiff and restrict him and so forth, but it was quite the opposite! I knew that a guy who's 18 percent body fat and trains down to, say, 4 percent is a trim fighter. A stronger athlete is a better athlete.*

Q: Getting back to you, you've been training in the sport for 17 years, and in that time you've undoubtedly experimented with every type of training routine and

technique there is. What have you found to be the best routine for putting on size?

LEE: *In my youth, I would say the four-day-a-week program. It was two-on/one-off and then two-on again. It would be a split routine where your first two days would be your heavy days, then your second segment would be Thursday and Friday, where you would use no more than 60 to 65 percent of your maximum weight. So you have a light day and a heavy day approach. I would do chest, back, and shoulders on one day and arms and legs the next, staying mostly with the basic movements. Once I turned professional, I needed a type of program that would allow me to grow while at the same time let me maintain a good degree of quality in the off-season. That's when I switched over to the three-on/one-off system, and I found it to be fantastic. I love that program!*

Q: In your videotape *Lee Haney's Mr. Olympia Workout,* you said you didn't feel that anyone ever needed to go below parallel for squats. What was your reasoning behind this?

LEE: *In doing squats, you've got to be careful about overburdening the joints. A guy around 5'11" like myself who doesn't have thick joints could end up hurting himself. You've got to be real careful; you want to stimulate—-not annihilate!*

Q: What about bench squats then—do you favor them?

LEE: *I don't like bench squats because if you lack control, you can jam the spine. You've got to use your natural instincts; you've got to have something to touch you in the butt to tell you it's time to go back up. Use your instincts.*

Q: What first drew you to the sport?

LEE: *Football. I wanted to be a professional football player. After injury after injury and setback after setback, I ended up becoming more and more involved in weight training, since I was using the weights in my rehabilitation. So I then decided to try my luck in bodybuilding. I didn't even place in my first competition; in my second I placed seventh, and then I placed fifth in my third, fourth in my fourth, and finally, after a couple of years, I started winning some shows! So mine is really a story of perseverance. I didn't just walk on the scene and start killing everybody. I had to work hard and learn and just stay at it.*

Q: With your hectic time schedule, what do you do to relax?

LEE: *I enjoy doing things with my family. Right now I'm into Walt Disney and Big Bird—kids, you know. I'm just running along with Josh [his two-year-old son], and we check our cartoons and go to movies and we do some traveling, so that's nice— but when I get a chance to do nothing, that's exactly what I do.*

Q: I understand that Josh has a little sister named Olympia. When was she born?

LEE: *Olympia was born October 16, 1990. It was really something, the way it happened. I was given a day in my honor by Atlanta Mayor Maynard Jackson. It was during Lee Haney Day that I had to take Shirley to the doctor. He told us that she was about ready to deliver. The next morning he told her she'd better come in—so we did, and the baby was born only three hours after we arrived! The doctor said it's a wonder she didn't have it right there during the proclamation—but she didn't have any pains whatsoever.*

Q: So what can Olympia's boyfriends expect from her dear old dad in, say, 18 years?

LEE: *Well, they'd better have their stuff together!*

Q: Lee, what is your philosophy of life?

LEE: *I try to live life from a holistic point of view; everything is connected to everything. I've always made sure that what I do, my family is always a part of it. Shirley is never left out of anything that I do; she's always right there by my side. And I've always maintained a very good spiritual relationship, which has given me guidance throughout the years. Now that I'm a father, all the things that helped to make Lee Haney, I'm able to pass along to my children. So my thing is to be happy! Be happy. That's the name of the game, and that's what I am.*

Q: At the Mr. Olympia last year, machines that you'd designed were on sale. There's talk that you're going to be stepping into films, you're starting to franchise your gyms, and you're still planning to compete in another Mr. O. How many business ventures can a fellow be involved with?

LEE: *[laughing] Just those, just those! I've got my own line of equipment plus I've endorsed the professional line for serious lifting and we are franchising the Animal Kingdom now, plus I've got some movie scripts that I'm looking into right now, but I don't know if I'll do them this year or not. It will depend on whether I go for an eighth Mr. Olympia title or not. Hopefully we'll shoot these films several months before the Mr. Olympia. There are a million things happening.*

Q: What kind of movie scripts are you looking at?

LEE: *Well, I'm a big guy in the scripts—I'm not doing any Pee-wee Herman stuff, that's for sure! One of them I'm looking at is comedy, and another is action. All I'm really doing is trying to rub shoulders with the right people. I have to get my foot in the door first.*

Q: As most of our readers don't want to compete but still want to put on muscle mass, what routine would you recommend to them?

LEE: *A four-day-a-week program. Just like the one I used early in my career. They'd do chest, back, and shoulders on one day, arms and legs the next. For biceps they might want to do barbell curls and preachers, just those two for a total of 8 sets. For chest they'd do 4 sets of benches, 4 sets of inclines, then maybe 3 sets of dumbbell flyes. For shoulders, presses in front of the head for one workout, then behind the neck the next workout. Then 3 sets of side laterals and three rear laterals and 3 sets of shrugs or upright rows—switch these back and forth from one workout to the next. And then for back it would be pulldowns behind the neck for 4 sets, barbell rows for 4 sets, and cable rows for 3 sets. The reps would always stay 6 to 8. And also use the Weider Pyramid Training Principle, which means starting with a light weight and working your way up. Never start with a heavy weight and work your way down. Then you'd have your legs. Now when I started out I would do squats first. Believe me, that was a boo-boo. Let's do leg extensions first to warm the knees up! So we'll do about 4 sets of leg extensions, reps will be a bit higher here, about 12 to 15 once again pyramiding—then we're going to do squats. We'll start here with one warm-up and then do about 4 sets of squats, reps 6 to 8 and pyramiding again. Then we're going to do leg curls, about 4 sets. The next workout, we'll do leg extensions, squats, and stiff-legged deadlifts. And we'd do about 4 sets of deadlifts and we'd switch them back and forth. Now I'm talking about growing—this* *is a mass routine. For abs, you can hit them a little bit every day. I suggest at least on the training day doing 4 sets of incline sit-ups and 3 sets of cable crunches or else 3 sets of leg raises on the vertical leg raise apparatus, where you prop your elbows up on the pads. Just remember to keep your reps in the 6 to 8 range. And for triceps, start with 4 sets of pressdowns on the cable and stay with 8 to 10 reps on triceps pressdowns because you want to warm those elbows up really good first. Then you'd go to lying extensions for 3 or 4 sets. So what I'd suggest when doing the workout is push/pull/push; chest [push], back [pull], shoulders [push]. Then the following day is going to be arms first, legs second. Then the third day you take off, or you may want to do a half-hour of some type of aerobic activity. As your body fat starts to creep up on you while you're bulking up, it'll be safe to include at least*

12 minutes of some type of aerobic activity after each workout anyway, and then a little extra on your day off. You have Wednesday off, then Saturday and Sunday off also, so if you're eating a lot, those are three extra days to get fat, and I don't want that to happen. You can't eat just anything; eat good quality stuff so that you bulk up and not fatten up.

Q: How would you like best to be remembered, Lee, I mean after you've hung it up?

LEE: Man, I'd just say as Mr. Olympia—period. There's heart, there's spirit—and that's everything. When Arnold left, he was known as Mr. Olympia. Sergio Oliva was remembered as Mr. Olympia, and that's how I want to be remembered—as Mr. Olympia.

And you may rest assured, folks, that he will be.

47

Mike Matarazzo

By all reports, Mike Matarazzo was something the other side of mammoth! To hear people tell it, Matarazzo has arms so enormous that the great Sergio Oliva would quickly cross the street if he saw him coming, to avoid comparison. Palpable nonsense! At least that was my outlook until I happened to spy some of the training shots that forced me to quickly reevaluate my rather hasty dismissal.

Although he may not yet be a household name, Mike Matarazzo is well on his way to being one; he has the size, the symmetry, and above all the genetics to go as far in this sport as he wants to. In fact, his calves when he started training were 18 inches in circumference, and I shudder to think what they measure now, such is the magnitude of this man's genetics.

According to Matarazzo, he was discovered by Gold's Gym's Ed Connors, who took one look at the physique on this young lad from Massachusetts and quickly deduced that if he trained in California, the magazine people would be pounding on his door for interviews, photos, and other avenues of exposure which, of course, always parlays into big professional bodybuilding endorsements. In short, moolah! Appropriately enough, the financial wheels of success have already started to turn his way, as Matarazzo has already appeared on cable television in the United States and in many magazines.

This is not to suggest that Matarazzo has just had all this good fortune dumped in his lap because he happened to be born with an arm the circumference of a small cement mixer. Matarazzo also happens to be one of the most fiery competitors on the posing dais today, having wiped the floor with Dean Caputo at the recent Mr. USA contest. So how did he get so huge? What role did genetics play in determining his ultimate muscular mass? And what are the Massachusetts Mastodon's plans for the future? Read on, for he reveals all in "20 Questions."

Q: Mike, what first drew you to the sport of bodybuilding?

MIKE: *Actually, I started bodybuilding to become stronger. I used to be into boxing—not a professional or even an amateur for that matter—and I found that it made me stronger and, because of that, a better boxer. Let me see, that would have been six and a half years ago. I wasn't an amateur or professional; that's just what I did to stay in shape. I used to spar and hit the heavy bag every day.*

Q: Alright, so you were originally into boxing, and that led you into weight training, but what eventually led you into bodybuilding?

MIKE: *I found that weight training gave me more confidence and increased my ability to take pain. Why I went into bodybuilding is that I made quick gains! I put on 30 pounds in just my first month, so I knew it was right for me.*

Q: What has been your proudest moment in the sport thus far?

MIKE: *Well, my proudest moment was my victory in the Mr. USA contest. It was great to defeat guys like Dean Caputo, whom I consider to be a great bodybuilder. Incidentally, this year's USA lineup was the biggest heavyweight class in the contest's history—there were 36 guys competing in it this year.*

Q: Mike, people tell me that your calves are the other side of phenomenal—and yet I hear tell that you don't even train them at all. What's the deal?

MIKE: *That's right. My calves are a blessing. I suppose I inherited them from my father. Before I even touched a weight I had 18-inch calves and 17-inch arms.*

Q: It would appear that much of your bodybuilding success would be due to genetics—but then, I suppose, whose isn't? In any event, for the purpose of comparison, what was your weight before taking up bodybuilding, and what is it now?

MIKE: *My weight when I started training was 210 pounds. That's at a height of 5'11". I now tip the scales at 255 pounds.*

Q: Your training has obviously accounted for at least a modicum of your bodybuilding success. What is your current training program that has allowed you to pack on some 45 pounds of muscle?

MIKE: *My current training routine is six days on, one day off, and I double split each day too. Day one would be on Monday, and in the morning I would do my chest and forearms.*

Q: What would your routine be for these body parts?

MIKE: *I always start my chest work with flat bench barbell presses for 5 or 6 sets. I should mention at the outset that I never count reps when I train. I do everything to failure. I never put a set number in my head—it's like a barrier. I gauge progress by the mirror—if I need beef somewhere I'll just put it on.*

Q: You start your chest work with flat bench, barbell presses. What's next?

MIKE: *I next do incline benches, again for 5 or 6 sets. For flat bench presses I'll work up to a top weight of 405 pounds. Inclines I'll max out at 315. After inclines, it's off to flat bench flyes for 4 sets—all to failure with 75- to 80-pound dumbbells. After that, I'd do cable crossovers (standing), and that's my final exercise for chest.*

Q: Would you describe yourself as an "instinctive trainer"?

MIKE: *Oh definitely! I do not even count exercises! I listen to my body! If it says go, I go, and if it says stop, I stop.*

Q: Next on the agenda is your forearm routine. What do you do for them?

MIKE: *For my forearms my routine is quite simple and very basic, consisting entirely of wrist curls on a flat bench with 135 to 155 pounds for 5 sets. That's it. Just to get the blood in there.*

Q: That brings us to day two, which if I recall was back only?

MIKE: *That's right, day two is back day. I will start with my heavy movements first, which means barbell rows for me. I'll work up to 405 pounds over 5 sets. From there, it's on to T-bar rows, again as heavy as possible, then single-arm dumbbell rows bracing myself on the flat bench. Then I move to seated cable rows to the front—again as heavy as possible, which, for me, is about 325 to 350 pounds or whatever the stack is. From here I would do seated pulley rows to my chest with a closer grip with a close-grip handlebar. I usually end it with something on the Hammer machine—they have very good back equipment on their close-grip rowing machine.*

Q: That covers back. What happens on day three?

MIKE: *Day three is my shoulder day, and I always start with press behind the neck— either with dumbbell or barbell. I have to do a lot of sets of these because I like to work up heavy on this exercise and I like to warm up thoroughly. I start the movement with a weight of only 135 pounds and then work up to 225 to 235 pounds with a barbell or similar poundages if I'm using dumbbells. From here, I'll go on to seated lateral raises with dumbbells. I do a variation of movements here as well.*

Q: Such as what?

MIKE: *Well, I do a lot of trisetting. I'll do the initial movement with heavy weights, lateral raises with 75-pound dumbbells, then I'll pick up a pair of 35-pounders to bomb them into failure. You really have to bomb your delts! From there I'll go to either upright rows or some form of cable raise to the front that will isolate the function of the anterior deltoid. Incidentally, all of these exercises I perform for 4 or 5 sets.*

Q: So day three is deltoid day. When do you train your legs?

MIKE: *I train them on day four—that's my leg day. For legs, I'll start with calves—but only if I'm in a precontest mode. Otherwise it's hamstrings. For my hamstrings, I found that weight training gave me more confidence and increased my ability to take pain! I'll start with deadlifts for 6 sets, and then I go to the Cybex leg curl machine for 6 more sets. That would normally cover*

hamstrings, as they'd be blitzed after that! So next I would move on to quads, and I'd start with squats. I take a narrow stance, again for about 6 sets, and I don't go too heavy, maybe only 405 pounds for reps. I feel that too many bodybuilders go too heavy on their squats and leg presses.

Q: Why is this?

MIKE: *Well, I believe that heavy lower body movements like those just thicken your waist. That's why I have a narrow waist—I don't squat or leg press all that heavy! I think your obliques kick in if you lift too heavy.*

Q: What is the remainder of your "non-heavy" leg routine?

MIKE: *I next move on to either hack squats or leg presses, again, for 5 or 6 sets, depending on just how I feel and what I want to work that day. Leg extensions round off the routine for 6 or 7 sets, and then after my last set of extensions I'll get up onto a multi machine and just do sissy squats to stretch the muscle fibers and get the blood in there. I'll do 4 or 5 sets of those. After each set, I'll squeeze the blood in there with some intense squeezing and flexing of the body part I've just trained. It's a misconception people have when they think that they can train more than one body part adequately in one day. I see them train arms and legs in the same day! You aren't giving your muscles enough time to grow when you do that! You've got* to allow enough time for growth and recuperation and also try to keep the blood in the muscle group for as long as possible in order to provide the cells with the nutrition they require for growth to take place.

Q: If you don't believe in training both your arms and legs on the same day, what day do you train your arms, and what is your routine?

MIKE: I train arms on my last training day of the week before I repeat my body part cycle. Arms are on the last day, and it consists of the entire arm—biceps, triceps, and forearms. I'll start off with bis, and 90 percent of the time I'll start off with heavy barbell curls—it's the ultimate biceps builder. I do about 5 sets and go up to 185 to 225 pounds on this one—and I'm not afraid to cheat it up! I'm a firm believer in cheating on this exercise—I'll do anything to get that weight up! From there, it's on to seated dumbbell curls for 5 sets, then I finish off with a cable movement just for isolation; usually a standing cable curl of some sort—it keeps constant tension on the biceps, from beginning to end, all through the movement. For triceps, I'll start with "nose breakers," more commonly called lying triceps extensions. It's the most painful but also the ultimate triceps movement. I go fairly heavy here too, up to 185 to 225 pounds for 5 or 6 sets. Then I'll do standing triceps pushdowns with a straight bar for 5 sets, and then I'll do standing bent-over kickbacks with dumbbells (with 50 pounds)

for 5 sets. I do this one slowly and really try to isolate the contraction. For my forearms it's really just a simple routine consisting of seated wrist curls—again for 5 sets.

Q: What about your abs? When do you train them?

MIKE: For abs, I train them in the off-season only twice a week. And then, I don't really pick a day to train them; I just make sure that at least two days pass since I last trained them before I train them again. If I have the energy, I'll do them on a given day, but always two or three days apart.

Q: So that's your mass routine, but what do you do to get ripped for a contest? Are you a calorie counter, or do you rely instead on aerobic exercise?

MIKE: To get ripped, I'm pretty much a calorie counter. For the USA, I went down from 8,000 to 2,000 calories a day. I was really depleted for the USA, but I was told it was a matter of hardness for the contest, so I did what I had to do. I don't even count exercises. I listen to my body. If it says go, I go, and if it says stop, I stop! As far as aerobics goes, I did aerobics for the USA; usually the treadmill, the bike, or the rowing machine. I was doing that every other day for one and a half hours in the morning and an hour before I went to bed. Hey, bodybuilding is a game of experimentation, and you have to experiment until you get it right. I wouldn't do that much aerobics again—that was overkill!

Q: I would like to combine two questions for my last question—if that makes any sense to you—and that is number one, what do you do when you're not banging around the iron in the gym, and number two, what are your future plans?

MIKE: *Well, when I'm not training, I relax by walking on the beach, or by throwing a couple of movies on the VCR or even just looking over some old issues of* Muscle & Fitness *magazine. I don't believe in clubbing or that sort of scene. I like sailing and fishing, those sorts of things. As far as future plans go, I want to win more contests. I'm going to the Mr. Olympia in September, and after that I'll be at the Arnold Classic. I'm gearing up for the Olympia, and I'm going to give It my best shot. I mean, it'll be an honor to be on the same stage as the rest of these guys! It's an honor for me, just like it was for me to talk to Joe Weider. I'm going to do the best I can for the sport and give it the best name possible, and I'll do my best to promote it. I'd like to thank some people who have helped me thus far in my career if I might. First of all, I'd like to thank my mother and my father for their support throughout the years, they are the best! I'd also especially like to thank Ed Connors of Gold's Gym. He made it possible for me. After I won the '89 Boston Gold's Classic, people wondered who I was. I took some time off and Lou Zwick flew me out to get a feel of what L.A. was like. Mr. Connors heard I was there and invited me into his office. He pulled out the tape measure and said, "Forget Massachusetts. You should be here." I call him Big Ed!*

48

Lee Labrada

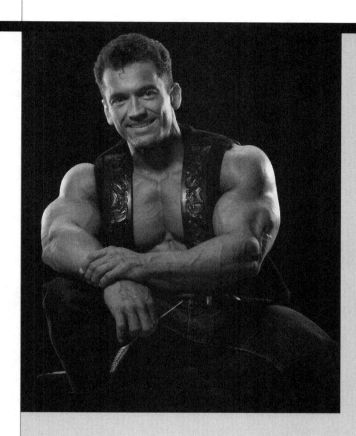

 One of the greatest bodybuilders of this age or, indeed of any age, is Lee Labrada. The man is a walking definition of the term *symmetry* and has enough muscle mass on his frame that Lee Haney himself was heard to heave a sigh of relief when he narrowly (and we mean narrowly) edged out Lee Labrada to take the 1990 Mr. Olympia contest, held in Chicago.

Yet Labrada isn't all sets and reps. He's an impassioned reader of philosophy and psychological tomes and claims to have found the secret to inner contentment and success in life in the pages of a 100-year-old book. He's an articulate and cordial individual who also happens to have one of the best physiques to ever grace a posing dais. Among other things, Lee Labrada will tell exactly how he built it when he answers "20 Questions."

Q: After last year's performance at the Mr. Olympia, where you finished runner-up, many people thought you should have actually won. What could you possibly have done this year to improve upon last year's condition?

LEE: *Well, I have improved upon that condition. I've basically put on some additional muscle mass this year, and my definition is as good as it was last year. It's funny, but it seems everyone, just hearing from the grapevine, has lost probably a good 10 percent of their body weight, and yet I'll be coming in at pretty much the same weight, or maybe just a couple of pounds more!*

Q: What is the weight that you competed at last year?

LEE: *Last year, I came in between 180 and 182 pounds. I'm at the same this year, in spite of the drug tests!*

Q: What were your thoughts when they first implemented the drug test to the men's professional ranks?

LEE: *I'm always open-minded, so I knew there had to be a reason. And, upon examining the reasons, which in my heart I feel are to clean up the image of the sport and have it accepted publicly, which will lead us to Olympic recognition and hence, lead us to more widespread popularity and lead us to more money in the sport, which leads us to et cetera. Not to mention the fact that it molds up a better image for the youngsters who are coming up through the ranks that it's not necessary to abuse steroids to become a champion.*

Q: Good point! One thing I'd like to touch on now with regard to your training is that, like Mike Mentzer in the late '70s, you tend to follow an abbreviated routine; for example, greater stress is placed on intensity, less upon duration and socializing in the gym. How then did you hit upon your current training system?

LEE: *Let's look at it this way: I don't have a carbon copy of Mentzer's style of training. However, I do not advocate the traditional styles of training where you would do, say, 20 sets per body part with lower intensity. I'm a firm believer that intensity causes the muscle to grow. Without getting into too much detail here, when you begin a set you have X amount of muscle fibers that are lifting the weight. As the set progresses, more and more muscle fibers are going to be recruited. So it stands to reason that the harder you push the set, the longer you push it, the more muscle fibers are going to be recruited. Then, and only then, can some kind of an effect take place that will induce greater growth. So if you do submaximal sets, the body's already used to that and has no reason to grow. Yeah, that may tax other aspects of the muscle; the endurance fibers and increased capillaries and things like that, but that's not going to affect the white muscle fibers, which are those that are in the greatest predominance with bodybuilders and are* *responsible for the greatest bulk of the muscle's size.*

Q: What was it in your training, and your own belief system, that led you to go from, say, "conventional" training to experiment with the Mike Mentzer system and then, ultimately, come up with your own training system?

LEE: I guess being an engineer by trade I'm a bit of an analytical type and, at the same time, I'm a big believer in empiricism. Not empiricism in the philosophical sense, but basing things on experience. Or, in other words, trial and error. At the onset of my bodybuilding career I tried a lot of different routines. I tried the standard six-days-a-week, 20-set routines, and I was getting nowhere fast. Then it happened that I came upon some articles written by Mentzer, and I followed his logic through the articles, and being of a scientific mind, they all made sense to me, and I tried it and started getting results. I kind of used that as a starting point and then evolved my own system of training. My training has changed; it's gone through different stages throughout the years. I used to do many fewer sets even than I do now. Typically, a chest workout might be only 6 sets for me when I first started out. Now I use a few more sets because I feel that I have to in order to tax the muscle more fully. I've kind of reached a happy medium, so to speak.

Q: In Mentzer's writings, he used to say that an individual would do a certain amount of sets to develop a muscle—intensity being the big factor—and everything else was related to diet. Do you believe that there is such a thing as "refinement" that is brought out by extra sets, or is it just a matter of growth stimulation and dieting for definition?

LEE: Yeah, I do believe in refinement to a degree. Let's look at it from two standpoints: Let's call additional sets "volume," the amount of work you do in a workout. If you do a greater volume it's going to necessitate a lower intensity; you're going to use lighter weights and higher reps, that sort of thing. That is going to tax a different part of the muscle fiber than heavy weights. Most physiology books will tell you that the makeup of the typical bodybuilder is about 80 percent white muscle fiber and about 20 percent of the red or endurance muscle fiber. So here's the neglected 20 percent for the guys who are doing the straight 6 to 8 reps all the time. So all of a sudden you start doing 15 to 20 reps occasionally and you start developing the other stuff. Yeah, that's going to amount to more "quality" in the muscle, number one, but I like to think of quality as something that you get over a period of time. A muscle reaches its maximum genetic size, and then it starts striating. And striated muscle only happens over a period of time, and that's what I call refinement.

Q: In preparing for this interview I read some articles that included some pictures of you when you were younger, and obviously the transformation was phenomenal. What was the most productive routine that you used to bring about that metamorphosis?

LEE: I would say a four-day-per-week routine, high intensity, using about three different exercises per body part and 2 to 3 sets of each, going to failure, using as much weight as I possibly can on each set.

Q: Are you a believer in the forced reps and negatives approach?

LEE: Yeah, forced reps, but certainly not negatives.

Q: Why would you then not perform negatives?

LEE: There's a physiological explanation for it, and it has to do with the way that the actin and myosin filaments within a muscle fiber operate. Both actin and myosin slide back and forth across each other along a little ATP bridge. When you get a contraction in the positive direction, a concentric contraction, you're basically using the muscle as it was intended, but when you start the eccentric or "negative" part of the motion, you are actually dragging the actin and myosin across each other, which creates internal friction in the muscle.

That's why people get sore when they do negative repetitions exclusively because they get microtrauma there.

Q: Indeed you would. You've mentioned that you've improved already over last year's condition at the Mr. Olympia. Is this again a matter of following a four-day-a-week routine, or have you evolved that routine to a different level as well?

LEE: I've used a two-on/one-off type of a system in the off-season, which incorporates three different workouts. The first workout would be chest, shoulders, and triceps, the second would be back and biceps, and the third workout would be legs.

Q: Since Mentzer and, I guess, some of the true intellectuals of the sport, you seem to have come along and filled that void in that your articles seem to possess an awful lot of insight into not only training physiology, but there also seems to be a certain logical consistency that runs throughout them. I'm curious, you mentioned engineering as being responsible for your inquisitive bent, but I think I detect something beyond that philosophy?

LEE: Well, thank you. You know, one of my big pastimes is to read a lot of things of a philosophical and theological nature, and I'm not one of those hellfire-and-brimstone types of Christians, but I do feel that I have a good relationship with God, and I feel when it boils right down to it, that that is the biggest source of energy and motivation in my life.

Q: Are there any books that have particularly influenced you, that is, apart from theology textbooks?

LEE: Yeah, I'll tell you what, there's one that I'd recommend to everybody [laughs]. I think the whole world would be better off if they read it! It's a book called As You Think, *and it's by James Allen. It is 100 years old, it's only about 75 pages, and the first time it came out in print it was called* As a Man Thinketh, *and man, it is just mind-blowing. It's so short in its message, it's all about taking responsibility for your own actions. I know you'd like it because you're right into philosophy—and that what you get out of this life is what you put into it and, basically, that you reap what you sow. You know, that positive thoughts beget positive action, negative thoughts beget negative action, and I am a big believer in that. I'm a big believer in taking control and taking responsibility both for my failures and for my successes, and I think that I'm where I am because I've worked hard for it, I've envisioned it, and basically, I've made myself into what I am like somebody in the gutter has made himself into what he is. Your mind is like a garden, you can plant seeds, and the positive seeds, thoughts, beget positive fruit or action and vice versa with the negative. If you choose not to plant anything, then weeds grow, but no matter what, something grows.*

Q: A very interesting simile. Touching on being responsible for your success or lack thereof, you seem to be one of the few bodybuilders who has volitionally taken control of, not only your life, but also your career. You're a very good strategist in terms of both marketing and promotions, A lot of other bodybuilders tend to sit back and lament the fact that a lot of offers haven't come to them, whereas you have sat back and mapped out your own strategy and made it happen. Could you comment on this dichotomy?

LEE: Well, thanks for the compliments. Yeah, it really irks me to see the attitude of most, and don't just say bodybuilders, let's say professional athletes in general, whether they are bodybuilders, or football players, or baseball players, they basically put all their eggs in one basket and think that they're going to get this big win or big break and then everyone and their mother is going to be calling them to get them on the cover of Sports Illustrated *and everything else. It doesn't work that way. The whole thing here is that you win a contest and then it's basically, "So what?" You have to make something of it then. It's just a tool with which you have to turn it into something for yourself. To give you an idea, when I won the Mr. Universe I didn't wait around for Joe Weider to call me. The first thing that I did was I grabbed Joe and we had our picture taken at the Mr. Universe. I literally dragged him out on stage, and the picture of course got* published. And then, when I came back to the United States, I had about 60 bucks in my pocket and I was sitting in a hotel room in Manhattan, and I whipped out the phone number for Weider Health & Fitness. I called the Woodland Hills office and got Joe on the phone. I told him, "I'm so and so, I won the Mr. Universe." He said, "Oh yeah, I remember you," and so forth and so on, and I said, "Look, Joe, I want to come out and get some photos taken, but I don't have any money." He flew me out, he put me up, and we took all sorts of photos, but otherwise it would never have happened. So what I'm saying is that you have to take your life into your hands, you have to do something.

Q: There were some great pictures of you at the Parthenon in Athens, Greece. It must have been quite an experience for you to stand on that hallowed philosophic, historical, and athletic ground there. How did that photo shoot come about?

LEE: And photographed by none other than the mighty Chris Lund! I'll tell you what, those were probably the best pictures that were ever taken of me. It was just terrific! You know I won the Greek Grand Prix and Chris invited me to go on a photo shoot, which of course I accepted because I knew where we were going to shoot. My God! It almost gave me chills when I stepped up onto those rocks and I realized where I was standing, the whole history and atmosphere of the place and its connection with

classical civilization. I knew that something magical was happening. I'll tell you what, I'm so proud of those pictures.

Q: What is your aerobic program before a contest, or are you just mainly relying on diet to bring in your cuts?

LEE: Bicycle! Bicycle! Bicycle! [laughs] Yeah, I find that the aerobic bicycle is one that tears my legs down the best. I feel that you should do maybe 30 minutes a day, maybe four times a week. That works real good to get the metabolism going.

Q: How many days per week do you think the average bodybuilder can train without overtraining?

LEE: I don't think it's so much on "average." Everybody has a different ability to recover from workouts, and you kind of have to gauge that for yourself. Keep in mind, however, that a muscle needs 72 hours to recover fully and that it's also possible to overtrain the body as a whole. You know, that's often the case; you overtrain the body on a systematic level, the entire body rather than just one or two body parts. Basically somebody can train maybe four or five days a week, tops, without overtraining, if they're really training hard.

Q: What are your future goals, both inside and outside of bodybuilding?

LEE: That's interesting that you asked that. My obvious goal at this point, professionally, from a bodybuilding standpoint, is to win the Mr. Olympia, and then after that, I'll probably compete for about another three or four years. I intend to be out of the sport when I'm 35, and I'm not 30. I've got my fingers in a lot of different business ventures now, and I'll probably take one of those routes and expand on it, but I fully intend to be a millionaire by the time I'm 35.

Q: That's a good ambition. Right now, you're probably well on your way to that goal, as you seem very successful. Do you have any advice to up-and-coming bodybuilders who may have won a few contests and are working their way up? How can they increase their potential fortunes?

LEE: *Well, first of all, be realistic. The fact of the matter is that bodybuilding is still not a big money sport like tennis or something like that, no matter what the magazines try to portray, it is not that way. The top five guys maybe make the good money, but again, you have to take the ball and run with it. If you don't have any business savvy, get a manager. Don't give away your life's earnings in the process. Then again, after that, it's just basically making good investments and realizing that you are a "product" and that you have to market that product and plan your career out and not just haphazardly follow that same happy-go-lucky path that you did when you were an amateur where you trained when you wanted and didn't train when you didn't want to. I always strive to improve. Every*

time I work out I have to get something out of the workout, and I don't like to just go through the motions.

Q: What is it that guides you through workout after workout after all these years of training? And what really keeps you motivated?

LEE: *It seems to go through different stages. When I'm in a growth stage then, yeah, I'll try and get stronger all the time. Whether it's an additional rep or another two pounds on a certain movement or something like that. In other phases of the month or year, whatever the case may be, my goal may be to improve circulation or a different aspect of training. Sometimes it's heavy mass training, sometimes it's high-rep training in order to improve the blood supply to the muscle and bring out more quality, and sometimes it's precontest training. However, I know what phase I'm in at each time of the year. It keeps me motivated, because if you don't have a plan when you go to the gym, it's useless.*

Q: You've competed against all of the top bodybuilders out there today, and yet most people see your only true competition being the big guy himself, Lee Haney. What are your thoughts on Lee Haney? What comes to mind when you hear his name?

LEE: *I think Lee Haney is a great athlete. I feel that I beat him last year and I can beat him again, and I don't see anybody* beating me unless they have my type of physique because otherwise it's just sheer mass. Plenty of guys are massive in one area or another, but they're not complete. The complete physiques are the ones that I have to watch for.

Q: As most of the people who read this are noncompetitive, but most of them, by and large, are looking to improve their muscle-mass stores, what routine would you recommend for them to do that?

LEE: Definitely the two-on/one-off system. Let's call it workout A, B, and C. I told you that A would be chest, shoulders, and triceps; B would be biceps and back, and the C would be legs. I would say workout A one day and workout B the next day. Then you take a day off, then it's workout C, then it's back to workout A, then you take another day off. See how that rotates? So it's two on, one off; with three different workouts; you rotate them around. This allows you to train each body part twice one week and once the next week, and it's terrific for mass. I'd say this is a great routine for the intermediate and advanced guys. For the beginners, four days a week is a great routine.

Q: We've touched on the topic of felicity a little while earlier in this interview. What is it that brings you happiness in this world, and I'm assuming that bodybuilding isn't number one in this particular realm of things?

LEE: Well the only thing that can bring you real happiness, regardless of what anybody tells you, is to be at peace with yourself. In other words, you have to like yourself; have a positive self-image. That's not based on winning or how much money you've got because the fact of the matter is that you came into this world naked and you're going to go out naked, you're not going to take any of it with you. Basically the only thing you have between point A and point B are experiences. I'm big on experience, and money is just a tool to garner more experiences. Coming back to what you are saying, I guess that being happy is just liking yourself, having a positive self-image. Loving yourself, and I don't mean that in a narcissistic sort of way, but it is necessary to love yourself before you can love others. Loving others, sharing, being giving, and being considerate of others, is what really brings the greatest satisfaction.

49

Tony Pearson

Whenever one talks of lat spreads, the name of Tony Pearson inevitably comes up. Let's face it, the man has the greatest V-taper in the sport. However, precious little is known about the man himself, what he believes, how he trains, and what routines he used to create one of the world's greatest physiques.

At this year's Arnold Classic in Columbus, Ohio, Pearson had electrified the crowd, not only with his incredibly ripped physique but with a posing routine that would have put Ed Corney to shame! It was while I was at the Arnold Classic this past year that I was finally able to corner Tony Pearson, "Mr. Lat Spread," and put to him "20 Questions."

Q: How did you ever get started in this sport, and what drew you to it?

TONY: *I started in 1976, and the reason I started was because I was wrestling in high school for three years. We were required to pump iron to get stronger and develop more strength for the sport. In* fact, I started showing improvements right away, my coaches and everyone else took an interest in what I was doing. Then I went to a real bodybuilding gym, which was in St. Louis, Missouri, where I went to school, and the owner of the gym took an interest in my progress and put me on a program and trained me for about six months. I made a lot of gains. In fact I put on 20 pounds in six months by squatting.

Q: Then what happened?

TONY: In 1976, I went to Venice, California, and trained at Gold's Gym. The first guy I saw there was Arnold on Venice Beach. Then I saw Robby Robinson and Frank Zane, who were the big guys at the time. I was only 19 then and weighed about 165 pounds [laughs] maximum! Then, two years later, after training there I became the AAU Mr. America for 1978. In 1979 I went to Europe for a couple of years, and then in 1981, I returned to America and the IFBB.

Q: What did you weigh when you won the Mr. America?

TONY: I weighed 178 pounds when I won the Mr. America [laughs]. I guess I made a bit of improvement from when I arrived in California. I've always had a fair amount of cuts or definition, but now the shift has changed to that of symmetry. Then I came back in 1981 and started competing on the pro circuit in the States and Europe. I won the Colorado Grand Prix in 1983, then I entered the Mixed Pairs, where I had five

different partners but won it six times [the last time being when he was paired with Carla Dunlap in France in 1988].

Q: How long have you been training then, altogether?

TONY: I've been training now for 14 years nonstop. Forced layoffs occasionally with maybe a month off here or there, but otherwise it's year-round all the way. [laughing] I'm one 100-percent bodybuilder.

Q: Given your 14-plus years of experience, what has been your proudest moment as a professional?

TONY: I suppose my proudest moment would have to be winning the Mr. America and then coming back and winning the Couples after losing it in 1987. But winning the Mr. America was really one of the greatest moments of my life.

Q: I think that you almost singlehandedly elevated Couples competition to a much higher level. Before a lot of people were very mechanical in their posing, and since you came onto the scene, the trend instantly switched to a more fluid style of posing. What was it that you brought to Couples competition that made such a dramatic change?

TONY: I kinda compare it to figure skating, or ballet, or dance. It's a combination of two people working together. It's an art form as long as your body's conditioned for it.

Q: What kind of practice goes into developing a Pair's posing routine?

TONY: *It takes a lot of rehearsal time and a partner that's compatible. You've got to have a partner that's compatible and that can work together with you. Most people are just into themselves, and they forget that this is teamwork.*

Q: At the risk of offending past partners, who was the one you felt you were matched the best with?

TONY: *Matched the best with? Definitely Carla Dunlap! We had the same feelings, height-wise we were good, body structure, the color and the muscle tie-ins were similar, and Carla puts together routines herself [laughs], so I just follow along with her!*

Q: You've mentioned that you've always had excellent definition. Do you rely heavily on aerobics to accomplish this, or are you that way genetically?

TONY: *Mainly genetics. I have a fast metabolism, I train twice a day year-round because I do seminars and exhibitions and I have a reputation for being in shape [laughs], I put the pressure on myself. Doing this makes it a lot easier for contests too—if you train all the time and are close to contest shape, it's easier to get there.*

Q: Don't you find that by training twice a day, year-round, you become overtrained?

TONY: *Yes, and to combat that I just take a couple of days off, eat what I want, relax, and then you start slowly back in again. You see, your body tells you when you've overdone it. Sometimes you don't listen, especially before a show. You think that the more you do, the better you're going to look, but it's really the reverse, and it ends up backfiring on you. Yes, I overtrain a little bit, but after so many years you do listen to your body and you realize, and you're getting older too, that maybe you'd better start easing off a little bit, eat more and rest.*

Q: In all of your years of training you must have used a lot of training routines. Which one have you found to be the most effective that you've ever used?

TONY: *It's still sets and reps to me with free weights. I mean that's how you get the best results—fast! It forces you to work. Whenever I go into a gym I usually pick the hardest movements and try to spend as little time as possible in there and still get the job done. Guys who spend three or four hours in a gym are wasting their time; you go for an hour and 15 minutes and then you leave—if you know what you're doing. If you're going to work chest and back, you work chest and back—one hour and 15 minutes. I compete against nothing but the clock and make it an aerobic workout as well.*

Q: Well, Tony, what routine do you presently follow?

TONY: I train straight through seven days a week. If it were off-season, I'd train six days a week, once a day, but with a contest coming up, I train twice a day.

Q: What kind of sets would you average per body part?

TONY: Per body part I would say between 15 and 18 sets. Each body part would be trained twice a week only. If you start overlapping three times a week, you're overdoing it. Each body part needs at least two or three days rest in between workouts. If you train each body part three days a week you won't grow because you're destroying it. Some body parts I have to work more than others, however. My arms, for example, I work them more than my other body parts, and yet they still respond. The more I train my arms, the bigger they look. The more I train my legs, the worse they look.

Q: It's been said that you have the best legs in the business. How often do you train them?

TONY: I train my legs every fourth day. I've altered my leg routine in recent years in that now I do a lot of lunges. I also do a lot of leg pressing and I squat but once every 10 days. I have found that when I lunge more or leg-press more, I have more mass. In fact, when I do squat I lose size. I have a lot less body fat in my legs than anywhere else, and that's always been a weak point because, as you know, when you lose size,

where do you lose it first? Your weak points. And by squatting 300 or 400 pounds, that destroys, and by the time it recovers it might take a week. Yet when I lunge and leg press, I always get that full, pumped look, and it stays. So I say, every third or fourth day I'm lunging and leg pressing. Occasionally I'll throw hacks in or squats. And when I do squat, I keep my back straight and my feet together and, really, seldom go beyond 315 pounds and do sets of 8, 10, to 12 repetitions only once every 10 days. I do the same with deadlifting too; the deadlift is a shock to the system, so I do it just once a week. Some people say that I train light, I don't train light. I train with intensity and control and technique. Technique makes it heavy.

Q: What are your thoughts on genetics in bodybuilding?

TONY: Genetics play a tremendous part. If I did not have good genetics it would be difficult for me up there against these young guys coming up who are so damn good. I'm fortunate in that I have very, very small hips and waist, which still gives you that illusion of size. Having big shoulders on top of this can give the crowd and judges the illusion that I weigh in over 200 pounds, and yet I'm only 198 or 200 max.

Q: Tony, your back development is the standard by which that body part is judged. Is it another case of genetics, and just what then is your back routine?

TONY: Genetically, yes, I've always been pretty wide, but there was not depth or thickness to it. So I did a lot of seated cable rows, wide-grip chins—both front and back, T-bar rows, and of course your normal barbell rows. I do basically the same things that everyone else does. I guess the seated rows and the chins would be the first and second exercise on my list. To get the depth in the center of my back, which I'm really getting now, you need to do close-grip barbell rows and T-bar rows.

Q: What are your thoughts on the drug testing being implemented in the men's professional ranks?

TONY: For me, I've never been a strong user of steroids—I mean anyone who looks at my body can see that. My skin is like a baby's skin, there's no pimples or stretch marks. I have never really been a believer in them. Yes, I've used them, but I won the Mr. America completely clean. I mean two years on nothing! Then afterward I indulged a little bit. And then, there's a certain point when I said to myself, "I don't need this anymore." I made slight gains, but for me, anyway, they were overrated. For the sport, I think it's a great idea! I think it's good because we're getting such a bad reputation in the media and with Ben Johnson at the Olympics. I mean I was just flying on the airplane, and the first thing that the stewardess said to me was, "Do you take drugs?" They forget about the 14 years that you sacrificed everything for and the

hard work that you put in. So I think it's great for the sport and its image, because we need that image—if it's going to be for the general public, we have to have a positive image.

Q: Given that most of those who train are noncompetitive, but still want to put on some solid muscular mass, what routine would you recommend for them to follow in their attempts to realize their bodybuilding training ambitions?

TONY: First of all, if they don't have any knowledge, read as much as possible. Then it's trial and error with your body. Go to as many seminars as you can and pick up some knowledge from each guy. Don't try and change every month, give a program a chance to work. Set a program and say, "I'm going to give this a chance to work. I'm going to try it." Then, three to four months down the road, you can change it again. Find someone who has some knowledge to help you out. I was very lucky in the beginning because I had someone always there who said, "Do this, this, and this." And I listened well, and you try it—it might not work, but you try it. And then be honest with yourself, look at yourself, be honest in your assessment and see what needs work the most. When I went to the gym before I won the Mr. America, the instructor there gave me a great program. It put 20 pounds of solid muscle on me. The owner, George Turner from St. Louis, Missouri, trained weight lifters all his life, and after watching me train in his gym for three hours—I'd never had a real workout in my life at this point—he walked up to me and said, "Come here a minute." I followed him into his office, where he wrote out a program and said, "Follow it every day." So I went to the gym, and he had me doing 10 sets of 10 at the squat rack on Monday, Wednesday, and Friday, which I did along with pullovers. Then, the next days, on Tuesdays, Thursdays, and Saturdays, he had me doing pullovers with chin-ups—and that's all he let me do. I didn't do abs, I didn't do rowing, and I must say that, in the long run, that's where I got the lats [laughs] from, 10 sets of chins three times a week! And I grew a lot in six weeks, and he had me eating a lot of protein in the form of steaks and protein drinks. After six months I said, "George, I'm leaving St. Louis, I'm going to California." He said, "No, you don't want to go to California because those guys out there are real bodybuilders!" So I went anyway and, first time out there, who did I see but Zane,

Robby, Manuel Perry, and Bill Grant was just going crazy! This is what I want to do! I want to be a bodybuilder.

Q: How many days a week do you think the average bodybuilder can train without overtraining?

TONY: If he's trying to make gains in muscle mass, no more than four or five days. But if you're trying to put size on, four or five days are really all you need.

Q: You seem a very optimistic fellow; you're not pessimistic at all. I'm curious as to what philosophy of life you would attribute that to?

TONY: I think it's a matter of knowing who you are and where you came from and facing reality. What motivates me is that I see improvements and I see changes. I'm 33 years old—aaagh! [laughs] I can see changes, and I feel that in the next few years I'm going to keep getting better and better—and that's what keeps me going. I have this picture in my mind of what I could look like, and I'm not there yet!

50

Bob Paris

When people first saw pictures of the Paris physique, many eyes opened and many jaws dropped; for what a number of bodybuilding purists believed they were witnessing was the reincarnation of the classic physique, with the lines, size, symmetry, and good looks of the incomparable (and now late) Steve Reeves. Not a bad comparison by any stretch of the imagination. But how did Bob Paris feel about such a lofty placing on the bodybuilding pedestal? In this edition of "20 Questions," he reveals the answer and a lot more.

Q: How did you feel about being thought of as the "new Steve Reeves"?

PARIS: *The man is a legend and it was nice in the beginning, but now I feel I've built my own identity, which means I have taken my body beyond being categorized in just one area. People often think of me as being just a symmetrical bodybuilder, but when you compare me onstage to some of* the biggest men in the sport, I can hold my own up there. I have developed what I call intelligent mass! What I mean by intelligent mass is the combination of size, symmetry, and basically everything. I feel that I am creating my own category in the sport.

Q: What is your usual weight at a contest?

PARIS: Well, at the Pro World I weighed in at 105½ kilos, which is 231 pounds, at a height of 6'.

Q: When you first came on the scene, you were branded with the "pretty boy" image, but now that appears to have changed. How do you feel about this today?

PARIS: Anyone who knows me well can tell you that I'm a jeans and T-shirt person. I mean, in the last year I've competed 16 times, so I'm as hard-core as they come. I can't help it if people attach something to my looks. Really, I'm just myself.

Q: In my opinion, just to complete the European Grand Prix is probably the toughest part of the sport. If you survive this European tour, then the next contest you train for, which will be the Olympia, must be simple. So, why do you do it?

PARIS: After a two-year break from competing I'm now giving the European countries perfect opportunities to let all the different markets know that I'm hard-core and available for promotions, etc. I'm showing that I support bodybuilding and willingly doing what I can to build the sport

in different markets. There comes the point where bang, I realize that I'm back on top again, which means the Olympia. That becomes the number one goal.

Q: Why did you suddenly get out of bodybuilding? You said that you would never return!

PARIS: I know I said that, and I fully believed that I wasn't going to ever compete again. You see, my success came very quickly as an amateur and I really hadn't set myself up as being a professional, goal-wise. In fact, I didn't see myself going beyond the Mr. America or Mr. Universe. I worked so hard during my first two years as a professional doing exhibitions and seminars. Then I was doing so much work on the maturity of my life that I eventually burned out. I also had other goals that I wanted to accomplish, so I just needed to get out of bodybuilding. Basically I thought I was finished with the sport for good.

Q: How did you feel, did you miss it?

PARIS: Oh yeah, and pretty soon I realized that I hadn't accomplished what I needed to in the sport. I felt that I hadn't set my place. Then, as I matured, I realized that I had to listen to my heart more. As I listened I knew that there was still something more to be accomplished.

Q: Were you still training, because you did become a whole lot smaller?

PARIS: *It was nice for a while because I felt very light and athletic, but I tell you, once I restarted training again the mass came back very quickly. Now, it feels real good to have everything nice and tight again, accompanied by good mass.*

Q: Do you feel that this time around you have more control over your eating habits, training dedication, and things of that nature?

PARIS: *I've always learned to listen to my body and analyze everything I do. But it was hard, because in the two years that I was gone the sport changed a whole lot. It went from "hardness" being the key, to "ultra-ultra hardness." It was as if the sport had moved light-years during the time I was gone. I actually had to relearn. It's always a learning process, and when you stop learning you stop growing and improving.*

Q: Do you still learn a lot on these tours? You know, being around other bodybuilders and seeing what they do?

PARIS: *Well, basically everyone eats the same things, chicken, rice, and so on. The best thing about these tours is that you have the chance to "peak" eight times, which means you have the opportunity to try out different things each week. What may have worked six months ago in preparing for, say, the sixth contest of a series might not work this time. So you have to make adjustments and stay smart.*

Q: Sometimes the guys are very inconsistent. They can look entirely different within two days. Is this just a case of excessive water retention?

PARIS: *Yes, the inconsistency may come from the stress of traveling or not being able to get the right food in that particular country. We've now developed a system where as soon as we arrive in a new country we head straight for the grocery store. The food situation and getting into our rooms easily really does relieve the stress.*

Q: Do you think the guys are more dedicated now, or maybe obsessed is a better word?

PARIS: *Yeah, you have to be obsessed, especially since there's a lot more money on the line.*

Q: Let's talk about training. Who was your inspiration?

PARIS: *Arnold, definitely! This was in about 1976, 1977. I saw an article in* Rolling Stone *on Arnold, and I was caught from there on. I told relatives that I would look like that in just a year, which they thought was the most conceited and strange statement that they had ever heard! It didn't take a year, though, and I'm still working on it. I actually started training in a small gym at school. I invented all the exercises and did as many as I could on the Universal equipment. It was a sort of a hit-and-miss process! I would do low reps, then feel as if I needed to do high reps. In* general, I mixed everything up. But then I found that I grew better on less sets. I did 3 sets of an exercise and pushed it as much as I could. I tried the system of training that Mike Mentzer used, but it just didn't feel right for me. I kept trying it because mentally it made so much sense. But, it didn't give me the diversity I needed to cover the various body parts. I do believe that you have to do what works for your own body.

Q: How hard do you personally train?

PARIS: I class myself as the hardest, quiet trainer. Rod and myself "bust butt" when we train, we don't put on a big show about it. It's very well focused and introverted instead of screaming and moaning. I consider myself a warrior in the gym, but I just do it in a very different way, and if people do a workout with me they're surprised as to how hard I actually push.

Q: And how often do you actually train?

PARIS: Basically, I train on a daily basis. I've found it's best for most people to develop a system like three days on, one day off. I'm at the point in my career where I can take a day off when I feel like it. Sometimes one day, sometimes three, because that is when my body needs rest. I'm not being lazy. My instincts govern the length of the workout. I may plan one that's entirely made up of supersets and giant sets, which means I can complete a body part in only 15 minutes. I could give

someone their ultimate biceps workout with a combination of three or four exercises, giant setted. I put them through that three times, which will only take 10 minutes, but they will have the most incredible pump, burn, and fatigue in their biceps! This is my favorite technique for bringing up a body part. Prior to a contest I usually use this system every other workout.

Q: What kind of training do you employ during the off-season?

PARIS: At that time I do basic, single-set movements with combinations of low and high reps. But, I like grouping the exercises together because this allows me to push to the limit.

Q: What would be a typical week's training for you then?

PARIS: I wake up at about six-thirty, have breakfast, which is usually oatmeal, egg whites, and coffee. I go to the gym at about 10 a.m. Monday would probably be chest and shoulders. I'd start out with incline barbell press, incline flyes, dips, and probably crossovers. My body thrives on anything from 6 to 30 reps, and I like to vary it from each exercise. Even when I'm doing a lot of reps, I still push it as intensely as a 5-rep set. Intensity doesn't mean heavy weights though. When it comes to training I'm a perfectionist, and that means strict form, which is probably why I've never been seriously injured.

Q: What about your shoulders then?

PARIS: Down-the-rack side lateral raises, with drops like 50, 40, 30, and maybe 10 reps each, with a rest period in between which is just long enough for the other person to do their set. Then I'd do a controlled press movement on the Universal. After these presses I do a sitting rear cable movement leaning back and crunching the delts. Then bent-over side raises down the rack again with probably three drops. When you're up on stage your deltoids are a major attraction. The judges always look for deltoids, waist, and calf impressiveness. Right after I finish a workout I take my amino acids. Then about half an hour later I'm ready to eat a meal comprised of potatoes, pasta, chicken, lean meat, and odd condiments.

Q: And what about the next day?

PARIS: The next day I would be back in the morning. I do chins first followed by close-grip pulldowns to the front, wide pulldowns to the rear, then two rowing movements, probably barbell row or cable row, with 4 sets of each movement. The arm routine at night would be incline dumbbell curls, barbell preacher curls, and close-grip EZ bar standing curls, 15 to 20 reps apiece. For triceps it would be pushdowns, overhead extensions, bench dips, and kickbacks.

Q: The next day you train legs, right?

PARIS: Yes, I love to do squats, I do them for really high reps. Then I do "down-the-rack" leg extensions, which means I'll start heavy and then gradually get lighter. I follow that with sissy squats and then high-rep leg presses. I have to watch it when I do squats because my thighs grow so easily and I have to make sure they don't get out of proportion. I don't like to do front squats because I feel unsure with that bar in front of me. But, if you master it, then I'm sure it's a good movement. I then do standing and lying leg curls plus stiff-legged deadlifts for my hamstrings, which must stay balanced. My calf training is very basic, just standing calf raises, nothing else.

Q: What kind of training approach would you follow when your competition days are eventually over?

PARIS: I would always do a combined training system of weight training, bike riding, aerobics, mountain climbing, and walking. I would probably bodybuild three or four times a week for about 45 minutes or one hour because I really do like training with weights. I always tell people that what I do works for me. I can give people information about my experience, but each individual must find their own paths and priorities. If you want to be a competitor learn everything you can and take every advantage. But, you must find the way that works for you.

51

Nimrod King

Any way you look at it, any parent that christens their child Nimrod in this day and age must have a very dry sense of humor. Yet that's exactly what Mr. and Mrs. King named their son, some decades back in their native land of Trinidad. And granted, the name's origins mean such lofty things as "great hunter," or "mighty ruler," but in today's jargon, when you call someone a "Nimrod" you're not referring to their ability to bring a fox home from the hunt!

It was with this later connotation that our protagonist is most familiar and, up until he started serious bodybuilding at the age of 12, people used to tease him about his name, but after the age of 12, the young Mr. King packed a rock-solid 215 pounds onto that 5'7" frame and people stopped making fun of his appellation.

I did find Nimrod King a genuinely decent chap, the sort of fellow who will patiently indulge your every question if he feels that you're sincere in posing it and who is quite willing to share his wealth of bodybuilding wisdom with those eager to acquire it.

Naturally enough, when one of the most massive bodybuilders on the planet agrees to share his secrets on how he came to be that way, I'll be front row and center waiting to ask him "20 Questions."

Q: Nimrod, what first drew you to the sport of bodybuilding?

NIMROD: *I just wanted to be big! I didn't want to better my speed or my strength in football or my kick in soccer, it was just that I wanted to be intimidating! I started weight training at 12 years of age, and I weighed 110 pounds.*

Q: You weighed 110 pounds at 12, what do you weigh now?

NIMROD: *It all depends because I compete just twice a year, which sees me diet for three months and basically, my weight is very up and down. Off-season, my weight is 235 pounds, but precontest, on the day of the show, I'm 215.*

Q: What has been your proudest moment in the sport so far?

NIMROD: *When I won my first U.S. Professional show, and my second proudest moment would be to win it again this time around.*

Q: Is there anything that bothers you about the sport of bodybuilding?

NIMROD: *I guess the fact that you get little respect for all the hard work that you put into the sport. People often don't understand that when they see a bodybuilder in a pro contest that this guy just went through a three-month hectic diet, 100 percent strict; no junk food, no alcohol, no greasy foods, no sugar, and the last five days before the contest, his diet has become 10 to 20 percent even more strict. This means, in fact, that he's going through sodium depletion, and the cutting out of certain liquids in your system. And most people do not give you the recognition and respect for all the hard work you put into that.*

Q: Do you include aerobics in your precontest phase of training?

NIMROD: *No, because my metabolism is so high and so rapid, and my style of training is so unorthodox; it involves very high reps and very low sets. I just don't need to put aside an extra two hours a day for aerobics.*

Q: How important do you think genetics are in bodybuilding?

NIMROD: *They're important! When you look at someone like Haney, for example, or a wrestler like Hulk Hogan, you'll see that Haney has very tiny joints, very tiny bones, so his muscles will stand out more onstage. Hulk Hogan, his bones are about four times the size of Lee's, so onstage,*

Haney would appear to be the most muscular.

Q: What are your thoughts on the recent move to introduce drug testing to the professional men's ranks?

NIMROD: *I do think it's well worth a change because, and this goes back to what I said before about getting little recognition, a lot of people attribute so much of what we do to drugs and don't realize the amount of hard dieting that we put into it. Maybe with drug testing, it will give the sport of body-building more credibility.*

Q: Who would you classify as the top 10 physiques of all time?

NIMROD: *Well, when I was younger, I admired the physiques of many bodybuilders, which included such greats as Robby Robinson, Sergio Oliva, Bertil Fox, Albert Beckles, Lee Haney, Johnny Fuller, Arnold Schwarzenegger, Mike Mentzer, Rick Wayne, and Serge Nubret.*

Q: Nimrod, you have perhaps the great muscle mass of any competitor today. What then has been your most productive training routine?

NIMROD: *For me, in my training, if you go back to how I trained five years ago, it hasn't changed at all! It's just basic, with maybe one or two things added on. I started with the basics and I was able to add on to that style of training, and I found*

that the basics were an excellent starting point and, bit by bit, my routine evolved to the one that I am currently using. I feel that this has been my most productive.

Q: Alright then, what is your current training routine, the one that's been so productive?

NIMROD: *Training for me is like this: I train on a three-day-on/one-day-off schedule. On the first day I do back and biceps; the second day would be chest, shoulders, traps, and triceps; the third day would be legs; and the fourth day would be a rest day before I would repeat the cycle once again.*

Q: How many sets would you do for each of those body parts?

NIMROD: *Well, on day one, for back I would do maybe 20, and for the biceps 12. On day two, chest 27, calves 20, shoulders 22, triceps, like biceps, about 12. Day three, which is leg day, I would train calves as well, but for legs I would do 30 to 32 sets, and then I would rest on the fourth day.*

Q: That's an awful lot of sets, and you've mentioned that you do very high repetitions as well, Do you ever find yourself overtrained on using such a system?

NIMROD: *No, I've never overtrained on it. I do feel, you have to understand that once you think of overtraining, your mind can condition your body to become overtrained and tired, and all the rest of it. So I try not* *to think of overtraining. I remember over the years that I've trained, getting frustrated at a lack of progress and asking myself, "Am I overtraining?" "Yes, I must be overtraining!" And I just got myself so confused that I would then disassemble my entire workout programs and have them all upside down and backward.*

Q: How many days per week do you think the average person can train without overtraining because, the power of the mind notwithstanding, overtraining is a very real and physical condition?

NIMROD: I would have to say that if their aim was to put on size, they should train no more than four days a week.

Q: For most people who work out, what routine would you recommend from your personal experience that would allow them to put on some really impressive muscle mass?

NIMROD: I would recommend just the basics, and for each body part no more than 12 to 16 sets. The highest amount of sets would be for the largest body part. For example, legs would be either 3 sets of four exercises, or 4 sets of three exercises, selected to cover the calves, hamstrings, and quads. They should train no more than four days a week with reps ranging anywhere from 10 to 15. How you would space your workouts out would depend basically on the flexibility of your time

schedule. For example, if you do work on Mondays and Sundays, then the ideal workout schedule would be Tuesdays, Wednesdays, Fridays, and Saturdays. If a person works a 9 a.m. to 5 p.m. shift, one of the busiest days in the gym is on a Monday, so I would try and avoid that Monday, but start my workout on a Tuesday.

Q: Nimrod, you're known for having, among other things, absolutely huge arms. What is your present routine for your arms?

NIMROD: Well, I would have to go back to when I first began training. When I first began, my arms were actually my worst body part and I was doing 20 sets for my arms. Then I was overtraining. But it did help in that it pumped me up—it didn't give me much mass, but it gave me shape and it did give me peak and roundness. When I was finally able to pack on some size, by increasing my calories and also decreasing my sets, my arms just got bigger and expanded from the inside. My routine at present is that I start off with biceps, 4 sets of incline alternating dumbbell curls, then on to 4 sets of preacher curls with dumbbells, and finally 4 sets of dumbbell concentration curls. Right now I only use dumbbells because I find that using dumbbells requires you to balance the weights much more, which involves more gripping and really helps in building up the forearms. I find that dumbbells are a lot more beneficial than barbells because my joints are quite small. Using barbells involves a lot of twisting of the wrist, and that puts too much pressure on my wrists. I remember years ago, coming out of the gym with my wrists just aching and hurting real bad. And I switched over to dumbbells and it took the pressure off my wrists. I could swivel them in various exercises, and it also helped to build my forearms. For me it was a big improvement. In any event, I use dumbbells now, but when training my arms I seldom train my biceps and triceps together. In fact, in my 12 years of training I would say that I've trained my biceps and triceps together for probably a four-month period one summer.

Q: Why do you prefer to train biceps and triceps separately from one another?

NIMROD: Well, I believe in getting the full-ness out of intense concentration on a muscle group like arms. You have to focus them to build them up. You have to make some sacrifices. Some people, you know, will never build their arms up because they're too much in love with the feel of the pump in the arm when both the bis and tris are pumped and hard. Mentally for them it's difficult to split up the biceps and the triceps mainly because once you pump the bis and you don't pump the tris, your arm's not as big. You can't concentrate on any muscle group properly when you're splitting your focus and concentration

between two muscle groups at the same time.

Q: What is your triceps routine, which you use on opposite days from your biceps routine?

NIMROD: For my triceps I do 5 sets of triceps pushdowns with a small bent bar. Then I move on to 4 sets of triceps knock-outs with a rope. Then it's 4 sets of one-arm reverse-grip triceps pushdowns. On most of my exercises, I don't pyramid the weights. What I do is keep the same weight for, say, triceps pushdowns, which is about 120 pounds, and then shoot for 20 reps each set until I've done 5 sets of 20 reps. I remember when I was in Germany last year, they thought my training was impossible! They went to University, and according to the University rules and books, my training was not a way to go about things. But my training has worked. And I must point out that when I'm doing barbell exercises, like flat or incline bench pressing, or any type of pressing for that matter, I try not to lock out. I never fully extend my elbows. I keep my elbows bent and only come up three-quarters of the way and then go back down.

Q: Tell us then, how do you perform your repetitions?

NIMROD: My movements are performed quite quick and, again, three-quarter lock-out style. I feel that this way keeps the tension on the muscle at all times and helps bring the muscle out even more. I know that a lot of people when benching, for example, will lock the weight out, take a deep breath, and then let the weight down. Then they take a breath, push it out, take another breath, let it down, and so on. There's just so much time wasted there, you could get twice the benefit in half the time if you're just speeding things up.

Q: Leaving the realm of training aside for a moment, what philosophy of life do you subscribe to?

NIMROD: *I believe that a person should, number one, believe in him or herself; and anything is possible in life, it comes from the inner determination. And therefore, anything is possible when you put your mind to it.*

Q: Well, Nimrod, we've touched on your prescription for mass, but we haven't yet hit upon the diet you follow to get so ripped. What sort of nutritional program do you follow?

NIMROD: *Diet for me is basically just to follow a very low-fat, moderate protein diet. I don't count calories mainly because of my body type, which is considered to be a mesomorph. There's no need to count calories because my metabolism is so quick. I've learned how to listen to my body and know just how much food I can consume and how much I can't in order to come in ripped for a contest.*

52

Kevin Levrone

Kevin Levrone is one of the rare breed of pro bodybuilders who has had an amazing career spanning years (a rarity in the highly competitive pro world) and not only captured the hearts of his legions of fans the world over; he had the physique, size, symmetry, and know-how to pose it that made photographers smile, competitors nervous, and fans gasp with approval. It seems as though Kevin's fans can never get enough of what the man says, and they're going to be happy to learn even more in this edition of "20 Questions."

Q: Kevin, what first drew you into the sport of bodybuilding?

KEVIN: *I guess it was a childhood thing. When I was growing up my brothers all trained with weights, and that kind of I inspired me a lot. I grew up around weight training, and seeing what it did for my brothers really instilled a strong desire to do likewise.*

Q: How old were you when you first started working out?

KEVIN: *I was 12 years old when I first got into weight training in any meaningful sense.*

Q: What has been your proudest moment as a bodybuilder since that time?

KEVIN: *My proudest moment would definitely be winning the National Championships. That was the greatest moment of my life.*

Q: On the other side of the coin, what has been your lowest moment in the sport? Or is it still too early in your career to have experienced anything but highs?

KEVIN: *Well, I haven't really had a lowest moment yet, to be honest with you. When it comes to bodybuilding, everything seems to have come my way. I'm really pleased with the way that things have been going, so I really haven't had anything negative to say about it.*

Q: Kevin, for the benefit of the readers who might not be familiar with your accomplishments, can you tell us what contests you have won to date?

KEVIN: *In the past I've won every "little" contest in Maryland—in short, every contest that Maryland has hosted, including the Maryland State that qualified me for the Nationals. I also won the Junior Nationals, and from then on I prepared for the Nationals.*

Q: How old are you right now?

KEVIN: *Right now I'm 25 years of age.*

Q: What is your height and weight?

KEVIN: *My contest weight at the Nationals was 235 pounds, but my off-season weight hovers about 260 pounds at a height of 5'9".*

Q: Do you use aerobics in your precontest phase of training, and if so, what do you do and for how often?

KEVIN: *I definitely use aerobics in my training. I have to, in order to get ripped. I typically ride the bike or use the Stairmaster three times a week for 30 minutes a day. I start my aerobic training some four weeks out from a show. I use aerobic training every other day.*

Q: What is your position on the importance of genetics in determining one's ultimate success in the sport?

KEVIN: *I think, without question, that my success in the sport has been a direct result of my genetics. For me, it was a blessing, and I definitely think that is why I'm where I am today. That's why I've won the shows that I have won. I've done the best that I could possibly do with my genetics. So, basically, that's what success in this sport is all about. Your body is built upon genetics, so it's vitally important with regard to your ultimate success. You either have it or you don't.*

Q: That's certainly true. Given the importance of genetics, there can also be no denying the importance of training methods in realizing one's genetic potential and, at a contest weight of 230 pounds, at a height of 5′9″, you certainly know a thing or two about how to stimulate muscle growth. What has been your most productive training routine?

KEVIN: *Heavy training! Heavy weights and basic bodybuilding movements such as the squat, barbell row, and bench press. My current routine also includes the basics as my core movements. Basic heavy squats, heavy bent-over rows, heavy chest movements, and then when I come to the smaller body parts I'll go to higher reps and higher intensity for the triceps, biceps, and calves.*

Q: Do you use high sets and lots of exercises, or do you subscribe to the heavy weights and low sets methodology?

KEVIN: *I typically use heavy weights and low sets. For back I'll do maybe 6 sets of 12 reps, depending on the weight, of course. Sometimes I'll use only 8 reps to get the job done, and it will be heavy. For legs I'll use 6 sets per exercise for maybe 10 reps and heavy again. For chest I'll do bench presses for 4 sets of 8 reps, then incline presses and flyes. Each set that I go to I'll do 4 sets of 8 reps.*

Q: Let's get down to specifics. Let's find out what your exact routine is, body part per body part, starting with legs.

KEVIN: *My leg routine consists of squats, hack squats, and leg extensions, and I'll alternate leg presses with squats from workout to workout.*

Q: Before we learn the rest of your exercises, sets, and reps, I would like to sidetrack to a particular issue that I've heard about your monstrous training poundages! What are some of your top poundages in various exercises?

KEVIN: *Well, in bench presses I've been up to 600 pounds, and I use 500 for reps. I can do 405 pounds for warm-ups too. Of course, I only do this to build my size. Hell, it's how I built my body! In squats I've been up to 800 pounds and 700 for reps. It's nothing to do 405 for reps either. In bent-over rows I've been up to 405 pounds and typically work out with 315 pounds.*

Q: Wow! People are always raving on about your arm development, so what's your magic arm routine?

KEVIN: *I'll do standing alternate dumbbell curls to start my biceps training. Again, I train them heavy, going up to 70 or 80 pounds. From alternates I'll go on to straight barbell curls. I don't do these all that heavy, usually with 150 pounds and then I'll do preacher curls with 110 pounds and really squeeze it up. Then I'll pick up a pair of 50-pound dumbbells and finish up with hammer curls. My reps are still in the 8 to 10 range. For triceps I'll start with regular pushdowns, overhead dumbbell* *extensions, one arm at a time, and I'll go heavy on this one as well with 60 pounds for reps. Gotta pump it up, man! In push-downs, I'll go up to 120 for relatively high reps, and reverse curls downward I'll also go to 120 pounds.*

Q: In the schematic of your training program itself, does it break down into a three-day-on/one-day-off system, or are you more of a four-day-on/one-day-off type of trainee?

KEVIN: *I train three days on and one day off, with the body part breakdown being chest, shoulders, and triceps one day with maybe some calves thrown in on that first day. Then on day two I'll train legs. When I say legs I mean quadriceps by themselves or with calves. The next day when I come to train, day three, I'll do back, biceps, and hamstrings. On day four I'll take the day off.*

Q: When you first started out in bodybuilding, who were your influences or heroes in the sport?

KEVIN: *Well, of course, Arnold Schwarzenegger when I first started out. Now it would have to be Lee Haney because of his overall view on the sport. He still has a level head, and if I ever have as much success in this sport as he does, I'd like to still be calm, cool, and collected and have total control of everything like he does.*

Q: How many days per week do you think that the average bodybuilder can engage in

weight training without getting into overtraining?

KEVIN: *I would have to say four or five days a week maximum, depending on how heavy the individual trained, with the heavier you train increasing the likelihood of overtraining. I think that you can work a body part maybe two times a week and still put on mass. Any more than that and you're training for definition.*

Q: To leave the realm of training aside for a moment, what philosophy of life do you subscribe to? What standards do you appeal to in order to guide your decision-making process?

KEVIN: *Well, I always believe in God. I come from a strong Christian background, so that gives me a lot of drive and determination. My early childhood days I still recall when my mother and father taught me responsibility and to treat everybody equal with regard to race, color, and things like that. So that background had a lot to do with how I've developed, mentally, and how I am today. Never give up no matter how hard things get. You've just got to keep going, and ultimately you will prevail!*

Q: What does a guy who bench presses 700 pounds do to relax? Perhaps press 300 pounds?

KEVIN: *I eat to relax. It really makes me feel good to eat a meal. I'm giving something back to my body after taking so much* away from it via training. When I eat, I feel real good about that.

Q: What tips can you offer our readers who are looking to put on size but who are not necessarily interested in competing?

KEVIN: Make sure that you definitely eat the proper foods, get a lot of sleep and proper rest. This is very important. You need a calm, simple life that is free of distractions. The reason for this is that you can't focus on your training objectives if you have a lot of distractions in your life. And train no more than five days a week, and know what you want and go for it.

53

Lenda Murray

She was born February 22, 1962, on the poor East Side of Detroit, Michigan. Lenda Ann Murray was one of five daughters delivered to the Murray family and, by all reports, was always outgoing and athletic. Now, being regarded as one of the greatest female bodybuilders of all time offends her modesty, but her physique and stage presence belie her sense of propriety. She was also a cheerleader in the state for a professional football team in Michigan and was about to sign on as a cheerleader in Dallas when the world of bodybuilding beckoned. However, lest you think that our reigning Ms. Olympia is all brawn and no brains, think again. The girl has a degree from Western Michigan University and served for four years as a human resources rep for the UNISYS Corporation before becoming the brightest star in the IFBB firmament.

You would not find a more thoughtful or considerate athlete in any sport competing today, and it's this scribe's wish that the business aspect of the sport of bodybuilding doesn't in any way jade her outlook on both

the sport and life itself. She's a great gal, a congenial interviewee, and a gracious champion. And she's about to answer "20 Questions."

Q: Lenda, how did you prepare for this year's Ms. Olympia?

LENDA: Oh gosh, I just worked really hard. I've been planning everything for this contest since the end of last year's contest. Likewise, I planned for last year's Ms. Olympia contest for a full year after the North American Championships in 1989. I put a lot of thought into my routine, into my music, I thought about what posing suit I should wear. I thought

and did research and looked at all the different posing suits and which one would best complement my physique. So I did a lot of work, as much as I could with the resources that I had.

Q: What about your diet? You always seem to enter a contest ripped to the bone! Are you a meticulous calorie counter?

LENDA: Oh yeah, I counted every calorie! I have a record from day one of exactly what I did.

Q: How many calories were you on for this contest?

LENDA: I was on 3,500 calories. I was high calorie-wise, but just this last week, leading up to the contest, I went down to about 2,500 calories, which helped me to maintain my leanness right down to the day of the show.

Q: What kind of training schedule did you follow for the Ms. Olympia contest?

LENDA: I train three days on and one day off. I've always felt that this allowed me the most recovery time and allowed me to give my all to each and every body part that I trained.

Q: What is your body part breakdown on such a system?

LENDA: I train my back and biceps together and legs or quads by themselves. I train my chest and triceps together, and that's it.

Q: How many sets do you find to be most effective for stimulating maximum muscle growth in these body parts?

LENDA: Actually it all depends on my intensity. For a large body part, like back or legs, I'll do four exercises, and if I do four exercises, I'll probably only do 3 sets for each exercise. I'm really into form! I'm not really into heavy, heavy weight. I'm into form so that I can concentrate on each repetition, instead of saying, "Okay, I have 12 reps, or 15 reps to complete." I think about each rep and go out max! I take each set to the point where I can't do another rep.

Q: To hark back on your definition again, what sort of aerobics program do you follow to get ripped?

LENDA: What I did for this show was to ride the bike or some other such aerobic activity for 45 minutes prior to my first meal, and then after my last meal I did an additional 45 minutes of aerobics. That really fired my metabolism up. That's why I was able to eat so much calorie-wise and still get defined.

Q: Hmm. Sounds suspiciously like a Parrillo-influenced aerobics program.

LENDA: Well, it is. I visited John Parrillo in Cincinnati and learned quite a bit about eating the right food as well as the role aerobics play in a bodybuilding program, and the diet tips paid off as I won the

North American Championships and two Ms. Olympia titles.

Q: Undisputedly. What do you think a Ms. Olympia should do—after winning the title?

LENDA: I think that she should do the best she can to represent the sport of women's bodybuilding and the IFBB. In my own example, I'll try and follow what Cory Everson did because she did an excellent job and she turned the sport around and people outside of bodybuilding know what bodybuilding is, they know about Cory Everson, and so I'd say a Ms. Olympia winner should carry herself well.

Q: What areas of the sport do you think there's room for improvement in?

LENDA: Well, I think, as with everything else, there's always room for improvements to be made. However, I think it will take time. The sport has only been around 11 years for the women, and that's not really as long as, say, the 26 years that it's been around for the men. So it's a very difficult thing to try and say what the women should look like, what they should be like, what they should do, and it's just hard when you're going by looks as opposed to a sport that's judged by who crosses the finish line first. I'm not denying that there are some things that definitely could be changed such as the variance over posing suits—that seems to change from year to year.

Q: If you were to set the standards for women's bodybuilding, tell us what would they be?

LENDA: *Definitely, I do like the drug testing element, mainly because I don't want women to look like men and get into that, because the drugs have a very different effect on the women than they do on the men. So to me it's very important that this issue would be a part of it to at least maintain some femininity in the sport. I've seen a change over the year when they implemented drug testing, especially in the way that the women look, and I think that's good in the sport.*

Q: Your home is Detroit. What has been the reaction to your success in Motown?

LENDA: *Oh, they can't believe it! They knew when I first started competing that I had the potential to do well. You know, the shape and physical structure to one day be Ms. Olympia, but they didn't really know if I had what it took—in terms of willingness to go out and work as hard as was necessary. I knew I had what it took because of my past experience in sports. I've been involved in sports for so long.*

Q: Gauging by your legs, I'd say that one of those sports was track.

LENDA: *Oh yeah, track. In running track I was a sprinter, which really laid a solid foundation for my hamstrings and quad development.*

Q: What about your shoulders? You have the most phenomenal deltoid development this side of Ron Love! What do you do for your delts?

LENDA: *Oh thank you. I love to do dumbbell presses and all types of dumbbell and barbell presses. Actually, it's funny you should mention Ron Love's name because when I first started training, Ron was the first one to approach me and tell me that I had a great physique and that I should seriously think about entering the sport of bodybuilding. And you know Ron's got great shoulders, so I got my shoulder workout from Ron 100 percent.*

Q: Alright then, now we get down to our futuristic questions. Do you intend to use bodybuilding as a stepping-stone of sorts, as Cory Everson did, to enter the world of films?

LENDA: *Oh yeah, sure. I think in my life, everything that's happened has been a stepping-stone to something else. Just like cheerleading and track and gymnastics gave me the foundation to build this physique. So, sure, I think that bodybuilding will lead to something else in my life. There will come a certain point, undoubtedly, like Cory, where she won the Olympia six times and now she wants to do something different. I'll be no different when my time comes.*

Q: Lenda, despite the fact that Ron Love thought you one of the world's most natural bodybuilders, a lot of work has gone into the building of your physique. What's been your most productive routine?

LENDA: I think my most productive training routine was when I trained four days on, followed by one day off. In this system I did my quads alone and my hamstrings separately. This gave me a little more time to concentrate on that body part instead of working my quadriceps, and by the time I got to my hamstrings I was too tired to train them properly.

Q: What was the breakdown of this particular routine?

LENDA: I trained my quadriceps on Monday along with calves. Then on Tuesday I would do upper body with back and biceps, which I trained together because you're already kind of working your biceps when you train your back. On the training day, Wednesday, I would train my hamstrings and shoulders, and then on the fourth day I'd train my chest and triceps.

Q: Would this include the same set range as the three-day-on/one-day-off systems you alluded to earlier?

LENDA: Yeah, pretty much. What I do when I train is just try to train really hard and high-intensity, and if I'm at a point where I don't feel I've done enough, or had a good workout, then I'll add something else, such as another exercise. I train pretty much instinctively. If my body doesn't respond to

an exercise, I'll drop it and move on to something else. Then if sometimes I'm in the gym and my mind starts wandering or won't follow what I'm doing, then I'll just end the workout then and there because if my mind is not into it then I can't concentrate on each rep—which can leave you wide open to possibly injuring yourself. At this time your body's telling you take a rest, go relax and sit back.

Q: What about your abs? They're so thick and cut. What do you do for them?

LENDA: I like doing crunches and reverse crunches. Actually, I got my abdominal routine from Lee Haney. I read an article that he had about three years ago; he does crunches and reverse crunches. Then I do things like twists. I don't like to do things with weights for my obliques because I like my waist to stay nice and small, so I just concentrate more on the rectus abdominus instead of the obliques. I still train my obliques but not as heavy or as concentrated as I do my abs.

Q: Lenda, you've touched on your approaches to diet and training and how John Parrillo influenced your dietary habits. However, you didn't really tell us what sort of habits you held, nutritionally speaking, before the encounter?

LENDA: I used to diet for a contest by starving myself. I'd go down as low as 1,200 calories a day, low carbs, you know. And I was dead on my feet. This, of course, means that my workouts weren't all that productive, and because of the diet, I was losing a lot of very hard-earned muscle tissue. However, after talking with John Parrillo, I started eating six meals a day with my calories reaching up to 4,500 on a daily basis. I'll reduce this number to 3,500 as the contest gets closer and even to 2,500, but never lower. Which, combined with the aerobics program twice a day, really lowers my body fat.

54

Mike Ashley

Some years ago, I had stayed at a resort in Ocho Rios, Jamaica. The resort had a health club, and it was not long before I decided to check out the equipment. While doing so, I met the resort trainer, a young Jamaican lad who possessed a tremendous physique. I asked him about training in Jamaica and what instructional materials existed for him to study from. "We get all the magazines like *FLEX* and *Muscle & Fitness*," he replied, "and I read all about the champions and their training systems."

His reply seemed to invite the next question, "Who then is your favorite bodybuilder?" Without a second thought he shot back, "Michael Ashley, because he's a local boy and doesn't use drugs to build his physique!" The lad went on to tell me about the time that Ashley had trained in one of the Island gyms and astounded everyone present with his phenomenal muscular development.

When I returned, I remembered my talk with the health club instructor and how Mike Ashley's drug-free reputation was truly of international renown. Ashley's physique had a similar impact upon the audience and judges at the Arnold Classic, held in Columbus, Ohio. The show was the first of the professional men's shows to be drug tested and, out of a field of 13 competitors, Ashley was, true to form, one of the nine who passed the drug test.

Furthermore, he was in such phenomenal shape, with a muscle density not previously seen on a posing dais, that even the great Arnold Schwarzenegger, the copromoter of the contest, told me afterward, "Ashley could have won this show [he would, technically, place second, but he was awarded first place a week later when the winner tested positive for steroid use], the difference between first and second is just so minute at this level."

And certainly if Ashley could look that good, drug free, and place well over other competitors who were on steroids, it seemed obvious that the man and his training methods were on the right track. But how did he train to get so huge? How did he diet to get so ripped? What were his thoughts on the current drug testing implementation? It was high time we had a talk with Mike Ashley and asked him "20 Questions."

Q: First of all Mike, congratulations on your excellent condition at the Arnold Classic in Columbus, Ohio. Did you do anything different in your training for that show?

MIKE: *Thank you. Yes, the real difference was in my diet and aerobic training; I'm on a much-higher-calorie diet. I ate everything pretty much the same as I do normally when leading up to a show, but the one thing that I did differently was to include aerobics twice a day, which is something that I didn't do before.*

Q: What made you decide to do aerobics twice a day?

MIKE: *I was talking to an NPC judge who told me about eating more food and doing much more aerobics, which tend to cause the metabolism to pick up and it enables you to come into a contest bigger, harder, and healthier. You really feel better. So I tried it, and it worked.*

Q: How many calories a day did you actually eat when ripping up for the contest?

MIKE: *5,000 calories [5,000? That's not even a diet!] Yeah, what I do is dehydrate potatoes and concentrate the calories, you know, like dried fruit. This enables you to eat more food, but it doesn't take up as much space in your stomach.*

Q: I'm amazed that you're able to get that ripped by consuming so many calories on a daily basis—what's your current body weight?

MIKE: *I'm currently 195 pounds. I was one of the lightest guys in the show. Steve Brisbois was in actual fact the lightest. My height is 5'8", so I'm not a really massive guy.*

Q: You may weigh 195, pounds but you look like you're 220 pounds. What does your aerobic routine consist of?

MIKE: *I have a stationary bike at home that I ride before my meals in the morning and then again after my meals at night. I either do the stationary bike, the Stairmaster, or else a rowing machine that I also have at home. I just rotate the various exercises and do each one for approximately 30 to 45 minutes per session, twice a day.*

Q: What has been your training leading up to the various pro shows that you've competed in this year?

MIKE: *Well, as far as training is concerned, I haven't done anything different for these shows. I just cycle my training; I train three on, one off. I have a heavy day, a medium day, and a light day. On my heavy days my repetitions go as low as 6, on my medium days 12, and on my light days up to 15 on my upper body and 20 on my lower body. I just cycle it; heavy, then the next workout medium, then the next workout light, and then back to heavy workouts again.*

Q: What is your routine these days that allows you to pack on so much muscle mass on your 5'8" frame?

MIKE: I start off with back and biceps, then on the next day I do legs and shoulders, and then chest and triceps, followed by a day off, and then I repeat the cycle. On my chest days, for example, I would do incline benches, barbell, or dumbbell; I rotate them from workout to workout. Incline dumbbell presses, flat dumbbell presses, pec dec flyes, and that would be for a heavy workout. On a medium chest workout, I would do incline dumbbell presses, flat dumbbell presses, dumbbell flyes, and dips or cable crossovers. On a light day, I'll do incline dumbbell presses supersetted with dumbbell flyes, flat barbell presses supersetted with pec dec flyes, and then superset cable crossovers with dips, and that would be my chest workout. For my triceps [which have to be the best in the business], I'll just do close-grip benches. I used to do a lot of lying triceps extensions, but my elbows did start to bother me from doing heavy (150 pounds) extensions, so now I just do close-grips, pushdowns, and dumbbell French presses. I see in the magazines people doing all those fancy cable curls for their triceps and all that, but I don't resort to that. I train very basic, and it seems to work for me. For my back I'll do barbell rowing, front and rear lat pulldowns, seated cable rowing, and one-arm dumbbell rows. For biceps, I'll do alternate dumbbell curls or barbell curls, depending on the day, followed by preacher curls and seated dumbbell curls, and I supinate my movements. As you can see, my routine is very basic. I think before a contest my biggest change is in my dieting. It's certainly the more important percentage, so I just generate more in the dieting aspect of the contest.

Q: What is the number of sets per exercise that you tend to generally follow?

MIKE: Well, it's 15 sets for my biceps and triceps, chest can be up to 20, legs can be as much as 30 because I've had a lot of problems with my knees. I had knee surgery last year, which is why I didn't compete last year. The doctors performed what they call a lateral release on my knee because my kneecap keeps shifting out of place, so they had to take some tissue out of the lateral muscle in order to align the kneecap, but it has been my third surgery, so I have to be careful.

Q: Do you ever find when you're doing upwards of 20 sets, that you ever become overtrained on this system?

MIKE: No, because I eat so much that my body can handle it. You see, I'm still eating fish and green beans, you know, I'm not cutting any nutrients out, and I'm able to eat normally!

Q: How did you get started in bodybuilding, Mike, what drew to you the sport?

MIKE: *I got started in high school.*

Q: How many days per week do you think the average bodybuilder can train without overtraining, or is that strictly diet related?

MIKE: *Well, it depends on how much the individual does. You can train six days a week and not overtrain. The fact that lots of other bodybuilders are doing that sort of thing proves it. But it depends on how much you do while you're in the gym. For the average type of bodybuilder, I would recommend training four days a week, like a Monday, Tuesday, Thursday, and Friday type of split routine. Sets would vary between 9 and 12, but, and this is where a lot of people get confused, when I say that I do 15 sets for biceps, I mean that I'm only doing 9 really effective sets out of those 15. The other 6 are just getting me up to the weight I want to use because I train really heavy, like standing alternate dumbbell curls with 80-pound dumbbells for 8 reps. Now, why would I start out by jumping right into a weight like that? My tissues and ligaments, they can't handle it. So I have to work my way up, and those sets are not necessarily as effective as those last few sets. That's why I say my total number of effective sets might not necessarily be as high for a particular body part. I would recommend that they perform maybe 9 effective sets with a few warm-up sets in there as well. It's the same with all body parts because a warm-up is very important.*

Q: What philosophy of life do you subscribe to? What attitude guides you in your day-to-day existence?

MIKE: *My thing is just to be the best that I can be in whatever I do. I'm a generally optimistic individual, and the thing about me is, if I'm doing the best that I can do, I'm not going to kill myself to do more, because then that's not me, that's something else, or someone else. I like to keep reality in perspective all the time. Once a guy looks at his physique and sees someone else's and he's like, "Gee, maybe if I change this or that, I can look like so and so," that's not being realistic. Reality is always there for me, and that is why I always tend to do my own thing. If I go out and I place high one day, or low the next, I'm still the same Mike. I'm not a follower. I'm a very stubborn individual, and I set the path for myself. We could say that 98 percent of the pros use steroids, why am I not using steroids? It's because I'm a stubborn Jamaican kid and I just believe in doing what I want to do. I don't want to do it, so why would I do it? When I was a kid, even the other guys would want to do this or that and I'd say, "No, that's not what I want to do." I was never a gang member, or in a cliquish group. I was the rebel! I did what I wanted to do.*

Q: What can we do to improve our sport of bodybuilding?

MIKE: I think we have to start thinking about ourselves more. One of the problems in our sport right now is that we're trying too hard to please the people out there. That's what's causing some of the guys to take all kinds of drugs. I'm really concerned about the drug issue. It's a fact that they all take these kinds of drugs and people say, "Ah well, look at him, he doesn't look that huge this year," and then the guy goes back and starts taking all sorts of drugs to make themselves into muscle freaks just to please the public. If you were to eliminate steroids from the sport, there would still be a winner and a loser.

Q: Do you train any differently in the off-season?

MIKE: Yes, I switch from a three-on/one-off to a four-on/one-off system. It's just a matter of taking more time before hitting that body part again, giving myself more recuperation time. This gives my body the ability to recuperate and again, grow. As it gets closer to the show, my major concern is in refining myself. I'm not concerned with growth, even though I like to maintain as much lean body weight as is possible.

Q: Do you like isolation movements?

MIKE: I don't think they're as effective as the basic movement.

Q: What advice would you give someone who wants to train naturally and build a great body?

MIKE: I'd recommend for them to eat a well-balanced diet, train hard, rest, and wish for the best! There's nothing more to it.

55

Thierry Pastel

One of the more introverted bodybuilders competing today is Parisian Thierry Pastel. Possessed of one of the greatest physiques to ever grace a posing dais, Pastel is nevertheless withdrawn when it comes to giving out information on how he created it.

Not that he's protectively belligerent or anything; it's just that his training methods are so instinctive that any description of what he did in his last workout will be obsolete by his next one. A frustrating task for a journalist asking questions, but there can be no disputing the results of his almost Taoist training methods. Pastel has been described as the most complete physique in bodybuilding today, and that may be correct.

Pastel possesses flawless proportions, excellent symmetry, and a stage presence that is second to none. He's a hard man to track down, but when I did I made sure that I had my tape recorder with me. After all, it was an excellent opportunity to ask the elusive Thierry Pastel "20 Questions."

Q: Tell me, Thierry, what first drew you to bodybuilding?

THIERRY: *Well I always seemed to be muscular. I've always had a fairly high metabolism, so I've always been lean, and I have good genetics, so I thought that I might have the potential to do well in a sport that had such things as requisites for success.*

Q: Well, how long ago would that have been then?

THIERRY: *I guess my first training session would have been in 1983.*

Q: What, thus far, has been your proudest moment as a bodybuilder?

THIERRY: *I'm proud to have been called a professional in the IFBB and also to be able to make a living from the sport. Not everyone can do that. I'm also proud in that I'm able to improve myself as a professional in every show that I enter.*

Q: What is your current training routine?

THIERRY: *I don't have any precise way of training. You see, I'm constantly trying to sharpen my physique, so I'm constantly using different training methods. I train pretty much instinctively, so I'm changing my training methods all the time.*

Q: I understand that you were training with Serge Nubret for a while. Can we deduce from this that you also train with the high reps that Serge does?

THIERRY: *I use every type of training method, including the one that Serge popularized. High reps, low reps, all kinds. You have to in order to constantly improve and shock your body into growth.*

Q: What kind of program split do you follow before a contest?

THIERRY: *I train six days a week with Sundays off for rest. I find I need to do this in order to come into a contest as hard as I need to.*

Q: How many sets would you do on average per body part?

THIERRY: *I do a lot of sets, sometimes I'll do leg extensions for 300 reps just to shock the muscles.*

Q: You are also known in bodybuilding circles as being very, very ripped. What's your secret?

THIERRY: *I think a lot of it has to do with my metabolism. A lot of my definition is natural due to my genetic predisposition. I eat a lot, but then I train a lot, too, in order to burn it off. Sometimes up to six hours a day!*

Q: Well, Thierry, you seem to have everything handed to you on a silver platter, at least in terms of growing on any training system and getting ripped on any diet. What then is your philosophy of life?

THIERRY: *It's a positive one. I believe that you should try and be positive about any situation. It benefits you in the long run.*

Q: Do you follow any sort of aerobics program in order to enhance your muscularity?

THIERRY: *Yes, sometimes I will do some running. A lot of running actually. In the off-season I'll run for one hour and only once a week.*

Q: What are your future plans?

THIERRY: *I'd like to win every Night of Champions contest I enter, as well as the Arnold Classic and the Olympia contests some day.*

Q: What are your thoughts on the standard of bodybuilding physiques over the years. Have they improved since Arnold's time, or was that as high as they could get and we have simply maintained the standards over the years?

THIERRY: *Bodybuilding standards are getting more difficult to attain, and unquestionably they're better than in the past. In Arnold's time, it was pretty basic. Now you could not even compare him with Lee Haney. The science and everything has evolved so much. Diet too.*

Q: What components do you think make up a great bodybuilder?

THIERRY: *I think a sense of the dramatic when you are on stage, with respect for your fans, and be amiable when approached.*

Q: How would you best like to be remembered after you retire?

THIERRY: *I'd like to be remembered as someone who gave something to bodybuilding. Someone who was always doing their best and who was always true to himself and never acted like someone he wasn't.*

Q: Back to training for a moment. Having trained with Serge Nubret, was he any kind of an early influence for you in respect to bodybuilding?

THIERRY: *No, not really. I didn't have any idols or influences. I just trained hard and inevitably grew.*

Q: You are renowned for having complete development. Do you have any tips on proportion that you could maybe pass on to our readers?

THIERRY: *Proportion is largely genetic, but I feel that, like art, you must train for balance and really concentrate on the muscle you're training. I always make a mental connection between my mind and the muscle I am training; this way, cheating is eliminated and the weights become merely an extension of my mind's will.*

Q: Your triceps are absolutely fantastic. Now I know you "do whatever you feel like" whenever you go into a gym to train, but what is your triceps routine?

THIERRY: *Well, thank you very much, but in all honesty, my exercises are the same as everybody else, the only difference is my concentration. I get right into the muscle,* and feel every inch of every movement—that's the secret to building muscle! However, in answer to your question, I'll tell you what I do—sometimes—for triceps. I always believe in thoroughly warming up the body part I'm training. For triceps, it might be reverse grip pulldowns. If I warm up with reverse grip pulldowns, I'll also start my real training with that same exercise. I put my hands about 20 centimeters apart and, again, I concentrate fully on the completed contracted position on every rep. I don't really count sets, but I suppose it would be in the neighborhood of 5 to 6 sets with reps in the range of 12 to 20. I'll do my pushdowns with an underhand grip for my first exercise and then move on to regular grip pushdowns. I'll then go to bench dips, which I find to be great for building mass, but I don't use any weight on this movement. Instead, I'll just do the movement very slowly, making sure I feel every inch of the contraction. I'll usually finish off my triceps with an isolation movement like one-arm extensions. I believe that to have perfect arms, you need to draw from a great variety of movements.

Q: How long does it take you to train a particular body part?

THIERRY: *It will depend on the body part I'm training. My biceps or triceps I'll train in 30 minutes. My chest would be about 45 minutes, and likewise for my back and* deltoids. Legs take the longest, and for me it would be one hour in length.

Q: What about this "feel" that you've talked about? How do you know when this feeling has arrived or even what it's supposed to feel like?

THIERRY: *I do train for the pump and nothing more. If you train too long, you will lose your pump, which defeats your purpose in weight training. Overtraining your arms, spending too much time on them, will reduce their size. It always does. I always look in the mirror to determine just how my arm looks; if it's full—as full as I think I can pump it to—then I will do no more exercises.*

Q: We've finally been able to pin you down regarding your training. Now we need to know about your diet. What the heck do you put into yourself in order to feed those bloody great muscles of yours?

THIERRY: *First off, I never really diet at all. I like to eat. And I eat almost anything I want, but I usually eat proper foods. However, I can do this because I train so hard, sometimes six hours a day, and this type of training burns a lot of calories! I see so many people in the States who just train for an hour or so and consequently have to eat like birds—and they end up looking like birds. I eat a lot and have the muscle mass because of it.*

56

Robby Robinson

It's pointless denying it: few bodybuilders in the history of this sport have come close to equaling the popularity of Robby Robinson. At the age of 44 years, Robinson has been competing and, more important, placing in competitions for well over 15 years (a feat in itself that is nothing short of phenomenal!) and shows absolutely no signs of slowing down.

Robinson's mid 1970s battles with Mike Mentzer have become legend in the sport, and Robinson's physique has (is it possible!) even improved since his former heyday in the '70s. He's won more titles than most of the current champions combined, from World Pro to Mr. Universe with a few Best in the Worlds and Night of Champions thrown in for good measure. He even placed high enough recently at the Arnold Classic in Columbus, Ohio, to qualify for this year's IFBB Mr. Olympia in the "Windy City" of Chicago.

Always a favorite with the crowd, with the most phenomenal peaked biceps in the sport's history, Robby has continued to display a rock-hard, almost statuesque physique with flawless proportions, gargantuan mass, and flawless symmetry. When the time came to speak to the legendary "Black Prince," it was too hard to resist asking him "20 Questions."

Q: Robby, what first drew you into the sport of bodybuilding?

ROBBY: I just liked to look healthy. I've always been involved in athletics of one shape or another, track, weight lifting, football, those kinds of things. In actual fact, it was powerlifting which really got me started out in bodybuilding. I'd work the basic movements, then pick up more and more knowledge on the sport as time went by, and then switched to bodybuilding entirely.

Q: How old were you when you first started bodybuilding?

ROBBY: I was just 13 years old when I first got into bodybuilding, just a little guy. [laughs]

Q: Well, you've certainly come a long way from being a "little guy." What has been your proudest moment as a professional bodybuilder?

ROBBY: I would say that actually coming back and standing on stage with all the judges looking at me. I knew them all personally, like Jim Manion, Art Bedway, and guys like that, and I think that they knew my physique from before, in the '70s, and yet they all knew that I had improved. You could see it in their eyes, and that

meant to me that my comeback was real, and not just in my own mind. They knew that I was back, and that was a great feeling, to have my own beliefs confirmed. It just motivated me to keep on working harder in the gym. And, after working hard, I qualified to go back into the Olympia in 1987, where I placed fifth. That was a great show. I remember standing onstage with all the guys like Gaspari and Haney. Then I went backstage and was standing behind Lee Haney. Wow, he was so wide! I couldn't see anybody else in front of him! I looked at my physique, then I looked at Haney's, then I looked back at my physique, then back to Haney's, and I thought to myself [begins to chuckle], damn! I'd better go do some more work! But just being at that show motivated me to come back and train hard again. I seemed to feed on it. I received more respect from the competitors, trained with more intensity, and I'd shoot for more reps, concentrate extra hard, and wrap my hands to the bar. I'd wrap my hands to the dumbbells, to the lat machines, everything to maintain the force that I knew I needed to qualify to be an Olympian. I'm also fired up for any of the Arnold Classics.

Q: On the other side of the coin, what's been your lowest moment as a professional bodybuilder?

ROBBY: I think after doing so well that year, coming back and placing seventh at the Mr. Olympia. That was also, ironically, one of my lowest moments, and I thought to myself, "Well, if a champion is truly a champion then he should be able to get back up." You know, you get down, so you get back up! So I went back into the gym and started right up training again. You can be a great individual or a great athlete, but you must learn that you can't be great all the time. You'll have your moments, and I figure that was one of my moments. If I was going to be the great professional that I'd seen written and heard talked about, then I had to get back up. And I think that I got back up.

Q: When you first really broke onto the scene in professional bodybuilding, back in the mid 1970s, there were some phenomenal photographs taken of you in Gold's Gym and you were, as you've mentioned, training with savage intensity. Has your training altered much since those days?

ROBBY: I think that I've become calmer. I used to be a really hyper person, I'm not 27 or 28 anymore, not that age has anything to do with it, but I've learned that I've got to take care of myself a little more. My wife has also had a tremendous effect on my life. She's very understanding of what I'm into as a professional body-builder. In fact, she's into it as much as I am! She helps me with my diet and really motivates me to train harder.

Q: Speaking of training, do you still use aerobics these days?

ROBBY: Oh yeah, I ride the bike. In fact, I'm on my way to climb the stairs after this interview. I like to ride the bike and I think that aerobics are one of the keys to keeping the body fat low and keeping the body muscular.

Q: How often would you engage in aerobic exercise?

ROBBY: I'd try and do it two or three times a week, perhaps a little more just before a contest.

Q: How important do you think that genetics are in determining ultimate bodybuilding success?

ROBBY: I do think a lot about genetics and, I'm not trying to sound arrogant, but I think that I had [begins to laugh] good parents. Both my mother and father were well developed. My dad was 6' tall and went at 220 pounds naturally. He had long muscle bellies and was just a naturally strong, lean, muscular kind of guy. I'm sure that's where I got my shape and my symmetry.

Q: What were your thoughts regarding the IFBB's recent move to implement drug testing to the men's professional ranks?

ROBBY: I think that it's going to improve the sport of bodybuilding. I think that when you're taking drugs they unquestionably help in the development of muscle mass, but at the same time they have a tendency to cause problems within your own body chemistry. I think that the move is going to be a turnaround for the sport. A lot of people are going to see great physiques up there still, the same Robinsons, the same Haneys, the Gasparis, the Bannouts, the Parises. All those guys will still have great physiques, and that's what counts—that's what this sport is all about! It's about bodybuilding, and I think that all of us realize that we have to work harder and watch our diet a lot more from now on. And, instead of blowing up to 255 or 275 pounds in the off-season, we're going to have to keep it tapered down now. The drugs do assist in the recovery ability and allow you to recover quicker, whereas now you have to find that medium another way.

Q: Given that many people who work out are noncompetitive, but are inspired by bodybuilders who are competitive, what routine could you recommend for them to follow to gain muscular size?

ROBBY: *I would say stick to the basics. You know, you can get fancy, cute, and do all those pretty little exercises, which are great, but they're not going to develop massive muscles for you. They'll give you that "pumped" look, but that's not going to last you for any length of time. You've got to work those basics, the bend press, inclines, dumbbell flyes, dips, squats, leg presses, leg extensions, leg curls, and for biceps, barbell curls, Scott bench curls, and concentration curls, low pulley rows, T-bar rows, chins, those are the basic exercises that I feel a person should stick with for at*

least a couple of years because they actually develop a foundation. You should include some powerlifting movements in this such as bench press, squat, and deadlift, they should be there too. You can always go back to the basics periodically to help build and maintain that structural foundation. The more you stick with those basics, the better progress you'll have. I mean, even as far as I've gone in bodybuilding, and I've been training since I was 13 years old, I still have to go back to the basics; that's the whole key to keeping the body hard. The other exercises add "polish" and a little "glitter" basically, but the basics are the key to success in bodybuilding.

Q: You've mentioned that you had an extensive powerlifting background, and in your years of training, you must have utilized virtually every training system at one time or another. Which method of training has been the most productive training system that you've ever used?

ROBBY: *Well, like I said, it would be my basics and "slow for growth." You know what I mean? It's like a lot of people today go through their movements like they're in a hurry to go somewhere. They don't give a lot of thought to what they're doing. I think a movement should be carefully looked at; it should be a moment where you're actually in touch with the muscle that you're training. Forget about the amount of weight in your hands and just concentrate on contracting your biceps and feeling the* movement. I apply this to all of my exercises, from declines to inclines, in all of my presses. I'm controlling the weight, thinking about what I'm doing and concentrating on the muscle I'm training. That's the method I've been using for years, and it's the method that I'm still using.

Q: How long do you think that a bodybuilder should use a training system before he or she alters it to ensure continued progress?

ROBBY: I think that if you're making progress on a system and it's working for you, then you'd be silly to change it. And conversely, if a system isn't working for you, then it's time to change it. You have to find out what works for you and use it, and like I said before, if you're not making gains on a system, then you ought to change it, but only when it's stopped working for you.

Q: How many days per week do you think the average bodybuilder can train without overtraining, or is this a highly individual thing?

ROBBY: Well, for me, I trained with Gary Strydom some three or four months back, and we trained like maniacs. I'd come home and sit down, sometimes I'd forget to eat, I was out of it! I was so tired. I've trained with Mike Quinn, I've trained with Rich Gaspari. Gary and I trained for about a month and a half together in preparation for him to enter the Iron Man Grand Prix and my going to Columbus, Ohio, this past March, and we were training so hard there

that at one time his wife was telephoning my wife saying, "Will you come to the house—please!" I was so tired that I'd come home and I couldn't even cook my food. My wife works hard, and she didn't want to cook either [laughing]! Ah, man, when I look back on those days it was touchy, but then it was worth it too. I think that if you stick to the basics and work hard, say, a four-days-on/one-day-off system, then that's great. In fact, I think that if you do a four-days-on/one-day-off system and work out hard with intensity, then that's enough! You take that one day off and do the bicycle, that's how you do it. Four hard days, then a day off, and then go back on four days, really working on the movements and feeling the muscles contracting, doing extra reps, forced reps, and things like that, but this time around with lighter weights.

Q: How do you know when to back off on a muscle group once you've trained it thoroughly and you don't want to then overtrain it?

ROBBY: Waking up not feeling very good in the middle of the night is one way I know that I'm doing too much. Or if someone is coming up real quick behind me and I get jumpy, then I know that my central nervous system is saying, "Give us a break, let's get away from this!" Or if I'm sore, even after a day off, or a shower, or a massage. If I'm still sore that's a sign that I'm doing too much. That's when I'll take a little break.

It's hard on me because I'm an athlete, so sometimes if someone gets on my case, like Haney [laughs] who might say, "Robby, you look tired today," I'll just say, "Nah," but inside, I'm dying! You've really got to be able to admit when you've overtrained.

Q: What physiques have inspired you the most throughout your competitive career?

ROBBY: *Gosh, all of them! I mean, I respect various bodybuilders for various reasons. Some guys were huge, others had great shape or definition. I remember when I lived in Europe for two and a half years seeing Berry DeMey when he was just 19 years old and saying that this is going to be a guy to watch for. I'm an athlete, and I can appreciate the work that they've put into developing their physiques, and that's what counts. I really would have to say that all of them have motivated me at one point or another in my career.*

Q: During the 1970s, your battles with Mike Mentzer on the posing dais were legendary. You'd win a contest, and then he'd win the next one, and you two would seesaw back and forth for supremacy. That must have been an exciting era in your career?

ROBBY: *Oh yeah! In fact, I was just shooting a cover with Chris Lund the other day and Mike walked up to me and said, "Damn it, Robby! It pisses me off! You look incredible, and it just pisses me off!" And, you know, I can admire him and respect the fact that we did have some great battles, and I still*

have some pictures of Mike in my old catalogue. He's such a great competitor that it bothered him that we weren't still competing against one another. Yeah, those really were some great battles!

Q: When you're not in the gym, what do you do to relax and unwind?

ROBBY: *Go to the beach or ride my bike. I also like to shop, there's just so many things. I love to read, I love poetry and just reading, anything. I'll go out and buy a book and a couple of newspapers and read them front cover to back page. I also like antiques, and I go to antique stores quite often. I also love to go house hunting, going and picking out houses.*

Q: You're also one of the most financially successful bodybuilders competing today. What financial tips can you offer other bodybuilders to protect what money they do make from the sport?

ROBBY: *Well, I was lucky enough to be able to come back and encounter an attorney by the name of George Zachary—he doesn't like me to talk about him, and he's put together some financial things for me that will probably last me until another lifetime. It's providing me with the financial security that I'll eventually need when I decide to get out of bodybuilding. I'm also in the process of working on a clothing line—I also love clothes—that has my likeness called Body Alive, and it should be coming out.*

Q: What do you think we can do to improve our sport of bodybuilding?

ROBBY: *I think the way that they have already started, with the drug tests, is a step in the right direction. Get that stuff under control and maybe find other products that will elicit the same response as the drugs but that aren't harmful. I think this drug test will definitely change the way the whole outlook on the sport will be from now on. The fact that bodybuilding is receiving more coverage from the media is also a step toward improving it, plus the magazines' exposure, all of these things add up to improving both the sport and its exposure.*

Q: Well Robby, this certainly wouldn't be "20 Questions" if I didn't' get your "magic" arm routine and back routine. So, if you wouldn't mind, what's your secret to developing these world famous body parts of yours?

ROBBY: *There's really no secret. To my mind, a lot of my success has been, again, just back to the basics. Each time I set out to train I stick to the basic exercises. For biceps, it's Scott bench barbell curls and standing barbell curls. I alternate between these two to keep the size in my arms. I'll do the alternate one-arm concentration curls—standing or kneeling, or on my thigh. I'll do alternate dumbbell curls too, and reverse curls, but those are basically it for my biceps. I'll alternate between two to three of those depending on how I feel or what I need the most. I'd average about 5 sets each, and on heavy days I'd do low reps and on light days high reps. For back, my basic exercise is chins because I just love chins. I'll start out doing 50 reps. Not all at once, mind you. My first set might be 12 to 15 reps, the next set might be 10 to 12 reps, but I'm going to get my 50! The whole idea is like a game I play with myself. And I love to change the grip, wide one set, narrow the next. Then I move on to my pet exercise, which is T-bar rows. Then barbell rows, again close and narrow grip, pullovers with an easy weight for 5 sets each, and that's it.*

57

Mike Mentzer

The late Mike Mentzer. To many, the name conjures up images of bodybuilding's foremost iconoclast: the man who single-handedly convinced bodybuilders to train less frequently but more intensely, to eat a balanced diet, and to shy away from unnecessary supplementation.

Others recall Mentzer as the one who reigned as the sport's first true intellectual, a man who could back up whatever opinion he expressed with reams of scientific copy. To me (John), Mentzer was a close friend, a student of philosophy, and, perhaps the rarest quality of all, a man of integrity.

Despite the odd article every now and then in *FLEX* or *Ironman*, Mentzer remained very quiet on the scene, opting instead to read the works of Ayn Rand or Victor Hugo or to personally instruct some of his bodybuilding clients such as Mitsuru Okabe, a Japanese bodybuilder who, under Mentzer's tutelage, shed some 40 pounds of fat and progressed from a physical condition where he couldn't even perform a single dip with his own body weight to being able to perform repetition dips with 180 pounds

was always out in the backyard doing calisthenics and high jumping, broad jumping, jumping over fences. And it carried over to one day when I was with my mother at a newsstand. And while she was doing some shopping, I was gazing over the vast array of magazines and my eyes came to rest upon a cover of Muscle Builder magazine [the forerunner to today's Muscle & Fitness], which had either Steve Reeves or Bill Pearl on the cover, and it was love at first sight and I knew instantly that that's what I wanted to be—whatever it was! It was my first introduction to bodybuilding, I just looked at the guy on the cover and there was this identification.

Q: What has been your proudest moment as a professional bodybuilder?

MIKE: My proudest was the condition that I attained for the 1980 Mr. Olympia contest. Even though I didn't win [and there were plenty of those in attendance that day who felt that he should have], I've always maintained that more important than winning was the process; the obtaining of your goal—which is getting into top shape, your best condition. I had started dieting that year in February, and the contest was in October or November, I can't quite remember. But I had applied myself longer than I ever had to obtain top condition, and I really did reach a peak of condition for that contest. My muscle quality was the best ever, and that was my proudest moment.

strapped around his waist. Mitsuru accomplished this miraculous transformation in a mere four months using Mentzer's Heavy Duty training system.

Whenever Mentzer spoke, he was worth listening to, as he tended to be rather controversial and always informative. He certainly proved to be plenty of both in this conversation we shared in 1990.

Q: Mike, how did you first get started in bodybuilding, and what first drew you to it?

MIKE: Well, I'd always been very physical. My father was a strong influence; he was into karate and basketball and sports of all sorts, and it rubbed off. As a young kid I

Q: What was your body-fat level for that contest?

MIKE: *Well, about a month before the show it was 3.8, and I lost a few more pounds before the contest itself. I would guesstimate that it would have been about 3 percent. It was very low.*

Q: That's a very low body-fat percentage! On the other side of the coin, what's been your lowest moment as a professional, your nadir, so to speak?

MIKE: *[chuckles] Interesting. My proudest moment was attaining the condition I achieved, just as I said, for the '80 Mr. Olympia, and on the flip side, at the same time, I lost the '80 Olympia in a very controversial decision. I had won the heavyweight division of the Mr. Olympia the year before, losing the overall to Frank Zane in a controversial decision. A lot of people, including myself, thought I had a very good chance of winning the '80 Olympia, and I thought I should have won—a lot of people thought so. That was my lowest point. I knew my career was over right there. . . . I'd always wanted to win the Mr. Olympia, and I was going to give it three or four tries. That was my second try, but because of the notion that it was fixed—and it did appear like it was fixed—I wasn't going to go back again and get screwed.*

Q: I remember you saying that the training for that was just incredibly intense.

MIKE: *It was incredibly intense, very draining and demanding. I had put more into it mentally and physically than I ever had before, and it really hurt very much. Not so much at the time, but in retrospect: if I had won that contest, or if it hadn't turned out the way it had, my whole life would be different right now.*

Q: After rereading some of your articles in preparation for this interview such as "Heavy or Light?," "Metabolic Momentum," and "Making Stress Work for You," I wondered, which do you think has been the most important one that you've written to date?

MIKE: *[laughs] The most important? Well, I don't know that any one that I've ever written is all that important; the most enjoyable article to write was "The Psychology of a Mr. Olympia Competitor."*

Q: Why is that?

MIKE: *Well, at the time I wrote it—after reading it—I thought I had written the best article I had ever written. It was well written from both a technical and artistic standpoint—at least at the time. In retrospect I can pick it apart and find flaws, but then I'm still evolving as a writer, so I don't think I've reached my apex. But I saw some of the Henry Miller influence creeping in there, and I like his style. And it read a little bit like a Henry Miller novel, so I liked it very much. That happened sort of unconsciously, by the way, I didn't set out to write* *an article in the Henry Miller style. Henry Miller, for those who don't know, was an American writer/novelist who achieved a certain amount of fame in this country and worldwide for writing. . . . That was my favorite article: "The Psychology of a Mr. Olympia Competitor." And the other ones you mentioned, "Metabolic Momentum" I thought was good because it was creative and incorporated concepts that had never been broached before in the annals of bodybuilding.*

Q: That's true. Well, I'm going to throw out a couple of quotes from you, culled from some of your articles regarding the adaptation response, and then I'm going to ask you a question relating to both of them: "Specific demands imposed upon the body result in specific physiological adjustments." The second quote is "Heavy exertion imposes a demand on the body that causes it to adapt by developing larger and stronger muscles." My question, then, is, can this "adaptation response" be triggered in an intermediate by, say, taking one set on one day (i.e., squats) to complete failure? Not doing six sets, but just one set? And then the next day hitting chest—same principle. Would the demand from that one set be sufficient, or would that not be sufficient sets for an intermediate?

MIKE: *Well, it's hard to say. [laughs] You're asking me to be omniscient here. As far as I know there haven't been any extensive—or even any—studies done with intermediates using that style of training. What I can say is that an advanced bodybuilder of my acquaintance made very good gains on that style of training. Back in 1983, Boyer Coe and I worked for Arthur Jones in Nautilus, and during the six months that I was there Boyer did do one set per body part, three days a week. His daily average workout lasted 17 minutes. When I arrived in Florida to work for Arthur Jones and I saw Boyer, I was surprised because he'd uncharacteristically let himself get out of condition; he had very little muscle mass in the upper body and very little definition. Six months later, following this program religiously, he transformed himself and became very large and muscular again— without steroids, by the way. So perhaps you can't make a general statement and say that it's going to work for everybody, or as dramatically as it did for Boyer. I think that the fact that an advanced bodybuilder was able to make that kind of improvement on a one-set-per-body-part program, three times per week, at least suggests that there is some merit to it.*

Q: Some publishers have categorized the Heavy Duty method as "one set to failure," "hard on the joints," "dangerous," "ultimately ineffective." As you've not been around that much recently, these comments have been made without fear of your rebuttal. I was wondering if you would care to set the record straight?

MIKE: *Well, I've never advocated just one set per body part.*

Q: I don't ever remember you saying that, but that's what they're saying; they're putting those words in your mouth.

MIKE: *I've never advocated training as heavy as possible just for the sake of heavy training. A lot of people still confuse Heavy Duty with just heavy, heavy training. It's high-intensity training, and it can be very low-force training where there's very little stress on the joints—or relatively little stress on the joints. A lot of people say things about Heavy Duty training based on hearsay and not having read my books and articles, so I don't put much stock in what they say.*

Q: Good for you.

MIKE: *I'm always open to a logical argument and reason, of course. I never even suggested that I had the final word or the last word on bodybuilding. If someone was able to logically prove that the conceptual framework that supported Heavy Duty was somehow in error I'd be more than ecstatic even to learn about my mistake. I'm more interested in the truth than in being proved right or wrong.*

Q: After a prolonged layoff you're now starting back into serious training. How long do you think it will take you to get back into peak shape, and what will your routine or routines be, including the progression in intensity to how many workout days per week, exercises, sets, and reps?

MIKE: *That's an interesting question. As I stated to you in an earlier conversation, I'm probably in the worst condition of my life insofar as my appearance is concerned. I haven't trained for the last 10 months, and my last period of training before that was only for two months' duration. I've been relatively inactive for the last several years, so I've slipped into, again, a very out-of-condition appearance. I started back training on February 25 at Gold's Gym on a typical Heavy Duty routine. It's going to be a four-day-a-week split. In my first workout I trained my chest, shoulders, and triceps using preexhaustion—about 4 to 6 sets a*

body part. Of course, my work capacity and strength were way down, so the intensity may not have seemed as high to an outsider as [laughs] they might have expected from "Mr. Heavy Duty," but again, it's going to take a while to get back into the condition where I can achieve that kind of intensity.

Q: So that was chest, shoulders, and triceps. So your next workout would be back, biceps, and legs? I'm just breaking down your workout here: it would be four days per week, sort of a Monday, Tuesday, Thursday, Friday?

MIKE: *Four days a week. Since I started out it's going to be Sunday, Monday, Wednesday, Thursday, and then I'll take a break. It's a four-day split, four days out of every seven days. Initially I'm too weak and too out of condition to overtrain; my main concern is to get in there, get in condition, burn calories, lose some of this fat, but as I progress and build muscle mass and my work capacity increases, I'll cut back to 4 days out of every 9 or 10 days because the likelihood of overtraining increases as you get bigger and stronger.*

Q: What sort of exercises would you be doing?

MIKE: *Well, for instance, on Sunday I did pecs: cable crossovers for pecs and incline presses. For delts I did Nautilus laterals and bent-over laterals. For triceps I did triceps pressdowns and triceps extensions*

on Nautilus. Then, yesterday, for back I did Nautilus behind-the-neck/torso, followed by close-grip/underhand pulldowns, followed by 2 sets of [barbell] rows. After lats, I did traps: shrugs followed by upright rows. After back was over I did biceps. On biceps I did Nautilus curls exclusively. After arms I went to legs, and I did leg extensions followed by leg press and leg curls.*

Q: When you were training back in the '70s, you were using some pretty monster weights on virtually every exercise, but I'm thinking on leg press, specifically, you got up to 1,200 pounds!

MIKE: *Yeah, I got up to 1,200 pounds. I don't plan to go that high again necessarily unless I start getting into condition and become more motivated. Right now my primary goal is to get back into reasonable shape and feel better about myself, but if I find that in so doing I enkindle that motivation that perhaps might lead to a peak condition, I'll certainly try to do it.*

Q: Will you be including aerobics in your training?

MIKE: *Not right now. Like I say, my body fat is up higher than it's ever been and I'm— at the moment—I'm more highly motivated to lose that than to build ultimate muscle mass. So later on down the line, in the next month or two, I'll incorporate some bicycle riding, perhaps, to increase my daily activity quotient and continue burning calo-*

ries as I lose fat. But at the moment, no, I'm just training.

Q: Will you be coming out with any new courses along the Heavy Duty line?

MIKE: *It's a possibility. It's been suggested, and I've thought about it myself. Again, as I get back in shape and perhaps some new ideas crop up I'll incorporate them into a new course or two. I probably will.*

Q: I was wondering if you could prescribe a routine for our intermediate readers who are trying to put on some serious muscle?

MIKE: *Well, the routine that I just outlined for myself is good for intermediates: incorporating preexhaustion, training to failure, forced reps. I would just suggest that no matter what methods you use, you don't do more than 4 to 6 sets per body part, use very good form—strict form—train to failure, use forced reps occasionally, and don't overtrain. The formula that Arthur Jones advocated was "Train intensely, briefly, and infrequently." That is, not too frequently so that you don't exceed your body's ability to overcome the exhaustive effects of exercise and that you have enough recovery ability left over for growth.*

Q: Just to get back to training for a minute, you've been renowned for many innovations in training, but certainly your arms have been the focus of a good part of it.

I was curious as what your most effective arm routine was.

MIKE: *There was nothing special; results are usually linked primarily to motivation and your willingness to apply yourself with 100 percent. My favorite arm exercises are Scott curls, Nautilus curls, and concentration curls for biceps. My favorite exercises for triceps are pressdowns, Nautilus extensions, and dips—although I can't do dips anymore because of my right shoulder.*

Q: What did you do to your shoulder?

MIKE: *Back in 1971 I dislocated it doing dumbbell flyes. It was a manageable injury during the '70s and early '80s, but in the last couple years the joint has undergone some kind of progressive deterioration. I'm not really sure what it is, but it causes me considerable pain in my chest exercises as well—and I'm finding that a little bit difficult. But actually I think dips are the best triceps exercise. It's also the best overall upper-body exercise—I call it "the upper-body squat." . . . It's a very good exercise. But again, the formula is brief training, intense training, infrequent training. Young bodybuilders reading this should be cautioned against doing too many sets on too many days for all body parts. Their enthusiasm is often a hindrance; they're so willing and able to train marathon-style to acquire a muscular physique that they often overtrain. I train in Gold's—when I do* *train—and I see this as probably the most pervasive mistake of all bodybuilders, including advanced bodybuilders. They grossly overtrain.*

Q: I was speaking with your former idol—when you were growing up—Bill Pearl, the other day, and I was completely shocked by his training approach, which is two and a half hours a day, seven days a week. And I thought, "This is the guy who was dispensing advice to you when you were growing up?"

MIKE: *Yeah.*

Q: Was it the same sort of thing that he was telling you? And did you make any progress on it?

MIKE: *Well, no I didn't. Earlier in my career, in the earlier '70s, I was training on the typical marathon type of training routine: 20 sets or more per body part for six days a week, and I hit a plateau in my progress which I couldn't overcome doing the 20 sets per body part. So I used the reasoning that "more is better," and I figured, "well, if 20 sets wasn't doing it, I need 30 sets." At one point, I even got up to 40 sets for my chest! I couldn't even get a pump after a while! And after months and months and months of no progress, I was about to abandon my training altogether; thinking it wasn't worth it. And that's when I had the good opportunity to meet Casey Viator at the 1971 Mr. America and was shocked to*

learn that he was only training 45 minutes, three days a week. And then in subsequent phone conversations with Casey and his mentor, Arthur Jones, I learned the theoretical framework and embraced it intellectually, and that made it easier to do in the gym and, of course, I went on to become a strong advocate and proponent of high-intensity training, which is what we've been talking about.

Q: You've also single-handedly led bodybuilders away from their aberrant dietary and training practices. How did you first hit upon the discovery of prolonged recovery periods and breaking out of viewing training within the seven-day confines of the Gregorian calendar?

MIKE: *Well, it was back in '79 or '80; my brother and I were training for contests together. We were training extremely intensely with heavy weights, training to failure with forced reps and negatives. And I remember it was on a Tuesday morning after a very heavy Monday workout. Ray and I met in the gym, as usual, and we were still hell-bent on making maximum progress. I was thinking about the workouts and analyzing them and analyzing their effects on my body from day to day, and I said to my brother, "Ray, how do you feel today?" And he—like me—was exhausted, having still not fully recovered from the Monday workout. And I reasoned; I said, "Ray, if we haven't* even recovered from our workout yesterday, we're not going to be able to invest our workout today with the intensity that is required to stimulate maximum muscle growth. And if we did, in fact, stimulate growth on Monday—which we probably did—we're not going to grow anyway because, again, recovery has to come first." Recovery and growth are two distinct physiological processes, both requiring time to fulfill or complete. And, again, "If we hadn't completed the recovery process, we're not going to produce any growth that we have stimulated." Growth stimulation and growth production are two distinct physiological processes, too; you have to stimulate growth in the gym and then allow growth to produce itself or manifest itself. Again, growth stimulation and growth production are two distinct processes, and the growth production has to be preceded by the recovery process. So what happens when you train again before you recover is that you short-circuit the growth process. And I explained this to Ray, and he agreed that he wasn't feeling recovered, that it was ridiculous to try and train again, let alone be concerned about growth. We would have been spinning our wheels, in effect, so we decided to take another day off, and that helped a lot and we recovered. And we found sometimes we even needed two days off in between workouts, so we started doing a 4 day out of every 9 or 10

day split—not allowing tradition and convenience and compulsion, at some points, to supersede logic and reason.

Q: That's good—and also you made probably the best progress of your life when you did that.

MIKE: Yes, we did make the best. We had hit a plateau there for a while; our gains had slowed down as is often the case with advanced bodybuilders, but when we adopted that program our gains skyrocketed again—even for advanced bodybuilders! At one point there I had gained 10 pounds of muscle in three weeks and lost four pounds of fat at the same time.

Q: So a 14-pound lean mass gain?

MIKE: Yeah.

Q: That's incredible. When you trained for the 1976 Mr. America, you trained three days per week on a full-body, predominantly Nautilus routine.

MIKE: Yeah.

Q: I'm just curious as to why you split it up when it appeared so successful. That is, why did you reduce your recovery days from four to three per week?

MIKE: Well, even in '76 when I was training for the America, a full-body high-intensity workout done three days a week was very demanding. I was going to school at the time, going to college carrying a full load, and also working in a doctor's office every day. And because my workouts came first in the morning, they would leave me so exhausted that I found it difficult to go to class and then go to work; I was just dragging myself around. It was too demanding, and I wasn't enjoying it. Because it was so demanding and so brutal I would find that my workouts were preceded by a period of anxiety—which I've heard from other bodybuilders who have tried the same routine.*

Q: I was going to say that was how I felt when I was doing the whole-body routine.

MIKE: Enjoying the workout is very important; if you don't enjoy it, you're not going to be at it for very long. So just out of practicality and because I wanted to enjoy it, I decided to break it up into a four-day split.

Q: And that proved to be every bit if not more successful than the three-day-per-week, whole-body system?

MIKE: Yeah, just as successful.

Q: Why, as the leading high-intensity advocate, have you never adopted the high-intensity line of just "one set to failure" per body part for advanced gains?

MIKE: Well, as I talked about earlier for the intermediates, besides from the study that was done with Boyer down there at Nautilus—and it was a scientific study—

I don't know of any other formal studies that have been done, so I can't comment on it extensively. But watching Boyer make that progress steadily and continuously for the six months, I think there's something to be said for it.

Q: Would you ever try it, do you think?

MIKE: Well, Boyer subsequently abandoned it, in part because he enjoys multiple set training and, again, there's something to be said for the joy factor.

Q: True.

MIKE: I think once I attain a peak of condition and my schedule proves more demanding at times I will probably adopt that kind of training.

Q: It would be interesting to see how that works with you as well. That would be an interesting experiment.

MIKE: I know darn well from past experience when I have been busy and I've been forced to reduce the sets that that kind of routine would at least be a maintenance routine.

Q: At the very least.

MIKE: For those who are working or going to school or finding the demands of a daily schedule very tough, a one set per body part routine will at least be a maintenance workout.

Q: What are your thoughts on drug testing being introduced to the men's pro ranks?

MIKE: *I'm very against drug testing and even drug laws. I think that drugs should be legalized. I believe very strongly in the notion that I was born a free, independent individual, and I should be able to take anything into my body that I want to—even if it kills me. It's my business. . . . Government has no business sticking its nose into private affairs, and I'm very, very much opposed to it. I think that the effort to get bodybuilding into the Olympics—which, ostensibly, is the reason for the drug testing—is futile; bodybuilding will never become accepted as an Olympic sport.*

Q: Why do you think? Because of the subjective nature of it?

MIKE: *It's very subjective, and subjectivity leads very strongly to nationalistic feelings, and the people that run the Olympics, from what I've been told, are concerned about taking sports on anymore that, you know, might lead to fights. And, again, bodybuilding with its very subjective nature would lead to that sort of thing.*

Q: Given your laissez-faire perspective on the drug testing element, would you—just in your own opinion—like to see the drugs continue to be in the sport, or do you think they're necessary? Or have they been over-rated or over-maligned?

MIKE: *Well, I think even your question is superfluous. I understand the reason for asking it, considering the moral climate in* bodybuilding *right now concerning drugs, but I don't think it's anybody's business, and I really don't care. I've always maintained that it comes down to a very personal decision. When asked at seminars or through the mail whether or not individuals should take drugs, I typically respond that, "I don't want any part of that. That's your decision. I arrived at my decision personally, having reviewed the literature and thought about it in reference to my career and goals, and that's what each individual has to do—and I don't want any part of that." I've got enough of a hard time taking care of my own life; I'm not going to make decisions for other people.*

Q: How important do you think genetics are in bodybuilding?

MIKE: *I'm the one who really started writing about genetics back in the late '70s and early '80s and I think raised the bodybuilding consciousness as to the importance of genetics. Genetics are very important. But I think, perhaps, they were overemphasized at various points, and the notion that you have to have good genetics to achieve a championship physique has demotivated some people. It's very difficult to accurately assess your genetic potential; you know, at best you might be able to get a suggestion of where you might go based on your muscle belly lengths, your bone structure, and metabolism and neuromuscular efficiency, but the most important* *thing, I think, is motivation. Everyone can improve themselves and that's important. Not everyone is going to become Mr. Olympia, but we can all improve ourselves. Again, that's the most important factor.*

Q: Well, here we go into another segue from your laissez-faire answer, and that is, What philosophy of life do you subscribe to?

MIKE: *The Objectivist philosophy of life.*

Q: And what drew you to it?

MIKE: *Well, I'd always been interested in philosophy, had read the works of various philosophers and discovered at one point that I was in a quandary as to what the real role of philosophy in life was. And then I came across the works of Ayn Rand and, as Ayn Rand said, "Philosophy is for living on earth"—pure and simple, that's all it is. Many people first coming into philosophy become confused because of the strong mystic/irrational element in philosophy. But once you read Ayn Rand, and you stay with it, you finally realize that it's not all that complicated. And the real role of philosophy is to help man make choices. As long as man is confronted with choices, he's going to need a philosophy, a value system. And after reading Ayn Rand's philosophy I realized that hers was the most thoroughly reasoned, the most logical, the most consistent. And I've adopted it and I've tried to live it—with lapses from time to time—but that's the*

responsibility of the individual over time; to consistently apply the philosophy, and that's what I'm still working on.

Q: I don't know if you find this, but in my own experience with Ayn Rand is that you read it and become so engrossed that it's like kerosene on a fire, but then in comes the "Crow Epistemology" sort of thing, and I find that I have to back off for a while to let the cells sort of cool down a bit.

MIKE: *Well you have to integrate it. You know, reading it is one thing!*

Q: But then I also find that after a lapse of it, where there's a void of reading any of that literature, I find a real hunger to get back into it again.

MIKE: *Well, this is the hard part of things that a lot of people have, not just with Ayn Rand's philosophy, but any philosophy; you can read about it and get excited about it and understand it, but it's the daily application of it that's important. You've got to think about it and, perhaps, write about it and apply it to every moment of your life— and this takes discipline. And this is one of the reasons why some people have steered away from Ayn Rand's philosophy. I tried to get a couple of friends of mine involved in it a few years back and they both, after a few months, said that it was too demanding. I thought it was a lame excuse; life is demanding. But yeah, I think the problem is daily application.*

Q: I find that once you read it, it is like a seed of truth has been planted and that when you're away from it, it begins to germinate a bit, and you find yourself saying, "Well, God, that's right."

MIKE: *Well it's very easy to read it and then go about your daily affairs and forget about it. If you're going to apply it, you've got to be obsessed with it for a while; you've go to think about it and how it applies to situations in your life. At various periods when I was reading the Objectivist literature a lot, I would take every opportunity to reflect on it during the day; when I was driving down the freeway, caught in traffic snafus, or during private moments when I had time alone. I would reflect on my own life situations and see where the philosophy applied and whether I did apply it or not and resolve to apply it more consistently in the future.*

58

Lou Ferrigno

Iwas quite literally speeding along the Santa Monica Freeway, and yet I was going to be late. Not horrifically late, mind you, perhaps 5 or 10 minutes at the most, but still one doesn't like to keep a man of Lou Ferrigno's stature waiting.

I began to pass all makes of cars with an increasing enjoyable frequency. I was now well over the usually well-enforced 55 mph, and there was not a police officer in sight. As I cranked up the radio in the rental car and began singing along, I didn't even notice that the car was now slowing down!

Suddenly, there was a very loud clunk as the transmission fell out of the car! As my rental car slowed, more and more car horns kept honking. In what had to be the worst case of bad timing, the transmission in my rental car chose to discard itself right in the middle of the freeway. Yep, I was going to be late. I would indeed be very late.

Finding a roadside telephone, I phoned for a cab, and after what seemed to be an eternity, a cab was dispatched and arrived to deliver me from being stranded on the Santa

Monica Freeway and also to my appointment with the Incredible Hulk.

On the way to Lou's home, I remembered that a friend once told me that if one was invited somewhere, it was only common etiquette to arrive 10 to 15 minutes late to allow your hosts extra time to prepare for your arrival. Feeling a bit more comforted, I now considered myself "fashionably late," a practice, I thought, that a jet-setter like Lou would naturally come to expect and not the least feel insulted by.

After the cab pulled up to the Ferrigno address, I got out and walked up to the big front door, knocked, and waited for the dainty sounds of wife Carla Ferrigno's advancing footsteps. Suddenly, the door opened, and what I assumed to be Carla turned out to be big Lou himself—all 6'5" of him! A few moments later, our interview began.

Q: First of all, for the benefit of your fans who want to know what you've been up to, what have you been doing?

LOU: Well, I've been doing theater for the last two years, stage plays. I've done one in Calgary, one in Edmonton, one in Texas, and I've just finished one in Chicago. So I've been training to keep in shape, and I think I may be shooting a "Rocky" story on bodybuilding.

Q: Did you write the script yourself?

LOU: The script is written, and they're finishing the financing now.

Q: That sounds good. When do you think it will come into being?

LOU: Christmas 1986

Q: Well that's more or less your future plans then, just to do the film.

LOU: Right.

Q: Were you the basis for the writing of the script of the film?

LOU: It is more related to my life story, but it is exaggerated, like Stallone did with Rocky. It will show competition, not like me and Arnold, but something different. Where I came from back east, and where I came to in California to make a living. It will include my meeting with Joe Weider, and the relationship between me and my father.

Q: After experiencing the footlights of the stage, do you have any plans to return to the medium of television?

LOU: Oh yeah, but by doing theater I'm perfecting my craft in acting. I still have a lot more to learn, but theater gave me a whole new dimension to acting, being in front of a live audience.

Q: Do you prefer that? Getting immediate feedback from the audience?

LOU: Yes, because when you go back to TV or feature films it won't be so strange, it will be more involved in the character. It taught me a lot.

Q: It is interesting in comparing the two mediums. I know Marlon Brando used to say that in the theater the actor could really get into the character he is portraying, whereas in films, it is so chopped up sequentially that it is hard to know the right emotional response as there is no logical emotional progression or buildup.

LOU: Yes, that's true. Acting is harder than bodybuilding.

Q: It is, is it?

LOU: Yes, mentally, because you have to listen, you have to know the character, you have to deliver lines, you have to feel the emotion of the character, so you end up doing four or five things at once. It's different, mentally, from bodybuilding.

Q: When you first took up bodybuilding, did you find it difficult to suddenly adopt a particular emotion? For example, if the script called for you to be sad, or unusually gleeful, was it hard for you to immediately snap into that?

LOU: Yes, it was difficult, and it has taken me some time to master it. It did take some time to get into it, but after a while, you develop your own little bag of tricks. For example, when it comes to bodybuilding, you go into a gym, and after you have trained for a few years, you learn how to psyche up and get into a really good workout. But a beginner, they're kind of lost. Acting is the same way, the preparation.

The Incredibe Big and Little Hulks: Lou Ferrigno with Flavio Baccianini

Q: What do you, being married now for six years, think are the ingredients for a successful marriage?

LOU: Sharing, open communication, giving and taking, and being your partner's best friend. Marriage, you know, is an art of negotiation, because you have to become equal partners.

Q: Do you have a particular philosophy that you subscribe to? When you live your life, base your decisions on, a certain code of values that you go by?

LOU: I really go by trusting my own feelings. How I believe in something, I trust my own

feelings, and my wife's opinion is very important to me also.

Q: Of all the film roles that you've played, what, to date, has been your favorite?

LOU: *I would say that it was the second series that I did, the medical series entitled "Trauma Center." It was too bad that the series was short-lived. But it gave me another dimension; it showed another*

side of me instead of just the body. Hercules *was fun, but I think that if we had had more time I could have been much better.*

Q: There was a movie that I saw on TV called *The Seven Magnificent Gladiators* which I enjoyed, and it starred not only yourself, but your wife, Carla, as well.

LOU: *Yeah, that's right. I enjoyed making that film too.*

Q: Does Carla have any more plans to pursue further acting roles?

LOU: *Carla used to be an actress, and she used to be a psychotherapist, but right now she has a career hosting a TV show.*

Q: On cable or public television?

LOU: *On both. She just got in from L.A., where she has just finished doing a tape for Matchbox toys, which is a variety show. She has her own show now called "The Honest Way to Success," where she interviews people to find out how people become successful and why.*

Q: Is this locally in Los Angeles?

LOU: *Yes, and she's got music on her show too.*

Q: What do you do for recreation?

LOU: *Believe it or not, it's my kids. My time is so involved with acting class, and I also train people one-on-one. I have a gym in* the back of my house. I train big people like jocks, producers, and directors one-on-one. It's something I enjoy doing, one of my hobbies. Plus I have the kids plus being gone on weekends, and training, so I have very little time to entertain myself with other activities.

Q: It's good that you spend a lot of time with your children, as so many people don't even find time for that.

LOU: Well this is the stage where kids need it [the attention] the most, "the growing years." I feel the more I spend with them, I'll get it back.

Q: Child psychologists say that from the age of birth to six years is the most important time in terms of the child's patterns for learning and development.

LOU: True.

Q: Who have been your greatest influences both in and out of bodybuilding?

LOU: In bodybuilding, do you mean when I was just beginning bodybuilding, or now?

Q: Both, I suppose. Who got you interested to get into bodybuilding, and who had an influence on your life outside of bodybuilding?

LOU: I would say that it was me from the beginning, but it had a lot to do with Schwarzenegger coming onto the scene. Because Arnold was the biggest body-

builder of all time until I came along, and he opened a lot of doors for me. And he has really been my idol, so he just made me very certain that I could go all the way in bodybuilding, and then on to television and feature films. That had a lot to do with it.

Q: So Arnold influenced you in viewing bodybuilding as a stepping-stone to broader career opportunities?

LOU: Right, but then again my father influenced me because he was big, and he had weights in the basement and all kinds of various muscle magazines. My father was big and I wanted to get as big as he was, and I saw that he was lifting weights. So I would try and work out myself to copy him. And little by little, I learned how to build up and utilize different exercises.

Q: In the movie *Pumping Iron* there was a photo displayed that showed you and your father posing together in what appeared to be your backyard. Your dad was in pretty fair shape himself.

LOU: Yeah, he really was.

Q: Here's an interesting question, How much of the movie *Pumping Iron* was staged, and how much was actually the documentary?

LOU: My father's involvement in the movie was just for the movie. He never really trained me at all in real life. It was only at the beginning that I wanted to learn from him, but he became more, I would say, of a fan. But the training relationship between me and my father was staged for the movie.

Q: Did you enjoy making that film?

LOU: Oh yeah. It's sad though that I didn't have more time because I was approached about nine weeks before the film to enter the contest, the Mr. Olympia. I trained for only 9 or 10 weeks because I was training for the ABC television network's "Superstars" competition. So I had to postpone training for that, and then train for bodybuilding. So with the fluctuation of body weight I didn't have time to cut up. It was very hectic, although I did enjoy making the film, the traveling to South Africa, competing with those guys like Arnold and Franco.

Q: Serge Nubret . . .

LOU: It was quite a rewarding experience.

Q: When you were shooting the *Hercules* films, what workout did you use to reach that absolute pinnacle of condition?

LOU: Well, I didn't have a great gym to train at, number one, I had a suite in which I put barbells and dumbbells. I had like eight different dumbbells, three barbells, one adjustable incline bench, that was it.

Q: Rather spartan conditions . . .

LOU: [laughing] Yeah. I trained for three hours every morning. I felt like I was starting all over again in my home gym. I had to clean and jerk the bar to do presses, so it was kind of awkward.

Q: Well, it paid off because your condition in that film was remarkable.

LOU: Thank you.

Q: How would your training for a film differ from your training for a contest?

LOU: It's much harder to train for a film because you have to be in top shape, plus you have to diet on top of that, and at the same time you have to film up to 12 hours a day. It is very difficult to get up in the morning and motivate yourself to train. When you are training for a competition, you train, lie in the sun, work on your posing; you can loaf around a little bit. But doing a film means being in top shape for five or six weeks. If you shoot a scene in which your condition is fine and then in the last week of shooting you have to retain that shape, whereas for competition it's only required to get into top shape for one day: you cut down or bulk up. Filming is much harder.

Q: So it's much more of a protracted peak that filming requires.

LOU: Right.

Q: Most of the readers are noncompetitive bodybuilders. Given that, how many sets would you say noncompetitive bodybuilders should perform to increase their size, as opposed to just keeping in shape? Also, how many sets per body part do you think a person should perform?

LOU: I would say 10 to 12 reps, 4 sets an exercise, three exercises per body part.

Q: In a related vein, how many days a week should a bodybuilder who is not competing train, without running the risk of overtraining?

LOU: I would say six days a week, 12 to 15 sets per body part, and the important thing is to train each body part twice a week, not three times a week. I would keep the repetitions from 12 to 15 with moderate weight. Watch your diet, and you should be about 75 percent of your best in the off-season. You shouldn't exceed 15 pounds over your contest weight, depending on your size. Like myself, it would be 25 pounds, a guy like you I would say 15 pounds, because if you take a guy 6'5", 15 pounds is like 5 pounds on a guy like you.

Q: For the benefit of our readers, I'm a towering 5'10" tall [Lou laughs]. How many calories per day would you consume during the course of an average day?

LOU: Now, I would say 4,000 to 5,000.

Q: That would be just to maintain your present body weight, wouldn't it?

LOU: Right, for me to cut up, I would have to go down to 2,000 calories, or 1,500, with a lot of aerobics.

Q: Would you do a lot of aerobics such a biking?

LOU: Yes. I also use the Stairmaster and treadmill. I like to run, but not too much, it hurts my knees. Normally when I run, I run on the beach.

Q: Do you find that to be much different?

LOU: Well the sand is much softer, and you don't have heavy pounding on your joints.

Q: So there wouldn't be as many problems with the knees?

LOU: Right, and you know, when you're over 30, you can develop a lot more injuries. You can't train as heavy; you have to warm up more. Well, actually, you train as heavy, but you have to warm up properly. Like now, I'm 34, but when I was 23, I could jump off the roof of this house, or I'd warm up with 225 pounds on the squat—for warm-up! Now, I have to gradually add on more weight, so it becomes harder when your body is more mature. I could be in better shape now than I was when I was 22.

Q: I was talking to Frank Zane about a month ago, and he commented that the older a person gets, the less body weight they should be carrying. Would you agree with that?

LOU: Yes, because as you get older, your bones get denser and you carry more body fat. For example, say you weigh 160 pounds at the height of 5'6", at an age of say, 21. You could be 45 and weigh the same but with a potbelly, your body gets fatter. So you should remove the fat as you get older and carry less weight. The older you get, the more muscles lose their elasticity. I mean look at Albert Beckles, that genetic freak that not every man can look like at 54 or 55. Oliva [Sergio] now is 54, but he doesn't have the same tightness Beckles has. I think it is because Beckles has been so ripped for so many years. Sergio has always been heavy, but it was hard for him to get cut, now that's working against him. It's like Frank Zane said, you should be lighter.

Q: Yeah, Beckles's metabolism must be very quick for him to get into condition like that. Anyway, back to the topic at hand, which is yourself, when you were shooting the *Hercules* films, did you do much research into Roman and Greek mythology, history, and/or philosophy in preparing for the role?

LOU: Sure, I read about his seven labors.

Q: There were actually 12.

LOU: [laughing] I've done a lot of reading and research, and I watched the old Hercules films.

Q: The ones starring Steve Reeves?

LOU: Yes.

Q: I'm going to interview him tomorrow, interestingly enough.

LOU: He's one of my idols. I thought that for his time he was fabulous! Ripped! Great! I mean I'm talking about without drugs, he had the perfect bone structure.

Q: Yeah, excellent genetics. He apparently has just turned 60 years of age this year.

LOU: I'll bet he still looks great.

Q: Well, we'll see tomorrow. [He did look great!] An obvious question: Will you ever compete again?

LOU: I don't know. I'd like to but it depends on all of my many movie commitments. I'll only compete again if I really have the desire to. It would be hard for me right now, but I often wonder about it. I'd guess right now I'd have to say that I don't know.

Q: There was a rumor last year that you were going to appear in the 1985 Olympia. Was there any truth in that?

LOU: I didn't have enough time. I had knee surgery.

Q: How did you hurt your knee?

LOU: Well, chondromalacia.

Q: Was that from running?

LOU: It was tearing from squatting, so they went inside and ground out the kneecap. It's much better now, but I couldn't come back like I used to. You see, if I train three to six months, I feel that I can compete with anyone in the world except Haney. To beat Lee Haney out, I would have to train for one full year. The man is awesome!

Q: Genetically, I think, you have superior proportion or symmetry.

LOU: Yes, but the way he's built, to beat him, it would never be a "wipe out" situation. To beat him, I would have to be at my all-time best because Haney is good!

Q: That's a fact. Who in your opinion, not including yourself, are the top 10 physiques of all time?

LOU: Steve Reeves, Arnold Schwarzenegger, Frank Zane, Bill Pearl, Reg Park, Larry Scott, Lee Haney, Serge Nubret, Sergio Oliva, and Casey Viator.

Q: Who did you consider to be your greatest competitor when you were competing?

LOU: Arnold. Arnold would still be my greatest competitor, more than Lee Haney today. He's the only that can motivate me—more than anybody! He's my greatest challenge to beat. I grew up with the guy, so, if you have an idol, you want to beat your idol, which is natural, but it was more fun when I competed against him, even though I wasn't at my prime. But I think Arnold is the greatest. I think right now, if he came back at his all-time best, I think he could beat Haney.

Q: How did it feel when you were actually in South Africa when you did actually compete against Arnold—but of course, you had already competed against Arnold

the year before in the 1975 Olympia, hadn't you?

LOU: Right, but I never had the opportunity to train out there [California] for a year. Arnold had no job, all he did was train, eat, sleep, and drink bodybuilding. He had Joe Weider behind him. I was working as a sheet metal worker; I trained like three months before the show. So I was young and immature. Arnold had all the advantages. If we were to compete today, it would be a very different contest, it would be very close. I might have a chance of beating him. But in those days, I just wanted to compete against him, to be Mr. Olympia. Even though I wasn't in my best shape, it was great fun.

Q: What did you think of Arnold's comeback in 1980?

LOU: Amazing.

Q: You felt his winning was deserved then, did you?

LOU: I thought it was pretty close. I thought that with his determination, charisma, and showmanship, he edged it out. But I found it very ballsy of him in a way. You have to give him credit to come out after training for only 10 weeks to meet those guys. He was nervous about it himself! It was quite a chance he took.

Q: Yeah, he pulled it off. Who are some of the people in the sport of bodybuilding who strike you as interesting, whether through them being distinct characters due to their personalities, sense of humor, or sheer knowledge? You must have met some really interesting people.

LOU: Well, Bill Pearl, number one, is very knowledgeable. Frank Zane also. I would say mainly the top bodybuilders, people like Sergio Oliva, they know so much. People who have been training like 25 or 30 years, they have vast experience.

Q: What did you think of Mike Mentzer when he was competing?

LOU: I thought Mentzer had a superior physique. I though he should have placed higher at times. You know, I thought he got screwed a couple of times.

Q: That's for sure. You also competed against him in the "Superstars" competition.

LOU: Yes I did.

Q: That must have been fun.

LOU: It was, even though I beat him at weight lifting, he was a good sport. I was nervous about losing. I couldn't afford to lose, you know, because I'm so much bigger than he is—but he's quite an athlete himself.

Q: It was quite a competition, both of you did well. What would you consider to be the most important factor in bodybuilding? Would it be the mind? Training? Nutrition? All three?

LOU: The mind. Because you can watch your diet, you can train hard, get the proper rest, but if your mind's not there, no way. You have to really want it. Like I could do all those things I said, the training and everything, and lose. But if I make up my mind that I want to win badly, I'll win the contest, the mind has everything, it gives you that extra push.

Q: In regard to supplements, do you believe them to be necessary in training?

LOU: I think supplements are good. I think that if you are getting a sufficient amount of vitamins, minerals, and protein from your diet, you shouldn't take too many supplements. I think a multivitamin tablet, vitamin E, B complex, and some aminos would be fine.

Q: I know your wife did a lot of research into training methods for pregnant women. Is there any particular way or any caution they should exercise when they are both training and expecting a child?

LOU: Well, as long as she doesn't do any exercises that will strain her stomach. If you feel a strain, then stop. That would be avoiding doing any heavy deadlifting, heavy sit-ups, heavy rows, heavy pull-downs, jerking, anything sitting down or standing up should be done lightly. Just do what you would normally do with a third of the weight and a third of the output.

Q: How about elderly people? People who are older but want to train to get in shape. Any particular precaution that they should exercise?

LOU: *Older people should train the same as younger people, but they have to train a lot lighter. If they have never weight trained before, they should take a treadmill test, or a blood test to check if they have signs of hypoglycemia, high cholesterol. All of these factors are very important, under 35 years of age no, but once you get older you should. There's no problem with weight training; it is just a matter of doing the exercises that don't hurt. They may not train as heavy, but they can begin slow and have a great workout.*

Q: You were one of the first champion bodybuilders to actively say that you used Nautilus equipment in your workouts, back in a time when a lot of bodybuilders, out of ignorance, shied away from it. What do you think of Nautilus equipment?

LOU: *I think it's great as a finishing exercise. I love their pullover machine—the plate loader—because you have a greater range of motion. Their leg extension is still by far the best leg extension in use today, compared with all other leg extension machines, because they're omni-directional. And even their chest machine is a great finishing exercise. I would say a good five or six machines I still include in my training. I would say my training is 75 to 80 percent free weights and 20 percent Nautilus.*

Q: That's good to know, because a lot of misinformed people say "Oh, Nautilus doesn't work," but you're proof that it does in that respect, as you've used it, and used it effectively.

LOU: *Sure.*

Q: Could you recommend a basic routine for the noncompetitive average person who wants to gain muscle size and good health?

LOU: *For the average person I would employ two exercises per body part. Like chest: 4 sets of bench press and 4 sets of flyes. The same procedure like all body parts: no more than 8 sets. Use 60 percent of your maximum and build up to 100 percent, still employing 8 to 12 repetitions and no more. That should be sufficient. Train each body part twice a week, train the back on Monday, shoulders and arms on Tuesday; and then legs, stomach, and calves on Wednesday.*

Q: You mentioned earlier that you've started personalized instruction in your home gym. How do you enjoy doing that?

LOU: *I love it. It's fantastic because I have people come to me who don't want to go to a regular gym. Mainly people such as businessmen, who have neglected their bodies for years. They have great intelligence, great minds, but they have no*

control over their bodies. So I have to motivate them, teach them, I take them under
my wing, so it's just me and that person,
no interruption, no one in your way, no
waiting for equipment, and they won't have
to worry about how other people think of
them, how they look.

Q: Do you find that a lot of them, being in
your presence, feel intimidated about
exercising?

LOU: Yes, at the beginning. Then they get to
a point where they want to impress me by
training harder and harder without me
saying anything, it just happens naturally.

Q: Do you eventually encourage them to
formulate their own training programs?

LOU: Sure, I'll outline a routine and tailor-
make a routine for their body, their diet,
everything. Then when they leave me after
three months or more, most of my clients
stay with me, they would go to a regular
gym, or have a gym at home and take over
what I've shown them. Mainly, they want to
lose weight, restore their bodies, and it's
amazing how weak and helpless they are—
like children. So after three months with
me, the progress they make is incredible.
The thing is that I don't hire people to train
with them. I'm with them. I'm there moving
the benches, I'm there doing the exercises,
showing them how to do the exercises and
watching every single repetition because I
feel that with the money they pay, it's my
time to be with them.

Q: I would guess that you encourage their
self-confidence too, as a lot of people feel
inadequate when they're training.

LOU: Sure.

Q: When you're doing plays and movies and
things like that, what do you do to keep in
shape when almost 100 percent of your
attention must remain focused on acting?

LOU: When you do a stage play, you usually
have to perform from 7:30 to 11:30 p.m.
You usually get out about 3:30 in the
morning. I would train the next morning.
You can't train hard, as the play takes a lot
out of you. So I would train just a little less
intensely than the average way I train to
keep in shape.

Q: Of all the plays you have yet to do, which
play would you ultimately like to star in?

LOU: I would like someday to do Requiem
for a Heavyweight.

Q: Yeah? Would you play the role that
Anthony Quinn portrayed?

LOU: Yes. It's a heavy, lots of crying, a lot of
emotion, a feeling of rejection.

Q: I recall, at one point, you being seriously
considered to star in a telefilm based on
John Steinbeck's play *Of Mice and Men*
alongside Robert Blake.

LOU: That's right. I couldn't do it because
Bobby [Robert Blake] had to shoot at the
same time that I was doing the "Hulk"

series, and the studio wouldn't let me have the time off to do it.

Q: Do you see Arnold anymore?

LOU: *I saw him two weeks ago at the gym.*

Q: Is it probable that the two of you will eventually do a film together some day?

LOU: *Probably. He came down to see my stage play in Chicago. He was filming* Raw Deal *there. He came down one night and I was doing the play—this was a theater in the round with like 1,000 people—and I turned for some reason [he begins to laugh] and I saw a guy that looked like him. I thought to myself "F***ing Arnold!" And he had that look, you know, like* The Terminator. *I couldn't believe it! I was happy he was there.*

Q: It was good that he came down to see you. How did he like the play?

LOU: *He liked it.*

Q: Arnold's never attempted the stage yet, has he?

LOU: *I don't think he'll want to attempt the stage, the way he's filming now. But I take it a step further. I just want to be a fine actor someday, but I'll tell you, you can spend 22 years bodybuilding, but acting is totally different. You're dealing with emotion. The hard part is that you can be in a class and show emotion, but suddenly when you're in front of thousands of people, you better be able to repeat those same emotions. If you don't, then you're only reading the lines, and the audience knows it.*

Q: Who is your favorite actor? Who inspires you dramatically?

LOU: *I have a few, like Cary Grant, Clark Gable, and in today's age, I would say Robert De Niro and Al Pacino.*

Q: Did you have any trouble making the transition from New York to California?

LOU: *None whatsoever.*

Q: Do you periodically return to New York?

LOU: *Maybe once or twice a year. My family is back there, but I wouldn't want to live there.*

Q: How's your dad doing?

LOU: *Good.*

Q: Is he still training?

LOU: *He runs a lot and fast walking.*

Q: Thank you for your time, Lou.

LOU: *You're welcome. It was nice talking with you.*

PART 5

My Most Productive Workout Routine

59

Dorian Yates

Massive Britisher Dorian Yates has, to understate things, a unique training system. Not only does he eschew the conventional six-days-a-week, 20-sets-per-body-part training methodologies utilized by the "ancients" such as Arnold Schwarzenegger, Frank Zane, and Sergio Oliva; he also has no use for the even more popular (and far more voguish) three-on/one-off systems employed by many top bodybuilders such as Lee Haney and Shawn Ray. This is not to say that Yates disrespects those who choose to train this way. In fact, it's quite the opposite; he has the utmost respect for all bodybuilders, from beginner to advanced, solely because they have opted to train with weights in a dedicated and systematic fashion. Yates just prefers to accomplish the same results in much less time.

Yates started his bodybuilding career at age 16, as a means to augment his martial arts training. Eventually his newfound love of bodybuilding outgrew his love of the combative arts and he made his transition full-time to the sport of bodybuilding. His early influences were the legendary Mike Mentzer who, history records, was the most vocal exponent of brief, high-intensity training.

The young Dorian Yates followed Mike's Heavy Duty training theories and, within a year, had packed 20 pounds of solid muscle onto his 5'10" frame. When he achieved a body weight of 230 pounds, he was not only bigger—he was massive almost beyond belief. But what was the routine that packed on those initial 20 pounds of beef? Further, what routine did Dorian Yates follow to continue to make gains and amaze both competitor and contest judge alike? Let's hear from the man himself:

"When I first started training, I would work out every other day, training half my body on one day, taking a day off, then training the other half of the body. I put on 20 pounds of muscle doing this program, and, I should mention, my sets were kept quite low.

"At this time I used to do chest, back, and shoulders on my first training day. The next day I'd take off to recover, and then the following day I would train my legs and arms. The next day would be an off day again to recover and grow, and then I'd just keep rotating it in a Monday, Wednesday, Friday, Sunday, Tuesday, Thursday, etc., sort of fashion. Just one-on, one-off all the time.

"I would space my workouts a full 48 hours apart solely to allow for recovery and growth." Yates obviously made great progress on such a restricted system, but didn't he, like the rest of us, at one time give in to the curiosity of doing a 'few more sets' or training 'just a couple of more days' a week?

"Shortly after I started training, I tried the more conventional four-day split routine that has the trainee working out on Mondays, Tuesdays, Thursdays, and Fridays, but even after a week on this sort of a program, I just knew that it was too much training—at least if your objective was to grow muscle. I was tired all the time and just couldn't recover properly."

THE MENTZER INFLUENCE

At this point in Dorian's life, he began to read up on high-intensity training in articles by Mike Mentzer that appeared in *Muscle and Fitness* magazine. "I'm the sort of person who, if he does something, does it 100 percent, so Mentzer's articles on maximum effort training made sense to me. That's why I switched over to the every-other-day split routine and, although I train somewhat differently now, I'll still just train three days a week at times during the off-season, training, say, Monday, Wednesday, and Friday, but using the two splits, which gives me maximum recovery and growth." So what exactly was this magic bulk-building routine of his?

"It was split up into two equal halves. The way I did it was, as mentioned, chest, back, and delts on one day, and the following day would be a complete rest day. The next day would be a training day and would consist of legs, calves, and arms, and the next day would again be a day of rest and recovery. Then I would just keep repeating the cycle. And sometimes I would even take an extra day off so that I would be training only three days a week. This way you would only be doing your chest twice and your legs once a week, which is fine, because if you take it over a period of nine days, it balances itself out equally.

"When I was doing this routine, I was also engaged in construction work, which consisted of heavy manual labor, so I really needed all the recovery time I could get from a training program if I hoped to make any gains at all. It doesn't really matter how you split up your body parts so long as it's a balanced split and you train your larger body parts first when you have the most energy. I have no reservations about recommending the three-day-a week routine to anybody seeking to gain muscle mass—it's a really good size-building program."

Does such a restricted program have any inherent flaws? "Well, not unless you're an advanced competitive bodybuilder, which, let's face it, few of us are. In that case, if you're going to have to train your chest, back, and shoulder, say, in one workout as a competitive bodybuilder, you're going to have to really do a lot of work to train the muscles from more than one angle to get at different aspects of it. This means inevitably that you're going to have to do more exercises and more sets which, when you're training three body parts in one session, is going to lead to overtraining and burnout. Some bodybuilders will say to me, 'I couldn't possibly train chest, back, and shoulders together,' but remember, when I was doing this I was doing only two exercises for each body part on average for only a handful of sets.

"For chest, as an example, my routine was flat bench presses and incline presses, and that was it. For back it was chins and barbell rowing—bam! Finished! For delts, press behind neck and lateral raises, and that was it, finished. Anybody can do that in 45 minutes. Here's how I'd work my chest: I'd just do bench presses and incline presses and I'd do a warm-up on the bench with 1 or 2 sets, and then I would take my heaviest weight on the third set, which would be my first real 'proper' set, which I'd take to positive failure. Then, on my second 'real' set, I'd drop the weight down a little bit to compensate for the fatigue that I'd induced with my previous set, so that I could still get an adequate amount of reps to stimulate more muscle fibers and, again, I'd go to positive failure. This would be a typical chest workout.

"On the bench press, I'd do two warm-up sets and two heavy sets. Then I would move on to the incline press. Now, I'd warm up before inclines because I find it easier to injure myself these days, but then, I'd just launch right into the inclines and just do my two intense sets on that. So that would be 4 sets total on the bench and 2 on the inclines and maybe, depending on how I felt, some dumbbell flyes, but mainly I would just do those two heavy, basic exercises."

LOW SETS, HIGH RESULTS

"I always used low sets in my training—again for the recovery factor—and even though I'm doing a few more sets now, I still use low sets compared to most bodybuilders competing today. For example, my biceps routine typically consists of a warm-up of concentration curls and then, like my bench presses, I'll do 2 more intense sets starting with my heaviest weight and then doing my second set with a lighter weight. After concentration curls, I would typically move on to standing barbell curls. I don't need to warm up on these, as I've already warmed up with the concentration curls, so I'd sail right into 2 intense sets of barbell curls to at least failure.

"Sometimes I'll even use forced reps on these, or descending sets, which really increase the intensity of the exercise. And that, basically, is my biceps workout, which is all of 4 sets after a 2-set warm-up. I only do 4 sets for my calves as well—that's all any body part needs, really, with the possible exception of back and legs where more muscle groups are involved."

Yates uses a variation of his former routine these days (at the time of this inter-view). It's still brief and intense to be sure, but it also features some subtle nuances in methodology. As it's his routine, we'll let him explain it to you:

"The format of my present routine is only slightly different from my earlier program. I've moved on from the every-other-day routine after using it religiously for three and a half years. In fact, I used it up until I won my first British Championship so, if I can use a three-day-a week program successfully up to that level, I'm confident that the majority of people will have equal success with it. Anyway, at that point in my career, after training on the every-other-day split for three and a half years, I wanted to get bigger, but I also felt that I needed to work on some of the different aspects of my muscles and refine what I had developed.

"I split up my program a little more to accomplish this. I wasn't successful right away. I started with the conventional three-day-on/one-day-off method which most of the top pros use, but straightaway I knew that I couldn't recuperate sufficiently on that to grow. I just couldn't do three all-out workouts in a row because by the time I got to the third one I was totally depleted. I mean, you could train with a three-on/one-off all the time if you weren't training at 100 percent, but then, if you're not training at 100 percent you're not going to get any results, are you? So I didn't see the point of the three-days-on/one-day-off system.

"What I came up with was cycling my workouts over a period of five days, during which time I would train my chest and arms on day one, legs and calves on day two, take day three off, train back and shoulders on day four, and take the fifth day off. That would be my five-day cycle, which I would then continue to repeat. I would work my entire body once over this five-day period, which allows me plenty of time to recuperate from my super-heavy training." (He's not kidding! We've seen Yates train with 200-pound dumbbells for strict one-arm rows and repetition bench presses with 405 pounds!)

"You see, my first workout, being chest and arms, isn't too depleting to the body, energy-wise, because the body parts being trained aren't all that big. Day two, where I train my legs and calves, is a killer day and takes a lot out of you, so you need the third day off. The fourth day, back and shoulders, is the other half of the upper body and is separated by a few days from the chest and arms workout so there's no overlap and plenty of rest and recuperation afforded the muscle groups you've trained."

Here is an example of Yates's routine:

Day 1: chest, biceps, and triceps

Day 2: quadriceps, hamstrings, and calves

Day 3: off

Day 4: back and shoulders

Day 5: off

In terms of exercises, Yates always preferred to train heavy and basic, utilizing ultra-strict form. Here is the routine that he used to successfully win the 1991 New York Night of the Champions.

DAY 1: CHEST AND ARMS

Chest

- Bench presses or decline presses (these exercises are switched from workout to workout): 2 or 3 sets of 12 reps followed by 2 sets of 6–8 reps.
- Incline barbell presses: 1 warm-up of 10 reps, followed by 2 heavy sets of 6–8 reps.
- Dumbbell flyes: 1 warm-up set, followed by 2 triple-drop sets of 6–8 reps. Yates likes to triple-drop each set of flyes he does; after hitting failure at the end of his first set of flyes, he will pick up a lighter pair of dumbbells and immediately perform another set. Then he performs one more drop set, again to failure.

Biceps

- Concentration curls: 1 warm-up set followed by 2 heavy sets of 8–10 reps. Yates sits on the edge of a bench and braces his upper arm against his inner thigh.
- Barbell curls: no warm-up set on this one, Yates instead launches right into heavy sets (the actual number could vary, but 2 sets was a good target) of 8–10 reps. These are performed very strictly, with no bending at the waist or cheating the weight up.
- Hammer curls (performed occasionally): again no warm-up here, Yates performs

2 sets of 8–10 reps, holding the dumb-bells with his thumbs up, and curls them either alternately or simultaneously.

Triceps

- Cable extensions on lat machine: 2 warm-up sets, followed by 2 heavy sets of 10–12 reps. Yates uses a narrow grip on these and pushes the weight straight down in front of him. Again, perfect form is emphasized.

- Lying triceps extensions: 1 warm-up set for 10 reps, followed by 2 heavy sets of 8–10 reps. Dorian uses super-strict form here, smoothly pushing the bar overhead for a complete contraction.

- One-arm dumbbell extensions: no warm-up, Yates instead launches directly into 1 set of 8–10 reps. Yates sits down on a bench, holding a single dumbbell overhead with one arm. He then slowly lowers it behind his head with his thumb facing down and then slowly extends it back overhead.

DAY 2: QUADS, HAMS, AND CALVES

In training legs, Yates does his first leg day heavy for sets of 8 to 12 reps and then, on the next leg day, Dorian goes with lighter poundages for reps in the 15 to 20 range.

Quads

- Leg extensions: 3 warm-up sets followed by 2 heavy sets (same protocol as with previous body parts). Again, super-strict form is employed here, particularly on the slow and deliberate lowering of the weight.

- Leg presses: 1 or 2 warm-up sets followed by 2 heavy sets.

- Hack squats: 1 warm-up set, followed by 2 heavy sets. Yates keeps his feet close together and goes as deep as he can. He will also substitute toes-out squats on the Smith machine from time to time.

Hamstrings

- Leg curls: 1 warm-up set, followed by 2 heavy sets, performed with special emphasis on keeping his hips down on the machine.

- Stiff-legged deadlifts: 1 warm-up followed by 2 heavy sets, done on an elevated platform for an enhanced stretch.

Calves

- Standing calf raises: 1 warm-up set, followed by 2 heavy sets. Dorian utilizes a variety of toe positions and follows the same set/rep scheme as for the rest of his leg training.

- Seated calf raises: Dorian doesn't use a warm-up set for this exercise, instead opting to launch right into 2 heavy sets to failure.

DAY 3: OFF

DAY 4: BACK AND DELTOIDS

Back

- Close-grip pulldowns: 2 warm-up sets, followed by 2 heavy sets of 8–10 reps. Like Mentzer before him, Dorian prefers to use a close grip on the lat bar with his palms facing upward.
- Weighted chins: 1 warm-up set (no weight), followed by 2 heavy sets of 6–8 reps. Yates uses up to 90 pounds strapped around his waist for extra resistance here.
- Bent-over rows: 1 warm-up set, followed by 2 sets of 8–10 reps. Yates alternates between barbell rows and one-arm dumbbell rows from workout to workout.
- Seated pulley rows: with no warm-up, Dorian wades right into 2 heavy sets of 8–10 reps.

Deltoids

- Seated dumbbell presses: 1 warm-up set, followed by 2 sets of 8–10 reps, performed either alternately or simultaneously.
- Seated dumbbell lateral raises: no warm-up, 2 sets of 8–10 reps. Yates uses the triple-drop system on each of his sets here.
- Bent-over lateral raises: with no warm-up, Dorian performs 2 heavy sets of 8–12 reps, again using the triple-drop system.

Traps

- Barbell shrugs: 1 warm-up set, followed by 2 sets of 8–12 reps. Yates uses wrist straps for these and shrugs the weight up in a smooth, steady fashion.

Erector Spinae

- Hyperextensions: no warm-up, followed by 2 or 3 sets of 12–15 reps.

Despite the fact that Dorian believes fully in the "Maximum effort equals maximum results" motto, he also subscribes to the importance of genetics. Hear him: "Obviously you can't go any further than your genetics allow you to go. It's physically impossible. But who can honestly say just how far that is? Has anybody ever reached even 50 percent of their genetic potential? If so, I'd like to meet them. I could have better genetics than the person reading this, but if they have even 50 percent more intelligence with regard to their training, diet, and other aspects of their bodybuilding, they could end up with a far better physique than I have. So at the end of the day, all things being equal, I suppose that the person with the best genetics will usually have the better physique—but things, as we know, aren't always equal. If you don't have great genetics, compensate by being smarter, by training better, and by using better nutrition and things like that. This is how you ultimately build a great physique."

60

Achim Albrecht

"**H**oly mother of Christ!" exclaimed a fat man in the audience. His rather unpious exclamation was issued in response to the sight of German (later residing in sunny California) behemoth Achim Albrecht as he stepped out upon the stage in Florida for the Mr. Olympia contest.

Albrecht looked phenomenal all right, if somewhat drawn from the strain of dieting. Yet there could be no disputing his incredible muscle mass. Apart from the man who would ultimately win the coveted Mr. Olympia title for an unprecedented eighth time, Lee Haney, and perhaps England's mammoth, Dorian Yates, there were none bigger on the Mr. Olympia dais at that time than Achim Albrecht.

Albrecht's look so wowed Joe Weider that the "Master Blaster" signed him on sight to an exclusive Weider contract. In a related vein, Albrecht seemed to win over a good proportion of spectators at the Mr. Olympia contest in much the same way. After he had completed his mind-blowing, muscle-popping posing routine, the chubby audience member just looked at the now empty stage and shook his head in disbelief at what he had just seen.

There was no doubt that Achim Albrecht had a phenomenally bright future ahead of him in bodybuilding, After all, a physique like his doesn't just pop up every day at Gold's gym (every two decades maybe, but definitely not every day). But how did he get so massive? What exercises gave him his best results? In short, what has been Achim Albrecht's most productive routine? The big guy himself answered this question.

"Unquestionably my most productive routine— in terms of really putting on mass—is the four-day-on, one-day-off system. That of course being to split up your body parts over a four-day cycle with the fifth day off for rest and growth. My personal split-up of these body parts would be chest and shoulders on day one, back and calves on day two; legs, calves, and abs on day three, and then arms by themselves.

"When I made my best size gains, I typically used about 4 sets per exercise and about four or five exercises per body part, and my repetitions may be as high as 20 on my first set and then drop to as low as 6 or 8 by my last one. Variety is the key; keep your muscles shocked and keep the variety of both exercises and repetitions constantly changing in order to ensure new growth stimulation."

GOOD GENETICS AREN'T EVERYTHING

Many bodybuilders are of the opinion that genetics are the be-all and the end-all of bodybuilding success; in other words, if you don't have it, you never will. Achim however, felt that approach is too simplistic. Hear him:

"Genetics are important, there's no question about it, but you still have to factor in the ultimate importance of both diet and training. Those are the 'Big Three' factors that ultimately determine a champion bodybuilder. Too many people think that if they just focus on one of these factors, then they, too, will become as successful as their favorite bodybuilding champion. I've heard people say in my seminars, 'I'll have an arm like Mike Mentzer's because I use barbell preacher curls with a wide grip—just like he does!'

"Hey, I'm here right now to tell you that training is only one part of the equation. The truth of the matter is that genetics, nutrition, and training are all required—in abundance in most instances—in order to create a championship physique."

AN ACHIM SAMPLE WORKOUT

Albrecht, as mentioned, breaks his training down into four days that cover each body part once and then takes the fifth day off before repeating the cycle. Here's how his routine breaks down:

Day 1: chest and shoulders

Day 2: back and calves

Day 3: legs, calves, and abs

Day 4: arms

Day 5: off

In terms of exercises, Albrecht's approach is basics all the way, preferring to train as heavy as possible utilizing strict form and basic movements. Here's the routine he used to pack on the mass that ultimately placed him ninth at Mr. Olympia and first at the World Championships:

DAY 1: CHEST AND SHOULDERS

Chest

- Bench presses: 2 warm-up sets followed by 2 super-heavy power sets of 8–12 repetitions.
- Incline presses: Albrecht likes to emphasize the stretch at the bottom of this movement again for 2 warm-up sets and 2 sets with as much weight as he can handle for 8–12 reps.
- Dumbbell flyes: 1 warm-up set followed by 3 progressively heavier sets of 8–10 repetitions each.

"Typically I'll only do these three exercises for my chest when I'm after mass, but before a contest I'll add an exercise like cable crossovers to bring out a little extra refinement. I'll do 2 warm-ups followed by 2 heavy sets to failure."

Shoulders

- Seated behind-the-neck presses: 1 warm-up set followed by 3 progressively heavier sets of 6–20 repetitions. "Sometimes when I'm feeling particularly strong, I'll add even more weight to my last set of shoulder presses and drop my reps down to as low as two."

- Seated dumbbell presses: 1 warm-up set of 15–20 reps, followed by 3 progressively heavier sets of 6–8 reps.
- Dumbbell lateral raises: 1 warm-up set in which he focuses entirely on the feeling inside the lateral head of the deltoid as he contracts it to lift the weight for 15 reps. The warm-up set is then followed by 3 progressively heavier sets of 8–10 repetitions.
- Bent-over lateral raises: 1 warm-up set followed by 3 progressively heavier sets of 8–10 reps. "I really try to isolate the rear head of the deltoid when I do this exercise," says Achim. "Too many bodybuilders have big but incomplete shoulder development because they never develop the rear head of the deltoid. Believe me, when you're standing on stage doing a rear double-biceps pose, you'd better have something in that rear delt cavity to show the judges."

DAY 2: BACK AND CALVES

Back

- T-bar rows: Achim performs 1 warm-up set, followed by 3 progressively heavier sets to failure (6–10 reps).
- Barbell rows: 2 warm-up sets, followed by 2 all-out sets to failure, which comes after 6–8 reps.

- Chins: Achim uses just his body weight with chins if they come third in his back exercise sequence (otherwise, he adds weight to his waist) for 4 sets of 6–12 reps.
- Cable rows: 1 warm-up set, followed by 3 progressively heavier sets of 8–10 reps to failure. "I believe in really training my back as heavy as possible, but not at the expense of correct exercise form, I also like to add forced reps whenever possible— particularly on my seated cable rows."

Calves

- Standing calf raises: 1 warm-up set followed by 3 heavy sets of 15–20 reps.
- Seated calf raises: 1 warm-up set, followed by 3 heavy sets of 12–15 reps.
- Calf raises on the leg press machine: 1 warm-up set of 20 reps, followed by 3 increasingly heavier sets of 12–15 reps. "I love my calf training," says Achim. "You must make sure to get a full stretch at the bottom or fully extended position and to really contract or cramp the calves at the top or fully contracted position. Force the blood in there."

DAY 3: LEGS, CALVES, AND ABS

Legs

- Leg extensions: 1 to 2 warm-up sets of 15–20 reps, followed by 3 progressively heavier sets of 12–15 reps to failure.
- Leg presses: 1 warm-up set, followed by 3 super-heavy sets of 10–12 reps.

- Squats: 1 warm-up set of 15–20 reps, followed by 3 progressively heavier sets of 6–10 reps.
- Leg curls: 1 warm-up set of 12–15 reps, followed by 3 heavy sets of 8–12 reps.
- Stiff-legged deadlifts: 1 warm-up set of 12–15 reps, followed by 3 progressively heavier sets of 8–12 reps.

"Leg training is the most important training day for me because all of my body parts respond better when my legs are getting stronger, but good form is especially important here as the knee joint is a very delicate one. If you have knee wraps, I'd suggest you use them and emphasize extra caution when descending in movements like squats and leg presses."

Calves

See Day 2's calf training section for details.

Abs

- Hanging leg raises: 1 warm-up set, followed by 3 sets of 12–15 reps.
- Crunches: 4 sets of 20–25 reps.
- Ab machine (occasionally): 4 sets of 12–15 reps. "I make sure to hold the contracted position of every crunch and then slowly lower myself back to the starting position. Remember with all training, it's imperative to 'feel' the contractions."

DAY 4: ARMS

Biceps

- Alternate dumbbell curls: 1 warm-up set, followed by 3 sets of 8–12 reps.
- Preacher curls: 1 warm-up set of 12 reps, followed by 3 progressively heavier sets of 8–12 reps.
- Barbell curls: 1 warm-up set of 15 reps, followed by 3 progressively heavier sets of 8–12 reps.

Triceps

- Pushdowns: 1 warm-up set of 12–15 reps, followed by 3 sets of 8–12 reps with progressively heavier weights.
- Lying triceps extensions: 1 warm-up set, followed by 3 progressively heavier sets of 8–10 reps.
- Cable pushdowns on lat machine: 1 warm-up set of 20 reps, followed by 3 very heavy sets of 6–8 reps.
- One-arm dumbbell extensions: 1 warm-up set per arm, followed by 3 progressively heavier sets of 10–12 reps per arm.

FINDING THAT OFF-SEASON MOTIVATION

It is a given that all professional bodybuilders train hard during the last six weeks before a contest. After all, it's the final stretch and they have nothing to lose and everything to gain. Few pros, however, train as hard as Achim in the off-season and, as a result, few pros carry the degree of muscle mass that this German freight train displays. Achim agrees with the assessment.

"Oh yeah, few pros train hard in the off-season. I train like an animal in the off-season because that's when I make my true muscle gains. That's also when I use this routine. Before a contest, I'll train seven days straight, but I won't insult your intelligence and tell you that I train heavier and harder than I do in the off-season because building mass—which is what my off-season program does—is a lot harder than refining the mass—what my precontest training does—once you've built it."

EATING THE RIGHT THINGS

"One reason that I'm able to build so much muscle mass in the off-season, and even for that matter precontest, is that I'm a big believer in eating healthy foods. What I mean by this is that I don't eat junk food. It's eating a balanced diet from the four basic food groups and supplementing with vita-mins, minerals, and protein if you need it whenever necessary. I definitely have to stay away from junk foods like pie and ice cream, or else my definition flies out the window."

A GREAT WORKOUT FOR NONCOMPETITORS

Alright, so Achim's outlined his off-season routine to build his incredible muscle mass. But what of those of us who have no inten-tions to compete but who still want to build up to a respectable size? Once again, the massive German has the answer.

"I would have noncompetitive trainers work out three to four times a week maximum. I'd also recommend that they follow a split routine not unlike the one I follow during the off-season. They should split their body parts up. The first workout day could be a split of, say, chest, shoulders, and triceps, with the second day being a split of legs, back, and biceps. Then on the third day of training they could repeat the program of the first day, and then take the fourth day off. Then they could just alternate back and forth between the two routines.

"As you can see, rest and recovery are factored into such a program, as certain body parts are trained twice in one week and only once the next week, so at least once a week certain body parts can rest up for the next week's assault, and then you would alternate the body parts that would be trained twice the next week.

"However I still feel the four-day-on/one-day-off program is the best training method there is for packing on muscle mass. You don't have to do a ton of sets to get results either; it's what you put into your sets that counts—not the sheer number of them. It's also important to feel the movement you are performing from full extension to full contraction. Use good form, don't overtrain, and eat a well-balanced diet and you'll have to get a whole new wardrobe—you'll get massive that quickly."

61

Doug Hepburn

The Canadian Colossus who throws around polysyllabic words like loose change saw a massive arm on a fellow who was getting on the bus and he knew right then that was what he wanted. He started to train and became acquainted with all the greats. His idols at the time were the great John Grimek and John David. He had Grimek's picture up on the wall. Mr. Weider came into the picture. "He did assist me financially to some extent, to help me out so that I could continue with my training and still get my food. He gave me protein supplements, and also a lot of articles that were written by Charlie Smith appeared in his magazines, and they made me famous in those early days. I must also say that Weider was the man, the one man, who took me in the beginning and recognized my potential ability and went ahead and promoted it. Nobody at the time did.

"Fundamentally the most productive way I discovered was to perform extended series of sets of low repetitions. What I mean by that is even 20 to 30 sets. My reps would go down to 3 or 5. I found out that this stimulated muscular growth because I don't believe that the average strength athlete, although they may more now than they did then, trained that way. They thought they could go and do 4 or 5 repetitions with a reasonably heavy weight. There's not enough repetitions there to stimulate maximum muscular growth.

"The principle of it was extended sets of 3 repetitions, combined with singles— possibly as many as 8. This is in a variation to the sets of threes. Then, for the other part, I used to do some sets of repetitions, up to as many as 8 for what you might call a 'pumping procedure.'

"I incorporated that basic routine when I was 54 years old. I decided to come back, and I went in there and I was way down in weight, weighing maybe 200 pounds. And I went in this gym and I hadn't been feeling too well. I used a routine similar to the one I've just explained the principles of and, when I was 54, I was doing repetition squats with 600 pounds, doing sets of 6 and 7. At 54 years of age, without wraps of any kind and of course without steroids, I did a standing press of 390 pounds."

ON OVERTRAINING

"You can train every day. If you organize it right, you can train every day—that's what I did when I was 54. When you're older, your strength will dissipate faster. Certain things happen. When you're young, you can get away with heavy workouts every three days or so because nature is working for you. As you age, you have to increase the frequency of your workouts. For example, now at age 66, I find that I have to train every day up to a heavy weight or I cannot maintain my strength.

"When you're older your recuperative powers are diminished, and your recuperative powers are essential to maintain strength. If I didn't train heavy on one given exercise at the most on every second day—and preferably every day—I'll go backward. So I've reached the point in my life now that I'll fall back to a point but I'll still maintain a basic strength. I could squat once a week for half an hour and always do a 350-pound squat—even at the age of 65. The reason for that is that I'm using the strength in the body that has been built there over a lifetime, and that level won't go down beyond a certain point unless you got sick or something. And also any exercise you do when you're older that involves tendons will give you more strength.

"Heavy weights influence the tendons as well as the muscle, of course. Great strength comes from tendons. More so than muscles. Steroids affect muscular strength, but not to the same extent in the tendons. It doesn't matter whether you do a partial or what, I don't think you can develop the strength of a full movement by doing a partial movement. To get strong, it's more built upon the structure of your routine."

DEVELOPING PRESSING POWER

"When I developed my pressing power I did it without using weights. I did handstand push-ups. When I was a young man on the beach at age 23, I weighed about 240 pounds. And I was a lifeguard, and there were logs on the beach. And from morning to night I would go up into a handstand with my hands on these logs and I'd begin to press myself up and down using my body weight like a barbell. I used to do it hour after hour. I could do sets of 10 reps. I got to the point where I was pressing upwards of 300 pounds without using weights just by using my own body weight. I believe that laid the foundation for my later strength in the shoulders. That developed it.

"It would be very good for a person to do handstand push-ups for any lift—they're excellent for training. Of course, when you're upside down, the blood rushes into your shoulders and, man, I think it's really good. Coupled again with your actual weight training. A lot of bench pressers can't do anything standing up. Standing presses give a better comparison of your basic body power. The whole structure of your entire physical structure is involved. If you've got a weak back, a weak waist, or a weak link in there, then you can't press the weight. I believe that the standing press is a better test of overall physical strength than the bench press."

LIFTS HE'S MOST PROUD OF

"I guess I did them all. I did a curl, and I never really thought of it at the time. After the British Empire Games in 1954, I believe that for pressing power, I was then as strong as I ever was. And I weighed about 300 pounds. I believe I had won the Games and I was out in the area where the university was with a little friend of mine, and we went into the gym where the guys used to train. Some of the athletes from the Games had not yet gone back to their own countries, and I remember there were some strength athletes there from Trinidad and Jamaica who I knew, one was a 198-pounder. I walked into the gym with a suit on, and I'd just eaten a big meal, and I used to like to puff on a cigar once in a while—Grimek likes cigars, you know. Stanko and Grimek each used to have a good cigar going during their lunch break.

"Anyway, I went into the gym and was feeling pretty good, so I took my suit jacket off and started to do some presses off the rack, which was set at about shoulder height. These guys were watching me, and I did a couple just to warm up and took 400 pounds off there and did it easy for 4 reps in the overhead press.

"This was back in 1954, and the funny part was, when I put it down, I looked at my friends from Jamaica—and they were white as a sheet, which is something for a native Jamaican, let me tell you! Their color was just

gone. They looked pale, and one of them walked over to me and tapped me on the chest and said, 'What have you got in there?' He wanted to know what I was made of because they never dreamed that a man would be able to do that.

"I always did my stuff through the mind. The mind gave me a pinpoint direction, the concentration of the mind. Two or three years ago, a fellow came to me who was a psychology student at the University of British Columbia. And he said, 'You know, the professor referred to you in his lecture in psychology? He said that Doug Hepburn had subjugated his libido.' He said, 'I don't know how the hell the man did it, but he did it.' He said it's virtually impossible for the average man to do that. I was in a state throughout those years that everything was completely subjugated to that one desire to develop strength, and I believe that it was what gave me tremendous power."

HIS GREATEST LIFT

"According to David Willoughby [strength historian], and he's probably right, it was not the press but the curl. I did a 260-pound strict curl and, I understand, I didn't get against the wall because I use my shoulder strength in curling and I can't use that when I'm against the wall. You also can't use a quick start. That doesn't reflect overall body power when you curl because you can't use your delts or trapezius.

"In training I could take a 360-pound barbell at shoulder level, drive it out away from my shoulders in a horizontal position, and pull it back into my shoulders before it had time to fall. My top press weight was 440 pounds. Although when I was a lifeguard in 1949, weighing maybe 235 pounds, I took a barbell that was loaded up with weights from a trestle and, wearing only my bathing suit and using a slight bend at the knee, rammed it up overhead. I found out later that the weight was 465 pounds."

STRONG MAN PHILOSOPHY

"The knowledge thus gained was the end product, so produced by intuition, trial and error, and an absolute integrity in the implementation of my daily procedure, coupled with an undeviating mode of conduct in my living habits and an unwavering belief in the morality of man's struggles to improve himself utilizing only the natural, God-given attributes that he was provided at birth. This paragraph represents my philosophy as a strong man."

MOST PRODUCTIVE TECHNIQUE

"When I trained, everybody was doing series of 6 and 8 reps. And I don't know why. Why would a man, who was living with people who had done something since the beginning of weight lifting, go out and then suddenly, for some strange gut feeling, throw the whole thing in the garbage can and do something entirely opposite to what everybody did? I don't why I did, but I started to do sets of threes—which was something that wasn't done. Mind you, I'm going back now to the '40s.

"I started out with the threes, and I believe what brought about the change in me was partially due to a somewhat good heritage, but also because I was the first one who discovered and utilized extensively that method of training, whereas nobody else did it. And I developed this power not because there were other men as strong as me, but because I was the first to conceive of it and utilize it!

"The principle was that I would do sets of threes, over and over and over for 20 or 30 sets. And I found out that all of a sudden my body responded unbelievably! And one thing I just want to mention, when you check into my lifting, at that period when I first came to be known, the gap that I established between myself and the other person in the world was the widest gap—strength-wise—of any other lifter in history.

"I'm fully convinced that the structure of sets and repetitions, coupled with the application as to the intensity and frequency of augmentation of the resistance, represents the keystone in the building of ultimate physical strength. I believe, as I've said, that the structure of the repetitions is more important than anything else you can do in regard to getting strong. Other than taking drugs. It's the structure of the routine and how it's used that develops ultimate strength.

"Protein and all that is fine, you know. Presently, I'm 66 years old and I'm still reasonably strong. I don't have any aches and pains although, of course, age takes its toll. I'm in a very unique position here. I'm inclined philosophically, and maybe to some extent scientifically, and I've been given the opportunity for probably the first time in history to approach the problem scientifically and study myself and the effects on my body of all different types of foods and different mental attitudes to see what happens and combat the aging process and the lowering of physical strength within a human being.

"I discovered that when you reach a point in your life a reversal starts to take place. In other words, you're dying faster than you're living. What actually kills the body is poisoning, the inefficiency of the body to function at its peak level. So it begins to poison itself, and then no nutrients are able to get into the muscles and so forth. So I say, 'How can we surmount this?'

"I say that as you get older you have to eat less, not more, in order to get strong. If you eat more when you reach that point of no return, it will make you ill. It will kill you. If you look at it logically, and I'm a great person for reasoning and logic, obviously when you're born, you go through a cycle of life and there's a point where the body begins to go the other way. It begins to die; it's going from life to death in the cycle. But they don't analyze the cycle and realize that during a part of that cycle, that reversals take place. When you think, they allow for the evolution of man in the material plane, but

do they ever think that thought may evolve and alter during the late cycle?"

MOTIVATION FOR THE OLDER MAN

"When a man is 75 and wants to utilize his strength and maintain it, he has no libido. Most guys now, as you know, are lifting weights and getting stronger to impress and get themselves a mate. But the reason the old guy doesn't still train is that he can't think of a damn good enough reason to do it. So therein is the problem. What does a man do to do this? Because this is also part and parcel of the aging process. I have to take these factors into consideration and say, 'How can I train, and push myself? What am I going to use for my impulsion to do it?' You cannot approach the training like you're going to set it down on a piece of paper and do 6 reps of this. You have to play it by ear."

WHY HE WAS POPULAR WITH POULTRY FARMERS

"I had a strong constitution genetically. I remember I was eating a lot one day in the summertime and I gained eight pounds in one day with water and food. I mean, I could eat! [laugh] One day I ate 65 eggs! I wanted to see how many I could drink in a milk shake."

DEFEATS ANDERSON

"Well, Anderson was a young man then— but he was strong. I think I was probably a little more experienced and a little older. Yes,

I did beat him, although his publicists claimed that he 'was never beaten.'"

ANDERSON'S MANAGER

"He was just back from his stage act in Reno where he had all these silver dollars that he used to lift. I remember I phoned down to the hotel where he was performing his act because Anderson had issued a challenge offering $15,000 to anyone who could match Paul's lift of a box filled with silver dollars. I called down to see if I could come down and attempt it. And you know what happened? And this isn't common knowledge either. About an hour later, Anderson's manager phoned—and this is documented because I have an article in the Oregon newspaper that documents this. Anderson's manager told me, 'Please don't come down, we'll do something with you later.'"

ANDERSON'S FALSE CLAIMS

"The other thing is this. . . . Anderson is undoubtedly one of the strongest men in history. I have a great respect for him. However, there are lifts and things that are given to him that are beyond the realm of what I believe to be possible. It's just gotten ridiculous, you know, 10 repetitions with 300 pounds in the one-arm press. Now, he might have done that in a one-arm bent press, but they're calling it a press! The point here is, it isn't only me, it ridicules all the other strong men in history. It's an insult. I look upon the strong man in terms of the world and what strength represents to mankind."

THE BENCH PRESS COMPETITION

"Anderson and I once had a bench press competition in his backyard. I had just come back from Hawaii, I'm not making excuses, but I was tired because it was hot over there and I'd put some shows on for a guy named Rex Ravalle. It was hot and I was a little tired, and when I came back I wasn't at my best, I weighed about 275 pounds. I went into Los Angeles from Hawaii because you have to go through there to get to Vancouver, where I live.

"Anderson's manager met me at the plane and took me to where he was staying, which was the manager's house. Anderson was training for a movie, and I met Anderson in the backyard. He must have weighed at least 360 pounds. I mean he wasn't young, but he was near his peak of strength. So I don't know how we ended up doing this, but we got down to a bench press and had a little competition. Both of us managed to do 500 pounds, which wasn't a bad bench in those days, but Anderson couldn't do an ounce more and neither could I—but I weighed 270 and he weighed 360 pounds.

"After the bench pressing, Anderson had an Olympic bar on trestles and he attempted to press 420 pounds, and he could not do it. Now I know he could do it, he was that close, and on any other day he might well have done it, but he couldn't do it that day. From that, and remember I did it at a body weight of 290 pounds, I standing pressed 440 pounds, and this was without any belt and on a gimpy leg and with no steroids.

"Taking a man of the present age who might have set his records while on drugs can't be compared to those of us who did it clean. It's an insult to all who have been before. I called the doctor on sports and steroids at the University of British Columbia. He told me that steroids became used and known to athletes at the beginning of the 1950s.

"Now before that, I had this gap between me and all the other strong men. How after the '50s, that's when all these other 'strong men' began to appear. It may be coincidence, but I'm doubtful. However, of the more modern crop, I appreciate a man like Kazmaier—he admits he took steroids. I mean, if a man admits it, that's great—he's an honest man, but for a man to do this and not admit it . . . that's all I'm complaining about.

"Anderson, all things being equal, would have been a great lifter at any time. I'm not trying to belittle Anderson, but I'm trying to save the credibility of powerlifting in the world. What the heck! Since when does a man like Anderson or anybody else mean more than the principle of sport and the morality of man in the world? I'm doing it for that and thank God that some people do!

"One of the greatest compliments I ever got was at the Goodwill Games when they were held in California. I was told by a writer friend of mine that the Russian weight lifting team was down there at that time and Vasily Alexeev was with them. We went down to see the weight lifters, and I could see Alexeev walking around backstage. I said to my friend, 'If you ever get backstage, which you might be able to do because you're a writer, can you do me a favor? I'd like you to ask the Russian coach if I would be allowed to correspond with Alexeev as one strong man to another.'

"So he phoned me back the next day and said, 'Well, Doug, I went down there and I got hold of the top Russian coach from their weight lifting team, and I showed him your pictures and I showed him what you lifted way back when, and then I asked the coach whether or not you could write to Alexeev, and you know what the coach said? He said, 'I think that Alexeev should write to Mr. Hepburn!' You know why? Because that coach knew that I did those lifts before steroids came into play. And as you well know, Alexeev was loaded with them.

"Terry Todd once told me that when a lifter gets all wrapped up in their support suits and takes steroids, they add 30 percent to their lift. And if you notice, take some of my old lifts and add 30 percent to them, you'll get up to just about what they're doing today with those aids."

62

Lee Labrada

Without question, one of the greatest Mr. Olympia competitors of all time was the mighty Lee Labrada. He has almost flawless proportions, terrific shape and detail, and, of course, the requisite muscle mass to go with it; and at his various Mr. Olympia competitions, he put it all together with a posing routine that always brought the house down.

Most bodybuilders would give up their jobs to experience the sort of gains that Labrada has made throughout his incredible career. Fortunately, there's no need for anyone of you to do anything so drastic, as I was able to obtain from the mighty Texan his most productive training routine, in addition to his favorite arm routine (always the muscle group of choice among bodybuilders) and the methods that he used to improve his already highly advanced physique for this year's Mr. Olympia contest.

According to Labrada, he has had two most productive routines: one when he was a beginner, the second being the one he hit upon for the Mr. Olympia. "Being an engineer by trade, I'm an analytical type, sort of from the empirical school, and I base things on experience and trial and error," said Labrada. "At the onset of my bodybuilding career I tried a lot of different routines, including the standard six-day-a-week, 20-sets-per-body-part routines, and I found that I was getting nowhere fast."

As fate would have it, it was at this juncture of his career that Labrada first discovered the writings of Heavy Duty training advocate Mike Mentzer, an articulate and physiologically informed former Mr. Olympia runner-up, and Labrada felt as though his eyes had been opened for the very first time. "I followed Mike's logic throughout his articles and, being of a scientific mind myself, it all made sense to me," said Labrada, "and so I tried it, and sure enough, I started getting results."

Labrada used Mentzer's training methodology as a starting point, and after meeting with varying degrees of success with certain techniques and exercises, gradually evolved his own system of training. "My own training has changed; it's gone through many different stages through the years," explains he of the watermelon-sized triceps, "I used to do many less sets than I even do now in fact. Typically, a chest workout might only be 6 sets for me when I first started out, whereas now it might go as high as 9 or 10 sets, which is still a lot lower than most pros use, and yet I was able to bring my chest up this year. I do use a few more sets now

before a contest because I feel that I have to in order to tax the muscle more fully. It's kind of a happy medium, so to speak."

But what was his first Mike Mentzer–inspired routine that brought about such fantastic results and sent him on to the intermediate and advanced levels of bodybuilding? "My most productive beginning routine was a four-day-per-week routine, high intensity, using about three different exercises per body part for 2 to 3 sets of each, going to positive failure and using as much weight as I could on each set. I trained on Mondays, Tuesdays, Thursdays, and Fridays, with Wednesdays, Saturdays, and Sundays off for growth. It was a simple formula, but it's worked like nothing else that I've ever done."

Such a program was just the ticket for Labrada's workouts, and he stayed with this program for a good many years. ("I won the Universe training on that one," he says with definite pride in his voice.) But in time, Lee noticed that his progress had come to a halt. Admittedly he was huge, with great shape and symmetry, but winning the Universe brought him into a whole new level of competition. Suddenly he had to compete against the pros, people with names like Gaspari, DeMey, Phil Hill, Mike Quinn, and, lest we forget, Lee Haney. To compete with the even bigger boys, Labrada reasoned that he would have to train more intensely in order to stimulate even more muscle growth, which in turn would necessitate a reduction in his training frequency.

"I knew that for this year's Mr. Oympia contest I would have to come in bigger than I did last year, so I upped the intensity and cut my training down to a two-on/one-off system in the off-season which would incorporate three different workouts. The first workout would be chest, shoulders, and triceps; the second one would be back and biceps; and the third one would be legs," says Labrada. "And I'd have to say that this format, which I'll explain fully in a minute, is the most productive routine that I've ever used for building big muscles fast. It certainly worked wonders for me this year!"

What then is the structure of this two-on/one-off method of Labrada's that made the system so productive? The Houston Hercules explains:

"This is how it works; let's call the three workouts A, B, and C. Chest, shoulders, and triceps would be workout A, back and biceps would be workout B, while workout C would be legs. You'd do workout A one day, workout B the next day, then you would take a day off. Then it's workout C, then it's back to workout A, and then you would take another day off and keep rotating the workouts like that. To reiterate, it's two days on, one off, with three different workouts that are rotated around. This allows you to train each body part twice one week and once the next week, and it's just terrific for packing on the mass in both intermediate and advanced trainees. It's a great routine!"

Labrada believes in positive failure and forced reps—but not negatives. "There's a physiological reason for my not doing negatives, and it has to do with the way that the muscle fibers function," he explains. "You've got actin and myosin (the filaments of the contractile fibers), which slide back and forth and are connected by a little ATP bridge (adenosine triphosphate), and when you perform a positive or concentric contraction, you're basically using the muscle fibers as they were intended. But when you start the eccentric or 'negative' part of the motion, you're actually dragging the actin and myosin across each other, creating internal friction within the muscle itself," says Labrada, who then adds almost as an afterthought, "That's why people get sore when they do negative repetitions exclusively, because they get microtrauma in the muscle fibers."

One high-intensity technique that Labrada does incorporate with devastating results is that of prefatigue. "Usually I start my workouts with an isolation movement for a given body part, whereas most pros start with a compound movement [i.e., bench press for chest]," he says before elaborating. "The reason I do this is to prefatigue the muscle that I'm training before beating the snot out of it with a heavy compound exercise. Using an isolation exercise such as leg extensions and then following that with a leg press or squat, or another combination would be concentration curls followed by a barbell curl. I feel that this warms up the muscle group thoroughly before I get into the real heavy compound movements."

But with all of these high-intensity methods of training to failure, prefatigue, and forced reps, doesn't Labrada think the average bodybuilder would overtrain and actually begin to lose size? Evidently not. "I don't think there is such a thing as an 'average' in terms of days per week that one can train without overtraining. I think that everybody has a different ability to recover from exercise and workouts, and you have to kind of gauge that for yourself," says the Titanic Texan.

"If you keep in mind that a muscle needs 72 hours to recover fully and that it's also possible to overtrain the body as a whole, then you should be able to structure your workouts properly," he adds. Like, say, a two-on/one-off type of system? "Precisely! The reason that most bodybuilders don't make any progress is simply overtraining; they overtrain the body on a systemic level, the entire body that is, rather than just one or two body parts, or something like that. I think that basically anyone can train four or five times a week tops without overtraining, if they're really training hard."

So, there you have it, Lee Labrada's most productive routines for both beginners and advanced trainees who really want to pack on the mass. And for those of you who would like to drop a little body fat along with building up on one of Lee's routines,

he has a simple addition to the program. "Cycling, cycling, cycling! The aerobic or stationary bicycle seems to be the best form of fat-burning aerobics that I've ever found. I feel that you should do about 30 minutes a day and maybe do this for four days a week to really get your metabolism going. It really works well, and it doesn't tear your legs down."

MY FAVORITE ARM ROUTINE

"My favorite movements for biceps are concentration curls, barbell curls, hammer curls (where the palm of the hand is facing the side of your rib cage throughout the movement, performed in an alternating fashion), alternate dumbbell curls, and preacher curls. These are my favorite biceps movements. I take three different exercises from this list and then do 2 or 3 sets of each. For triceps, my favorite exercises are triceps pushdowns, lying triceps extensions with an EZ curl bar, and seated French press, also with the EZ curl bar. I also like this absurd little movement I do in my triceps routine, called the lying alternate triceps extension, which is like a lying triceps extension with a barbell, only this way you have a dumbbell in each hand. It's a real ass-kicker! And, again, I'll pick two or three of these movements for 2 or 3 sets, depending on my energy levels."

63

Shawn Ray

If there was any bodybuilder who could honestly be said to be the "uncrowned Mr. Olympia," it was California native Shawn Ray. It was a given among bodybuilding reporters that this man had the most symmetrical and aesthetically appealing physique on the dais, but what was often overlooked in their commentaries was that the man was huge. Shawn has defeated most of the sport's top professionals, such as Phil Hill, Rich Gaspari, Vince Taylor, and Mike Ashley, to name but a few, and he gave multi–Mr. Olympia winner Lee Haney fits, despite Haney's claim to no less than seven consecutive Sandow statuettes.

I've interviewed Shawn Ray four times and have always found him to be a lot of fun (he enjoys good-hearted ribbing—which he can dish out as well as he receives!), honest (if you ask him a question, you'd better believe that he'll answer it straight up, regardless of the consequences), and very much in tune with his physique and just what it took to develop it to the phenomenal degree that it's at presently.

"My most productive routine has been, largely, the instinctive training routine," he said. "I don't like to train too much with a partner or even at the same gym with the same exercises because I like a change of scenery. I get bored easily doing the same things day in and day out, that's why I like to constantly change the order of the exercises that I do, the sets and reps, and I never favor any particular body part."

That's well and good, but it doesn't do much for our readers who want to know just what it took for the man to get those massive great muscles of his! Shawn laughed at the suggestion. "Hey, I can't be any more specific than I'm being now because that's the way I live. My bodybuilding lifestyle is variety. That's one of the reasons that I stay so motivated, because I never do the same routine and I never eat the same things and I never subscribe to rules when it comes down to a bodybuilding philosophy. I can tell you one thing today, and tomorrow, I'll do another thing entirely.

"My most dramatic jump in muscle size came during my growth spurt, which came between the ages of 18 and 21, which is when you're supposed to grow, and that's also when I became more educated on nutrition and more intensively involved in my training."

So was he saying that there was no "magic" exercise or routine that made him as a bodybuilder? [Darn, if he didn't laugh again!]

"People always ask me, 'What did you do during that point when you grew the most?' And all I did was the same thing I did when I started lifting. I just continued to eat five or six meals a day; I trained my chest, shoulders, and arms and my back and my legs twice a week, I trained on a three-on/one-off routine, I trained on a six-day-on/ one-off routine, I trained on a four-day-on/one-off routine, and I grew on all of them.

"I was just training with weights, I didn't really follow anyone's routine, or even my own, I just went by the feel. My progress wasn't the result of doing low repetitions and high sets, or putting more emphasis on exercises such as the squat, the bench press, or the deadlift. It was just a situation where I was eating more of the right food and still hitting my muscles from every possible and conceivable angle. I could be training with a 50-year-old man one day and a 14-year-old kid the next—it didn't matter. I was just training to train, I didn't know any better. And to this day, I think that this approach has still kept me motivated and kept me from getting burned out and fatigued because I do what I feel like doing.

"When I go to the gym I don't know what exercises I'm going to do until I get there, and it comes to me like an artist sitting down at his drawing board. I think that a three-day-on/one-day-off routine—or any routine that you're not doing presently, is a step in the right direction."

All right then, what guidelines could Shawn Ray offer those of us who want to pack on the muscle mass, but aren't as in tune to our bodies' fluctuating training needs as he is?

"I'd recommend and yes, I guess this would be a routine that I've used quite successfully, so maybe you would call this my most productive routine, but it would consist of training three days on as heavy as you can, followed by one day off, and then three days light with one day off so that there would be adequate time allotted for recuperation.

"Day one would consist of training back, biceps, and triceps; day two would be legs only, and the third day would be chest and shoulders. Calves you could train three days a week and abs every other workout. On the heavy days what I do is shoot for 6 to 8 reps per set, and on the lighter days I'd go for 12 to 20 reps per set."

What about aerobics for reducing body fat—or is this also determined by instinct (as opposed to steadily advancing stores of adipose)? "I always ride the stationary bike at least four days a week for 30 minutes, first thing in the morning, and I usually strive to ride the bike five days a week. It's a good precaution to keep the body fat down.

"In terms of exercises, I change them around constantly. I'm always searching for new angles to train a muscle. I do, however, believe in strict form, which means full repetitions in good workout style and, generally, I follow the pyramid system, doing about 8 to 12 reps per set, and if I can only do 6 reps, I'll reduce the weight. I use primarily four exercises per body part for about 5 sets each,

but 2 of those 5 sets will be warm-ups, so I'm really only doing 3 sets per exercise."

Does Shawn subscribe to the same technique that Lee Labrada does, in starting with a heavy weight and then reducing the poundage with each succeeding set? "Nope. Bodybuilders who subscribe to that theory usually end up injured. There's a lot of ligament problems and tendinitis out there because guys don't thoroughly work their way up in poundage to thoroughly warm up the muscle that they're training. A good and safe system of training has you working up in weight each set until you max out with 6 to 8 reps, and then work your way back down again."

"My personal three-on/one-off program would consist of starting with chest and shoulders. I'd do 2 or 3 sets on the pec dec to warm up my shoulder girdle, and then I'll go right into incline dumbbell presses, followed by flyes and then barbell bench presses. Occasionally I'll finish with parallel dips— but again, these exercises might well change the next time I go into the gym.

"In training shoulders, I'll usually start with dumbbell lateral raises, and from there I'll move on to either seated barbell or dumbbell presses, followed by bent-over laterals, and finish up with dumbbell shrugs or barbell upright rowing. I'll alternate these two exercises from workout to workout.

"On Tuesday, my second workout of the week, I'll start with legs, which means that after my warm-up, I'll train my hamstrings with 5 sets of leg curls. I'll move into squats and then leg presses and, finally, lunges. I like lunges, as they keep my glutes tight all year round.

"On Wednesday, it's back and arms, starting with 3 sets of chins to warm up and then 3 sets of chins behind the neck. Then I move on to seated cable rowing, where I attempt to squeeze my scapulae together at the back when the handle reaches my chest, and then it's on to barbell bent-over rows, followed by lat machine pulldowns to the front. My arm training is largely instinctive. I just select three exercises for biceps and three for triceps and perform 4 sets of each."

The California Colossus offered this advice: "One thing that I do caution body-builders about is overtraining, and you can tell when you're becoming overtrained. It's when, instead of getting stronger, you start to actually feel weak. At this point, you've got to eat a little more and get out of the gym a little quicker. But when you train, get in there, break that sweat and try and achieve that goal, and the confidence will come from your trying to achieve it."

A FAVORITE ARM ROUTINE

"There are a lot of ways to approach arm training, and no one way is better than any other. However, while I subscribe to instinctive training, there are four exercises that are fundamental for full biceps development and three for triceps.

"For biceps, it's standing barbell curls, preacher curls, one-arm preacher curls, and concentration curls. For triceps, it would be triceps pushdowns on the lat machine, triceps extensions, and one-arm dumbbell kickbacks. I use at least two from each group during any off-season workout and three as a contest approaches. I'll also include isolation exercises before a contest such as dips between benches and one-arm cable curls. I'll do 4 to 5 sets of each exercise for 6 to 8 repetitions with about one and a half minutes of rest in between sets."

64

Robby Robinson

One of the greatest bodybuilders of all time was Florida state native Robby Robinson. Dubbed the "Black Prince" by bodybuilding journalist Ricky Wayne back in the mid-1970s, Robinson certainly lived up to his royal moniker.

Robinson possessed what most bodybuilders would refer to as "the perfect physique": huge shoulders, flaring lats tapering down into a wasp-thin waist. His thighs were massive, yet aesthetically appealing, and let's not even mention those biceps of his! It was a longstanding joke that whenever Robby went to take a sip out of a glass of water, his peaked Kilamanjaro-esque biceps leaped up and smacked the cup out of his hand! Robinson competed and, more to the point, placed, in contests that spanned three decades (the '70s, '80s and '90s).

Robinson was one of the greatest body-builders of all time, but how did he get that way? Certainly he had incredible genetics, but genetics alone cannot adequately explain the Robinson physique. For the answer to this paradox, we must go straight to the words of the man himself, who told about his diet, his motivation to compete, and most important of all, his most productive routine.

ON BEING MOTIVATED

"I've never had a problem with motivation. I've just always been really turned on by looking healthy. I've always been involved in athletics of some shape or form whether it was track and field, football, or weight lifting. Bodybuilding is just the same—I love it so much! When someone else competes in a sport, they do so in order for 'the team' to win, or to make their coaches and trainers proud of them. For me, I train because I want to look good and to be healthy. I do it for me, as both of these objectives serve my personal best interests in the long run."

THE AEROBIC FACTOR

Robinson was also a big believer in the value of aerobic exercise, not only to the heart and lungs, but also in hardening or defining a physique. Hear him:

"I ride my bike all the time! I think that aerobics should be performed by bodybuilders whether they're preparing for a contest or not because of how it reduces body fat. Somebody who's fat isn't a bodybuilder in my book; you should always look muscular. Not freaky muscular, like we do for a contest, because that's a one-shot deal where you try to get as defined as possible for one day in order to bring out maximum muscularity on your body. I think you should

look defined and trim but not ripped to the bone all year round.

"Aerobics is one of the keys to keeping the body fat low and keeping the body muscular. I always try to perform my aerobic exercise two or three times a week in the off-season, and then I increase that, depending on my definition levels, just before a contest."

ROBBY ROBINSON'S MOST PRODUCTIVE ROUTINE

"My most productive training routine has always been centered around the basics. That is, basic, compound exercises. My training philosophy has always been to stick with the basic exercises because they're the ones that involve the most amount of muscle mass, which of course should be what you're after. You can get fancy and cute and do all those pretty little exercises, but believe me, they're not going to develop massive muscles on you. At least, that's not how I built my muscle mass.

"Isolation movements and machine work will give you that pumped look, and it even puts size on some people, but if you want size that's going to last you a lifetime, you'd better be prepared to bust your butt on the basic exercises every time you hit the gym. Exercises like bench presses, incline presses, dumbbell flyes, and dips. They've always formed the core of my chest training workouts. They're basic, they're traditional, and they're traditional because they've been proven to work over time.

"For legs, the same thing: squats, leg presses, leg curls, leg extensions. Just get in the gym and do 'em! Your legs will grow as a result. For biceps, it's barbell curls, Scott bench curls, and concentration curls; for back, low pulley rows, T-bar rows—which are my personal favorite and have really given me a lot of width and density in my back—and of course chin-ups, which are probably the most basic exercise there is.

"These are the basic exercises that I've always used to build my physique and that I feel a person should stick with for at least a couple of years because they help to develop what I call a foundation to your physique upon which you can build, add, refine, polish, whatever, once you've built your basic mass."

POWERLIFTS ARE IMPORTANT

"I've always included some powerlifting movements in my routines over the years and always in the routines that I found to be the most productive in terms of packing on some serious size. By powerlifting movements, I mean bench presses, squats, and deadlifts. These should be in anybody's program who's serious about putting on size because they stress so many of the body's muscle groups. If they hit 'em, use 'em; after all that's the purpose of exercising with weights.

"If you want to deviate from the basics from time to time, that's fine, but you can always go back to the basics periodically to help build and maintain that structural foundation. The more you stick with those basic exercises, the better the progress you'll experience. Even as far as I've been able to go in bodybuilding, and I've been training since I was 13 years old, I still have to go back to the basics. That's the whole key to keeping the body hard. The other exercises add polish and glitter, but the basics are the key to success in bodybuilding."

GO SLOW FOR GROWTH

"I've always believed in a 'slow for growth' approach to my set performance. A lot of people training today, even some of the pros, rush through their movements like they're in a hurry to go somewhere. They don't give a lot of thought to what they're doing. I believe that a movement should be carefully looked at when you're training; it should be a moment where you're actually in touch with the muscle that you're attempting to train.

"Forget about the amount of weight in your hands and just concentrate on, say, contracting your biceps and feeling the movement itself. I apply this to all of my exercises, from declines to inclines. In all of my exercises, I'm controlling the weight, thinking about what I'm doing and concentrating on the muscle I'm training. That's the method I've been using for years, and it's the method that I'm still using!"

THE FOUR-DAY SPLIT

"I think that if you stick to the basics and work hard, say on a four-on/one-off system, you'll find yourself packing on the muscle mass. In fact, I think that you'll find it to be as productive for you as it has been for me. Working out on a four-on/one-off system and training really hard with high intensity will be enough for anyone. I'd even recommend that you do stationary cycling on your off day to keep yourself hard and defined.

"Also, when training on a four-days-on/one-off system, use your first four-on/one-off series to train heavy and your next four-on/one-off to train a littler lighter, really working on refining the movements you're performing and feeling the muscles contracting, doing extra reps, forced reps, and things like that but this time around using lighter weights. I'll give you an example of my biceps and back routine to show you how I utilize the basics.

"For my biceps, it's Scott bench barbell curls and standing barbell curls, alternating between these two exercises to keep the size in my arms. I'll do the alternate one-arm curl as a concentration curl, standing or kneeling, or with my arm braced on my thigh. I'll do proper alternate dumbbell curls next and reverse curls, but those are basically it for my biceps. I'll alternate between two or three of those depending on how I feel or what I

need the most. I'd average about 5 sets each, and on my heavy days I'd do low reps and on light days, high reps.

"For my back, my basic exercise is chins because I just love chins! I'll do 1 set of 50 reps! Not all at once. My first set might be 12 reps or 15 reps, the next set might be 10 to 12 reps—but I'm going to do 50 reps! The whole idea is like a game I play with myself. And I love to change the grip, wide one set, narrow the next, then I move on to my pet exercise, the T-bar row. From there it's barbell rows, again with a close and narrow grip, followed by pullovers with an easy weight for 5 sets each, and that's it! That's my most productive routine.

"I try to change my routines from workout to workout in order to perpetually confuse muscles. By choosing different exercises each session, I keep my muscles off balance, in a state in which they can't adapt to a consistent routine. Doing this forces them to respond much more quickly than if I were to do the same program day after day.

"Just remember the real key to building up your body is mental—get into your workouts mentally, establish that mind-muscle link, and feel what you're doing. Believe me, you'll grow!"

65

Paul Dillett

Quick! What do you call a guy who's 6'1" and 282 pounds of solid muscle? Well, if you said "Sir," you'd certainly have a case. However, in this instance, you'd call him Paul. Paul Dillett, to be exact, and this man was *big*. "How big," you ask? How's a 23-inch arm with 18-inch forearms sound? Not bad, eh? But how does one slap on over 100 pounds of muscle mass without damaging one's natural symmetry? And was Dillett a so-called "genetic freak," one who gains muscle mass quicker than an escalation in the national debt? We asked the man himself.

"Well, I don't know if I'm a genetic freak, but I did get growth in my muscles almost immediately when I started barbell training," he said with a wry grin. And then, as if to underscore his point, he hit us with this eye-opening verbal shot, "In fact, within two to three months of first having started training I went from 175 pounds to 205 pounds! I grew like a weed."

So what was the routine that packed on all this muscle during Dillett's genesis in bodybuilding? "Actually, I didn't even have a routine. Basically I'd do chest one day, go in another and do back, go in another and do legs [he laughed], sometimes I'd even do chest twice in one day! I just did about everything I could think of!" In assessing this nihilistic approach to training, Dillett concluded that his routine was "so unorthodox because I was just starting out on my own and I'd not have the foggiest idea of what proper training was or what I was doing in the gym. I was like a mad man who would just go into the gym and do everything that he could possible think of."

All right, so in the beginning it was hit-and-miss for Mr. Massive. In retrospect, then, would he advise young neophytes to the sport on how to train properly—given his current level of bodybuilding acumen?

"Knowing what I know now, I'd recommend trainees go three on and one day off for rest. If they have the time, I'd recommend a split routine with an hour of training in the morning and another hour at night, with a body part breakdown of chest in the morning with arms and calves at night. Then, the next day it would be quads in the morning with hamstrings and calves at night. Seeing how back is such a big body part, I'd just train it once on day three by itself, and that would be it. Day four would be a rest day, but day five would see you coming in again to train shoulders in the morning and arms in the evening, and then

you'd repeat the cycle, making sure to take every fourth day off for rest. I think this would be a good cycle."

What follows is one of Paul Dillett's personal size-bustin' routines that he used to build his phenomenal muscle mass.

DAY 1: BACK

- T-bar rows. "I will do 5 sets of this exercise, starting with 150 pounds, and work my way up to 350."
- Low cable rows. "I will do 4 sets of 10 reps, making sure to get a good stretch at the bottom of the movement."
- Hammer machine rows. "I like this machine a lot, and here I'll do 3 sets of 10 reps, then stay with this machine and do . . ."
- One-arm hammer machine rows. "This again, would be for 3 sets of 10 reps, and that would be my back training that day. The next week, my back training would change totally except for the T-bar rows, which will stay in there always for the thickness quality they impart to my back. Then I would move to wide-grip lat pulldowns, lat pulldowns to the back, and long pulley rows, again for 4 sets of 10 reps."

DAY 2: SHOULDERS

- Hammer machine shoulder press: 5 sets of 10 reps.
- Icarian pec dec for rear delts: 4 sets of 10 reps.
- Upright rows: 4 sets of 10 reps.

- Seated lateral raises: 4 sets of 12 reps.
- Unilateral cable side laterals: 4 sets of 10 reps.

ARMS

"Sometimes I'll train both triceps and biceps together, and other times I'll just do triceps or biceps."

- Triceps machine pressdowns: 4 sets of 10 reps.
- Triceps extensions: 4 sets of 10 reps.
- Reverse triceps extensions: 4 sets of 10 reps.
- One-arm triceps extensions: 4 sets of 10 reps.
- Icarian machine curls: 5 sets of 10 reps. "I work my way down on this one, starting with 80 pounds and working my way down until I'm using the whole stack, which is about 130 pounds.
- Preacher curl machine: 5 sets of 10 reps supersetted with the concentration curls (following).
- Concentration curls: 5 sets of 12 reps.
- Standing dumbbell curls: 4 sets of 10 reps. "I don't go heavy in this one, maybe 50 pounds, for the full 4 sets."
- Hammer dumbbell curls: 3 sets of 10 with 40-pound dumbbells.

A side note to Paul Dillett's arm training is that he performed no direct forearm work. Here's why: "My forearms are so big that if I ever did any sort of forearm work I'd probably get them bigger than my arms!"

DAY 3: LEGS

- Leg presses. "I start out with three plates on each side and then work my way up the entire stack, or however much it will hold. My first 4 sets see me doing 20 reps. I work my way up to 12 plats on each side, reducing to 10 reps for 10 sets in all with my top weight being 1,080 pounds, plus the carriage."
- Hack squats: 3 sets of 50 reps. "My knees aren't that great, so my main exercise is the leg press. On hacks, I figure 3 sets of high reps should be enough to give them the shape I want."
- Leg extensions supersetted with unilateral leg extensions. "I do a total of 10 sets, with my two-legged extensions being for 10 reps each set and one-legged extensions being for 12 per set."

CALVES

- Toe presses on leg press machine: 8 sets of 15 reps.
- Seated calf raises: 5 sets of 15 reps.

HAMSTRINGS

- Lying leg curls: 5 sets of 12 reps.
- Seated leg curls: 5 sets of 10 reps supersetted with stiff-legged deadlifts (following).
- Stiff-legged deadlifts: 5 sets of 15 reps. "The weight I use for stiff-legged deadlifts is very light; usually only 100 pounds."
- Unilateral leg curls: 5 sets of 10 reps.

DAY 4: REST DAY

DAY 5: CHEST

- Incline barbell presses on Smith machine. "I start off with 225 and work my way up to 375. I do 6 sets of 10 reps. The first set is 15 reps, the second set is 12 reps, and then every set after this would be 10 reps."
- Hammer machine incline presses: 3 sets of 10 reps.
- Hammer machine decline presses: 4 sets of 10 reps.
- Bench press machine: 3 sets of 10 reps.
- Pec dec: 4 sets of 10 reps.

The cycle continues with the repeat of Day 1 and Day 2 training routines before a rest day is taken, and the three-day cycle is picked up again from where it was left off.

You may have noticed that Dillett favors machines in his training, a view that would have more than a few bodybuilding "purists" spinning their twist-key barbell collars in frustration. Certainly there can be no dispute whatsoever in terms of the results he's achieved. But why this departure from the "hallowed halls" of bodybuilding conventions?

"I love machines because right now, with all the technology that's gone into their invention, I honestly think that they are a lot better than free weights. With free weights you can cheat a lot, and you can't go as heavy and you always take the risk of hurting yourself. If you think of the longevity of your competing in the sport, machines are a lot safer and a lot better for you than free weights. And you have to look at things like you're thinking in terms of longevity, otherwise you'll be here today and gone tomorrow."

66

Mohammed Benaziza

One of the tragedies of bodybuilding was the death of Mohammed Benaziza, a great bodybuilder who passed away in 1993 after competing in the Holland Grand Prix. It was determined that Benaziza's death was the result of an abuse of diuretics. It was a blow to those of us who knew and liked Benaziza and a wake-up call to other bodybuilders that perhaps the sport was heading in the wrong direction.

Back when we knew Benaziza there was a popular misconception that the Algerian strongman never trained at all except for the last eight weeks before a contest. And even then, all he did supposedly was walk into the gym, look at the weights, leave, and his muscles began to grow while he was sipping on some Beaujolais in a fine French bistro. "That is ridiculous," laughed "Momo" as he prefers to be called, when we told him this, slapping his hand onto his granite-hard thigh to emphasize his merriment. "But I'll admit that I've heard it before. People say, 'Oh, Momo was born that way. His contest training consists of sitting in front of a television set and changing the channels with one of those remote controls." He laughed out loud again.

"Man, these people, where do they get these things? Ha! Ha! Ha! Ha!" Momo was in a particularly good mood. He'd just finished a good chest workout—and it showed. His pecs were still pumped and swollen to ale keg dimensions—and this was a full 30 minutes after he'd finished his workout, showered, and sat down to browse through a paper in the gym. Despite his levity on the subject, his phenomenal physique was the product of many long and torturous hours of heavy and brutal training. At least that was his story, and he stuck to it.

HEAVY WEIGHTS AND HIGH REPS

"I always use heavy weights, even up to the day of the contest. The secret for me has always been to train with heavy weights for 10 to 20 reps per set. I think that using heavy weights with relatively high reps hardens the physique and also keeps the muscle mass levels up while dieting for a contest."

FOOTBALL STARTED IT ALL

"When I started bodybuilding, it was largely to improve my speed for soccer. I was in the French semipro system. I started at a body weight of 125 pounds, and after six years of training I entered my first contest at a body weight of 152 pounds, and I actually won it!"

EARLY DAYS AND LOWER REPS

"In those days I was training with relatively heavy weights for 8 to 12 reps a set, but after that contest, which was in 1987, I increased my reps to the 15 to 20 range. It was at this point that I was able to pack on yet another 40 pounds of muscle to my frame at a height of 5'2", and 192 pounds looks pretty impressive, let me tell you."

YEAR-ROUND DOUBLE SPLIT

"I should point out that I follow a double split system year-round. I don't train casually until I'm eight weeks away from a contest. It's twice a day workouts, all year round. The only difference is that I'll switch over from a three-on/one-off format to a six days straight/one-off system. Before a contest, I'll increase my reps slightly from 10 to 12 to 20 to 25—but I'm getting ahead of myself."

THE "FOUR BY FOUR" SYSTEM

"My most popular routine consisted of doing four exercises per body part, and my sets are also fixed at four. I also used straight sets exclusively, as I prefer to superset only before a contest for a little extra jolt to my muscles. I find it helps them hold their edge before a contest."

BE INSTINCTIVE

"Nevertheless, my training methods once I hit the gym are very instinctive. I tend to adjust my choice of exercises and the order in which I perform them as I see fit, or, in fact, based on how I actually feel once I have hit the gym. My training routine looks something like this:

Day 1

- Chest, lower abs (a.m.)
- Thighs, upper abs (p.m.)

Day 2

- Triceps, abs, hamstrings (a.m.)
- Lats, lower back, abs (p.m.)

Day 3

- Biceps, abs, calves (a.m.)
- Shoulders, abs (p.m.)

Momo Benaziza's Back Workout

- Behind-the-neck pulldowns: 4 sets of 10–20 reps.
- Bent-over barbell rows: 4 sets of 10–20 reps.
- Seated pulley rows: 4 sets of 10–20 reps.
- Hyperextensions: 4 sets of 20 reps.
- Stiff-legged deadlifts: 4 sets of 10–20 reps.

HITTING ABS EVERY DAY

"As you no doubt have noticed, I train my abdominals every day, even in the off-season. The reason for this is that it's far too easy to fall into the habit of letting your abs go, thinking that because they're stabilizer muscles, they're receiving adequate work from all the other exercises you do. This is one reason why so many of my competitors lose out at shows—they don't have enough time to bring them up to par in the eight weeks they allot themselves to prepare for a contest. I just don't have that problem because I do work them hard every day, with the exception of the fourth cycle day, which is a rest day for my whole body."

RIDING THE BIKE DAILY

"I'll also ride the stationary bike for an hour in the evening to sort of wind down my day's training. It also helps to keep my body fat in check and improve my overall muscularity."

VARY THE TRAINING

"As my routine is so instinctive, it would be silly to say that 'this is my routine, this is what is responsible for my muscular development today' simply because I've used so many exercises and the order in which I do them while at the same time keeping within the framework that has packed on all of my muscle mass. Therefore, I won't say that this is the 'magic' routine that has done this. It's just train heavy, with reps between 10 and 20, pick four exercises a body part and do four solid sets increasing the weight with each set. And that's my 'secret,' if you choose to call it that."

USE CONTROL

"I'll also make a point to lower my weights slowly and under control; I like to *lift* heavy, not heave heavy, and you can only lift heavy if your muscles are actually lifting the weight and not momentum. I also don't rest long between sets, maybe a minute at the most, as this also brings out maximum muscularity, which is, after all, the name of the game."

INCREASE THE INTENSITY

"Forced reps are also employed from time to time as a really good way to burn in extra growth to the muscles, although I don't use forced reps all that often. They are, however, a really good 'shocking' movement for the muscles, to jar them out of complacency."

DIETING FOR SIZE

"As far as dieting is concerned, my precontest diet will see me drop my calories down from 1,600 to 1,800 calories in order to rip up, and I'll break my meals down to five meals a day, consisting of the following; chicken, fish, egg whites, pasta, potatoes, whole wheat bread, rice, sweet potatoes, and fresh fruit, combined with gallons of water. As you can see, it's not that much different from how many other bodybuilders diet before a contest.

"As far as eating for size goes, my recommendation is a joyous one . . . eat! I make sure I eat a low-fat diet, but my daily calories are in the 4,500 to 5,000 calories per day range. If you want to get huge, then you just have to eat huge, but it's got to be huge amounts of the right kind of foods, not candy bars and ice cream. And if you follow my dietary and training advice, I'll guarantee that you will pack on so much size that you'll need a whole new wardrobe of clothes and will never be small again!"

67

Francis Benfatto

Even superstar Shawn Ray was impressed with the physique of Frenchman Francis Benfatto. He said, "I just love the lines on the guy! Benfatto's physique fills me with awe—much more so than even that of Lee Haney." High praise indeed. The "appeal" factor, for want of a better adjective, lay in Benfatto's lineage to the "classic" bodybuilding look.

Like Frank Zane before him, and the great Steve Reeves before Zane, Benfatto was the bearer of a proud tradition that never allowed size to supersede aesthetics. As a result, the physique of the Frenchman caused women to swoon and their dates to turn to green with envy. Benfatto didn't believe in the "heavy weights equal massive muscles" approach, either.

In his words, "If you want to be the best in bodybuilding, then forget about what you weigh or how much you can squat! You must remember that bodybuilding's a visual activity, so your training must reflect attention to the shape and muscularity, not simply body weight and training poundages."

For all his worldliness, Benfatto was not one to prescribe a "one size fits all" training philosophy, believing instead that each individual must be his own investigating agent, experimenting with various techniques, sets, reps, and methodologies until the one is discovered that is right for him.

"I personally use many techniques," says Benfatto. "I even change them up between off-season and precontest, nothing stays the same. Stagnation is death, both in life and especially in training. To grow, to improve, and to become the best you can be, you must first discard the notion that there is only one way to train—there are instead thousands, and each has something positive to offer your physique."

In the off-season, Benfatto worked out at what some might rightly consider a precontest pace, his workouts being twice a day for up to six days at a crack.

"I take a little more time in the moving between sets and exercises during the off-season," conceded Benfatto, "and I'll typically pyramid my poundages for the first 3 sets before stripping off the weight for my last two sets to failure." Precontest, Benfatto became a virtual "gymaholic," returning to the gym no less than three times a day, seven days a week.

"This is when my training really becomes fun," he mused. "I take no rest at all between sets and hit my weak areas every day to force them to respond to my will. Like I said, you must find out what works for you—this certainly works well for me."

There's no disputing this. However, what kind of aerobic program could Benfatto possibly follow on a three-workouts-per-day/seven-days-a-week system in order to "rip up" for a contest—and, more to the point, where the heck did he get the energy for it?

"I would not have the energy for it, which is precisely why I'll never do aerobics before a contest," said he of the pronounced V-taper. "I find that my nonstop training approach, coupled with a reduced-calorie diet, for seven days a week, three times a day is more than adequate for ripping up for a contest."

THE LINES

All right, so the secret to Benfatto's success (at least for him) has been in lengthy workouts. Certainly, he had plenty of mass, but it was his famed "lines," the same ones mentioned by Shawn Ray, that had everyone gaga over him, so how in the heck did he attain what became the envy of every other top bodybuilder?

"I have a training credo," he said, an impish grin beginning to form on his visage. "I believe that if you train for shape and proportion, size will come, and when it does, it will flow out smoothly and magnificently from your insertion points." Now if anybody else made such a statement, you'd be forgiven for guffawing in his face, but when Benfatto made such an utterance—darn it if it doesn't somehow seem appropriate.

"I fully expect to add progressively more and more muscle mass to my frame over the next 10 years—but never solely for the sake of putting on size. I train for shape and proportion. Size just follows as a natural effect of such training."

SHAPE TRAINING

If, when you read about Benfatto speaking of training for shape, you think of isolation exercise and a lot of dumbbell work being performed, you'd be right. "Dumbbells allow me greater isolation and the potential to hit much more of the target muscle fibers than with barbells," he said.

Benfatto trained by breaking his body parts up into a four-day cycle. He started with chest and shoulders. The second day would be devoted to back by itself, the third day would consist of training his legs, calves, and abdominals, and the fourth day was devoted to arms and forearms.

"I would recommend, though, that those trainees seeking to gain muscle mass should take a day off after four straight training days until they're at a more advanced level physiologically," cautioned Benfatto. "The beauty of this four-day split is that each body part is given four days of complete recovery for growth to take place."

All right then, so Benfatto recommended a four-day split—but what exercises, sets and reps? "I can't tell you that!" he exclaimed with a twinkle in his eye. "The reason being that you should use every exercise for a given body part that you can until you find the ones that create the greatest effect in your own body. Use them all at various

times. Experiment! That's the key to both success and longevity in this sport. I make it a point to add at least one new exercise each successive training session as new exercises serve to offset stagnation and add the element of quality to the muscle that I'm training."

THE TWICE-A-DAY SPLIT

Another interesting component of the Benfatto workout is the fact that his twice-a-day sessions consisted of the same body parts being trained. That is, whereas most bodybuilders on a double split system will train, say, their chest in the morning and their back in the evening, Benfatto trained his chest and shoulders in the morning and then popped into the gym in the evening and trained these same two body parts again—albeit differently.

"I will do one heavy exercise for the first muscle group that I'm training in the morning and then do only shaping movements for the second body part during the morning session. In the evening, I will reverse the procedure for the two body parts. For example, if I'm working my back in the morning, along with my chest—and, again, my body part combinations will vary as well as the exercises I will use to train them with—I might do heavy barbell rows as my basic movement and then use shaping exercises such as pec dec flyes, dumbbell flyes, and high-rep cable crossovers for my chest. In the evening, I'll come back into the gym and hit chest with heavy barbell bench preses and then train back with the various isolation/shaping movements in superset fashion. My heavy movements are done for approximately 8 to 10 sets."

THE MAGIC ARM WORKOUT

For the purpose of elaboration, Benfatto agreed to share his current arm routine, in which he incorporated the preceding principles:

"When I train my arms, I train them both in the morning and again in the evening, like the rest of my body parts. I train my triceps first in the morning, followed by my biceps, and then in the evening, I'll perform my heavy biceps movement first, followed by my shaping exercises for the triceps. In my morning workout, I'll typically start with lying triceps extensions with a barbell for 6 sets of 6 to 8 reps—and that's it for triceps for the morning.

"Next comes biceps, and I'll start with a superset of preacher bench curls in which I'll alternate between a wide and narrow hand grip each set of 12 reps. Then I'll immediately proceed to standing barbell curls, but I'll do them in 21s fashion, wherein I'll do 7 half reps from the bottom to the midway point in the range of motion, followed immediately by 7 half reps from the top to the midway range of motion, and then, finally, 7 full-range reps, going all the way up and all the way down.

"Then it's on to concentration curls for 3 sets of 6 reps with a heavy dumbbell, from which I then grab a lighter dumbbell and rep out for 12 reps. Two such sets make one superset here, and I'll do 3 such supersets. I'll finish off with one-arm cable curls supersetted with hammer curls, each done for 12 reps for 2 to 3 supersets.

"Then in the evening, I'll return and perform 6 to 8 sets of heavy barbell curls for my biceps and then work my triceps by starting with lying triceps extensions with a barbell for 12 reps. I'll triset this with another set of lying triceps extensions, but with a lighter weight, and then finish the triset with an even lighter set of lying triceps extensions with a reverse grip which, I feel, hits the lower areas of the triceps very thoroughly. I'll do four of these trisets and then proceed to cable pushdowns, where I'll do three descending sets of 10 reps each to failure. I'll repeat this strip-off method for 3 sets. My final triceps movement is dumbbell kickbacks while lying facedown on a slightly inclining bench. I'll do 5 sets of 12 reps."

Benfatto applies this heavy and light system to all body parts that he trains, from calves to forearms, with, as mentioned, a host of different exercises to do the job of ensuring fiber stimulation from a variety of angles.

"I also train very slowly, making sure that I feel the movement from start to finish. Granted, this reduces my training poundages, but then, as I said at the beginning, successful bodybuilding emphasizes shape and proportion; this is a visual sport and really has nothing to do with how much you lift."

68

Renel Janvier

When it came to massive ripped muscle, combined with deeply etched lines and dynamic stage aura, one professional who stood out was Renel Janvier. He had enough muscle to rival a bull elephant and was so ripped that even the ultra-shredded Austrian Andreas Munzer was rumored to awake at night in a cold sweat.

Despite his awesome size, Janvier was a soft-spoken man. Quiet, in fact. Yet his words carried considerable weight in the bodybuilding world, particularly when it came to the question of how he built his muscular mass. Fortunately, Renel wasn't averse to sharing his wealth of training secrets with his fellow trainees and, in fact, agreed to tell all about his most productive routine.

THE GAINS CAME QUICKLY

"Results for me came very quickly during the first few years," explained Renel, as he kicked back into a chair that seems to be straining to contain his coconut-sized delts. "I originally used a three-day-a-week routine when I first starting training. I didn't really know what I was doing then, but I'd some guidance from a fellow named Carlo Bursi who consulted with me from time to time about how to work out. I seem to recall that, in the beginning, I made some pretty good gains on that system."

THREE-ON/ONE-OFF

Familiarity breeds contempt, so the saying goes, and Renel found that his progress eventually ground to a halt on the system, which led him to seek an alternate method of training. "At this point I went from three days a week to a three-on/one-off system. In retrospect, the three-days-a-week program didn't really work all that well for me. It was more of a breaking-in program in which I would go in on one day and do chest, back, shoulders, and arms, take off a day, and then go in again and do legs and something else—but it was so long ago that it's hard for me to remember now exactly what I did."

ALWAYS CHANGING THINGS

One thing about Renel Janvier, the man hated routine. His workouts were never the same from one session to the next, nor were his training schedules always followed "come hell or high water." With such an outlook, it's little wonder that the three-days-on/one-day-off system would also eventually go the way of the three-days-per-week routine. To hear him tell it, though, the decision was the natural result of a typical evolutionary process of training.

"After I was on the three-on/one-off system, I found that it wasn't right for me either, and so I changed it after a while to a straight seven-days-a-week training schedule. I moved out to California and received better guidance, and I stayed with the three-on/one-off for a year. However, when I didn't do so well at the Los Angeles championships I went back to the East Coast and won the Nationals. Then I moved back again to California, where I won the L.A. Championships in '87. After winning the L.A.s, I started training seven days a week, which I've found, for now at least, to have been my most productive routine."

THE PROBLEM OF OVERTRAINING

Training seven days a week, week in and week out, would seem to be inviting the scourge of overtraining to rear its ugly head. Renel agreed that it had happened. "I have overtrained on this system before," he said with a laugh as his giant arm slapped down upon his thigh. "However, I've since learned how to cut back on it, especially before competition. I used to train seven days a week right up to the Thursday before the contest, which led me to overtrain. Having said that, I should point out that I don't really believe in the term 'overtraining.' I rather believe that it is possible to both under eat and under rest. I find that it's best to take a week off from training before a show and just relax, meditate, and concentrate more on the contest itself than the training. It seems to work better."

A SAMPLE WORKOUT

"I train seven days a week, which is broken down into chest and triceps on one day, back and biceps the second, shoulders and maybe triceps. Sometimes I'll skip triceps on my first day and do them with shoulders to mix them up a little bit on Day 4. In any event, Day 3 is legs day, and then I would start the whole cycle over again the following day."

If you want a definition of difficult, just try and ask Renel what his workouts consisted of. "I can give you base of what I do, but they change just about every day. In any event, here's the base: For most of the major muscle groups I never do more than 10 to 12 sets, except for back, which is a body part that I put more emphasis on. For back I will do anywhere from 12 to 30 sets, but I don't do that every day. I'll just do that occasionally to shock the muscles."

DAY 1: CHEST AND TRICEPS

"For chest I'd start out with incline dumbbell presses, incline barbell presses. I do mostly incline work for my chest, and dips to finish off. All of these exercises are done for 3 or 4 sets, and I'll quite often superset my dips with cable crossovers. Some days I'd do just straight supersets with these two exercises, while on other days I'd just go heavy on the dips and not rush so quickly to the crossovers. I'm definitely old school when it comes to my core exercises. I think that dips and chins are the primary source of building mass. If I do chest and triceps on the same day, I won't do as much for triceps, as they've

already been blasted by the chest work. Mainly if my triceps training falls on a chest day, I'll just do triceps pressdowns on the lat machine and maybe some individual cable presses for a total of 8 sets for my triceps."

ENJOYS HIGH-INTENSITY TRAINING

"I tend to do a more high-intensity, lower-set system for my body, but then my system changes so much, it depends on the mood that I'm in when I hit the gym. In some instances I'll conclude my chest workout in 20 to 30 minutes. I'll go really heavy and intense, while other days, when I don't feel so great, I'll go in and spend more time and not train so intensely. Basically every other day, I'll do an intense workout."

DAY 2: BACK AND BICEPS

"On Day 2 I'll train my back, which normally starts with pulldowns to warm up. I'll do 4 sets of pulldowns and then move on to chins for 5 to 6 sets with reps up to 15 and no less than 6. From there it's cable rows for pretty much the same thing, with reps ranging from 8 to 12 and then dumbbell rows for 3 sets up to 200 pounds, depending on where I am and if that kind of weight is available. Then I'll conclude with pullovers on a machine if available. If not I'll use dumbbells. Often when I do back, it's like when I train my triceps after chest. My biceps are so fatigued from an intense back training session that I'll only do 4 sets of direct biceps work to finish off. If I were training my biceps after back I'd typically do standing barbell curls, preacher curls, and alternating incline dumbbell curls. My workouts are very instinctive and, again, a lot of my training is based upon how I feel on a given day when I go to the gym."

DAY 3: LEGS AND THIGHS

"Day 3 would be my leg day, so that the upper body has a chance to rest for a day. I've actually cut down on my leg training. I no longer do squats, as I've already profited a lot from my younger years when I trained my legs with heavy squats. Now when I perform squats I find I have problems with my knees or back. So I've stayed away from squats for the last three to four years and I use mainly leg presses. For leg presses I'll do 5 to 6 sets going from 30 reps down to 6. I'll warm up with about 30 reps, then go to 25, then 20, 15, 10, 8, and at my heaviest, I would go up to 1,600 pounds for 6 reps."

USE FULL-RANGE MOVEMENTS

"I believe in full-range movements depending on the muscle group. Back, for example, is an area in which I don't always do full-range movements, but I would make up for it by doing an isolation movement such as a dumbbell row, which I would perform slowly. Other movements though, like cable movements, I don't exactly do a full range all the time. But on legs I think it's important that I do full range, especially on the leg press. After leg presses I'll go on to 4 sets of hack squats for 8 to 12 reps. Then I'll finish off with leg extensions and stiff-legged

deadlifts for 3 sets each. I don't do leg curls very much anymore. I should mention that in the beginning years, when you first start off, it is important to squat for overall development, not only the legs. You see, heavy squatting stimulates the whole body to grow, so you're not only working legs with squats, you're working the whole body too."

CALF TRAINING

"For calves, I'll go right away to the leg press machine and do the inverted toe press. Then I'll move on to the seated calf raise. I'll do 4 to 5 sets on each movement with my reps in the range of 15 to 29."

DAY 4: DELTOIDS

"The following day I would come into the gym and do shoulders. I'll start out with seated behind-the-neck presses, which I'll alternate between barbell and dumbbells from workout to workout. I'll do 4 to 5 sets of presses for roughly 8 to 12 reps. From there, it's on to side lateral raises for 3 to 4 sets of 12 to 15 reps. Then I go on to bent-over lateral raises with dumbbells or I'll do them on a rear delt machine if it's available, and I'll do 3 to 4 sets of 8 to 15 reps. From there, it's on to upright rows for 3 to 4 sets of 12 to 15 reps, and that looks after my shoulder training."

SPECIAL TRAP MOVEMENT

"I do a combination of upright rows and shrugs in order to work my traps as well. It's hard to explain, but it involves starting out with a straight arm lateral to the front for the delts, and when I can no longer perform the exercise, I'd switch the movement to an upright row for the traps. As I mentioned earlier, I try not to do many sets. My theory in training is more along the high-intensity track. I use as much weight as I can handle. If I'm doing leg presses, for example, I'll use 1,600 pounds for 5 to 6 reps, then I'll do strip-offs on the weight until I can't even do one rep. So eventually I end up with 50 to 60 reps in that set, but they all feel the same because I continue to work the muscles to their maximum via descending sets. I use this principle on a lot of exercises."

A WORD ON DIET

"I follow a high-protein diet. A lot of steak and eggs. In fact, when training for mass I'll eat up to two dozen eggs a day and two pounds of beef a day. I don't eat the yolk per se, I let the yolks run out. However, I do feel that if you follow this program and eat a lot of protein from meat and egg sources, you'll pack on a tremendous amount of mass."

69

Bertil Fox

Muscle mass run amok! Huge—and then some! Big and beyond! These are all terms that have been applied to massively muscled Bertil Fox. And, I might add, they have been applied accurately. Fox, or Foxy as he became known among his inner circle, was quite possibly the "purest" bodybuilder (in the hard-core sense of the term) that competed in his day.

Bertil was a throwback to the golden years of bodybuilding, when training solely for the love of moving heavier and heavier chunks of iron was the order of the day, when you lived to break a hearty sweat from your first set of heavy bench presses, and when the gyms were sweatshops with benches, heavy dumbbells, and a few Olympic bars, not chrome palaces with spandex-clad "athletes" primping and preening before the multitude of gym mirrors as they pose their way into the next set of iso-lateral, omni/quasi extensions, or some other such absurd title.

Foxy was from the school that said, "Don't think about it, just do it!" and "Train basic, heavy, and skip the fancy stuff!" There's certainly no disagreeing with the results of the other "classmates" who've graduated from the same school. The roll call reads as a listing of bodybuilding's Who's Who: Reg Park, Sergio Oliva, Robby Robinson ,and Arnold Schwarzenegger, among others. "I don't believe in all those fancy machines," stated Bertil. "I mean, they're fine for fitness and keeping tone, if that's your goal, but if you really want to put on some serious size, listen to what I've got to tell you!" Hey, Mr. Fox, we're all ears.

PRECONTEST AND BEYOND

"First of all, let me say here and now that I'm a power bodybuilder, first and foremost, and I always will be. However, before a contest certain changes must take place in one's training, as judges aren't looking for bulk alone. On my first workout day of the week I'll train my chest and back, usually with barbells exclusively. The reason behind this is that I don't have to worry about balance with a barbell; I can just concentrate on the movement and getting the poundage up. My precontest chest work consists of flat bench presses, incline presses, hand dumbbell flyes which I superset with weighted dips. Man, I love that exercise! I finish my chest work with some cable crossovers.

"Back comes next, and I'll use T-bar rowing to start my workouts nine times out of ten. I follow this with lat machines pull-downs to the front, as this not only puts a great pump into my lats but also helps to work my upper back a bit. I should also mention that precontest I'll do 4 sets per exercise. Continuing with back, I move on to low pulley rows and follow this up with pullovers and my favorite standby, chins. Talk about a pump!

"Of course, you can't train for a contest and neglect your abs, so I'll train my abs on my chest and back day as well, and my ab workout consists of Roman chair sit-ups for 5 sets and then some quick-rep leg raises on the floor. I don't want to forget the showy intercostal muscles either, so I'll throw in 4 sets of twisting kneeling hyperextensions and close-grip pulldowns. After a few hours' break, I'll return to the gym to train my legs.

"Like I said, my off-season structuring of workouts doesn't change all that much. In any event, I'll start my legs with either hack squats or leg extensions, depending on my temperament on any given day. I'll finish off with hamstrings for reasons already given and perform several sets of leg curls and then many, many sets of calf work. And, just like my earlier workout, I'll finish off my precontest workout with abdominals, usually back on the Roman chair apparatus and floor leg raises. I'll finish off my precontest work with aerobics, usually the stationary bicycle for 10 to 15 minutes.

"The next day I'd train my shoulders with seated press behind the neck and seated lateral raises, which I superset with front barbell raises. Then I finish off my shoulder work with another superset, this time involving both bent-over laterals and dumbbell shrugs and then 3 sets of cable bent-over laterals. I'll finish off my shoulder work by training my abs and then doing some more aerobic work. I'll train my arms with my shoulders as well, and that consists of triceps pressdowns, lying EZ curl bar extensions, reverse-grip pressdowns, and dumbbell kickbacks.

"During a precontest phase, I'm more concerned with my reps than my sets, so I'll cut my sets back to 3 per exercise and my reps to 8 to 12. After triceps, I'll move on to biceps, which is always preacher curls, for 4 sets of 12 reps, again pyramiding the weight as best I can. Then I perform 4 more sets of dumbbell incline curls and then 3 or 4 sets of one-arm pulley curls and 1 dumbbell concentration curls.

"I should also mention that before a contest I train my legs seven days a week and, in fact, I increase my training days to seven days a week as well. However, on my weekend workouts I'll only train once a day, the rest of the time it's twice, with legs in the evening."

WHAT TO EAT?

To pack on muscle mass, Foxy had some simple advice . . . eat! "Hey, if you eat like a bird, you're going to look like a bird," he laughed, "I love to eat! Not junk food all the time though. I eat good food and lots of it. That's why I'm able to put on quality muscle mass as opposed to simply size, which could

be made up of fat—something you definitely don't want on your physique. By good food, I mean steak, beef, chicken, vegetables, whole grains and fruits, as much as you can handle. Milk also is very good for some people, although others might have an allergy to it. So eat a lot, train hard, and rest well between workouts and you'll grow muscles, man. I mean, great big bloody muscles!"

IT'S ALL ABOUT BEING YOURSELF

"It's important to train heavy and hard, but don't get hung up on trying to match your current bodybuilding hero's training poundages. Remember we're all individuals. What is dangerously heavy for one person is someone else's warm-up weight. I use super-heavy poundages because they don't feel that heavy. However, there are some powerlifters who lift heavier weights than me, but I don't let that bother me. I train according to my body structure and what feels heavy to it. So should you. Don't lift the poundages that I think are heavy for my body. Instead, lift the poundages that feel heavy to your body. Be an individual, train hard, and get ready to grow."

TRAINING TIPS

"All right, it should be stressed right off the top that my precontest routine is different from my off-season routine. It has to be, because the results I seek from my training vary depending on whether or not I'm training for a contest. When you train for a contest, your goal is maximum definition with as much mass as you can retain while ripping up. Off-season, I train exclusively for size. Mass! That's what it's all about and, quite frankly, off-season training is what I enjoy the most because that's when I'm at my strongest and my weights are at their highest.

"Let me outline two routines for you. The first is my basic 'Mass Blaster' routine, which I guarantee will pack size on your body, providing you eat properly too, of course. The second routine is my current precontest routine, which I'll get to in a moment."

MONDAY AND THURSDAY: LEGS, CHEST, AND BACK

Legs

- Squats: 4 sets of 8 to 15 reps. "I love squats! If one exercise could be said to have paced on the most size on my body it would be this one (although dips would be a very close second). I always use the pyramid system with squats whereupon I'll increase my training poundage with each succeeding set until I'm at my fourth and final set with a weight that allows me just 8 reps. I'll start with a warm-up set for 15 reps, then move the weight up for 12 reps on my second set, increase the weight again for my third set of 10 reps, and then increase it again to blast my quads for a final set of 8 reps. You gotta love squats!"
- Leg curls: 3 sets of 10 to 20 reps. "Leg curls are perhaps the best hamstring

exercise you can do. Too many people worry about building up great huge thighs but completely neglect their hamstrings. This is stupid for two reasons: one, nothing looks worse up onstage than having well-developed thighs and piddly little thigh biceps. I mean, what would an arm look like with great thick biceps and spindly little triceps? Think about it. Second, you can injure yourself by overdeveloping one muscle group at the expense of its antagonistic muscle group. That's one of the reasons why footballers often suffer pulled hamstring muscles; they're just not as strong as the quadriceps which are used and strengthened more from running."

- Calf raises: 4 sets of 60 reps. "Calves are a very stubborn body part to train effectively because they have a very high labor threshold. That means that you've got to hit them with something they're not used to, like 4 heavy sets of 20 reps calf raises. They'll balloon after these."

Chest

- Bench presses: 4 sets of 8 to15 reps. "Here we go. This is one of the greatest upper body exercises there is. The bench press has been called the upper body squat and with good reason. It works just about every muscle in the upper body, including your lats, believe it or not. Again, I pyramid this exercise just as I did with squats. I'll start with 15 reps on my first set to warm up, add weight, then bang off 12 reps, add weight again and crack off 10, then add more weight for my final set of 8 reps. My pecs are usually on fire after 4 sets of these, and on days when I'm into it, I'll do 6 to 8 sets of benches. They're just such a great exercise."

- Dumbbell flyes: 3 sets of 12 reps. "I'd do 3 sets with as heavy a weight as I can for 12 reps. This really is a great chest movement in itself, as the primary function of the pec muscle is to draw the arm from a position behind the body to one in front of the body—which just happens to be the exact movement that flyes duplicate. Again, this is a great chest-building exercise."

Back

- Chins: 4 sets of 12 reps. "I say 4 sets of 12 reps, but don't fret if you can't do a full 12 reps in one whack. Just do as many as you can until you hit 12 reps all told for that set, and do 4 of them. Chins really stretch your lats and strengthen not only your back muscles but also your delts and biceps."
- Bent-over barbell rows: 4 sets of 8 to15 reps. "I also pyramid my weights on bent-over barbell rows because the heavier you lift, the bigger you get! I start out with a moderately heavy weight for 15 reps to really warm up my lower and upper back muscles, and from there it's right into the heavy stuff. My next set is for 12 reps, then weight is added again

and I'll bang off 10 reps, add more weight and finish with a tough set of 8 reps."

TUESDAY AND FRIDAY: DELTS AND ARMS

Delts

- Seated dumbbell presses: 4 sets of 8 to 15 reps. "This is the 'basic' delt exercise. It really doesn't matter if you use dumbbells or a barbell, but I prefer dumbbells because it allows me a better stretch. Like my earlier exercises, I'll pyramid my poundages, starting with a warm-up set of 15 reps and adding weight each succeeding set, for 12, 10, and finally 8 reps on my last set. Remember to really push on this exercise, as it's the one that's really going to pack the mass on your delts. It's one of my favorites."
- Dumbbell side laterals: 3 sets of 12 reps. "I'll usually add weight to each set I do of dumbbell side laterals, but that's just because I love to lift heavy weights. For most bodybuilders, keeping the weight the same for 3 sets of 12 reps will pack the meat onto your delts. Just remember to keep a slight bend in your elbows as you lift the dumbbells straight out to the sides of your body and to lower them back down under control."
- Bent-over dumbbell raises: 3 sets of 12 reps. "The same principles apply to this exercise as to the previous one. Laterals of the bent-over variety, however, hit the rear delts directly and really give a great

pump to the whole shoulder area and the upper back region as well. Don't forget to train this vitally important body part."

Biceps

- Incline dumbbell curls: 4 sets of 6 to 12 reps. "This is a great biceps exercise. Remember to really squeeze the contraction at the top of the movement to stimulate more of the muscle fibers. I pyramid this exercise too, starting with 12 reps, adding weight and doing a second set of 10 reps, then adding weight again for a set of 8 reps and finally putting on my top weight for that final set of 6 reps. Talk about a burn!"

- Preacher curls: 3 sets of 6 to 10 reps. "It's very important to try and stretch at the bottom of this movement and squeeze the contraction at the top. Again I'll pyramid the poundages, starting with a warm-up weight for 10 reps, adding weight for my next set. I'll heavy up the poundages and just squeeze out 8 reps before increasing it again to get my final 6 reps."

Triceps

- Foxy close-grip bent-over pushdowns: 4 sets of 6 to 12 reps. "This is a special movement that I invented but that's packed more size onto my triceps than any other I've done. To start, select a heavy poundage and hold it at chest level. Now, bending over slightly from the waist, push it straight down with a bit of body English. The movement sort of resembles a close-grip bench press, but it really packs size onto your horse-shoes. I'll typically start with a warm-up weight for 12 reps, then pyramid my poundages for sets of 10, 8, and 6 reps respectively, finishing with my top weight for 6 reps."

- Lying EZ bar curl extensions: 4 sets of 6 to 12 reps. "This is also an excellent triceps-building movement. Again, I pyramid my poundages, finishing off with my top weight for a triceps-quivering 6 reps. It's a bloody killer, but if you want big guns, you've got to pay the price in sweat."

PART 6

Personality Profiles

70

A Few Last Words from Andreas Munzer

In the world of pro bodybuilding, few pros are impressed by the sight of other pros. At that elite level, they all have size. They all have symmetry. And they all have cuts. But few had the striations of the late Andreas Munzer. Andy, as his friends called him, sadly passed from this earth in 1996 at the age of 31, but he left an indelible mark in the minds of those who ever wondered how a physique could look if taken to the nth degree.

One week before his passing, I [Bob] had the opportunity to talk to Andreas. We talked about many things, from his training to the sport of bodybuilding he loved. Here is some of what he said.

HOW A PHYSIQUE SHOULD LOOK

Andreas said he believed that the symmetry, posing, and quality of the physique is being overlooked. The emphasis is on mass rather

than quality. He felt that the weight of an athlete should not matter nor be important. What should matter is how the bodybuilder looks. If he looks great, then he is great. When a bodybuilder is too heavy, just for the sake of being big, then the physique suffers.

FOLLOWING HIS BODYBUILDING PASSION

Andreas said that when he decided to become a pro, he developed his body his way and not because of what the judges wanted or the latest trend. If they liked what they saw, great. If not, then, that's great too because he didn't get into bodybuilding to please others—only himself.

Munzer admitted that he worked a long time to develop his body, and how much he weighed was not important to him. What was important was the kind of body he built. He said he wanted a high biceps peak, deep striated triceps, round shoulders, a big shredded chest, separated hamstrings, and striated and shredded quads with very deep cuts. For Andreas, this is what made a real bodybuilder. A big leg without deep cuts is just a big leg.

HOW HE ACHIEVED HIS PHENOMENAL CUTS

Andreas was known for his amazing cuts, and he said his cuts were not so much genetic as they were from training and diet. He wasn't a last-minute bodybuilder who turned up the workout intensity a few months before a show. Andreas was a bodybuilder all year round. He had had lots of training partners over the years, and each of them went from little or no cuts to deep cuts simply by doing his way of training.

The key, Andreas said, was to use a weight that will allow you to do 8 good reps. Then, with the help of a partner, do another 2 or 3 reps, for a total of 10 to 11 reps. You must train very intensely. It's not important if you can lift 300 pounds. Forget the amount of weight. Focus on taking whatever weight you use and making the muscle work very intensely. Doing those extra 2 or 3 reps beyond failure on every set is the difference between calling yourself a bodybuilder or a champion.

While many believe that exercises like squats and bench presses are for mass and leg extensions and pec dec are only for definition, Munzer disagreed. These are only exercises, and it's not the exercise that matters. It's how you do the exercise. Andreas said that since 1987, he had been training six days per week and twice per day during the off-season. Today, you don't see many pros training like that.

ANDREAS MUNZER'S WORKOUT ROUTINE

Monday morning: chest and stationary bike

Monday evening: back and abdominals

Tuesday morning: biceps and calves

Tuesday evening: shoulders and stationary bike

Wednesday morning: triceps

Wednesday evening: legs

Thursday morning: repeat Monday morning workout

Sunday: rest day

He varied his sets for off-season and precontest as follows:

Large body parts: chest—20 sets off-season, 24 to 28 sets precontest

Small body parts: biceps and triceps—16 sets off-season, 20 to 24 sets precontest

TRAINING MIND-SET

The mind is very important in everything, especially bodybuilding. Andreas's mind-set was that he liked doing one body part per workout because he felt he was able to fully concentrate and work that body part 100 percent harder than if he was working it with other body parts in the same workout. Then, later that same night, he could come back in the gym and give the next body part 100 percent intensity.

Munzer realized that not everyone can or wants to be a serious bodybuilder. Nor do they have the time to train twice a day, six days per week. For these people, they can still get great results by training once a day, four or five times per week.

NUTRITION

So what did a bodybuilding phenomenon like Munzer eat? He said he ate five meals a day. He believed this was important to keep the body full of nutrients. He advocated keeping the protein intake up. Andreas said he believed three grams of protein per pound of body weight is ideal, and he got that protein from egg whites, turkey, chicken breasts, low-fat cheese, and protein powder.

For carbohydrates, Andreas ate potatoes, rice, oatmeal, and a few other kinds of vegetables. He didn't eat a lot of fruit, and he stayed away from sugar. He drank 8 to 10 liters (over two gallons) of water per day. Andreas also said he put magnesium in his water, just to be sure he got a good mineral balance along with the potassium and sodium he was getting from his food. For supplements, Andreas said he took multi-minerals and vitamins along with amino acids and extra vitamin A and zinc.

71

Porter Cottrell

ittle did Porter Cottrell realize when he picked up his first physique magazine more than 20 years ago that one day he would be a world champion body-builder. But he did and went on to beat such bodybuilding stars as Albert Beckles, J. J. Marsh, Nimrod King, Phil Williams, Milos Sarcev, and many others.

MAKING CHANGES

Cottrell trained hard for his first crack at the pro ranks, but according to the man himself, not all that differently than when he was training for the NPC Nationals. Porter said that when he first started his preparations for one of his big pro shows, he tried some different things in his training but noticed they weren't working for him, so he went back to what he knew worked best for him in the past.

Porter said that with every year that passed, he learned something more about nutrition and training—at least as far as contest preparation is concerned—but his training approach, strangely enough, turned out to be exactly the same for his first pro show as it was for his last amateur win.

HIS TRAINING SYSTEM

Porter said that he would typically train two-on/one-off 365 days of the year and tried to keep his caloric intake at 2,700 a day. Trying to keep his caloric intake high and increase his cardiovascular work didn't really work for him. Instead, he was doing an hour and a half a day of aerobics, sometimes two hours a day both in the morning and sometimes right after his workout.

KEEP PEDALING

Cottrell also learned that some aerobic devices worked better for him than others. He preferred the bike over anything. He tried the Stairmaster but got too much of a depletion of glycogen from that. The treadmill didn't really seem to work on his lower body like he wanted it to, so he went back to the same simple old basics that he knew had worked for him in the past.

ALL ABOUT SETS AND TEMPO

Something he said he didn't really believe in, especially before a contest, was the light weights/high sets for definition theory so popularized by bodybuilders of the '70s and '80s. Porter said that when he prepared for a show, he tried to stay as heavy as he could. On the average, he would do 10 to 15 sets for body parts like chest and shoulders. In fact, it was basically 10 to 15 for every body part except quads, where he might go as high as 20, but then his hamstring work was included with that too.

Porter liked to work out at a moderate speed and stay as heavy as he could. He believed this was what enabled him to come into contests bigger and with the same degree of hardness he was known for.

A DIFFERENT WAY TO PEAK

Another thing that separated Porter from the majority of his fellow competitors was the diverging beliefs about peaking for a show. He didn't believe in the so-called philosophy of peaking. To Porter, either you're in shape or you're not in shape; either you're retaining fluid or you're not retaining fluid. Fortunately for him, he didn't retain a lot of fluid.

FORGET THE FOUR-DAY SPLIT

Porter wasn't a huge fan of conventional bodybuilding systems. For example, while many competitors were training four days on, one day off, Porter preferred his two-on/one-off system all year round. He said he tried the four-on/one-off routine before, but it just fatigued him to the point where his progress not only slowed down, but actually started regressing instead of progressing.

Here are three sample workouts Porter said he did that gave him excellent results.

WORKOUT 1: CHEST AND DELTS

Chest	

- Bench press (barbell): warm-up—4 sets of 15 (135 pounds); pyramid sets—4 sets of 15 (working up to 315 pounds)

- Incline barbell presses: warm-up—1 set of 15 (135 pounds); pyramid sets—3 sets of 10–15 (working up to 315 pounds)
- Incline dumbbell flyes: warm-up—1 set of 15 (light dumbbells); pyramid sets—3 sets of 8–12
- Cable crossovers: warm-up—1 set of 20 (light weight for pump); pyramid sets—3 sets of 15–20 (working up to 90 pounds per side)

Delts

- Dumbbell presses: warm-up—1 set of 15 (70-pound dumbbells); pyramid sets—4 sets of 8–15 (working up to 90-pound dumbbells)
- Standing side lateral raises (dumbbells): warm-up—1 set of 15 (15-pound dumbbell); pyramid sets—4 or 5 sets of 8–20 (working up to 65-pound dumbbells)
- Bent-over dumbbell laterals: warm-up—1 set of 20 (45-pound dumbbells); pyramid sets—4 sets of 8-15 (working up to 65-pound dumbbells)
- Dumbbell shrugs: warm-up—1 set of 15 (light dumbbells) same weight; 4 sets of 12 (using 65-pound dumbbells and holding contraction at the top of movement for as long as possible)

WORKOUT 2: BACK AND BICEPS

Back

- Lat pulldowns: warm-up—1 set of 15 (60 pounds); pyramid sets—5 sets of 12–20 (working up to 280 pounds)

- Bent-over barbell rows: warm-up—1 set of 15 (135 pounds); pyramid sets—4 sets of 6–15 (working up to 295 pounds)
- One-arm dumbbell rows: warm-up—1 set of 15 (125-pound dumbbell); weight is moved up to 157 pounds and kept there for 4 sets of 10–20
- Parallel-grip pulldowns: warm-up—1 set of 15 (160 pounds); pyramid sets—4 sets of 15 (working up to 200 pounds)

Biceps

- Barbell curls: warm-up—1 set of 15 (just Olympic bar); pyramid sets—4 sets of 6–12 (working up to 135 pounds)
- Standing alternate dumbbell curls: warm-up—1 set of 15 (with 20-pound dumbbells); pyramid sets—4 sets of 6–15 (working up to 65-pound dumbbells)
- Preacher cable curls (optional): warm-up—1 set of 15 (20 pounds); pyramid sets—4 sets of 15–20 (working up to 70 pounds)

WORKOUT 3: TRICEPS AND LEGS

Triceps

- Triceps pushdowns: warm-up—9 sets of 20 (moving the pin down the stack so that he does 20 reps with 10 pounds, 20 reps with 20 pounds, and so on, until he's finished his warm-up by doing 20 reps with 90 pounds); pyramid sets—6 sets of 8–20 (working up to 150 pounds)

- Lying triceps extensions: warm-up—1 set of 15 (110 pounds); pyramid sets—4 sets of 8–15 (working up to 170 pounds)
- Reverse-grip pushdowns on lat machine: warm-up—1 set of 15 (light weight); pyramid sets—4 sets of 10–15

Legs

- Leg extensions: warm-up—4 or 5 light sets; pyramid sets—4 sets of 10–20 reps (working up to 150 pounds)
- Leg presses: warm-up—2 light sets; pyramid sets—4 sets of 15–30 reps (working up to 22 45-pound plates)
- Squats: warm-up—1 set of 20 (135 pounds); pyramid sets—4 sets of 15 (working up to 365 pounds)
- Seated leg curls: warm-up—1 set of 20 (150 pounds); pyramid sets—4 sets of 8–20 (working up to 275 pounds)
- Lying leg curls: warm-up—1 set of 15 (100 pounds); pyramid sets—5 sets of 8–10 (working up to 120 pounds)

KEEP THIS IN MIND

Porter cautioned that although some of the poundages he used in training were considerable, he wouldn't increase the weight he was using at the expense of proper exercise form. He thought it was vitally important to maintain very strict form and didn't cheat on his movements. He also took the tempo of the rep into account for form, meaning it took him roughly two to three seconds to perform the positive portion of a rep. However, Porter said he wasn't the type of person to really lower the weight slowly. Mind you, he was in complete control of it, but it wasn't a negative type of thing.

Porter said his reps, although he didn't like to use the terminology, were more of a "pumping" movement. On high-rep exercises, such as cable crossovers, the duration of the rep would last between four and six seconds because even when he contracted that muscle fully, he would really squeeze it and then let it out slowly with complete control of that movement.

72

John Carl Grimek

John Grimek's name is legendary within the sport of bodybuilding, as it has come to be synonymous with hard work, dedication, superhuman strength, and a physique that was years ahead of its time.

Grimek was a product of the Depression era of American history. Of Czechoslovakian stock, Grimek hailed from middle America and would in time come to embody the much heralded "work ethic" of his era. When Franklin D. Roosevelt was in office, a young John Carl Grimek was just beginning to hit his stride in what was then the little known sport of bodybuilding.

He was born in Perth Amboy, New Jersey, in 1909 and became interested in training at a very young age after witnessing the results his older brother had obtained from lifting weights. He trained initially for strength, and man-oh-man, did he develop it! He could jerk 370 pounds overhead with ease and simultaneously press two dumbbells weighing 125 and 110 pounds. In fact, he became so strong that he was asked to represent the United States in the sport of weight lifting at the 1936 Olympic Games in

Berlin, which he did proudly, competing in the heavyweight division.

Along with his prodigious strength was an almost feline flexibility. Grimek could, at any time, drop down into a full splits or perform any one of a dozen other gymnastics techniques. In fact, his name was often invoked as the standard rebuttal to the then-popular assertion that "bodybuilders aren't really strong and certainly aren't really athletes."

Despite his many athletic talents, it would be the little heralded sport of bodybuilding with which Grimek would ultimately cast his lot. He built his physique up to a rock-solid 203 pounds with a 50-inch chest, 30½-inch waist, and 18½-inch arms simply by the application of his two maxims, "hard work and consistency." It's comforting to note that Grimek accomplished these impressive stats without the aid of any kind of anabolic agent. In fact, at the time of his greatest bodybuilding achievements, steroids were still 16 years away from being invented!

That Grimek was drug-free is probably the reason why his physique continued to look so good for so long. In fact, his muscular development was so astounding that he won the AAU Mr. America title in 1940 at 31 years of age, and when he repeated the victory the following year, the powers that existed within the AAU decided that he could well continue to win the title indefinitely, so they immediately laid down new rules stating that a man could win the title only once.

Grimek's competitive success didn't stop there, however. At age 39, Grimek traveled to London, England, to compete in the Mr. Universe contest against another bodybuilding legend, Steve Reeves. Reeves, as we all know, possessed what some have called "the most genetically perfect physique of all time," and yet Grimek drubbed him handily, winning the contest with ease. Perhaps Grimek's finest hour came at an age that most of us would have considered past his prime, when he decided to compete for the 1949 Mr. USA title at the Shrine Auditorium in Los Angeles.

More than 7,000 fans turned out to watch the "Old Lion" battle it out with the most formidable physiques in the world. Men such as Armand Tanny, Clancy Ross, and George Eiferman were there to compete as, indeed, was the legendary Steve Reeves, still smarting from his defeat the previous year at Grimek's hands and burning to avenge the loss. Nevertheless, once the smoke of the battle had cleared, Grimek again had emerged victorious—at 40 years of age! With this professional victory under his belt, Grimek retired undefeated from bodybuilding—the only athlete in the history of our sport to have successfully done so.

I [John] was fortunate enough to both meet and interview the legendary John Grimek at the Arnold Classic in Columbus, Ohio, where he was the personally invited guest of Arnold Schwarzenegger himself, and let me tell you, at 83 years of age, the man still cuts an imposing physical figure!

He's also a very straightforward guy; no airs or pretenses about him, and his bodybuilding philosophy is, not surprisingly, formulated along these same lines. When I asked him what special things he did, in order to build his awesome physique, he just smiled and said, "In our time, we didn't do anything special—we just trained hard." And with that, our interview with this true legend of bodybuilding began.

Q: How did you train?

GRIMEK: *I really didn't have anything different that somebody before me hadn't already tried. If anything, I just was more consistent in never missing a training session. In fact, in my case, I would have tried anything to get bigger. I wanted that to happen more than anything else.*

Q: Did anyone teach you anything that really helped you to pack on size?

GRIMEK: *No, they didn't really want to show you anything in those days because their attitude was "What the hell, why would I disclose my secrets to you, when it might work better for you?" So they ended up not saying anything. They'd keep it to themselves. It wasn't until I started getting some recognition and started getting friendly with some of these professional men from stage and so forth that they started to disclose anything I sought or asked. But prior to that—hell! I'd written to dozens of them, and that was just a waste of time.*

Q: Who were your idols, peers, or influences when you were training?

GRIMEK: *Well, that was way back in the '20s and, you know, it would be men like Sandow of course, he was very popular, and some of the other men were Europeans like Chrysinski and so forth, who were terrific, but then there were the Americans and Canadians, like Jowitt and all the others who, over the years I was fortunate enough to meet most of them, and I was influenced by them and I tried to get their secrets, but [laughs] no one would tell me anything.*

Q: How many days a week did you train when you made your best progress?

GRIMEK: *Well, like most anyone who's a beginner, it was recommended that three times a week would be the maximum time any person should exercise. However, when I started, I was stupid enough that I didn't read the training system correctly. It said that you should do so many exercises and so many repetitions and so forth the one day, and then the next training day you did another program. Now it didn't say, "rest a day in between sessions," it just said "the next training day," so I took it for a fact that the next training day was, in fact, the very next day—so I did the same thing again. Then the course said to try and increase the repetitions you're using every third workout, which I tried to do if I could. And as a result, I trained every doggone day, seven days a week. And after three or four weeks of this, my ass kept dragging. Boy, I was ready to give it up. I thought, "This is hell, I can't stand this!" And I wasn't gaining, I was losing, but worse yet, I was so damned tired all the time. I mean, I was training seven days a week, every day, and I was just a beginner. In later years, after I came to work, and I was doing some training, well I could train six or seven days a week—it didn't mean a damn. But in those days when I just began, the training every day nearly killed me. And believe me, I was ready to give up. It wasn't until my brother, who was then working in some lumber camp up around Canada somewhere, came back and said, "How you doing in training?" And I said,*

"Oh, Christ! It's killing me! I don't know if I can take it!" He said, "Why?" and I explained it to him, and he said, "You stupid so and so"—he called me a lot of names—"you're supposed to only train three days a week!" I said, "How? The course says increase the repetitions every three days!" And he said, "Yeah, you're supposed to train every third day, which means that the day after a session is a rest day!" Well, when I found that out and tried it, things went terrific after that!

Q: Where did you do your training in those days?

GRIMEK: *I used to work out in our attic. In the summer time, it got too damn hot, so I had to quit training by mid-June or the end of June, and then I began again later in September, but then I had to quit again when it got so damn cold [laughs]. It was something in those days. There of course were no sweat pants in those times and often, because of the bar being so damn cold, my darn hands would stick to the bar and I couldn't even shake it loose! So it was a miserable time, but I've got to admit that I made better progress through those times than I can ever remember.*

Q: Why do you think that was?

GRIMEK: *It just happened that way. I don't know how. I guess I was more methodical; I did so many reps, and if I could do an extra 1 or 2 repetitions, I did, which meant the following workout day I would have to* increase the weight by maybe five pounds more or so. In that way, I guess the program worked quite well, but throughout the course of an entire year, I could only train maybe five, six, or seven months a year because of the climate conditions.

Q: So what did you do to keep in shape during those months when you couldn't train?

GRIMEK: Oh, nothing more or less, except that I would be going to the beach or things like that. Sometimes I would be doing chinning or, when I would go to the YMCA, I would do some parallel bar work and things that you might normally do. I didn't know anything about it, but I just did it. I remember when I was working for a while as a soda jerk and we would work to midnight, and when I'd get home, which would be around midnight or little later, I would often train in the backyard in the moonlight, and that was kind of productive.

Q: So you were training three days a week in those days. How many sets were you averaging per body part?

GRIMEK: In those days there were no sets. You trained one set per exercise, which was one exercise for each part of the body. In other words, presses for the arms and shoulders and back and curls for your forearms, wrist, and biceps and so forth. And squats would be your sole leg exercise, but I did, besides squats, since I couldn't get enough weight on my back, I would do

what they called "the Jefferson lift" and exercises of that sort which were very good leg exercises.

Q: So what would a typical workout be for you?

GRIMEK: Whatever the old Milo Barbell Course consisted of, which was all standard exercises. That was the one that I followed but then, I didn't know anything about it, I didn't even know the difference. All I followed was the suggested list of exercises, and that was it.

Q: So would that consist of a "baker's dozen" exercises?

GRIMEK: Oh yes, that would be at least a dozen, probably more because you would include everything from curls to pullovers, to squats, deadlifts and stiff-legged deadlifts, and all the others, which was a continuation, but there was also in that course what they called "advanced" training. Well, since I was only a beginner I wasn't attempting to go into the advanced level, although some of the exercises looked good to me and I would include them occasionally. It was also at this point that I fashioned what they called "supporting feats," which is isometric in a sense.

Q: What was that?

GRIMEK: Well, I had rafters in the attic, and I fixed up where I had some sort of support straps where the bar would be suspended and I could load it up with weights and support it or maybe do partial presses with it from the top of my head overhead, so forth. I could make it very heavy this way. Then for a while I got into a point where I trained three times a day.

Q: How did that work?

GRIMEK: Well, I'd do a regular warm-up or regular bodybuilding exercises during the morning because I wasn't working at the time, then I would do some of what they called "lifting movements." Some of them I'd do for several repetitions and repeat it until I felt I'd had enough. And then in the evening, after supper, I would do what they called "supporting feats," which were isometric exercises.

Q: Were these worthwhile movements to engage in?

GRIMEK: Yes. I recall that they worked quite well. I recall that I got quite strong. I mean, for my size and age and so forth, I was much stronger than anybody around at the time. It was all a kind of a hit-and-miss type of thing where you'd say, "Try this," and I'd say, "That sounds good." It was also at this time that I made several different types of training apparatus.

Q: What were they like?

GRIMEK: They weren't perfect, that's for sure. But at the same time, they were good for stretching myself, and at the same time it provided a lot of lat work and arm work by . . . how shall I explain this? It repre-

sented a kind of M shape, with two pulleys hung on the rafters, and the lower part of the M would be a kind of a halter type that you could put your head in or, at least, keep your head in contact, and then when you pulled the outside handles, it would stretch you and you got a lot of exercise from it. It was an interesting piece of equipment, but I never fashioned it enough to be more practical and to try and improve its benefits. Actually, I think it would still benefit the gymnast who wanted to do what they call the "iron cross." That would be the ideal training method for perfecting that movement.

Q: You mentioned that it was your brother who put you straight about training three days a week. What was his training background?

GRIMEK: He and some of his group had been training together, and they'd bought all the courses that were available at the time and they would exchange them. They'd work on one course for about a month or so, and then change with the other one and just pass them around. And when he left, of course, he left most of his stuff at home, so I used it. That's how I got into it, because he did make fairly good progress at the time so I figured, "Geez, if he can do it maybe I'll try."

Q: How important a role do you think genetics play in developing a championship physique?

GRIMEK: Well, I guess they're very important, but I can't believe that it is all-important though. I have some cousins, one of which is a twin. I mean identical. And what happened was that his twin died very early; within the first six months after he was born. Now the surviving twin is the only one that's left of that whole family. He had two or three other brothers, and they all died, and everyone else died. His mother lived to be quite old too, but if everything is genetic, why didn't he pass on long ago as his twin did? That's the thing that bugs me, I can't believe it. When people talk about it and say how important genetics are, I say, "Yeah, that's true but!" And then I bring this thing up because it's been bugging me ever since I stopped by about two years ago when we were going down to Florida to see him, and he's in terrific shape. He even likes his beer, and the other brothers didn't drink that much, apart from socializing with friends, but nothing like this guy does, and yet he's around still. He's in good shape though. I remember when I was training for the 1936 Olympic Games, why, he was thinking of doing it too. "I'll do it the next time," he said, and that would have been for the 1940 Games which, of course, never came off because of the war. The point is, he was one of the most interested persons in the athletic way there was.

Q: What do you think was the high point of your career?

GRIMEK: I don't know if there was any high point that I can remember. It's hard to say. I mean, even competition-wise, it was just something I got into and that was it. If I won, fine.

Q: I recall interviewing Steve Reeves back in 1986, and he said that he considered you to have been among his toughest competition. Do you remember that contest?

GRIMEK: Yes, that would have been in London. I remember it because people sometimes bring it up, and at that time, he was very egotistical himself. This was years ago, mind you, I'm talking about in the '40s. I didn't expect that, although we treated him very good when he was here. We really did everything we could because we wanted to send him over to Europe, well, London, England, specifically, which we did, so that was the highlight of his entire career because he missed it the first time, but he went back and picked it up. And he made a hit there.

Q: What do you think of some of today's training methods such as the six days a week or three days on, one day off?

GRIMEK: Well, as I said, you can get used to it where it can be productive, but if you are a beginner and you have no experience and your muscles aren't acclimated to any kind of a rigid or sustained training, you're going to have problems like I ran into. Once I came to York and I had the *gym at my beck and call anytime I wanted it, it was often that I began to do whatever I wanted. I'd train every day without wanting to. It wasn't that I wanted to train, I simply got into the gym and I was encouraged to try something and, before you knew it, you were actually training. You can get adapted to it, but it would be impossible and actually detrimental to a person to begin with such a system. I think it's too rigorous for anybody who doesn't have either the experience or the endurance to keep going for hours. Stand-ford and I, a couple of times, would train for six to eight hours a day! It didn't matter because we didn't even feel tired or exhausted and say, "Oh boy! Am I beat!"*

There was no such thing then, it was just as a matter of fact.

Q: What routine would you recommend to the average trainee today who wants to gain size?

GRIMEK: *Oh, I would think that anyone who is going to start should include at least one exercise for each part of the body, but specifically for the leg and chest regions. The reason is that as you get older, you see a lot of people who can't even walk, and getting up out of chairs is a problem, so if you don't keep them at least half strong, you're going to run into problems, and some of us do a little earlier than others. That's a big problem.*

73

Shawn Ray

In all the years we've known Shawn Ray and spoken with him, he impressed us as a guy who not only had his stuff together business-wise, you could count on him to always come to a contest "ready," and he would be one of the few consistent top competitors. Many people gave him the reputation of "the man who was always in shape."

So, what was it that made Shawn so successful? Many things. The mind-set. His belief in himself. Great genetics. Smart training and nutrition and . . . well, perhaps it would be enjoyable to read about a few of the things we learned from him.

When it came to competing, Shawn always came to win. It really didn't matter who his competition was or if they were in shape or not. He came to do battle, and they had better also. He also didn't mess too much with the things that brought him success in the past—like his training.

What did change was his continual will to succeed. It seemed like each year, it became sharper and more focused (not that it wasn't before, mind you). For a guy who came on the scene at age 21 as a National

Shawn Ray gives a "sneak preview" the night before a big event.

champion, then at 22 he was onstage at the Mr. Olympia, Shawn already had a wealth of experiences at such an early age. Things could only get better.

We asked him for one of his classic game plans that had brought him success, and this was what he said.

Shawn's training style was very instinctive. More on that in a moment. He said that in the off-season, he trained four-on/one-off, and then before a contest, say, six to twelve weeks out, he upped it to three-on/one-off.

On his four-on/one-off schedule, he said he did back and shoulders. On day two, he did legs and calves. On day three he did chest by itself, and on day four he did arms and calves. For day five, he said he would

ride the bike for 20 to 30 minutes. Shawn said that he rode the bike every day whether he was training or not. For abs, he did those every other day.

When Shawn made the switch to the three-on/one off schedule, he did back with shoulders and calves on day one, then legs on day two. On day three he did chest and arms. Shawn said that he would split his three-on/one-off training sessions into two parts, training once in the morning and once at night.

When it came to the workouts, Shawn said that he would choose four exercises that would change almost every workout and then do 5 sets of each, inclusive of 2 warmup sets. Before a contest, he would do pretty much the same thing except that he might implement a few drop sets, consisting of sets of 30 repetitions with three drops per set.

For example, he might do 1 set of 10 reps, then he'd drop 10 pounds or so and do another 10 reps, then break it down again and do another 10 reps for a total of 30 reps, however all of that would equal 1 set. He was a big believer in using the best form he could since he wanted to feel it in the muscle that he was training.

What may surprise many people was that Shawn didn't train super-heavy. He said that a lot of times when you get too caught up in trying to lift heavier and heavier weights, you run into nothing but joint and ligament problems and, possibly, torn muscles, so in the long run, longevity is the key, so you have to be careful.

An example of Shawn's training approach would be his arm workout. He would typically use three exercises for both biceps and triceps and do 2 warm-up sets and then 3 sets for each exercise, doing between 10 and 15 reps on each set.

Shawn believed that how hard you focus on your exercises determines to a large extent whether or not you're overtraining. He trained with a good focus, but didn't train with weights that were so heavy that he needed a spotter or forced reps. As the contest date drew closer, say, only two weeks to go, Shawn's workouts became much quicker paced, and he would normally reduce his total number of sets to 3 per exercise at that time.

He said he didn't superset. The only variations he would typically do would be to add drop sets to his routine, but even then, he would break it down to only 3 such sets per exercise and then start adding drop sets and training at a quicker pace. He said he would also start adding isometric posing more often and for longer periods immediately following his training sessions.

It is at this point that Shawn said he would also cut back a bit on his aerobic activity. He said he would normally just reduce the times that he used the Lifecycle and the Liferower. So instead of two 20-minute sessions, he might only do one.

Shawn said he would also be paying more attention to his abdominal details as far as upping the repetitions from 35 (which he said was standard for him) to possibly 50 reps for maybe 3 sets of four different exercises. For lower back, Shawn said he got good results with hyperextensions.

Food-wise, he said he might reduce his carbohydrates a bit and up his protein intake, but he really didn't manipulate that process too much because it was too hit-and-miss. At this stage, he was also drinking lots of water (two and a half to three gallons a day). Shawn said he tried to drink as much water (distilled) as he could and found it helped keep his muscles full and his body flushed.

Shawn said that water at this stage was very important to him because he was training twice a day and he was also lying in the sun bed or lying out in the sun tanning and losing a lot of water when he was posing, so it was important to replace that water because—at two or three weeks out from a show—it wasn't time to drop the water yet. But make no mistake, his mindset was so focused at that stage of his contest preparation that a bomb could drop and he'd still continue training.

SHAWN RAY'S KEY TO SUCCESS

Many people, if having the opportunity to talk one-on-one with Shawn Ray, would be quite impressed with the fact that the man is intelligent. College educated, in fact. And he accredited his education for a large measure of his success.

He said he majored in social psychology and found himself using it every day. Shawn's family were actively involved in businesses of their own, from his sister right on up to his mom and dad, so he knew that he didn't want to become dependent on anybody but Shawn Ray.

Shawn thought his schooling gave him an entirely different realm in his life, that is, capable of functioning outside the gym; dealing with people in social settings, knowing and understanding different cultures, different environments, and different social issues such as interracial marriages, death and dying, and various family issues such as group confrontations and conflicts and a whole host of other courses and subject matter that he believed helped him become a well-rounded individual.

HEAVY WEIGHTS AREN'T THAT IMPORTANT

Despite the fact that Shawn Ray was quite strong, he didn't stress the use of heavy weights in training for quality muscle mass. He said he didn't think his physique was built on strength so much as it was built on moderate repetitions with medium-heavy weights.

Shawn said that rarely did he go below 12 repetitions but, if he was going medium heavy, he could go as low as 8, not lower. He also trained at a very quick pace by comparison to many guys, but that was just the nature of his training. It took a lot of stamina, it didn't require slow training, which heavy weights necessitated, because he liked to feel the muscle work, and when

he trained with heavy weights he just didn't feel it. Shawn also felt that a muscle is taxed far more with higher repetitions, you got a lot more lactic acid buildup and you got a killer pump.

What was interesting was that Shawn said he didn't monitor his progress by strength. He said he didn't monitor his progress by size, and he didn't take measurements. However, he did say he used the mirror, and if his mirror told him that he was getting a bit out of condition, then he would do more aerobics and eat lower carbohydrates. Conversely, if he needed to gain weight, he'd eat more carbohydrates and lower the aerobic activity. For Shawn, the mirror was the best monitor. Strength was not the most important factor.

A SHAWN RAY SAMPLE PRECONTEST WORKOUT

For precontest, Shawn worked out three days on, one day off.

Day 1: Back and Shoulders

- Warm-up: 3 sets of front chins, followed by 3 sets of behind-the-neck chins.
- Seated pulley rows. Shawn would squeeze his elbows together when the handle reached his chest.
- Then it's barbell bent-over rows or T-bar rows, followed by lat machine pulldowns to the front.

- For shoulders, it's dumbbell side laterals (single-armed or two-armed). Then he moves on to seated dumbbell presses or seated barbell presses, followed by bent-over dumbbell laterals. Shawn finishes up with either dumbbell shrugs or barbell upright rows.

Day 2: Legs and Abs

Shawn warms up with stretching movements and light leg extensions before launching right into his first exercise which, surprisingly enough, is leg curls for 5 sets. Then he proceeds to squats or front squats, and then it's leg presses and lunges. Shawn said he did lunges all year round.

Day 3: Chest and Arms

Shawn always warms up with 2 to 3 sets on the pec dec to warm up the shoulder girdle, and then he moves right into heavy incline dumbbell presses, flyes, flat bench presses, and weighted parallel bar dips. Arm training could be anything, which could be three good biceps exercises followed by three hard triceps ones.

74

What It's Like to Make a Comeback Mike Matarazzo Style

The history of bodybuilding is rich with those who achieved great heights, then faded off to oblivion, and then came back again—sometimes much better. Mike Matarazzo was one of them. Known for his unbelievable arms and calves, Mike was also one of the sport's favorite guys. People just liked hanging around him.

Matarazzo is a guy who loved the sport. But it was years of brutally intense workouts, along with competition after competition and years of travel and nonstop seminars and guest posings that burned him out physically and mentally. He said he needed time away from the sport and to sit back and take a good hard look at the sport he loved.

He was looking to get that competitive rush back again.

Matarazzo said he knew that so many guest appearances would not allow him to prepare properly for a show. He knew that his body needed to be trained hard, and it needed time to recuperate and grow. He also knew he wasn't giving it either.

Mike said he realized a painful truth that many pros face: they work out hard, but find their body is no longer changing or growing. A classic case of burnout. After taking a much-needed respite from the sport he loved, the fire inside was beginning to burn hotter. As what happens with many pros, Mike's body was finally getting the recuperation and down time it needed. It was also heavier, but its hardness, endurance, and

Mike decided to make a comeback, and he said he went back to the things that gave his body the best results: the basics. He also said he started out very slowly (a hugely important thing when making a comeback) to give his body plenty of time to adjust to the weights. He went back to his old split training schedule of five days on, one day off, working one body part a day. The workout was split like this:

Monday: back

Tuesday: chest, abs

Wednesday: shoulders and rear delts

Thursday: quads, calves, hamstrings

Friday: arms

He said his sets and reps varied for each body part. For big muscle groups like back, he did 12 to 15 sets total using 3 or 4 exercises, and for smaller muscles like arms, he did 4 to 8 sets total using 2 or 3 exercises. He went to failure on every set of every exercise for every body part.

To get his endurance back, Mike said he rode the stationary bike for 30 minutes a day, gradually working his way up to an hour every day. Soon thereafter, he switched to the treadmill. Mike said he liked the treadmill because he found it to harden his body up all over more than anything else. It took only a month of doing one hour a day on the treadmill to get his body into terrific shape.

Of course, nutrition was a very important part of Mike's comeback, and he said he got back on a good eating plan by eating five to six small meals a day of clean, healthy food (chicken, rice, steamed vegetables, etc.) and substituting two of those meals with a good protein shake. He had a shake for breakfast and the other right after his workout. He also said he would double up serving size just so he could give his body the extra protein, carbs, and other nutrients it needed for growth. He found that when he did this before his workout, it gave him an amazing pump.

The story of Mike Matarazzo's success and comeback could be your story if you always remember that it's the basics that got you to where you are and it'll be the basics that'll bring you back. In this age of so much information instantly at your fingertips, never lose sight of the fact that whether you're an amateur or pro, the right training, the right nutrition, and the right amount of rest will take you as far as your genetics allow and you believe possible.

PART 7

Wisdom

75

One-on-One with Rachel McLish

She would be the last to admit it, but Rachel McLish is an icon to women everywhere. Even though she hasn't competed in eons, since she won the first ever Ms. Olympia, her name and image are still talked about to this day by women and men alike as someone whose gorgeous body and face turned heads, but brought with them a sense of elegance and class that so many have tried to emulate.

Perhaps one of the most impressive things about Rachel is that she never forgot where she came from. Her faith, her roots, her family, and her friends come first and foremost in her life. She never let success, fame, or fortune change who and what she was. And in the fickle and fleeting world of bodybuilding and entertainment stardom, that's huge.

Here are a few of her interesting (and spot-on) observations on a number of subjects we think you'll find enjoyable reading.

WHY SHE BECAME A BODYBUILDER

Rachel said she thought it was her upbringing that led her to become a body-builder. Her father was always physically fit, and that influenced her a great deal. Even at the age of five, she said, she could remember being very impressed with the strength and musculature of the human body.

Then, around 1979 or 1980, bodybuilder Lisa Lyon was getting lots of publicity, and Rachel thought she looked fabulous. She wanted to enter the competition that Lisa was promoting in Atlantic City, New Jersey.

Rachel said she trained hard for that show, and something inside of her kept telling her that this new phenomenon called bodybuilding was a part of her destiny. She believed that she could win and knew she had a message to give to women, and winning that show and the first Ms. Olympia gave her the opportunity to do it. She said she always preached the good news of being fit, strong, healthy, and sexy, even as a kid living in Texas. Bodybuilding gave her the platform to share this terrific secret with women all over the world.

For Rachel, the essence of her passion for bodybuilding was that if you work out hard with weights and eat smart and healthy, you're going to have a body you're proud of and you're going to feel great in your skin.

THOSE WHO INFLUENCED HER

Rachel said that as a child, her strongest influence was her father. He really molded her character. To watch him go through the struggles of life and see how he handled some tough situations positively influenced her. He taught her to be herself, be honest and strong, and always hold her head up high and not be a coward.

Rachel said her mother was a major influence in her life too. She raised five children and was always there for Rachel's family, and she had the patience of a saint. Rachel said that her mother had the ability to rise above any adversity, and she said to be like her mom is, to her, to be a godly woman. She lived for other people with a real servant's heart, and Rachel admired her very much.

Even though Rachel was blessed with great genetics and looks, she said she was never influenced by the looks and beauty that someone possessed. It was more of a deeper thing for her; those qualities that make us each uniquely human. When asked about other influences, she said Joe Weider and his bodybuilding philosophy and Mother Teresa for her compassion and love for all people. Talk about diversity!

BODYBUILDING FAME AND SUCCESS

Rachel said that bodybuilding fulfilled a lot of her adult and childhood dreams. She's been able to see the world and meet many incredible people, and she believed this is one of the richest experiences that bodybuilding has given her.

Make no mistake, bodybuilding has also given her many opportunities, and she's prospered financially. However, to Rachel, money has never been a motivating factor.

She said she really must be passionate about what she does or she won't do it, regardless of how much money is involved.

Rachel has a great philosophy on money, success, and fame. She said that having lots of money and all those things will only make you an exaggerated version of who you already are. If you're a selfish person, more money and fame will only make you more selfish. If you're a giving person, then lots of money and fame will only enable you to give more.

GOALS

Rachel said that her mind was continually flooded with new dreams and new goals, so it's an ongoing process. She believed that if she did whatever she was doing in the present, the best that she could, it would automatically and naturally generate the next steps for the attainment of whatever goal she was working toward.

WHAT KEEPS MANY FROM SUCCESS

Rachel said she found that most people fall short of their fitness goals because they are missing one small element of the fitness puzzle. Maybe it's too much aerobic, not enough weight training, too many carbs, or not enough protein. Yet if they change one small variable, like magic, they achieve success.

Whenever people are frustrated or have reached a sticking point in the nutrition and training program, she might tell them to take a few days off, forget what they know about nutrition and fitness, and start with a clean slate and get back to the basics. This will give them a much clearer perspective and help them look forward to experiencing new results.

EXPERTS AND INFORMATION

She felt there was just too much conflicting information out there in the magazines and on television. She was amazed at the number of "experts" who keep giving people misinformation and throwing out facts out of context just to make believers out of those to whom they want to sell their products, whether they be nutritional supplements or fitness products. In fact, she said she quit reading many of these magazines a long time ago and now only reads newsletters. She found the information to be more cutting-edge, accurate, and without all the commercial hype.

PERSONAL TRAINERS

Rachel had an interesting take on personal trainers. She said that when she was competing, she found it very insulting if someone asked her if she had a trainer. When it came to her body, she was the expert, and nobody knew how to train that body better than she did. It was she who got her body to reach its level of conditioning according to her goals, her desires, and her agenda. Training for a championship was highly personal.

Rachel said that to her, a training partner was much better than a personal trainer.

Granted, a background in kinesiology, physiology, and nutrition is essential in providing the basics for your training program, and she thought it was smart for bodybuilders to use those services and integrate the information into their strategy. However, Rachel said she's always believed that if you trust somebody with your physiology, you'll eventually become dependent upon them for your psychology.

BIG MISTAKES PEOPLE MAKE

Rachel said one thing bodybuilders should do is eat more to be leaner and weigh less. She said that eating breakfast was, at times, tough for her because she's not hungry, but she did it because she knew her day would go better and it stoked her metabolism and helped her stay leaner. She believed that people need to realize that having that first meal in the morning will empower them to make wise choices about food the rest of the day and not be so susceptible to the urgings and cravings of starvation and temptations of junk food from skipping breakfast.

THE PRESSURES WOMEN FACE IN SOCIETY

Many women look up to Rachel as a role model and for words of guidance. When it came to the subject of the pressures put on women by society, Rachel said that many women—especially young girls—have it tough. It's such a visual world that women can't get away from a superficial image of what they're supposed to look like. All of that perpetuates the eating disorders, marathon workouts, and other nutrition and fitness obsessions.

Rachel said she tells women that what's helped her is to remember that we are each unique individuals, with our own special gifts and abilities. Don't compare your body, looks, and anything else to other people. Use what is yours, and use it to your best advantage. Be the best that you can be because nobody can do that better than you.

TRAINING TIPS FOR WOMEN

Rachel offered some training and nutrition advice for women:

- Do four to five 30-minute cardio workouts (such as brisk walking, stair-climber, or treadmill) per week. You simply don't need more than 30 minutes per workout if you're doing it right.
- Do two whole-body weight training workouts per week. Sets will vary from body part to body part, but do at least 15 reps per set.
- Be sure you're working out hard enough to breathe heavily and sweat so you will burn sugar and fat at the same time. Keep your rest between sets to 35 seconds or less.

ONE OF HER WORKOUTS

Rachel gave an overview of her workout and nutrition strategy. Here's what she did:

- Work out five days per week.
- Stretch before, during, and after any kind of training.
- Cardio training consists of either mountain hiking (two to three hours), biking (approximately 10 miles), running (slow jog for five minutes, then stop to stretch groin and hip joints, then resume running), sprinting/walking, stair-climber, or rowing machine for 30 minutes.

WHAT SHE EATS

Rachel frequently changes what she eats, but this is a typical menu.

Breakfast: high-bran cereal or oatmeal with fruit or egg white omelet with whole wheat toast

Lunch: salad with chicken or vegetable burger or fresh vegetable juice and fruit

Dinner: fish, chicken, or pasta with fresh basil and garlic

If she eats protein in the morning, she'll have carbs in the afternoon or vice versa.

Rachel keeps protein powder on hand in case she needs some extra protein or wants to make a protein smoothie to replace a meal. She starts out the day with a liter of water before she'll eat breakfast or have herb tea or coffee.

Whenever she got the urge to really watch her diet, she'd begin the week with a juice or vegetable fast and the next day have only fruits and lots of water. Then she'd slowly introduce clean, lean protein and vegetables back into her diet. She said you'd be surprised how much energy you'll have

and how many toxins you'll eliminate from your body by doing this.

TRAINING FOR YOUR BODY TYPE AND GOALS

Over the years many women have said they'd like their bodies to look like Rachel's. Rachel said (although she was flattered at the compliment) that people need to realize that despite their best intentions and years of hard work, they would never be her, or look like her or any other person for that matter. She believed that each of us has our own unique body, and that's the beauty of it, to develop it so it makes a statement about who each of us is, without being a copy of someone else.

She said that in a world of copies, developing your body is what it's all about. If having the kind of body she has is an inspiration for someone, then try to think of her as a guidepost and not as the ultimate goal. You are the ultimate goal.

HAPPINESS

Rachel said that on any given day, she was happy and fulfilled. She also remembers each day how blessed she is. Her faith is very important to her, and she takes time out of each day to talk to God and just give thanks. What she has experienced in her life has far exceeded her wildest dreams. That's not to say that Rachel doesn't have other dreams, because she does. She realizes that it's all in God's master plan for her life.

HER LIFE'S PURPOSE

Rachel said she thought about her life's purpose every day. She believed it was to do God's will and use her abilities to help make other people's lives better, to be the very best that Rachel can be.

HOW SHE'D LIKE TO BE REMEMBERED

Rachel said that first of all, she'd like to be remembered by people with a smile on their faces, and she'd like to be remembered in a lot of different ways. To be one that uplifted and edified everyone she came into contact with in some special way. Rachel has certainly done that!

76

Arnold Speaks: Arnold Schwarzenegger's Tips on Success

Over the years, we have had the opportunity to interview and talk with Arnold Schwarzenegger. Besides being quite an influence to many of us, there was no denying the Schwarzenegger charm, enthusiasm, and his belief in himself and making his goals and dreams come true. When it came to success—be it in sports, bodybuilding, or life—he had much to say.

DISCIPLINE, BODYBUILDING, MARTIAL ARTS, AND SPORTS

Arnold said that whether it was boxing, martial arts, or weight training—all of those things need a tremendous amount of discipline and follow-through. And he thought that this was one of the reasons why those things go very well together. He also thought those kinds of activities were all very good for recreational sports, things that are important to give one a sense of total fitness both inside and outside the gym.

For training and staying fit, there were so many similarities. He said that when he went around and talked about fitness, he would mention martial arts as a good example of a sport where you didn't just get physically fit and strong, but you also got mental discipline.

Arnold said that from these sports you also learn about things such as camaraderie, you learn about setting goals, about sacrifices you have to take, and about self-esteem—how you build self-esteem and self-worth. So there are so many things one gets out of it.

VISUALIZING HIS SUCCESS

When asked about how he used visualization, he said, "Let me tell you how I came to believe in this method of visualization for success." First of all, he knew that the whole idea of achieving your goals starts in your mind. You first have to dream it, you first have to see it or visualize it. Then, when you can visualize it, you can go after it and you can accomplish it and turn it into reality.

But you have to have a clear picture or idea of what you want to achieve, for if you have no vision, then what do you go after?

There's nothing to go after! He compared it to the analogy that you can have the best ship in the world, but if the captain doesn't know where to go it's just going to drift around.

Arnold used sports and martial arts as examples of having a clear picture and goal to shoot for. The coaches and the trainers and the martial arts teachers all tell you your goal: you have to break through this piece of wood; you have to get this kind of a style to accomplish your goals in fighting; this is the belt that you go after; the brown belt, the black belt—there were always these little goals, and when you accomplished them, then you knew it was through hard work (and let us add, having set specific goals). And, he said, the message that you learn from accomplishing these tasks, of course, you could then apply to anything you do in life.

WHAT TRAINING CAN TEACH YOU

Arnold said that the psychological foundations that one has to cultivate, bringing up the will to train hard and to have the willpower to excel, the discipline that you have to have to continue to stay with it and not slack off—and the things that you learn from it—had broad applications for success in any endeavor.

THE BENEFITS OF WORKING OUT

Arnold said there were many benefits of working out, and apart from the mental and goal-setting rewards achieved by such activities, there was obviously the dividend of the health benefits.

He said you feel better physically, you get in better shape, and you learn how to control your body. And as a result of this, you begin to feel more confident because you can do things with your body when you train now that you couldn't do before.

Arnold was a big believer that whether you train in bodybuilding, general fitness, or in the martial arts, all of these benefits were very, very great assets that would lead to success in all areas of life.

77

Lee Haney One-on-One

One of the most popular body-builders of all time was Lee Haney. Even years after he last competed and won his eight Mr. Olympia titles, to this day, people ask about Lee Haney and want to know more about the man, his training, his life, and what made him tick. Here are a few of the things Lee said.

THOSE WHO INSPIRED HIM

Lee said that Joe Weider was a big inspiration because he looked at his story of where he came from. Lee had a chance to go out and visit Joe Weider's home, and it looked like a museum. But, Lee said, Joe came from another rags-to-riches story. So did Arnold. Lee said he liked that, and that was inspiring to him.

Lee said that Joe had always given him good words of wisdom. They always stayed in touch, and they had their little discussions, but always remained friends, no matter what. He will always respect Joe and care for him.

WHAT MADE HIM WANT TO TRAIN

Lee said he grew up with this thing inside of him wanting to pick up and lift things. He told a funny story that happened when Lee was around four or five years old.

Lee said he wanted to test his strength on this one particular day, and he and his brother, who was about nine years old, were out horseplaying.

His father had a baby blue Ford Fairlane that was his prized possession. Something inside of Lee said that he was strong enough to throw a huge rock over that car. So he told his brother to "Watch this!" and he picked up the rock, and he muscled it over his head and pushed with all his might—and the law of gravity took over. That boulder fell right in the back glass of his father's car!

Lee said his father came out yelling, "Who did it?" and Lee pointed to his brother and said, "He did it," and his daddy beat the crap out of his brother. (Lee laughed as he told this.) Lee said it was only when he was about 22 that his dad found out who really did it. Lee laughed and said he was really into that kind of stuff back then, being raised from the Bible and so forth and reading the story of Samson's feats of strength.

Then Lee told about his grandpa. He was a powerful man. Lee said he watched him hold the hind legs of a boar pig while he was kicking. He said that even at age 75, his grandpa had striations in his chest and triceps. So Lee grew up being amazed at feats of strength and muscles and seeing Hercules movies. All of those things, he said, were inspiring.

WHEN HE STARTED WORKING OUT

Lee said his father got him a set of weights when he was around 14 years old (weighing about 140 pounds), and he used them religiously. Lee was approached at that time by a coach at his school who wanted him to play football. He told Lee that he was a big guy to be in junior high school, and he asked Lee to play ball for him. Lee told him yes, and that was when he got more into weight training. Lee said he wanted to become a football legend like Jim Brown. Lifting weights made him stronger and faster. However, during his junior year in high school, Lee broke his leg. So back into the weight room he went, and within a few months, his weight shot up from 150 pounds to 180 pounds. He played six games, broke his ankle on his other leg, and back into the weight room he went. This time, he weighed 185 pounds going in. His body responded well to weight training. Hoping to get a football scholarship, he came out of the weight room weighing 214 pounds.

THE CONTESTS HE WON

Lee said he entered the Mr. South Carolina bodybuilding show and didn't place, but people at the show told him he had a lot of potential. He weighed about 218 pounds for that show, where he was the youngest and second-largest guy in the whole show.

He first won the Mr. South. Then he won the Mr. Palmetto at 18. In 1979, he won the Teenage Mr. America at 19, and in 1980, he placed fourth in the heavyweight division in the USA competition when he was 20 years old. In 1982, everything began to click. He won the Atlantic USA, the Junior Mr. America, the NPC Nationals, then the Mr. Universe. After that, Lee said he knew he had arrived.

HIS BIGGEST BODYBUILDING INFLUENCES

Lee said he read every piece of material that he could pick up regarding Arnold Schwarzenegger or Robby Robinson. Especially Robby. Lee said he was a big fan of Robby. Robby Robinson *back*! Robby Robinson *chest*! Robby Robinson *arms*! Everything.

He also admired Arnold and said Arnold was an ongoing story. You wondered when it was going to end, but he hoped it never ended. Lee liked the fact that Arnold did something that everyone said couldn't be done. He took it from one step to the next step to the next step. He was still going, and Lee liked that.

HIS OTHER INFLUENCES

Lee said there were many people and things that influenced him. He thought it took a lot of different things and influences to make a holistic and complete person. Lee's grandfather was one important influence. He was a very religious man and a very strong man. He didn't believe in weakness. He didn't believe in wimpy men or crybabies, people who feel sorry for themselves. He didn't believe in that whatsoever.

Lee said his grandfather had a mule and a plow and raised 12 kids. This was during the Depression; but there was no such thing as a depression to him. As long as he had soil and God made rain and sunshine for his seeds to grow, he was always able to feed and take care of his family. Lee said he learned a lot of his morals from him.

Then, Lee said, there were his fat little old schoolteachers, God bless their souls. It was during a time that schools were not integrated, and there were a lot of hardships placed on black people during that time. It was a time when one wasn't treated or looked upon equally.

Lee said that it was up to those schoolteachers to teach their students that they had to grow up and be somebody. They had to try extra hard in order to be somebody, and they could be anything they wanted to be. But you have to work hard. Lee said those teachers instilled in their students much of the rich black culture that was lost in the past, and they let them know that they were special.

BODYBUILDING STEREOTYPES

Lee said that when he started competing, one of the biggest stereotypes was that you couldn't have a family and be a top pro bodybuilder. You had to spend hours a day in the gym, and all you should ever think about was your training. Yet he proved that wasn't true. Lee said that in all his years as Mr. Olympia, he never had stress. He was always the same Lee Haney.

He felt that too many of the pros sacrificed relationships because they thought they had to in order to be a champion. Lee said this was hogwash! He advised that one should enjoy life, experience life, and don't hold your breath waiting for a certain event to happen before you'll allow yourself to be happy.

WHAT'S MISSING IN THE SPORT

Lee said he had talked with Franco Columbu about what was so different about the sport today, compared to when they were competing. Basically, there's more money involved now, and this is a huge motivation for today's pros. As a result, many can become very materialistic.

Lee said that when he competed, he did it because it was something he loved. If he could make money at it, great, but that wasn't his primary motivation for competing. He had fun and he loved it. That was a time when guys wanted the best for each other. They weren't selfish, jealous, envious, and wouldn't talk bad about each other. They were a family, a brotherhood. If someone jumped down on one guy, he'd better get ready to take on the whole group.

THE INFLUENCE OF HIS WIFE

Lee told the story of how he and his wife, Shirley, came all the way from grade school to college together. Neither one of them came from a substantial financial base, as far as their home environment as they grew up, so to come from a sort of rags-to-riches story was fantastic. He said it was something that they both wanted very badly. Lee said Shirley was dedicated to being there and being supportive, and he was dedicated to making it a happy-ever-after story.

Shirley was Lee's second-grade sweetheart, and she's been his number one fan and supporter for many years. In 1983, he proposed to her, and soon after that they were married. In 1985, she was his training partner, and besides being a wonderful wife and mother, she's Lee's best friend.

As Lee put it, Shirley is his hero in life. She inspires him. He said he knew if he had her support, he could do anything. Amazingly, he said that in all the years he had known her, he had never seen her with doubts or a negative attitude. Lee said that Shirley's a beautiful person and he knew she was a gift from God.

COLLEGE AND BECOMING A PRO BODYBUILDER

Lee said he had a plan for his life. His number one thing at the beginning of his career was deciding what college he wanted to go to. His major was criminal justice, and he has a degree in youth counseling. So he had a plan for his education, and as he trained, if something nice happened it happened.

He started to compete. He still wanted, and Shirley was in agreement with his sacrifice (at least for a few years), to see if Mr. America or Mr. Universe could become a reality. Lee said he recalled getting ready for the Nationals. He had just won the Teenage America in 1979 and the Junior Nationals in 1982. He told her that he understood that she had been with him and very supportive for years, and that if he didn't win the Nationals, he would not ask her to make any more sacrifices and he would go ahead and get a job in his profession.

BEING REALISTIC OF HIS DREAMS OF BODYBUILDING SUCCESS

Lee said he was a realist, and that if one has the potential, great. But if one lacks the potential, don't beat your head against the wall because you are not one in a million. Don't beat your head against the wall for something that is not there. Lee believed that one should enjoy life. And Lee said he enjoyed himself and his training. It was sheer enjoyment. To him, if it all happened, then great! So Lee and Shirley decided to go for it, and the rest is history.

THE POWER OF BELIEF AND FAITH

Lee Haney is a man of powerful faith. He said that ever since he was a kid his parents, especially his mother, had always told him that he was special. When one grows up believing that you are someone special, that you could be anything that you want to be, then amazing things can happen.

He said his father and mother always told him that if you work hard, are dedicated to your dream, and always put the greater source at the head of those things—for Lee, this is Christ—it can become a reality.

Lee said that having that greater source has been extremely important to their lives. Lee and Shirley left South Carolina in 1983 in a Nissan 280-Z with one little bag of clothing and a promise from Joe Weider, God bless his soul. Joe asked Lee if he would like to train in California, and Lee told him that he would love to. Joe asked Lee if he had a girl, and Lee said he did, and Joe told him to bring her along and he'd make sure that she had a job there with the company.

So Lee said he told Shirley that he didn't know what was in California, because both of them came from a really small town of maybe 60 to 100 people. He said that he didn't know what to expect, but Joe had offered him the opportunity to come to California and train under him, and Joe was going to cover his expenses while he trained for the competitions. Lee told Shirley that Joe said he would take care of her by giving her a job in the company. He told her that if she wanted to come, he wanted here there. But, if she was afraid and wasn't sure, then he would understand and he would just send for her later when everything was taken care of.

Lee said Shirley just looked at him and said, "When are we going?!" But Lee wanted to do one very important thing before they left for California: marry her. He said coming from where they came from, he was a strong believer in respect. Respect in things that you do and don't do. One of those things was to marry her and not shack up with her. So they set a wedding date, got married on May 14, and a week later he won the New York Night of the Champions and they moved out to Los Angeles.

LIVING IN CALIFORNIA

Lee said he fell in love with the people in California. He said Arnold made him feel very at home, and when Lee first came to Los Angeles Arnold asked him if everything was okay and said if there was anything he needed to let him know. Lee said he met a lot of special people who are still his friends today.

AVOIDING THE GYM-RAT MENTALITY

Unlike some of the pros and would-be pros, Lee never got caught up in the gym rat mentality. Lee said his thing was that bodybuilding was his job and his profession, and he worked hard at it, but he didn't hang around the gym and become a gym rat. He'd work out, say hello to friends, then he was out of there. Simple as that.

Lee offered me (Bob) some advice years ago prior to me moving to California to work for Joe Weider, and he said that California can be full of mystique. Two years go by, a year goes by just like that! He said you can have a great time and get caught up and the next thing that you know, you've blown a lot of money and a lot of years have gone by. And that can happen easily. He watched it happen to a lot of athletes. That was good advice then as it is today.

THE EVENTS LEADING UP TO HIS EIGHTH MR. OLYMPIA VICTORY

Lee said that after he won the seventh Mr. Olympia, he talked with Shirley and asked her if he should go for eight Mr. Olympias. The record was six consecutive Mr. Olympia titles, and he felt safe having won seven consecutive Mr. Olympias. But going for eight meant it was all or nothing— everything was on the line. He said Shirley looked at him and without hesitation said, what was he talking about! Of course he had to do it! Once he had her support, he decided to go for it, as he and Shirley believed that if he had the opportunity to make history, such as being the first man to win eight Mr. Olympias, then he should do it. Things like that only happen once in a person's lifetime.

WHY HE STOPPED COMPETING

Lee said that ever since he began competing, he's looked at bodybuilding as a job and a career. Arnold used bodybuilding to promote his future successes, and Lee said he made sure to do that too. After he won eight Mr. Olympias, Lee decided it was time to devote his time to Lee Haney's World Class Fitness Center in Atlanta and to the Haney Harvest House, which is a nonprofit 40-acre youth retreat that Shirley and Lee set up in 1994.

HIS EARLY TRAINING METHODS

Lee said he started with the basics and was inspired by powerlifters like Chuck Braxton with his strength. During the early years of bodybuilding competition, the bodybuilders would go on after the powerlifting competition was over, and he said that sometimes they wouldn't go onstage until one or two in the morning. In the meantime, Lee had the opportunity to watch a lot of powerlifters train and see their technique and form.

He also said that he trained in the same gym as a lot of powerlifters, and that gave him the insight on how to train properly and how to get big. Lee said that just watching powerlifters and studying their reps and the amount of explosiveness they used when training and seeing that they used only the basic exercises was helpful.

What also helped, Lee said, was studying the other routines that were written in Joe Weider's publications as it surrounded Arnold, Robby, Franco, Boyer, Padilla, and Roy Callender and people like that. Information he found here helped to incorporate the finishing touches to the basic routines. He said he stayed with the basics, and then he incorporated the other quality movements

without overdoing it. All told, it was a lot of years of studying and reading.

Lee said he did a lot of experimenting and trying different things until he found what worked best for him. For example, he said the same routine that he used when training for the teenage Nationals, the same barbell curls, the same bench press, the same squats, the same barbell rows and presses, were the same ones he still used. He just incorporated other finishing touches with them. However, they still were the backbone of his training. Lee said that if he did nothing else and still did the basics, he would still be big with muscle size and mass.

HAVING A TRAINING PARTNER

Lee said that a training partner can be really important. He made his best gains with a training partner. To be able to squeeze out those extra few reps, you've got to have somebody who will really push you. That's where you are able to go beyond.

CYCLING HIS WORKOUTS

He said that he cycled his training and didn't go heavy all the time. The joints can't stand that kind of pressure. Lee said he might go heavy for three or four weeks, then he'd back off to medium. However, he felt going light was a waste of time and stayed with going from medium to heavy. Lee cautioned that the intensity level is something that you have to take into consideration. For example, if you had a knockout workout, then you don't want to come back three days later and repeat the same thing. It is important to give the body plenty of time to rest and recuperate.

TRAINING IN THE OFF-SEASON AND FOR A MR. OLYMPIA

Lee said that the last 10 weeks before the show was when he really kicked in and did not let up. He trained every day—however, not necessarily with weights. On his weight training day off, he would do one and a half hours of aerobics, so there was never a day off when he was getting close to the Olympia.

His workouts during the off-season were three-on/one-off or three-on/two-off. Then when the Olympia approached, he kicked his training up a notch and kept it there for a good 12 weeks before the show.

HOW TO AVOID INJURIES

Lee was a careful and smart trainer and said he let the joints recover in his off-season training. The last thing he wanted to do was prepare for a competition with his joints hurting. So he let his joints recover so they would last those 12 weeks before the competition. That is why you have to be careful in cycling your training and not go heavy all the time.

HOW TO GET THE BEST RESULTS FROM ANY EXERCISE

Lee said it was important to learn how to think and feel the movement as it relates to the muscle that you are working. At first, he said, he counted reps, but now he went by instinct.

MISTAKES PEOPLE MAKE

Lee thought there were two combinations of mistakes: Overtraining and overeating. Overtraining and undereating. People were also not doing the basics and developing a solid enough foundation before moving on to the specialty movements. Lee laughed when he said that he would see guys doing cable crossovers when they hadn't even grown a chest yet.

Another mistake he said people made was getting away from the basics. In other words, they seemed to think that there was some secret to Lee Haney's training that was different from Arnold's or Sergio's. But it all goes back to the basic movements.

Lee used the example that when you look at Arnold and Sergio, they all did the basic movements. As a result, they got meaty physiques—real nice thick meaty physiques that still are amazing. Lee advised to get back to the basics.

TIPS THAT CAN HELP YOU LOOK GREAT

When we asked Lee for some tips that would help people (both men and women) look great, here's what we learned:

- Train each body part twice a week.
- Do 6 to 8 sets for smaller muscles like arms, 9 sets for delts, and 12 sets for bigger muscles like legs.

- Keep the reps in the 12 to 15 range.
- Do squats once a week.
- Always stay with the basic foundational movements like presses, rows, curls, and squats. However, you can add finishing and machine movements each workout if you feel the need.

WORKOUT TIPS FOR WOMEN

- On Monday and Friday work the lower body.
- On Wednesday work the upper body.
- The following week, work the upper body on Monday and Friday and lower body on Wednesday. Every week change the order.
- On the days you are not weight training, do some type of aerobic activity for 30 minutes.
- On the weight training days, do 30 minutes on the exercise bike, treadmill, or some form of speed walking.
- Keep your metabolism up, and remember that you don't need to train heavy to get great results.
- To rev the metabolism up, eat more simple carbs like pears, pineapple, and bananas. Of course, carbs from a salad will also help.
- Only eat complex carbs—potatoes, rice, pasta, etc.—before you are most active so they will burn more efficiently. Lee said he found the best times for women to eat complex carbs are between noon and 3:00 p.m.
- Do not eat any complex carbs after 5:00 p.m.

- Keep the lean protein intake up. Lean meat, chicken, fish, egg whites, and even two whole eggs a day is fine.
- For the average woman who weighs 130 pounds, he suggested she take in 40 to 50 grams of protein less than her body-weight number, or about 80 to 90 grams of protein per day.

NUTRITION AND REST

Lee said a lot of interesting things when it came to nutrition and rest. First, he thought nutrition and rest were the backbone of everything. He said nutrition was 75 to 80 percent of his success, because people can push and pull things all day long, but if they don't eat right and get enough rest, they are not going to make any progress whatsoever.

As some bodybuilders can be known to be a bit fanatical about their eating (numbers of meals, etc.), Lee said he sometimes got tired of eating and would catch himself eating only two or three meals a day, and then he would quickly get back on track. About six or seven months away from the contest, he said he would get in the groove and start eating four and five meals a day about every three hours.

EATING FOR A MR. OLYMPIA COMPETITION

Lee said that for a Mr. Olympia competition, typically, he would take in about 3,500 calories a day. Then he would step up the pace and go to 4,000 . . . 4,500 . . . 4,800, because as the activity rises, so should the caloric intake. However, he said he didn't like starving and liked to eat when he wanted to eat. One thing Lee has always been known for is the great shape he stays in all year round, and he does so by keeping his body-fat levels low.

As far as diet went, he said it would consist of potatoes, pasta, beans, rice, spinach, greens, fruit, whole grains, whole wheat, sugars like honey and pure maple syrup, chicken, fish, eggs, and plenty of water. He kept his diet at 65 percent carbo-hydrates, 25 percent protein, and 10 percent fat, and that minimum amount of fat was nothing to be worried about because the body needs it.

EATING AND LISTENING TO THE BODY

Lee said he was fanatical and had to eat every three hours. He always let his body tell him when he needed to eat. He said that the harder he trained, the more he needed to eat and vice versa. Lee said he told people to let the scale, their appearance, and their level of activity dictate the amount of calories they should be eating. If you flatten out, feel weak, or you're losing up to three pounds in a week, increase your calories, but do it gradually.

SUPPLEMENTATION

Supplements come and go, and at the time we talked with him, Lee said he liked crea-tine, choline and inositol, L-carnitine, and the combination of ornithine, lysine, and

methionine. He thought the cleansing effect on the liver of choline, inositol, and methio-nine was excellent.

He said when he made the jump from 233 pounds at the '83 Mr. Olympia to 243 pounds at the '84 Mr. Olympia, he used the combination of arginine and ornithine and had stayed with that supplement combina-tion and had used it for the athletes he worked with.

Lee also said that he liked free-form amino acids after workouts. In addition, he liked a good multivitamin and a mineral replacement drink while training if the athlete needed it. He said he liked extra vitamin C with bioflavonoids, as well as herbals like saw palmetto berries, Siberian ginseng, wild yam, smilax, and damiana.

HIS TRAVELS AND SOME FUNNY EXPERIENCES

Lee told of the time he almost set a restau-rant on fire in Germany. He said his buddy and he were in the restaurant having a bite to eat, and as they got up to use the restroom, Lee dropped his napkin on the floor. He picked up the napkin and tossed it on the table as they walked away. The candle on the table caught the napkin on fire, and as they came out of the restroom, the whole place was full of smoke. Lee said he asked his buddy what was going on, and his buddy told him he almost set the whole restaurant on fire.

He also told of the time he was in Greece and he had a guy tell him that he did squats to build his chest muscles. Try as much as he could, Lee said it was hard for Mr. Olympia to explain to this guy that squats don't build big thick chest muscles.

MAKING A DIFFERENCE

One thing one takes away from being in the presence of Lee is that he is a godly man who wants to make a difference. Lee said that what he tried to do in life and what he tried do in his approach to people in general is always remember where he came from. He wanted to keep the same heart that he had when he first walked into the sport and that nobody along the way could say that Lee Haney was this or Lee Haney was that or he developed an arrogant attitude or he treated a person less because that person wasn't a somebody. He said that no matter what, we are all precious in God's eyes. We are all special people, and each and every one of us is important, and we all have a very important contribution to make.

THE PROBLEMS KIDS AND ADULTS FACE

Lee Haney has a special place in his heart for kids. He also felt it was a big mistake for people to adopt new kinds of thinking to fit the times and to sacrifice morals to do so. Good morals will never change. He said that we have to address the problem of morals as it relates to our children and old people. We need to take care of those (of any race or color) who made this country what it is.

GOAL SETTING

Lee said goals are very important, and he always kept them in mind. He set short-, medium-, and long-term goals in everything that he did. Lee said the big plan was that he wanted his life story to end as one of success and happiness. Happiness was success, and you couldn't have one without the other. Knowing that all of the hard work that he put into his career and shaping his life and making sure that his family was taken care of and secure was also important. Lee said he always lived by the creed of be somebody, work hard, and be dedicated.

THE SECRETS TO SUCCESS

Lee said he worked hard, he prayed hard, and he believed that great things would happen. Sometimes, he said, success comes to people before they have the wisdom, and then they get into trouble. Whereas God was slow in giving him success until he had the wisdom to use his success in a good way.

He said he never ever feared defeat when he walked onto the Mr. Olympia stage because he knew what he did before he got there, and there couldn't be anybody training harder than he was. Definitely not praying as hard. Lee said he had a higher source within him and that he never worried about what happened because he knew that it all fit into God's plan for his life.

THE ATTITUDE OF SUCCESS

To Lee, attitude was everything. He said that he had an attitude. Not a bad attitude, but an attitude that said, I will outdo that weight and I will be the best and I will make myself the best that I can possibly be. And I will use that iron in order to do that. That was the kind of attitude that the old Gold's Gym had, and that was what helped make Arnold who he was.

THE TRAINING ADVICE TO BECOME A CHAMPION

Lee said that the number one requirement to become a champion was to be patient, to be consistent and remember that Rome wasn't built in a day. Lee said it was important to give yourself time to breathe and time to live.

I (Bob) have always remembered what Lee said about success and postponing happiness for some future event to happen. He said that some people hold their breath for so many years while they are waiting to achieve something. They miss so much along the way. You've got to enjoy the journey to whatever destination you are going to. Lee said that he lived his life to the fullest while he was Mr. Olympia. He has lived and not held his breath. He has a wife. He has kids and a happy marriage and family life, all of which has made him a happy man.

Lee said that he always felt that the end result to hard work, dedication, and discipline was success. Success didn't always mean ending up with a first-place trophy. Keeping that in mind, he was able to maintain his focus because he knew what the end result of hard work would be.

He also had that spiritual side of him that taught that you receive according to your faith. If you have little bitty faith, you get little bitty results. Lee said he had big faith and he wanted *big* results. He wanted to walk away the winner. He believed in big stuff and didn't believe in anything little . . . period. Amen to that!

BEING THE BEST YOU CAN BE

Lee said that life was a journey. Each day, you should strive to be better and become more than you were the day before. He said that as he looked back on his life, he knew that it was through the grace of God and not his own power that he has been as successful as he has.

THE IMPORTANCE OF BALANCE

To Lee, balance was very important. He said when he was 17, he prayed a prayer and asked God that if He saw fit to allow him to rise up and become the best in the sport, he would be sure to give Him the glory, and he would use his success to make the world a better place.

Lee said that soon after that prayer, he won the Teenage Mr. America, Junior Nationals, Nationals, and the Mr. Universe—all in the same year! That was almost unthinkable! No one else has ever done that in that order in just one year. Lee knew God heard his prayer, and it was up to him to fulfill his end of the agreement.

THE IMPORTANCE OF A SPIRITUAL CONNECTION

Lee believed that if you could not edify and uplift other people with what you know or do, then there was no use knowing it or doing it. He believed we're placed on this earth to help and love other people. That's our purpose.

He said that if he knew something good that could help somebody, he wanted to tell them about it. Lee said he always wanted to bring inspiration to the lives of those who are impacted by our sport and that one could have a wife, children, and a relationship with God, which is the most important thing. Lee said that you can make lots of money and achieve great worldly success, but if you don't have the spiritual connection with the Source of all power, it can all slip out of your fingers.

LIFE AFTER BODYBUILDING

At the time we spoke with him, Lee said he was doing a lot of motivational speaking in schools to help kids set goals and give them a head start in life. A big dream of Lee and Shirley's came true when they bought a 40-acre retreat they named the Harvest House. This nonprofit, nondenominational retreat is for kids—inner-city, abused, abandoned, and disabled kids—and teaches them morals, values, discipline, responsibilities, and respect for themselves and others.

Lee took me (Bob) to see Harvest House, and it was a wonderful idea that would help so many people. Lee said they had nature trails, a petting zoo, ball fields, and many other activities that would give these kids a chance to learn about and enjoy nature and develop their potential as fully functioning people in our society.

For Lee Haney, making a difference in people's lives is a great feeling. He said that one of his big goals was to create jobs for people. To give them hope and a future. Lee said he always told his employees that if I eat, you're going to eat. If you suffer, then I suffer. We all depend upon each other.

He said he believed in sharing the wealth and success with those who work for him. They all work hard together, and they all benefit together. Lee has been so blessed in his life, and as long as he was looking out for the welfare of others, he knew he would continue to be blessed.

WHAT HE WOULD'VE DONE IF HE HADN'T BECOME A CHAMPION BODYBUILDER

Lee said that if he hadn't become a champion bodybuilder, he knew he would be very much involved with helping people. Lee has a degree in youth counseling, and when we spoke with him, he was working on a youth developmental program with the mayor of Atlanta that would teach kids skills and get them off the street.

HIS PURPOSE IN LIFE

Lee said his purpose in life was to be a blessing for people. To whom much is given, much is expected. Lee said he wanted to continue to take his successes and plant those seeds and spread them around (Harvest House was a great example).

HOW HE THINKS OTHERS DESCRIBE HIM

Lee said that he felt blessed that over the years, people have told him that he's given the sport a sense of class and that they admired his morals and family values. Those kind of comments, Lee said, meant a lot to him. He has always treated people like he wanted to be treated and said he never wanted anyone to think of Lee Haney as more than just a person, someone who was willing to work hard and be the best at what he does.

HAPPINESS AND SUCCESS

Lee said he believed that if he had never become a bodybuilder, he would've been the best at something else. He was a happy man regardless of what he did. Lee said that when he was young, his parents instilled in him the belief that he was special and that he could be anything he wanted to be, if he worked hard enough and put his mind to it. For a guy who has a head full of dreams and goals, Lee said there were a lot of things that he loved doing. Yet, he said, God pointed him in the direction of bodybuilding, and he became the best he could at it.

HOW HE'D LIKE TO BE REMEMBERED

Lee said he wanted to be a man that God blessed who fulfilled God's purpose for his life. He wanted to be remembered as a good steward of the gifts he was blessed with and one who took that which God gave him and did the right things with it.

He said he wanted to help others and to love others and for it to be seen that Lee Haney lived his life by faith. Lee said that when it was time for him to leave this world, he wanted people to say, God, that was a cool dude. He did something *good*.

78

The Wisdom of Steve Reeves

"No one in the Midwest had seen him. A few days before the contest we heard rumors about a man that had throngs of people following him along the Lake Michigan beachfront, and we could not imagine who could draw crowds by merely walking along a beach. I was anxious to see this man, and when we did, we knew he was the Mr. America for that year."

—George Eiferman (circa 1947)

The amazing Steve Reeves. It's hard to find words to describe this man. When Steve passed from this earth, he left a huge empty place in everyone's heart who so admired him, ourselves included.

Some years prior to his passing, a dream came true for John and me (Bob) when we were chosen by Steve to write his book on training called *Building the Classic Physique*. We were, and still to this day are, deeply honored by the man who so inspired us and whom we greatly respected.

On a number of occasions, Steve invited us to his ranch just outside of San Diego, and it was always a treat to drive down there and see him. Hours upon hours would pass as we'd talk about training, nutrition, horses, the movies, life, philosophy, the good old days of bodybuilding and strength, his travels, and so much more.

One of the more enjoyable experiences for us was when Steve would take us into his private gym (which he called "The Barn") and personally put us through his workout on the same classic pieces of equipment he customized and for years had trained on. Often, after such a workout, or enjoyable talk, he'd invite us to stay for lunch or dinner, and what a treat it was sitting at the same table with Hercules!

While we highly recommend you pick up a copy of Steve's book for training and nutrition information you'll find hugely helpful, we also think you'll enjoy reading excerpts from one of the very first interviews John did with Steve back in 1986.

Time may pass, but as you'll read, wisdom and good information doesn't change. Enjoy.

Q: In your training routine for the Mr. America and Mr. Universe contests, there have been conflicting reports of just what exercises you did, how many sets, etc. I remember that in one year alone, there were three magazines each purporting to contain the "exact" routine that you used—and each one was different!

STEVE: *Well, the routine I would do is as follows: I would start off by warming up, doing a few dumbbell swings and things*

like that. And then after the warm-up—and I consider the warm-up very important, especially on a cold day—I would do front deltoids. You see, I believe in working my body in a certain system. When you start with the deltoids, you pump blood into the deltoids, then the second exercise [muscle group] would be the pectorals; the blood runs down into the pectorals. While working the pectorals, the triceps are already getting worked, the blood is there, so the blood is already in the upper back area. So you work lats next, which in turn warm up the biceps. So you work biceps next and end with triceps, and that's it. You see the way the blood goes: deltoids, pecs, lats, biceps, triceps. You're not pumping blood to the calves, then up to the deltoids, then down to . . . . Toward the end I started doing incline presses, incline curls, and things like that. I'd use dumbbells, and would use about 110 pounds in each hand.

For incline presses I'd use really good style. I would go parallel to my body and parallel to the ground. Back and forth like this. [He demonstrated the proper form for the exercise by having his palms facing forward at the bottom of the movement at his chest and slowly rotating, via supination, his palms toward each other at the peak of the dumbbell's ascent.] Swing them in and let them [the dumbbells] touch plates, go out like this and down again. Just level out with your chest, and I'd do 3 sets of those. Then after that I would do flying motion.

Q: Supine flyes?

STEVE: Yes. But what they call flyes these days, they're not doing flyes. They're doing bent-arm laterals. . . . They call them flyes, but they're not flyes. Bent-arm laterals are performed with the palms facing each other. . . . I'd use dumbbells, and would use about 10 pounds in each hand.

Q: What, then, are "proper" flyes?

STEVE: Proper flying is performed with the thumbs in. Thumbs-in with arms bent, it makes a difference. [He then showed me how the exercise should be performed; when your arms are extended above your chest in the starting position, your palms should be facing your feet so that your thumbs are side by side. Your grip should be off-center so that your thumb and index finger are touching the plates at the top of the dumbbell.]

I do flyes offset. In other words, what I'll do is to put the plates, jammed against my thumb, and have the remainder or lower part of the dumbbell hanging down toward the ground, thereby once again providing more resistance throughout a greater range of motion. Bent-armed laterals (like close-grip bench presses) start out difficult and then get progressively easier toward the top or finish of the movement, which means an imbalance in resistance. But when flyes are performed my way, with the thumbs in, the resistance is constant and difficult all the way up. I call them offset flyes.

Q: Did you find that the resistance could in some way be altered by having more or less of a bend in your elbows?

STEVE: I'd bend my elbows to let's say a 30-degree angle and then keep them there. If I were to tell someone how to do the exercise, I'd tell them to do it as if their arms were in a cast at about a 30-degree angle, and then keep that degree of angle on the way down and on the way up, or all the way throughout the movement. And offset your plates. In fact, if I really wanted to get a good workout, if I was home or something, I'd put two or three plates on the inside and about five on the outside to keep a real angle of resistance on my pecs via an offset grip. So the people of today are doing the wrong thing. They're doing bent-arm laterals. . . . Just like they used to say "prone presses." It's impossible to do "prone presses" because "prone" means that you're lying on your stomach.

Q: [Laughing.] That's right.

STEVE: What they should have said was "supine presses," right? [Laughing.] They called them "prone" for years, didn't they?

Q: Some still do.

STEVE: They're still wrong, aren't they? Okay, my pecs would be through then. Then I'd go to lats. I would do chin behind neck, and then I would do the low pulley or low pulley rows. And another thing that they do wrong today, even Arnold and Lou and all those guys—they all do it wrong, and I've seen pictures of them doing it—they will start low pulley rows with their arms fully extended all the way forward, and then they row in, and they will move their upper body all the way back with the pulley handles. That's not the right way to do it. The right way to do it is to keep your body forward at all times and move your arms only. Don't swing that body back and forth; you're working your lats, not your whole body! I can't believe it when I see these guys doing it—even Arnold. No, the correct way is to go all the way forward and to keep yourself there and move your arms only.

Q: It would seem to me that their poor form is the result of trying to use too much weight.

STEVE: *Exactly. Trying to use too much weight and watching some other guy working out, and he's using poor form and you're, let's say, only 18 years old or 16 years old and that guy is 25 years old and he has big arms. So you would automatically think that must be the right way. However, it may have taken him 10 years to get those arms, while it would have taken him only 2 years if he did it correctly.*

Then I would do one-arm rowing, bent over, with my arm completely extended, and then I'd pull the weight up to my hip. Bring it forward once more and then back to the hip again with a real smooth action. And that was my lats; 3 sets of one-arm rowing.

Q: How many reps are necessary to stimulate a muscle?

STEVE: *Oh, I used to do between 8 and 12. I figured that was a good amount. But sometimes I would mix things up. For instance, I don't believe in keeping the same routine all of the time. In fact, I don't even like to call a workout a "routine," I prefer to call it a "schedule." A routine means doing the same thing over and over and over again. What I like to do is change my schedules. For example, I may use the same exercises, but maybe one day a week, I might do 5–7 reps, another day during the week, I'll do 7–11 reps, and another day 11–15. That way you confuse the body. The body's used to really exerting for those 7 reps, when all of a sudden you hit it with 15 reps, and it has to change completely. It really works out well.*

Q: It doesn't have time to adapt to any one routine.

STEVE: *Right. Or a person can do it this way; work out one month with 5 to 7 reps, then jump to 11 to 15, and then go somewhere in the middle again. Back and forth each month, instead of changing each week, which is difficult—you have to remember, "How much weight did I use when I did 7 reps on an incline bench curl?" You would have to remember three different routines, you see, with all those different weights, which is difficult for some people unless they keep schedules. But I believe in mixing it up to kind of confuse* the body, so that it doesn't get into a routine and stay there.

Q: I'm not sure how long, physiologically, it takes for the body to adapt to a particular stressor, but it's very quickly, and that's when progress stops.

STEVE: Right. Okay, then I would go and do triceps. I would do 3 sets of the overhead pulley or triceps pushdowns with hands about six inches apart, elbows to the side, slightly back from the pulley so that I would get a long, sustained push. From there, I would go to the bench and do triceps bench curls (what is commonly known as lying triceps extensions) with dumbbells, with arms parallel and elbows stationary. After that, I would do one-arm curls (lying dumbbell cross-extensions; performed by lowering the dumbbell to your opposite shoulder), where you lie down and you let the weight cross over just in front of your ear.

Q: What is the advantage of doing that particular exercise? I've never tried it, but I've seen others use it. [In response, he leaned toward me and rolled up his sleeve.]

STEVE: The advantage of that is to get this [he proceeded to contract the lateral head of his triceps, which stood out from his upper arm like a 30-foot iceberg in a 12-foot swimming pool], the "horseshoe." It allows you to hit the triceps from a different angle. You see the reason I do only three different exercises for each

muscle group is to work the muscles from a different angle. Except for incline curls, which I find are so outstanding, and which do get the biceps from every angle if you do them correctly.

Q: How are they done correctly?

STEVE: No swinging, and also with your plates offset. In other words, the plates should be jammed against the inside or heel of your palm, and the remainder of the bar would be hanging down from the thumb side so that your biceps are not only under constant tension, but supinate naturally, due to the offset grip, at the top of the curl.

Q: This offset curl would seem to be just what the biceps would need, as both of its functions are fulfilled.

STEVE: Well, even if they just have a regular stock dumbbell, all they have to do is to jam their hand against the inside of the plate (the plate by the baby finger) so that the majority of the dumbbell is hanging down the thumb side, and start at the bottom from a straight or pronated position, and then, as you curl the weight upward, slowly twist or supinate your palm so that the heel of your palm is higher than your thumb at the top of the curl. It really works well.

Q: You mentioned in one article that when you did incline curls, you used something called a "rear-stop bar." What is that?

STEVE: *In back of the incline bench where you would place your back you would put little rings there through which would be placed a stop bar so that your arms are held in one position at all times. This prevents you from swinging, which is cheating, either forward or backward. When your arm is braced against the bar, it's your biceps, and your biceps alone, that do the work. What I would do was to make brackets and bolt them to the bench, and then I would get an I-bar to go through there; about 18 inches long or 24 inches long, whatever. And then I'd get some collars that I had made out of aluminum. They were about three inches in diameter, so that you wouldn't have the pressure in one place on your triceps. You see, if it's only a one-inch bar, you kind of get pressure on your triceps. But if it's a three-inch bar, or padded, you can't feel any pressure, as it's dispersed and not concentrated; it just holds your arms back. That was really great. I really liked that a lot. So then when I finished with my triceps, I would go to my legs. For legs I would do half squats, 3 sets; hack lifts, 3 sets; and then I would do some front squats, 3 sets; leg curls, 3 sets; calf raises, 3 sets; and then 1 set of sit-ups for my abdominals and a set of hyper-extensions for my back, and that was it.*

Q: How many repetitions did you do for your abdominals?

STEVE: *I would do 20 repetitions,*

Q: Did you ever do any direct forearm work?

STEVE: *No, never did. Never had to.*

Q: When you performed half squats, was that primarily for the upper thigh or rectus femoris?

STEVE: *No, "half squats" are parallel squats. People call them "full squats" today. In other words, parallel squats. To us, parallel squats were when you put your butt against your knee, that's full squats. So half squats, to us, is what they recommend today; parallel squats, when your foreleg and your thigh are at right angles to each other. So those are called "full squats" today, but we called them "half squats."*

Q: Front squats I guess would work more of the lower thigh, the vastus medialis and vastus lateralis?

STEVE: *Yes, they would.*

Q: And you would get more range on that exercise than, say, parallel squats?

STEVE: *Yes you would. You see the front squats and hack lifts build or develop similar areas of the thigh. What I find with a lot of bodybuilders today is that they have upper thighs that are too big, or disproportionate to the lower thighs, the area right above the knee. This area should not be neglected as fully developed; they not only look good, but also provide the legs with a lot of strength.*

Q: That's true, there isn't a lot of lower thigh development today.

STEVE: *Well, there's lower thigh development, but not in proportion to the upper thigh. In other words, the lower thigh development is there, but the upper thigh development outshadows it so much that it doesn't look like it's so developed there. Proportion is not there. So that was my routine.*

Q: Of the 9 total sets that you did per body part, were each of those sets "all out," or were a few of them warm-up sets?

STEVE: *All out.*

Q: Every one was all out, was it?

STEVE: *Right, and just enough time between sets for another workout partner to grab the apparatus, or the weight, and hit it. In other words, very, very intensive, or very high intensity.*

Q: Very little rest between sets.

STEVE: *Very little rest, just enough to do the exercise and to let the other person do theirs afterward. But if you have three people, it's too much already.*

Q: So just enough rest to recover momentarily?

STEVE: *That's right, just enough for another person to go through it. Or if you don't have a workout partner, figure how long it takes your partner to do the set, and rest*

about the same length of time only. However, between body parts you can rest five minutes.

Q: Would the weight be increased each set, or left about the same?

STEVE: *No, the weight would be the same. But you go to your limit; as many reps as possible. It's possible, say, on the first set, that you might hit 12 reps; on the second set, 10 reps; and you might have to go down to 8 on the third set because if you give [each set] your all, you're not going to be able to recuperate that fast—especially if you go just one after the other with your workout partner.*

Q: Were your repetitions different for your lower body than for your upper body, or were they still in the 8 to 12 range?

STEVE: *No, they were always the same, except for calf raises. And the calf raises were done for about 20 to 25 reps.*

Q: When you employ such high repetitions, is it possible or necessary to employ very heavy weights?

STEVE: *Well, if I planned to do 20 reps for my calves, I would use a weight that allowed me to do 20 reps. I wouldn't use a resistance that would only allow me to get 10 reps, I wouldn't cheat. I'd go all the way up and all the way down, and I'd concentrate on having all the pressure and all the weight on my big toe. A lot of people do* *calf raises with their toes pointing out, their toes straight ahead, and toes in; you don't need to do that. That's a waste of time. All you have to do is point your toes straight ahead and put down all the weight on the big toe as you go up and down.*

Q: And that covers it all?

STEVE: *That's right. You see [rolling up his pant leg], here's my calf today . . . [At which point his ascending pant cuff revealed quite possibly the largest and most intricately developed calf muscle that has ever existed! I could hear the thud of my jaw hitting the ground in bewilderment as this man—who claimed an age of 60—had better developed calves than anyone I had seen, including the current crop of champions training at Gold's the previous week!]*

Q: That's not a calf, that's a cow!

STEVE: *[Laughing] Yeah, well, that's my routine.*

Q: And you only did 3 sets of calf raises to achieve that degree of development?

STEVE: *Right. And I didn't do those at all the first year that I started training. When I started working out, I wasn't proportioned right. In other words, I had pretty good legs, but the upper body wasn't developed because I never worked it. But I did a lot of bicycling, so my legs were in pretty good shape.*

Q: How big were your arms when you started working out?

STEVE: *When I started working out, my arms were 13½ inches and my calves were 16½ inches, so they were 3 inches out of proportion initially. So I didn't work my calves at all until I got my arms to 16½ inches, and then I built my arms, my neck, and my calves up to 17 inches together; 17½ inches together; 18 inches together; 18¼ inches together, and I left them there. That was plenty for me.*

Q: Eighteen and a quarter inches. Wow, that's very big. Especially today. I was talking to some of today's bodybuilders and trying to get some accurate measurements from them, and it's like trying to pull teeth, nearly impossible. And some that they claim are so obviously exaggerated.

STEVE: *Another thing that they do is give measurements after they are pumped up. We would take our measurements when we got up in the morning. Before we exercised, or anything like that. It wasn't measured after exercising, or having pumped up or anything like that. It was just cold, I mean ice cold, when we got those measurements taken. And in those days, the guys would let each other take the measurements, you know? I'd measure George Eiferman's arm, Armand Tanny would measure my arm, it didn't matter. I mean, we knew what we had, we weren't conning anybody. And we knew it was going to be there tomorrow; we knew that what we had was not there because of steroids—which we didn't take—but because of training,* *and therefore it would not disappear if we stopped taking steroids. I mean, these guys today, if they don't take their steroids, a week later their arms are going to be an inch smaller or something like that. We were not worried about that because we didn't have to rely on those things.*

Q: What sort of supplements did you take?

STEVE: *Oh, we would take things like Knox gelatin and brewer's yeast. However, the thing with gelatin is that it's about 87 percent protein, but your body can't utilize the protein because it's missing a key amino acid, which you'll find in eggs. So if you're going to take gelatin for protein, you have to have eggs with it or else it won't work for you.*

Q: What sort of gelatin is this? When I think of gelatin, I think of Jell-O, the dessert. Is it like that or something else entirely?

STEVE: *Well, it's that but without the sugar. Without the sugar and flavoring. You can buy it in any health food store or in any grocery store—Knox gelatin or just plain gelatin. Like I say, it's about 87 percent protein, so that's where we got our protein from right there. However, the guys who didn't eat eggs with it didn't get developed fast because they were missing one amino acid. And if you don't have all of them, you're not going to grow.*

Q: How many calories would you consume to build up when, for instance, in a "bulking" stage?

STEVE: *I never was in a "bulking" stage.*

Q: In a "building" stage, then?

STEVE: *In a building stage, right. What I'm trying to say is that a lot of people would in fact "bulk up," then trim down for shows, contests, pictures, or whatever. But every pound of muscle that I put on was good muscle all the way up. When I first started, I was 16½ years old and I weighed 163 pounds. I worked out for a month, and I went on the scale looking a little better; more firmed up, more in shape, and I still weighed 163 pounds! But that month served to tone my body up and get my metabolism working well for me. And then the following month, I went on the scale and I weighed 173 pounds. I had gained 10 pounds of solid muscle, you could see it growing! The following month, I gained another 10 pounds of solid muscle, and the following month, another 10 pounds of solid muscle. In other words, after working out with weights for four months, I was the best-built guy at the gym. There were guys there who had been working out for three and four years before me, and they couldn't believe it! They thought a miracle had happened there.*

Q: What do you think accounted for your rapid muscular progress?

STEVE: *I think it was because, number one, I didn't give myself any limitations. I didn't know it was difficult to build muscles.*

Q: Obviously!

STEVE: *For me it wasn't. Not that I was different, but for the fact that no one said, "Boy, that's really hard to do," or "You have to work for years before you can gain an inch on your arms," or things like that. I had no limitations, and I used extreme concentration. In other words, when I worked out, I'd concentrate exclusively on the muscle being worked. I'd concentrate on the movements, doing them nice and slow so that I could really feel the movement all the way up and all the way down. I used a full range of motion, and it really worked out well for me. What you have to do is to create a superior line of communication between your brain and your muscles. And you can only do that two ways: by concentration and by practicing muscle control in your spare time when you're not working out. When you can flip those muscles [e.g., getting your biceps to twitch through brief, voluntary flexion], that means you have great communication between your mind and your muscle tissue. So by building up a greater, superior line of communication between the brain and the muscles, I was able to develop much faster and easier. In other words, I didn't put so much time into it. I'd work out three days a week for about two to two and a half hours a day. Probably two and a half hours counting my upper body and lower body, and the other four days a week I would rest because rest is just as important as working out.*

Q: Yes, if not more so.

STEVE: *A lot of these people, they don't have the recuperation period in there. They work out, then they work out, and they work out, and they work out again—they're tearing down more muscle than they are building!*

Q: Did you ever find that performing 9 sets per body part, two and a half hours per workout, three times per week left you feeling overtrained at all?

STEVE: *Never.*

Q: Really? Not even with that combined volume of work (62 total sets per workout)?

STEVE: *No, because I got all of four days rest. In other words, I was putting in maybe seven hours a week in training, that's all. There's 168 hours in a week, so I'd never feel overtrained, never. In fact, I would never have to take layoffs or anything like that because I'd never feel overtrained. I would always go into a workout looking forward to it; seeing if I could do a few more reps today, or maybe raise the weight a little bit, or whatever.*

Q: Would you recommend to bodybuilders following your schedule to include aerobics on their off days, or would this workout more than cover that aspect?

STEVE: *It depends on what the person wants to accomplish. To anybody who just wants to keep in shape, he doesn't want to get any bigger, then I would say to do aerobics a couple of times per week. But, if you're trying to get big, then I would* *suggest performing aerobics maybe just once a week.*

Q: When you were training for the Mr. America and the Mr. Universe contests, when you wanted to become more defined, would you include aerobic activity of some description to supplement your weight training?

STEVE: *No, I didn't.*

Q: Primarily an alteration in diet, then?

STEVE: *No, like I said, I was always in fairly good shape. I would just train a little harder. In other words, I would just train a little faster. I would increase the intensity by having less time in between sets and each muscle group.*

Q: So basically you did absolutely nothing different before a contest.

STEVE: *No, just increase the intensity.*

Q: You would just roll out of bed and go to the contest.

STEVE: *That's right. In other words, what you have to have to build the body is a good balance of intensity and duration. If you have too high an intensity, you can't work out very long. If you have low intensity, you can go for long duration but you're not getting any benefits because it goes on and on and on; you're wasting your time. It's a waste of time unless you have a balance of intensity and duration and a rest period for recuperation.*

Q: So there is a definite threshold of intensity. You have to do a certain number of sets, and anything below that is too high and therefore nonproductive.

STEVE: *That's right. And I guess that each individual is different. Probably a person with fast-twitch muscles should probably do low reps, say, from 5 to 7 reps, because that best suits their predominant fiber type. But a person with slow-twitch muscles can do something with more endurance, say, from 12 to 15 reps, because they can maintain it for a longer period of time without getting tired. You kind of have to go along with what fiber type you are, but you can modify it slightly.*

Q: The incline bench that you used, was that a standing or a seated incline bench?

STEVE: *It was a seated one, not that it matters, but it was a seated one. It really doesn't matter which you use. There is one other thing that I should mention regarding training, and that is that body-builders must take in a lot of fluid when they exercise.*

Q: So they should drink water continuously while they're working out?

STEVE: *That's right, yes. Because water helps them metabolize their fat. In other words, if you're going to work out, you're going to burn all [exclusively] glycogen and you're going to "poop out" too soon. If you can find a way to burn fat, if you take in a lot of water, it will help you burn fat.*

Q: In your training, you seemed to hit upon a lot of principles naturally that your fellow competitors missed and that in time would be adopted as physiologic law by exercise physiologists (i.e., training briefly, infrequently, and intensely). Did you have any similar foresights into the realm of nutrition?

STEVE: *I automatically did something correct when I was working out. I didn't know what I was doing [biochemically] at the time, but I did it instinctively. I used to drink a lot of water, and I used to mix lemon and honey with my water, and that way I was able to replace all of my electrolytes that would be lost through perspiration, about 40 years before a similar product came out, commercially, for athletes.*

Q: That's right. What you were consuming was the forerunner to what eventually would become Gatorade.

STEVE: *Yes, 30 or 40 years before they came out, I was already having my electrolytes, and it worked out great. Something instinctively said, "That's the thing to do, I must do it," and I did. By having lemonade, you know, I alkalinized the system and I was able to work out more without my muscles getting too much "pump" in them too soon. In other words, the muscles would not tire out before they were tired. [The muscles would fail due to muscle fiber fatigue and not due to localized congestion of blood.]*

Q: That certainly was a revolutionary biochemical/physical idea. What would a typical diet consist of for you back then? A daily diet?

STEVE: *It was just a mixed diet. A lot of salads, cottage cheese, and fruit. Complex carbohydrates like corn, beans, oatmeal, things like that. Whole wheat products.*

Q: I suppose that living in California would allow you to acquire a tan naturally. However, was there anything special that you did before a contest to deepen your tan?

STEVE: *Well, I would eat a lot of iron, in the form of raisins, and drink a lot of carrot juice. The reason that I did this was that iron in your system makes your skin a little reddish, a blush color, and carrot juice makes you a little orange-ish. So red and orange together, with a little sun, will give you a real brilliant tan.*

Q: Did you train any differently when you were in training for the Mr. Universe than when you trained for your movie roles as Hercules? You've said that there would be a period where you wouldn't train at all, and then a month before you began filming, you would train again. Would you employ the same Mr. America/Universe routine, or would you use a different routine when training for a film?

STEVE: *I would use the same routine, I would just eat a little less. I wouldn't go on a diet, but I wouldn't force-feed myself either.*

Q: How about older people who have recently come to embrace bodybuilding? People about 70 years old or so, who are just starting weight training. Is there any particular advice you would give them when they are just starting out, aside from getting a medical checkup?

STEVE: I would say to get a medical checkup first. Then to maintain a body, or if you're just starting to work out and you're, let's say, 50 or over, and want to get into better shape, or a person who has been working out for years and wants to stay in shape; all they need is 3 sets for each muscle. They don't need to do 9 sets. All they need is 3 sets for each muscle, so I would advise them not to do more than 3 sets for each muscle. I would say that an ideal routine for anybody, whether young or old, is to work out three days per week but have the maximum amount of rest in between workouts. Say, working Monday morning, Wednesday night, and Saturday morning.

Q: Oh, I see, so that you can prolong the recovery phase.

STEVE: Right. You get yourself another 12 hours or whatever, rest. Or let's say if you can't do that, you can work out Monday night, Thursday morning, and Saturday night. That way you have a prolonged rest in between workouts to recuperate and to balance it. If I were to work out again and really try to get in shape fast or gain size,

or whatever I wanted to do, that's the routine that I would definitely go on because you have just the right amount of time to recuperate in between. However, Monday, Wednesday, and Friday is fine also, as you have Saturday and Sunday to rest. But sometimes you rest too long and it's hard to get started again. And it may be that those 48 hours you have between workouts might not be enough. Maybe 60 hours would have been better. So I think that's the ideal routine.

Q: Well, as you say, recovery is a very important factor.

STEVE: Right. If I had somebody who had my potential, I could train them to hit the top—if they had my same mentality. But you can find the guy with the greatest potential in the world, and if he doesn't have that certain mentality, that drive, you can't help at all.

Q: Mike Mentzer actually commented on that very issue. He said that as far as the genetic potential for bodybuilding goes, perhaps one in 100,000 males have it. Of that, an even lesser percentage would possess the intelligence to know how to train correctly to realize their genetic potential.

STEVE: Right, exactly. Not only do they have to have intelligence to train correctly, they have to have enough intelligence to follow someone who knows how to train correctly. Also, they must have the drive and the desire and the discipline.

Q: How do you keep in shape at the present time? I mean you're obviously in great shape.

STEVE: Well, two days a week, I'll take bicycle rides. For instance, there's a long pass up the mountains, it's 12 miles on an 8 to 9 percent grade all the time. I'll get on my bike and I'll pedal solidly for two hours, really giving it a go, boom, boom, boom, boom, not letting up. Not missing one beat at about 75 revolutions per minute. I have a little computer on my bike, about the size of a four by three. I'll get on that, put it in a certain gear, and I'll pedal about 75 revolutions per minute, all the way up that hill, and it takes me about two hours.

Q: That seems like a lot of exercise.

STEVE: Well, I worked into that because about five years ago, when I started biking again, there was a hill close to where I lived that has a 9 percent grade and about three miles long. It took me, I believe, three months before I made that hill. I was able to make the first half before my legs would puff up and shake and tremble, and I'd be breathless. So then I trained on a level ground and a few hills for about a week, and then I went back to that same mountain again and added a quarter mile to my previous best distance. In other words, each week I had myself programmed for a schedule that would add an additional quarter mile. I knew I would do it. If I had given myself a half-mile progression each week, I might have failed, and that would have set me up for failure, psychologically, for the future. I didn't want that. I would rather do what I thought I could do and stick with it until I could hit the top of the hill, which I eventually did. It took me about three months to do it, but each time I would do it, instead of my initial quarter mile. So I'll do that two days a week, and on those days when I come back from bicycling, I'll do a little upper body work afterward. . . . I have a machine out in my garage, which simulates riding a bicycle—only with your upper body. . . . You pedal with your arms. So I can get a complete workout by just riding my bicycle, coming back and using what I call the "torso-trainer." Just pedaling with your arms like you're pedaling a bicycle, with the effect being that when your arm goes forward you're hitting your triceps, your pecs and deltoids; while on the way back, you're getting your biceps, your lats, and your lower back. . . . And afterward I'll do a set of stretches and a set of sit-ups, and I've had a terrific workout!

Q: And you do that twice a week?

STEVE: Yes.

Q: Well, after that two-hour uphill bike ride, a person would need about five days to recover.

STEVE: [Laughing] No, no, no. Actually, sometimes I feel so good after I get back from that ride that I'll ask my wife, "Do you want to go out for a walk for about two hours or so?" And she'll say yes. So we will either go for a walk, or else I'll put on weights. I'll put on 40 pounds of weights; I'll put 20 pounds around my waist, 5 pounds in each hand, and a pair of combat boots with 2½-pound ankle weights. In other words, I am weighing about 195 to 200 pounds now, so I'm using 20 percent of my body weight, which would be 40 pounds. I do that for about an hour, twice a week. I bicycle twice a week, and then, in between, I do just short bicycling to prepare the muscles for the hard ride and to get them relaxed after a hard ride. So that's what I do to keep in shape now. Another thing that I do is this, I found it really works, and I think it might work for bodybuilders too—I'd like for them to try it and let me know. On the day that they work out, before they work out that day, in the morning have your carbohydrates, but after the workout for the rest of the day have predominantly protein. But the day before your workout, have predominantly complex carbohydrates. It really works well. For my biking, it works terrific!

Q: For those who are unfamiliar with the term *complex carbohydrates,* would you please give them one or two examples?

STEVE: Well, oatmeal with a few almonds thrown in and apples and raisins would be a good breakfast, a high-carb breakfast. Have as many bananas as you want during the day, and whole wheat spaghetti with a sauce that doesn't have any meat or oil in it. This would be on your high-carb day, and some corn bread, or cornmeal mush and buckwheat, things like that, I find it really great. Sometimes I have so much energy that I feel like going and tipping my truck over! I mean, literally, I have that much energy after I've been on my high carbs! And then after I get back from my ride, on my exercise days, after I exercise, for the next day or so, I'll have about half-and-half carbohydrates and protein, to rebuild what I have torn down. And it works fantastic! In other words, before your exercise routine, have complex carbohydrates, and after, have half carbohydrates and half protein. Eat your protein after your workout, and on the day before you work out, you eat your complex carbohydrates. . . .

[For protein, they could have] tuna, or chicken, or turkey, or even real lean beef. If they want to mix the Knox gelatin, for every heaped tablespoonful of Knox gelatin, you should have one egg. Preferably soft-boiled. Or if it has to be fried, fried so that it just barely turns white. That would be a good proportion. . . . What I would do was to mix orange juice, a banana, honey, and the gelatin together in a blender. It makes a heck of a good drink, and then eat the eggs separately, maybe with a little bit of whole wheat toast if you want, but the complex carbs eaten before you train, and protein eaten after you train is a combination that really works well. I've been trying it now for about six months, and I've really noticed a difference. I'm 60 years old now, and I can do things now, endurance-wise, that I couldn't even dream of at 20 or 25 years old! . . . In fact, many times I'll be riding my bicycle along the highway alongside some guys on racing bikes, and when it comes to a hill, I'll pass them like they're standing still.

Q: [Confronted with the monstrosity that Reeves calls his calf] I'd believe it.

STEVE: [Smiling and pointing to his legs] I have the power there. In fact, sometimes during the winter months when it's raining here, one day a week instead of going on a long bike ride, like I would normally do, I'll go out to my garage, where I have a complete Universal Gym set up. I'll go to the leg press unit that is equipped with variable resistance [the farther you extend your legs, the more the resistance is increased via levers], and I'll put 200 pounds on it, and I'll do 1,000 leg presses in a row continuously. It takes me 46 minutes.

Q: One thousand leg presses in a row?!

STEVE: In 46 minutes. I worked up to that too. I started with 100 repetitions, then 200, then 300, until eventually I worked up to 1,000.

Q: You must have unswerving concentration to be able to perform an exercise in good form for 46 minutes straight!

STEVE: Well, I do. It takes me 46 minutes; it takes about one second each way; one

second down, one second up; one second down, one second up, etc. I have a certain rhythm there, and breathing I find to be very important when working out. You have to think of yourself as a giant carburetor; you have to get that oxygen in there in order to metabolize the glycogen in your system. You have to mix them together; that is, the glycogen and the oxygen together in your bloodstream because that is what gives you energy.

Q: What is the advantage in performing such high repetitions?

STEVE: For endurance. For biking, for training for the hills. You see, if I can't go on the hills that day, I'll want to make sure that when I do go on the hills the next time, I'll be in better shape than I was the last time. So I'll do leg presses specifically for that; 1,000 of them.

Q: Your legs must just blow up like balloons when you finally get off the leg press machine

STEVE: A little bit, yes.

Q: Does your wife exercise also?

STEVE: Yes, she exercises, she does her own type of exercise. She'll do a little bit on the machines, and aerobic dancing to music, especially in the pool. She likes to do aerobic dancing in the pool. When she's in the pool she'll wear ankle weights and little wrist weights to make her aerobic exercises more difficult.

Q: Plus she would have the resistance of the water itself.

STEVE: *That's right, she also has that to contend with. She prefers mainly to use the ankle weights in the water because she encounters more resistance. The water itself makes a person buoyant in a certain way; it makes you buoyant if you're going up or down or sideways, the ankle weights serve to counter this somewhat. In addition to the added resistance of the water itself, as you mentioned.*

Q: What are your thoughts regarding today's six days per week and 20 sets per body part training?

STEVE: *I think it's ridiculous and a waste of time! I think those who engage in such training would get twice as much benefit with half as much work, and much more pleasure. Here's what I figure: on my system, when you're working your muscle groups, you're also working your nervous system. You know, the concentration; the stress of trying to get that last rep in and think about something else. You don't worry about it, and your whole body recuperates again and even gets stronger. But if you're going to exercise twice a day, six days a week, when do you have time to recuperate? You don't have it! And if you're going to do that, you can't be giving your all (two workouts a day, six days a week), because it wouldn't be possible. You just couldn't. It's just like jogging, compared to running. I believe in running. In fact, I used*

to run the mile just for exercise years ago, and I always used to try to be within five minutes or five minutes and a few seconds. I used to do that about twice a week and try to get within five minutes at that time. The world record wasn't even four minutes at that time. I worked up to that too. I paced myself. The point is this: when people jog they have to kind of hold back, for instance in a marathon. If they were going to run a marathon, they would have to hold themselves back because if they were giving their all they would be out of wind at about 200 yards! The same thing applies for those guys who train twice a day, six days a week. They can't be giving their all because it's impossible to give your all that many times per day, that many days a week, without getting stale and starting to hate your workouts instead of enjoying them. I think it's a waste of time, and I think it's ridiculous. I think Mike Mentzer thinks the way that I do. He's probably one of the only people who does, but he got good results in a short period of time, and he enjoyed himself in life.

Q: That's true. He's also one of the few people in this sport who has outside pursuits. He is not by any means one-dimensional.

STEVE: *That's right.*

Q: The steroid problem in bodybuilding; why do you think it came about?

STEVE: *I think it's a terrible thing because bodybuilding should actually be a health-*

oriented sport, instead of a drug-oriented sport. I think it came about because people wanted to take the easy way to get there. If one guy took the easy way and started getting results, and then somebody else thought, "Well, if he did it, I'll do it," and it went back and forth. The magazines, instead of discouraging it, were encouraging it. And the judges then started giving trophies out to the person with the "biggest" legs, not the "best developed" legs; the "biggest" arms, not the "best developed" arms, and so on. It just got out of hand. I've talked to many professional football players who take steroids to get bigger, and they say that they would rather be 24 pounds lighter and play the game, but the other guys facing them on the line weigh about 250, 260, or 280 pounds, and they're only weighing 220 pounds. They can't really function well against people who outweigh them by 50 pounds. However, they said that if everybody would go off steroids, they would all be playing at their ideal weight. By the way, I think for an athlete the ideal weight would be according to height. Let's say a person is 6' tall, he should weigh about 200 pounds, and then as you progress each inch over 6', add 15 pounds (i.e., 6'1", 215 pounds; 6'2", 230 pounds; etc.). And under 6', you just drop 10 pounds. Let's say a person who is 5'11" should weigh 190 pounds. Even for bodybuilders I think this would be great. It worked for me; I was 6'1" and 215 pounds, and it seemed ideal for me.

Q: Well, I can't dispute that. As in your reported workout, where magazines have printed conflicting reports on how you trained, a similar morass has arisen over your top form measurements. In order to set the records straight, once and for all, what were your measurements when in top shape?

STEVE: *My best measurements were as follows:*

Height: 6'1"

Weight: 213 pounds

Shoulder breadth: 23½ inches

Neck: 18¼ inches

Pecs: 52 inches

Waist: 29 inches

Biceps: 18¼ inches

Forearms: 14¾ inches

Wrist: 7¼ inches

Thigh: 26 inches

Calf: 18¼ inches

Ankle: 9¼ inches

Q: How about genetics and training? Do you feel that an individual can only improve so far? That is, does DNA somehow limit your ultimate potential?

STEVE: *Well, there is a limit, yes. But you can off-balance that limit by having deep concentration and making sure that you have all the amino acids in your diet along with the proper vitamins and minerals. You can offset it. In other words, a person who has a great potential, genetically, but doesn't eat right, and doesn't train right, can be outclassed by a person who has* *less genetic potential, but who does every-thing right. Just like a lot of athletes, for instance Pete Rose. I mean he's out there giving his 110 percent at all times. He's a good athlete, but he's not really "gifted." But he excels, he's a champ because he wants to be; he has concentration! He's in there at all times, giving his 110 percent. Whereas another guy who's always been good, he'll give about 90 percent, but his 90 percent isn't as good as the other guy's 110 percent, if you know what I mean.*

Q: Yes. The one fellow has always been able to get by without having to improve through effort, and consequently, even though his potential may be greater genetically, his lack of effort retards his ability to reach his potential, and he stagnates, incapable of becoming what he ultimately had the power to become.

STEVE: *Exactly.*

Q: When you were competing in contests, and you had to go through the usual precontest ritual of shaving, was there any particular method that you used to shave down?

STEVE: *I just used electric clippers. Real fine electric clippers.*

Q: And you'd use them perhaps two or three weeks before a contest?

STEVE: *No, actually I'd shave down just one week before. Maybe even two days before so that I'd be clean clipped. They were clippers or electric razors from the barber's*

like what you'd find in a barber's shop. They were ones that shaved real clean.

Q: Jumping over to the "personal" category, what has been your personal favorite film of all the movies that you made?

STEVE: *My favorite film was my last film, which was called* A Long Ride from Hell. *It was a western, of which I was the star, coauthor of the script, technical director, participating producer, and it was very diffi-cult to do it. But I loved the Old West, and it was based upon a book that I had read one winter in Switzerland. I read about 100 Western novels, and out of the hundred I found three that I liked. So I wrote to a literary agent in New York and said that I would be interested in taking an option on these three, or one of these three. "I'm sorry," he said "Wayne has the option on one, and Clint Walker has the option on the other two. However, I understand that he is going to drop the option on one of them in February." He dropped the option on the one I wanted, so out of the hundred books that I read, I got the option on the one I wanted.*

Q: Did you read a lot of Zane Grey?

STEVE: *Yes, he's good. My favorite authors are Ernest Hemingway and Zane Grey. . . . [Hemingway] was very descriptive. . . . I like to read adventure stories.*

Q: What business or entrepreneurial avenues are you currently pursuing?

STEVE: None, I'm retired. I've been retired for, or rather I thought I would retire at the age of 45, which I planned for, but then I got the idea for this Powerwalking, and I've been working with this for the last six or seven years. I've actually been Power-walking for 10 years, but working with the book and its validation for only the past 5 years.

Q: How did you create Powerwalking?

STEVE: Well, I wanted to do something that in no way would be jarring or damaging to the knees, because I was getting bad knees from running. So I thought I'd use the progressive resistance principle, instead of just using my body weight over a certain [mile or so] distance. I'll add a little weight to it and move it [his body plus this weight] over the same distance and get the same results. So, actually, it came about as an aerobic exercise. I was training my Morgan horses to walk out real fast. I had a couple of them trained real well, so some friends of mine said, "You know the country hills, why don't you lead us on a trail ride from Anza to Borrego Springs?" which is about 30 miles through the mountains and desert. So I thought this would be okay, as I was in good shape and my horse was in good shape, but I realized that these other riders, they were not in very good shape; they only came out on weekends to ride, and their horses were not in that great a shape, so I thought I would conduct the ride cavalry-style, where you ride for 50 minutes and get off and walk beside your horse for 10 minutes. So when I got off my horse to walk for the 10, he started walking out real fast. So I thought well, I'll lengthen my stride. So I lengthened my stride, and I was keeping up pretty well, but I felt a little off-balance, so I started swinging my free arm, and I was doing okay but then I was getting breathless. So I thought, well, I'll do rhythmic breathing. So I breathed for three steps, out for three steps, in three, out for three, and it felt great! And after 10 minutes of this, I stopped and looked around, and the people were about half a mile behind me. I thought, "Hey, this is a great aerobic exercise!" I mean I felt good, my heart was beating a little faster but not too fast, you know; it was accelerated but not to danger-ously high proportions. So then I started walking up hills, and then I got in such shape that the mountains felt like hills and the hills felt like I was on the level. So then I thought, "Well, I've got to add weight myself," and so I started adding ankle weights and waist weights and hand weights. I worked up from 1 pound in each hand to 10 pounds in each hand. However, I found that 10 was too heavy in that it interfered with my stride. So I broke it down to 5 pounds, and I've found that that's the best. A person shouldn't walk with more than 20 percent of their body weight; 10 percent around the waist, and the rest divided between the wrist and the ankle weights.

Q: How far a distance would you recommend people to cover?

STEVE: *Three miles is enough.*

Q: Would you be the first pioneer in that particular field? Because I've seen other people come out with weights (i.e., "Heavy Hands") and courses trying to copy what you've originated.

STEVE: *Yes, I am the sole pioneer in that field. They've copied my concept. I definitely came out with it before they did, and I can prove it.*

Q: Good, because I think it should be made clear on principle that you invented Power-walking, and that they merely copied it.

STEVE: *Yes, I invented it. These other people have some form of walking, but they don't have any progressive, physiologically precise routine. I mean mine is "Do this; then, with this much weight at this time; for so many miles; at a certain age; at certain body weights; with this much weight added," things like that. In other words, I have a carefully thought-out system, a routine. It isn't just "If you want to do this, just do this; if you don't like to do this, then do that." Most of those books are that way. My book has from beginning to end laid out the best way to condition yourself.*

Q: When you were preparing for your roles in Hercules, did you study or read much Greek or Roman history, philosophy, or mythology?

STEVE: *No.*

Q: You just went over and donned the sandals, so to speak?

STEVE: *That's right. But I must say, I was fated to do Hercules.*

Q: How so?

STEVE: *When I was about 24 years old, I didn't have any money to buy things. But there was an artist in Redondo Beach whose name was Hubert Stowitz, and through a mutual friend, he asked if I would pose for the 12 Labors of Hercules. And for some reason I did it. I use to go over there every Thursday for about three hours in the evening and pose for the guy while he did the sketches. I don't know why I did it; I wasn't getting paid for it, I was burning my gas driving there, I was wasting my evenings, I thought, but something said I must do it! So I went over there and did it, and a couple of years later I was offered the role of Hercules, and [laughing] so Hercules has been good to me, I guess, because I was good to him! Anyway, It was a strange idea.*

Q: It must have been something to travel to and visit those places in the ancient world that were significant historically.

STEVE: *Oh yes, it was. I loved to make pictures in all those different countries. I've made pictures in Egypt, Greece, Yugoslavia, Italy, Spain, Ceylon (modern-day Sri Lanka), India, and probably a few others that I can't remember.*

Q: That's a very impressive list. Which was your favorite country to visit?

STEVE: Well, I loved Egypt, it was great. . . . I loved the shape of the Pyramids. To me the pyramid is very important, very positive. In fact, I think I'll have my tombstone made in the shape of a pyramid. . . . I just feel it's the right thing to do. . . . I just like the shape of the pyramid itself. I just think it's a very positive symbol.

Q: While we're on a rather esoteric topic, what philosophy of life do you subscribe to?

STEVE: Well, my philosophy of life is to be able to function regardless of your means in life. In other words, to be able to adjust. I can live in Buckingham Palace and be very comfortable, or I can live in some little tent somewhere and be very happy with the outdoors, the fresh air, and things like that. So don't have too many material expectations in life.

Q: So your philosophy of life is one of adaptation?

STEVE: That's right. To be able to adapt and to always try to lead a balanced life; don't try to be a fanatic in any way.

Q: Who has been your greatest influence, in training and also in life?

STEVE: Well it's hard to say. As far as training, when I first started training I used to look at pictures of different bodybuilders, but there was no one bodybuilder that made me think, "I want to be like him." For instance, I would look at, say, John Grimek and say, "You know, I'd like to have legs like that. Now there's a good pair of legs; he has calves and thighs that balance, I'd like to have a pair of legs like Grimek's." Then I'd look at Allen Stephan and I'd say, "Now there's a great pair of lats, now there is a great back. I'll have legs like Grimek and lats like Stephan." Then I would choose arms like somebody else and maybe a chest like John Farbotnik's or whatever, and maybe definition like Clarence Ross, and that's the way I'd do it. I would just be making a composite of these different bodybuilders, putting them all together and working that way.

Q: What do you do to unwind and relax aside from barreling up very steep hills in two hours?

STEVE: Well, I like to listen to good music, and I like to read

Q: What sort of music do you classify as good?

STEVE: I like musicals, operettas like Kismet, The King and I, and all of those musicals. Sometimes I like to listen to great opera singers, too, but not in an opera, just singing their different songs, individually.

Q: How many years have you been married now?

STEVE: It's been around 25 years, I guess.

Q: What would you say is the secret to a successful marriage? What ingredients would go into it?

STEVE: I guess compromise and not preventing the other person from being themselves. Not trying to change a person too much. Giving a person a little space to be themselves and not always trying to have the person being what you'd like them to be. Not expecting a person to change when you marry a person. If they change the way that you would like them to be in your style of life, that's fine, but don't expect it and you won't be disappointed.

Q: So it is imperative in a successful marriage not to have unrealistic expectations from your partner?

STEVE: Exactly.

Q: Do you still keep in touch with any of your former training partners?

STEVE: I keep in touch with George Eiferman, who used to be a good training partner of mine. Actually, when I think of George Eiferman, I was thinking of when I was training for the Mr. America contest. What I would do was this: I had a training partner, and more or less, I would try to do 10 reps, and he'd count "1 . . . 2 . . . 3 . . . 4 . . . 5," and on the sixth rep he would name one of the competitors that was going to be in the Mr. America contest. See, I knew who they were, but they didn't know who I was because I didn't want my

pictures in there until after I had won the contest. So what I would do, say, on number 6, would be to have my training partner say "Eiferman!" and I'd go [mimes a very determined bench press] Vooom! That means that in my own mind [with that rep] I had beaten Eiferman. For my next rep, instead of "7" he would say "Farbotnik!" . . . Vooom! [There goes Farbotnik.] Then instead of "8" he would say "Eric Pederson!" . . . Vooom! I knew who the five guys that I had to beat were, so instead of "6, 7, 8, 9, and 10," the reps became "Eiferman, Farbotnik, Pederson, and Joe Lauria, Kimon Voyages." In fact, that's the way they placed. They were in the first six, and I was number one. Using that substitution of people for numbers would inspire me! . . . I was mentally winning the contest before the contest had existed, before I was actually on the stage. I believe that if you can't conceive of an idea, you can't realize it.

Q: Back in your competitive days, who did you consider to be your greatest competition or rival?

STEVE: Eric Pederson and Reg Park. . . . Eric Pederson to start and Reg Park secondary, because he came later. In other words, he was not in the European contest.

Q: How was Grimek as a person?

STEVE: I didn't really know him that well. I competed against him, and he was always very pleasant with me, but I never really knew him that well. He inspired a lot of people, and it's a good thing that he came along when he did because he set new standards. Like I said, I admired his arms especially, and his legs, which served for a time as my role models. He was a good poser, and he was quite limber and athletic. He could do the splits and handstands and a few things like that. He was a good person to have come before and to look up to.

Q: Aside from yourself, who do you think has developed the greatest physique of all time?

STEVE: *Well, it's hard to say, there have been quite a few. The top five in my opinion would be Arnold, Frank Zane, Mike Mentzer, Casey Viator, Robby Robinson, and I would also have to include Chris Dickerson in that list.*

Q: What is your opinion of the advance made by machines in training, for example your Universal Gym machine and Nautilus machines?

STEVE: *Well, I don't know if they're advances or not, but they're different. In other words, I think that the greatest advance of those machines is that they're safer for the average person to use. Whereas with free weights, a person might drop them on themselves or hurt themselves, but with these machines they kind of have a safety factor built into them. That's their greatest advantage. I would like to add that their versatility is another advantage. The*

machines provide resistance where there wouldn't be any otherwise, in the form of variable resistance. For instance, with a barbell, it's either hard or medium or easy. Whereas with a machine you get difficult resistance spread evenly all the way up and down. So the greatest advantage by the machines has been the introduction of variable resistance training. However, what I really like are pulleys! I think with pulleys you get greater resistance over a greater range of motion than with barbells. I like pulleys a lot. In fact a person can get a complete workout on pulleys and would not have to do anything else! They're just that efficient if you have them set up right.*

Q: Is there a secret to setting them up? To make them more efficient?

STEVE: *Have cross-pulleys. Have a wall that's about 12 feet wide, and have a pulley on one wall and a pulley on the other, so that you can do all sorts of "crossing" exercises for your shoulders, for your chest, for your back, and things like that.*

Q: Speaking of shoulders, how is yours coming along? [With that, Reeves leaped to his feet with the agility that one would normally associate exclusively with members of the feline genus and raised his arm in front of his body to just below shoulder level.]

STEVE: *(Straining) I can't lift it any higher than this. . . . That's it, but when I get on* *my machine (the "torso-trainer") pedaling and things like that, I'm all right, and if I get under my Universal machine, the machine balances the weight and holds it still and I can press the weight up to about the top. Otherwise I can't train my upper body; I just have about half motion no matter what I do. It doesn't hurt me anymore.*

For those readers who are unfamiliar with the brutal shoulder injury that severely hampered Steve Reeves's upper body training, here is a synopsized account of its occurrence. While filming on the penultimate day of shooting the 1959 picture *The Last Days of Pompei*, the chariot that Reeves was driving slammed into a tree, dislocating his shoulder. He forced it back into place by himself and finished the shooting for that day. The next day and final day of shooting happened to involve the lion's share of action scenes, and Steve was called on to perform a 20-yard underwater swim beneath flaming oil that had been poured onto the surface of the water. Not being able to surface through the flaming liquid, he was compelled to swim the 60 feet. With each stroke, he was keenly aware that he was tearing ligaments in his injured shoulder. He finished the stunt, but paid a tremendous physiological price.

Q: So it's just the range that's gone?

STEVE: *The range has been gone, you see it's been screwed up for 25 years. And over the 25 years, the pectorals and the lats and everything have foreshortened, and it's now like an unseen cable that's holding my range back; my shoulders are capable of pulling up, my lats and my pecs are capable of pulling down, so I can only get about halfway there. If I really stretch it and get a machine, I can get fairly good range of motion, but then a half-hour after, there it is again back to where it was. In fact, for many years, I couldn't do any kind of weight exercises at all because no matter what movement I tried, my shoulder was a limiting factor. If I tried frontal raises, I'd be hurting my shoulder; and if I tried curls, the movement would be pulling down on my shoulder; triceps exercises would be jamming my shoulder, so I couldn't do anything.*

Q: You went down to Deland, Florida, for a while to have some physiotherapy, didn't you?

STEVE: *Yes. Actually, Arthur Jones invited me down to Florida to check out some of his new machines; he valued my advice in what he was doing there and he wanted to see what I thought of them, so I said okay. He gave me a plane ticket, and I went down and spent a week there. While I was down there, I talked to his doctor, who is one of the greatest orthopedic surgeons in the world. In fact, he was the one who discovered that if you drill little holes in the kneecap, your knee will heal faster and build up new cartilage. He checked my* shoulder out and gave me an x-ray and things like that. . . . So he checked it out and I had the shoulder operated on, and it was a successful operation as far as clearing up the bone spur was concerned. I had partially pulled a tendon there, and it had formed a calcium bone spur, like a knuckle on your hand. So the ball was not even to rotate in the socket. It would previously rotate until the spur and then stop. And then when I had it removed it would go there, but by that time, the muscles were foreshortened. So during rehabilitation, they wanted to give me size and strength, and I said, "Look, you give me range of motion; I know how to build the size and the strength." So I had no faith in those people. In fact, I've done better on my own, creating pulleys with certain angled handles that work a little better and things like that. I've done better on my own than I did with them. . . . The operation was good, but that was it.

Q: Given your colorful career, you must have met a lot of interesting people both in the entertainment medium and also through exercise. Is there anyone or any group of individuals who stand out in your mind?

STEVE: I liked Errol Flynn. He was very dashing, just like he was on the screen, in regular life. And Tyrone Power had a lot of magnetism, and he was a real gentleman, a real nice guy. And I met John Wayne over in Majorca when my wife and I were there on our honeymoon. He was sailing over

there in the yacht, and we were staying at the same hotel, and we had dinner together one evening and he was real nice.

Q: What does a typical day consist of for you?

STEVE: Well, I get up maybe about 6:30 a.m., and I have the same thing to eat every morning. I'll have a tall glass of orange juice, freshly squeezed from oranges that I've picked off of my own trees, a banana, and some bee pollen tablets. That gets my energy up, and then I'll go take my bicycle ride or my walk, and then I'll come and do a little work in the garden or on the fruit trees around the place. I'll have lunch say about 1:00 p.m., and I'll take a nap between 2:00 and 2:30 p.m. Get up at 3:30 p.m., go ride my horse for an hour. Come back, shower up, watch the news, and that's the day.

Q: How often do you ride your horses?

STEVE: Well, I used to have five that I used to ride on the same day. At one time I used to ride five hours a day. I'm down to about one hour now because I found that before, the horses used to provide me with my exercise; now I get the exercise on the bicycle. So the time I would spend on horses, I now spend on the bicycle, and I'm better off for it, and maybe the horse is too [laughing]!

Q: Any last bit of advice for our bodybuilder public?

STEVE: Yes, I would like to recommend that their daily diet be composed of this: 60 percent complex carbs, 20 percent protein, and not more than 20 percent fat.

STEVE REEVES ON BRIEF WORKOUT STRATEGIES

Steve knew that most people didn't have much time to train, or as much as they might like, so he gave us a great little circuit training workout we think is a terrific alternative to the same old sets and reps workout you might find getting a bit boring. First, keep these points in mind:

1. Try to do the workout three days a week. For example, Monday morning, Wednesday night, and Saturday morning.
2. Be sure to move from one exercise to another without resting.
3. The workout is designed so that you do an exercise that tones and reduces the waistline in between the weight resistance exercises, so that you will get a breather (so to speak) between the more demanding exercises, while still keeping your circulation and heart rate up to a desirable level.
4. Start the workout with a 5- to 10-minute warm-up on the treadmill or stationary bike.
5. You will then do 20 repetitions of dumbbell swings. To do them, stand in a straddled position, bend at the waist, swing a light dumbbell back between your legs, then swing it forward and overhead, in a smooth movement as you straighten your legs and upper torso.

Now, you're ready for the rest of the workout. Move directly from one exercise to the next without stopping to rest.

Exercise 1: Upright Rows

Muscle group emphasis: shoulders

Repetitions: 12–15

Weight: moderately heavy

Exercise 2: Forward Bends

Muscle group emphasis: firms and strengthens the lower back

Repetitions: 20

Weight: no weight on this exercise

Exercise 3: Bench Presses

Muscle group emphasis: chest

Repetitions: 10–15

Weight: moderately heavy

Exercise 4: Breathing Pullovers

Muscle group emphasis: develops lung capacity

Repetitions: 20

Weight: 10 pounds

Exercise 5: Bent-Over Rows

Muscle group emphasis: upper back

Repetitions: 10–15

Weight: moderately heavy

Exercise 6: Side Bends

Muscle group emphasis: front and sides of waist

Repetitions: 20 per side

Weight: no weight on this exercise

Exercise 7: Barbell Curls

Muscle group emphasis: biceps

Repetitions: 10–15

Weight: moderately heavy

Exercise 8: Trunk Twists

Muscle group emphasis: front and sides of waist

Repetitions: 20 reps per side

Weight: no weight on this exercise

Exercise 9: Triceps Extensions on the Overhead Pulley

Muscle group emphasis: triceps

Repetitions: 10–15

Weight: moderately heavy

Exercise 10: Bent-Knee Curl-Ups

Muscle group emphasis: waist

Repetitions: 20

Weight: no weight on this exercise

Exercise 11: Squats

Muscle group emphasis: thighs

Repetitions: 10–15

Weight: moderately heavy

Exercise 12: Bent-Knee Leg Raises

Muscle group emphasis: waist

Repetitions: 20

Weight: no weight on this exercise

Exercise 13: Calf Raises

Muscle group emphasis: calves

Repetitions: 20

Weight: moderately heavy

Exercise 14: Neck Extension and Contraction

Muscle group emphasis: neck

Repetitions: 20 (in all four directions; front, back, left side, right side)

Weight: no weight in this exercise

Epilogue

Congratulations! Just think about what you've done: you've now read more information and learned more lessons about training than most people will ever do. So, what are you going to do with all this knowledge? Well, we have a few ideas.

First, take the words and ideas you found most interesting right now and begin to act on them. That's right, make those ideas a part of your bodybuilding/strength program and begin to incorporate them into your workouts. While some of them may not work, you'll find others will work amazingly well. Keep those elements that do work, and don't worry about those that don't.

Next, go back and reread the chapters and stories that you found entertaining. Maybe these stories and ideas didn't give you specific training and nutritional advice, but they did give you insight into how these athletes looked at life, success, and training, and this can be very important in helping you plot your next course of action for success both in and out of the gym.

Remember, success in your life is not just about weights, sets, and reps. If you like the philosophy and approach of anyone you read about, then experiment and see what it feels like to make some of those ideas your own. Refine them. Create new ideas. Put it all together into something that feels really good to you and one you can say, "This is my life!"

Finally, go back in a month or two, then six months, and then a year from now and reread the book. You will be amazed and pleasantly surprised at how much you've grown (physically and mentally) and that the words you read that didn't impact you previously, you'll now find interesting and relevant to the road you are on in your life right now. With more than 180,000 words in this book, we think you'll always find one of them that will inspire you and could be just what you need when you need it.

We say enjoy the lifetime of good health and happiness. Let this book and its words be only one of many of the guideposts on your road to building your body and life just the way you want them.

Index